STUDIES IN ORIENTAL CULTURE
NUMBER SEVEN
# IQBAL

# IQBAL

## POET-PHILOSOPHER OF PAKISTAN

*edited by*
*Hafeez Malik*

NEW YORK AND LONDON
COLUMBIA UNIVERSITY PRESS
1971

Hafeez Malik is Professor of History and Political Science at Villanova University in Pennsylvania. He is the author of *Muslim Nationalism in India and Pakistan* (Washington, D.C., 1963). From 1961 to 1963 and from 1966 to 1968 he was Visiting Lecturer at the Foreign Service Institute of the U.S. State Department.

The Asian Literature Program of The Asia Society, New York, and Villanova University have generously provided financial assistance toward the publication of this volume.

Copyright © 1971 Columbia University Press
ISBN: 0-231-03320-6
Library of Congress Catalog Card Number: 75-135475
Printed in the United States of America

STUDIES IN ORIENTAL CULTURE
*Edited at Columbia University*

BOARD OF EDITORS
Ivan Morris, *Professor of Japanese*
Wm. Theodore de Bary, *Horace Walpole Carpentier Professor of Oriental Studies*
Ainslie T. Embree, *Professor of History, Duke University*
Charles P. Issawi, *Ragnar Nurkse Professor of Economics*

*For my son (Saki)*
## Cyrus H. Malik
*who inherits the East and the West*

# Foreword

MUHAMMAD IQBAL—lawyer, jurist, and poet—rests in a simple tomb just outside the main entrance to the Badshahi mosque in Lahore. That simple tomb is a place of pilgrimage for me. For Iqbal was a man who belonged to all races; his concepts had universal appeal. He spoke to the consciences of men of good will whatever their tongue, whatever their creed.

This man who was the spiritual godfather of Pakistan filled his poetry with songs. He sang of many things, from simple daily events to metaphysics and philosophy. He was passionately religious and devout.

The Westerner will find in Iqbal's philosophy of religion a challenging outlook on life and the universe, and a universal concept of God. More than this, he will find concrete proposals for building the future world along new lines.

The great contribution of the West to the East is the scientific attitude. One great contribution of the East to the West is Charity or Love, as epitomized by Muhammad and Christ, Buddha and Confucius. Another is the East's emphasis on relaxation and reflection. The machine tends to make man an automaton. The slower reflective pace of the East tends to develop unlike people, men with striking diversities. Iqbal recognized what science introduced to ancient Asia might do. He saw its potential for good, its potential for evil:

> Love fled, Mind stung him like a snake; he could not
>   Force it to vision's will.
> He tracked the orbits of the stars, yet could not
>   Travel his own thoughts' world;
> Entangled in the labyrinth of his science
>   Lost count of good and ill;
> Took captive the sun's rays, and yet no sunrise
>   On life's thick night unfurled.

And when we view the nuclear discoveries of this age we can say with him, "and yet no sunrise on life's thick night unfurled." Iqbal recognized that if science were to treat kindly with Asia, not make it a sweatshop of capitalism on the one hand or the victim of communist regimentation on the other, it must be controlled in the public good:

> The object of science and art is not knowledge,
> The object of the garden is not the bud and the flower.
> Science is an instrument for the preservation of Life,
> Science is a means of establishing the Self.
> Science and art are servants of Life,
> Slaves born and bred in its house.

The most remarkable phenomenon of modern history to Iqbal was the new spiritual understanding between the East and the West. He put this thought into verse:

> In the West, intellect is the source of life.
> In the East, Love is the basis of life.
> Through Love, Intellect grows acquainted with Reality,
> And Intellect gives stability to the work of Love,
> Arise and lay the foundations of a new world,
> By wedding Intellect to Love.

The great need these days is for bridges of understanding between East and West. The need is for bridges of understanding at the highest intellectual levels, so that divergent civilizations—each great in its own right—may come to know and understand each other and, knowing, come to tolerate, respect, and even admire each other. Iqbal was a voice from the East that found a common denominator with the West and helped build the universal community that tolerates all differences in race, in creed, in language.

In deep humility we pay tribute to the name of Iqbal and send up our prayers in gratitude that this man was permitted to pass among us.

For these reasons I say that although Iqbal was a son of Pakistan, we of America also claim him.

WILLIAM O. DOUGLAS
*Associate Justice,*
*The Supreme Court of the United States*

Washington, D.C.

# Preface

By a consensus among historians the twentieth century is described as the century of nationalism. Although this statement is relevant to all the continents of the world, it is particularly germane to Asia. Within Asia, however, the least understood phenomenon of nationalism is that of Pakistan. Often influenced by political considerations, scholars have tended to explain away the creation of Pakistan in terms of religion. Undoubtedly, Islam, like Hinduism in India and Catholicism in Poland, is the central dynamic of Pakistan's national life, yet it is by no means the only component of the Pakistani mind. The collective consciousness (or, to use Professor Hans Kohn's language, the corporate will) of the Indo-Pakistani Muslims was the product of a thousand years of history. Modern trends were shaped by numerous scholars and poets and political movements and leaders, such as Shah Walīullah (d. 1762), Sayyid Ahmad Shahīd (d. 1839) and his coworker Mawlana Ismaʿīl Shahīd (d. 1839), and Sir Sayyid Ahmad Khan (d. 1898). In the post-Sir Sayyid period no intellectual or political leader influenced the Indic Muslim mind as profoundly as Dr. Muhammad Iqbal (d. 1938).

Although Iqbal did not coin the name Pakistan, he made a significant contribution to its creation in three basic ways. He formally enunciated the two-nation theory (1930), which the All-India Muslim League adopted a decade later, and he presented an updated Islamic ideology for the Muslim state of his vision. Second, he persuaded Muhammad Ali Jinnah, the founder of Pakistan, to ask for a separate Muslim homeland. In a letter to Jinnah on June 21, 1937 Iqbal stated unequivocally: "A separate federation of Muslim provinces . . . is the only course by which we can secure a peaceful India and save Muslims from the domination of non-Muslims. Why should not the Muslims of North-West India and Bengal be considered as nations, entitled to self-determination just as other nations of India and outside India are?"

Third, his philosophic doctrine of *khudi* (ego, or self-affirmation) expressed in his captivating poetry, provided a frame of reference not only for the individual but also for the Muslim national identity.

Against this background it is not inappropriate to describe him as the poet-philosopher of Pakistan. Yet it would be an injustice to Iqbal if the impression were given that he was a parochial nationalist, whose mental horizon was not wider than the boundaries of a Muslim national state. Before Iqbal, Muslim political thought was primarily concerned with Muslims in India. For instance, to Sir Sayyid love was like a pyramid; at the top was the noblest form of love—love for the universe. "This kind of love," he had stated "was unattainable." In the middle was love "for those who share human qualities with us." Lofty though this sentiment is, for Sir Sayyid, it "was far too elusive a quality to be comprehended." He reasoned that "at the bottom of the pyramid is placed a sentiment which I call love of nation, which I understand and am capable of."

On the other hand, Iqbal's intellectual evolution was the reverse of Sir Sayyid's. In his early works, Iqbal was absorbed in himself, lamenting his disappointments and personal sorrows. From himself his emotional horizons expanded to include India, particularly the Indian Muslims and the larger world of Islam. Then his love enveloped mankind, and at still a later stage it changed into a passionate involvement with the universe. Despite his commitment to the concept of a separate Muslim state, he remained a philosophic humanist, and humanism was truly his message.

It is precisely for this reason that the advent of Pakistan has not greatly tarnished his popularity in India. In India Iqbal Day is still celebrated, his poems are sung on the All-India Radio, and periodically literary journals publish special issues exclusively devoted to his life and thought. Although Pakistanis feel that by virtue of Iqbal's support for the creation of Pakistan they have a better claim on the poet-philosopher, Indians, with considerable justification, call him their own. After all, it was Iqbal who wrote a truly nonsectarian national anthem for India, which India failed to adopt in the heat of political passions.

In Pakistan, however, Iqbal is the patron saint. His books are prescribed as texts in colleges and schools. At weddings sets of his poetical works often form part of the bride's trousseau. Politicians often recite appropriate verses from Iqbal before they deliver their orations. The modernist ahl al-Qur'ān and the fundamentalist Jamā'at-i Islami (the two most influential movements in Pakistan) claim to have received inspiration from Iqbal, and aver that their interpretations of Islam are in accord with his ideas.

Nor has the Government of Pakistan lagged behind the citizens in appreciation of Iqbal. On the suggestion of some eminent Pakistani scholars (including Khalifah 'Abdūl Hakīm, Mawlavi Muhammad Shafi', Professor M. M. Sharīf, Sayyid Nazīr Niyāzi, Dr. S. M. 'Abdūllah, and Justice S. A. Rahmān), in 1950 the Government of the Punjab established the Iqbal Academy in Lahore. Three years later the Government of Pakistan, by an act of the National Assembly, founded another Iqbal Academy in Karachi, forcing the old Academy to change its name to Bazm-i Iqbal (Iqbal Society). Staffed by outstanding scholars, the Academy and the Bazm have regularly published learned quarterly journals—*The Iqbal Review* from Karachi, and *Iqbal* from Lahore, which are subsidized by the provincial and federal governments of Pakistan. They have also published translations of Iqbal's works into Bengali, Sindhi, Pashto, and into almost every European language. In addition they have published scholarly treatises on the life and thought of Iqbal in Pakistani and in foreign languages.

There is not any country in the world except Pakistan where a poet and a scholar has been raised to the position of a national hero. Yet a lively debate about Iqbal's social class affiliation has persisted among scholars. Some have emphasized his modest family origins and his proletarian sympathies; others have identified him with the Muslim bourgeoisie and its aspirations; and those who failed to understand his philosophical system resolved the dilemma by explaining simultaneously what they called progressive and reactionary trends in Iqbal's thought. Professor V. G. Kiernan's assessment comes closest to the truth: "Iqbal, a man of the middle class, was close enough both to the landlords and princes above it, and to the labourers and peasants below it, to be able to look at life through the eyes of all of them, and his ideal of religious brotherhood derived from this fact."

Despite Iqbal's eminence in Pakistan and in the Muslim world, he is not well known in the West, and especially not in the United States. Although British scholars translated his works into English in the 1920s, American academic circles have generally remained unaware of Iqbal's philosophy and his contribution to the creation of Pakistan.

## Preface

Some years ago a small number of Pakistani and American scholars, inspired by Justice William O. Douglas's admiration of Iqbal's poetry, started to meet informally in Washington, D.C. for discussions of Iqbal's poetry and philosophy. Out of these meetings developed the idea that an authoritative study of Iqbal's life and ideas should be published in the United States. A list of important topics was drawn up and in 1964 outstanding scholars from countries where significant publications on Iqbal have appeared were invited to contribute chapters on those topics. Thus came into being this international symposium on Iqbal, which includes contributions by seventeen Soviet, Czech, German, Indian, Pakistani, and American scholars.

I was particularly heartened by the cooperation of the Soviet Academy of Arts and Sciences and its Institute of the Peoples of Asia in Moscow. Several publications on Iqbal, and the publication of his poetical works in various Soviet languages, testify to their serious involvement. Consequently, after the Pakistani contributors, the Soviet contributors are the largest contingent in this symposium. It must be pointed out, however, that their view of Iqbal's philosophy and politics is based upon Marxist-Leninist theory. The Soviet scholars submitted their drafts in Russian, which was subsequently translated into English by professional translators. The authors were given the opportunity to examine the English version, and they have indicated their approval. Each chapter has been especially written for this symposium and has not appeared previously in any book or journal. Also, these contributions indicate a significant collaboration between the scholars of Socialist and non-Socialist countries about the life and philosophy of the spiritual godfather of Pakistan.

This study would not have seen the light of day had it not been for the generous help and cooperation of Mrs. Bonnie R. Crown, Director of the Asian Literature Program of The Asia Society, New York, and Rev. John M. Driscoll, Vice-President for Academic Affairs, Villanova University. During the course of my work on this symposium I greatly benefited from the advice and encouragement of my friends —Wayne A. Wilcox of Columbia University, Khalil I. Semaan of the State University of New York at Binghamton, S. A. Vahid of Karachi, B. A. Dar, Director of the Iqbal Academy in Pakistan, William F. Merrill, Director of Jones Library in Amherst, Massachussets, Marguerite J. Fisher of Syracuse University, Mr. and Mrs. Irving G. Pollock of New York, Patrick J. Nolan of Villanova University, and Prof. W. W. Kulski and Mrs. Antonina Reutt Kulski of Duke University. My wife, Lynda P. Malik, in addition to being coauthor of the biographical chapter, brought to bear upon certain sections of the symposium her usual sensitivity of judgment, which solved many ticklish problems. In the final organization of the manuscript I received valuable assistance from my friend Ainslie T. Embree of Columbia University. He extended his critical judgment to many crucial and sensitive issues, and thus greatly improved the quality of several chapters, including my own.

Last but not least, I gratefully acknowledge the splendid cooperation of the contributors, who cheerfully endured my editorial suggestions. Despite their physical separation from each other they readily accommodated fellow contributors in order to maintain unity and consistency in the book. Without their scholarly give-and-take, many of Iqbal's ideas would have suffered from repetition and unharmonized treatment. I endeavoured to achieve unity and a comprehensive coverage of Iqbal's philosophy, and have in no way tampered with the interpretations of the contributors. Consequently, they alone are responsible for their views, just as I am responsible for my own.

HAFEEZ MALIK

Arden Road, Village of Gulph Mills
Pennsylvania

# Contents

## I · BIOGRAPHY

1. The Life of the Poet-Philosopher
   *Hafeez Malik and Lynda P. Malik*   3
2. Glimpses of the Man
   *Muhammad Daud Rahbar*   36
3. Iqbal: My Father
   *Javid Iqbal*   56

## II · POLITICS

4. The Man of Thought and the Man of Action
   *Hafeez Malik*   69
5. Ideology of Muslim Nationalism
   *L. R. Gordon-Polonskaya*   108
6. The Development of Political Philosophy
   *Riffat Hassan*   136
7. Perceptions of International Politics
   *Jan Marek*   159
8. View of Democracy and the West
   *Freeland Abbott*   174

## III · PHILOSOPHY

9. Inspiration from the West
   *B. A. Dar*   187

|    |                                           |     |
|----|-------------------------------------------|-----|
| 10 | The Heritage of Islamic Thought           |     |
|    | *A. H. Kamali*                            | 211 |
| 11 | Conception of Time                        |     |
|    | *S. Alam Khundmiri*                       | 243 |
| 12 | The Doctrine of Personality               |     |
|    | *N. P. Anikeyev*                          | 264 |

## IV · ISLAMIC MYSTICISM

|    |                                           |     |
|----|-------------------------------------------|-----|
| 13 | Attitude toward Sufism                    |     |
|    | *Abu Sayeed Nur-ud-Din*                   | 287 |
| 14 | The Demise of Fatalism                    |     |
|    | *M. T. Stepanyants*                       | 301 |
| 15 | Mystic Impact of Hallaj                   |     |
|    | *Annemarie Schimmel*                      | 310 |

## V · POETRY

|    |                                           |     |
|----|-------------------------------------------|-----|
| 16 | Conception of Poetry and the Poet         |     |
|    | *Hadi Hussain*                            | 327 |
| 17 | Iqbal and Western Poets                   |     |
|    | *S. A. Vahid*                             | 347 |

## APPENDIX

| Letters of Iqbal to Jinnah                  | 383 |
|---------------------------------------------|-----|

| Notes                                       | 391 |
|---------------------------------------------|-----|
| Selected Bibliography *by Hafeez Malik*     | 416 |
| Contributors                                | 430 |
| Index                                       | 433 |

# {I}
# BIOGRAPHY

# I

## The Life of the Poet-Philosopher

HAFEEZ MALIK & LYNDA P. MALIK

IQBAL, the poet-philosopher of Pakistan, was born on November 9, 1877 at Sialkot,[1] and died at the peak of his glory and fame in the early hours of April 21, 1938 at Lahore.

Sialkot is a border town of the Punjab; only a few miles beyond the city begins the state of Jammu and Kashmir, now a bone of contention between India and Pakistan. At the beginning of the nineteenth century the Sikhs, who had established their rule in the Punjab, ousted the Afghans from Kashmir with the help of a Dogra chief, Raja Gulab Singh. The Sikhs rewarded him by establishing Gulab Singh's control over the province of Jammu. In 1837–1839 he extended his rule by seizing from Tibet the northern areas, Ladakh and Baltistan. Seven years later the British waged war against the Sikhs and ordered them to relinquish their hold over Kashmir. Taking advantage of his former allies' military defeat, the Dogra chieftain offered the British 7.5 million rupees (£750,000) for the possession of Kashmir. This arrangement was consummated in the Treaty of Amritsar, signed in 1846. From then on Kashmir was to belong "forever, an independent possession to Maharaja Gulab Singh, and the heirs male of his body."

Thus began the modern history of Kashmir. Commenting on the Dogra rule of Kashmir, Josef Korbel says: "It was for the Kashmiris another tragic experience in a millennium of tragedies. Though once Hindus, they had for 500 years been Muslims. Now, by the terms of the Treaty of Amritsar, the Hindu Dogras possessed the territory; they immediately set out upon a policy of unlimited cruelty that seemed to vent upon the hapless Kashmiris pent-up hatred of the Hindus for the five centuries of Muslim rule."[2] Consequently many Kashmiri families migrated from Kashmir to the Punjab. Iqbal's grandfather Shaikh Rafiq left his ancestral village of Looehar in Kashmir not long after

1857, and came to settle in Sialkot along with his three brothers. Although the family never returned to Kashmir, the memory of the land and its people was never erased from the mind of Iqbal. Lamenting the fate of the Kashmiris, Iqbal wrote several verses which evoke deep sympathy and pathos.

Shaikh Rafīq was a peddler of Kashmiri shawls, whose two sons Shaikh Nūr Muhammad (the father of Iqbal), and Shaikh Ghulam Qādir were probably born in Sialkot soon after the family's arrival at their new home. Shaikh Nūr Muhammad learned the trade of a tailor and embroiderer, and Shaikh Ghulam Qādir eventually found a job in the Department of Irrigation, probably as an unskilled worker. Neither brother acquired any formal education, and like many Kashmiri families who followed them they joined the ranks of the working classes in the urban areas of the Punjab.

Shaikh Nūr Muhammad, Iqbal's father, was not only endowed with the gift of native intelligence and natural curiosity, but also was complimented with a handsome appearance. He had a ruddy complexion, a platinum white beard, and a pair of penetrating, keen eyes. He was generally respected by his peers because of his religious piety and mystic temperament. He kept the company of the Sufis, from whom he acquired a great deal of mystic knowledge. Out of affection Shaikh Nūr Muhammad's friends used to call him an *un parh falsafī* (untutored philosopher).

Iqbal's mother, Imam Bibi, was also a deeply religious woman. As the child of a working-class family she acquired no formal secular education except an elementary knowledge of the Qur'ān, different forms of *'ibadāt* (religious duties), and deep consciousness of *imān* (belief) and *ihsān* (right-doing). These qualities she firmly instilled in their three daughters and two sons—Shaikh 'Atta Muhammad (the eldest child, born in 1860) and Muhammad Iqbal.[3]

Shaikh Nūr Muhammad acquired a reputation as a highly skilled tailor. A local official, Deputy Wazīr Ali Bilgrami, had hired him and purchased especially for him a new Singer sewing machine, which was then an object of curiosity. Imam Bibi suspected the legitimacy of the Deputy's income, believing that a large part of it had been derived from un-Islamic and illegal pursuits and thus refused to spend any part of her husband's income on herself. This eventually compelled Shaikh Nūr Muhammad to leave his job, and he opened a small millinery of his own, specializing in embroidering the caps of Muslim women's *burqa* (the outer garment concealing their appearance). As a capmaker he was a modest success, and eventually hired a few skilled workers to meet the increasing demand. When Shaikh Nūr Muhammad grew old he transferred his shop to his son-in-law, Ghulam Muhammad. Under the latter the trade soon languished and in a short time the shop closed.

Despite his skill and enterprise as a tailor, Shaikh Nūr Muhammad had a hard time supporting his large family. His oldest son, Shaikh 'Atta Muhammad, did not even complete high school, and his parents married him to the daughter of a retired soldier of the British Indian Army. His father-in-law secured a position for him in the Army, and after a few years he entered the Engineering School at Rurki. A few years later he graduated from the school and rejoined the Army as an overseer of the Mechanical Engineering Service. Shaikh 'Atta Muhammad's success paved the way for the progress of Iqbal, and raised the social status of the family from a working-class to a middle-class position.

## EARLY YEARS IN SIALKOT

THE Sialkot which saw the childhood of Iqbal and his brother was no longer the Mughal city of splendor. The renowned *makatīb* and *madāres* which once flourished in the city had disappeared with the empire. In February, 1846, three decades before the birth of Iqbal, the British had defeated the Sikhs and established the *Pax Britannica* in the Punjab. After 1857 the Aligarh movement of Sir Sayyid Ahmad Khan (1817–1898) had won over the Muslims of the Punjab, and *nai' ta'līm* (modern education) of the west was becoming popular. Western missionaries, particularly the Church of Scotland and the Reformed Churches in the Netherlands, had already established in 1889 a junior college—The Scotch Mission College (currently named Murray College)—in Sialkot. The Scotch Mission College simultaneously offered courses in liberal arts then currently taught in English universities and some courses in Arabic and Persian in keeping with the classical traditions of Muslim India. The advantages to be derived from this dual curriculum lured a sizable number of young Muslims to the college. Persian was no longer the official language of the British Indian government nor the medium of instruction in schools. The supremacy of the English language had, by this time, been firmly established. However the Muslims of the Punjab were taking to Urdu under the influence of the Aligarh movement. Only sixty-five miles away from Sialkot, Lahore, the former Mughal capital, was vibrating with new intellectual trends. In Lahore Urdu poetical symposia were in vogue, and Altaf Husain Hali (a pillar of the Aligarh movement), and Maulana Muhammad Hussain Azad were the shining literary stars. The cultural life of Sialkot echoed the trends prevailing in Lahore.

Iqbal's childhood and adolescent years in Sialkot were no different than the life of most young children of poor and middle-class parents. He was athletically inclined, and used to spend hours in the arena wrestling with his friends. Also, he loved partridges and until the end of his life retained very tender feelings for pigeons. Javid Iqbal, the son of the poet, recalls that during the last years of Iqbal's life when he kept indifferent health "he had a great desire that on the roof of our house he should get a large cage built, full with pigeons, and that his bed should be placed in the middle of them." Iqbal's teacher, Sayyid Mīr Hasan, often observed him learning his lessons while tenderly holding a partridge in his hand. Once he asked him: "My dear boy, what peculiar enjoyment do you get out of this?" Iqbal promptly answered: "Please master, just hold it and feel."[4]

The atmosphere in the house was deeply religious. Although Shaikh Nūr Muhammad never tried to cash in on his religious piety as a professional holy man, he had the reputation of an accomplished Sufi. The Shaikh's family believed that he had intuitive knowledge of future events. 'Abdūl Majīd Sālik stated that Iqbal once told him that he was hardly eleven when the following incident occurred.

One night I awoke from a deep sleep . . . and saw my mother going down stairs, and I followed her. Finally we stood in front of a half-opened door of a room and saw rays of light streaming out of the room. Mother went in, and she peeped through the window; I also did the same. We saw that my father was sitting in the open courtyard surrounded by a halo of soft light. I wanted to go to my father, but mother put me to bed with some explanation [of this phenomenon].

Next morning I rushed to father and found mother sitting next to him listening to his intuitions. "I intuitively comprehended," said father, "that a caravan has come from Kabul and was encamped some miles out of

Sialkot. There was a sick man among the people desperately in need of help. I feel I should go to their help." Then the parents hired a *tonga* (horse drawn carriage), and we proceeded to the camp of the caravan. Father inquired from the head of the caravan about the sick man, and asked to be taken near his bed. Father discovered that the patient was in critical condition due to a severe infection. Then he took out something from his pocket which looked very much like ashes and rubbed it on his infected limbs. Father said *Inshā Allah* (God willing) the patient would recover. No one believed it but within twenty-four hours the condition of the patient turned for the better. [In appreciation of this] his parents sent money to my father, but he did not accept it. A few days later the caravan came to Sialkot, and we discovered that the patient had regained his health.5

It is entirely probable that Iqbal had this experience in his dreams, and later confused it with actual reality. Be that as it may, stories like this provide us with significant insight into Iqbal's psychological and religious orientation. Khalīfah 'Abdūl Ḥakīm, who knew Iqbal intimately, has stated that in his old age Iqbal often said that "he did not develop his philosophic *Weltanschauung* through philosophic speculation, but has inherited it [from his parents]."6 There is a measure of truth in this statement. Some of the lessons learned in his early years remained ever with him; one is tempted to hypothesize that Iqbal's broad humanism also owes much to the religious orientation of his parents. Iqbal has highlighted this aspect of his character in *Asrār-i Khudi* (The Secrets of the Self).7

"A beggar once appeared at the door of our house," Iqbal tells in his elegant Persian verses, "and incessantly demanded alms. I lost my temper and hit him with a stave. Consequently, the harvest of his beggary spilled from his hands. My father saw this and in anguish tears rolled down his cheeks. He said 'On the day of Resurrection the followers of the Prophet Muhammad including the *ghazian* (warriors of the *millat*), the martyrs, the learned and the sinful, will gather around him. Then in the midst of this company the suffering beggar's cries will attract the Prophet's attention, and he will ask me:

> When this the Prophet asks me: 'God to thee
> Committed a young Muslim, and he won
> No portion of instruction from my school;
> What, was this labor too, too hard for thee
> So that that heap of clay became not man'?

'What am I to say to my master?' Finally father advised me, saying:

> Reflect a little, son and bring to mind
> The last great gathering of the Prophet's fold;
> Look once again on my white beard, and see
> How now I tremble between fear and hope;
> Do not thy father this foul injury,
> O put him not to shame before his Lord!
> Thou art a bud burst from Muhammad's branch;
> Break into bloom before the genial breeze
> Of his warm spring; win thee the scent and hue
> Of that sweet season; strive to gain for thee
> Some fragment of his character sublime!"[8]

In the choice of early teachers for Iqbal, his parents also reflected their devotion to Islam. During the period of Iqbal's childhood four *makatib* in Sialkot (those of Mawlana Ghulam Murtaḍa, Mawlana Abū 'Abdūllah, Mawlana Muhammad Muzammal, and Mawlana Sayyid Mīr Hasan) enjoyed a reputation for scholarship and were, even in those days of decline, reminiscent of the Mughal days. Although the first three concentrated exclusively on Islamic studies and theology, the last one also included offerings on Arabic and Persian literatures.

Sayyid Mīr Hasan (1844–1929), who recognized early Iqbal's poetic talent, was not only an acknowledged scholar of Arabic and Persian literatures, but was also in sympathy with the aims of the Aligarh movement. He knew Sir Sayyid personally, subscribed regularly to the *Tahdhīb al-Akhlāq*, and often sought Sir Sayyid's help in understanding his *Tafsīr* (exegesis of the Qur'ān). In fact when Shām Bihari Lāl, the treasurer of the Anglo-Muhammadan College at Aligarh, embezzled Rs. 100,000 from the college, Sayyid Mīr Hasan, in order to partially compensate Sir Sayyid for this loss, regularly contributed from his personal funds and also collected sizable donations from others.[9] Sayyid Mīr Hasan knew no English, nor did he ever make an attempt to learn it, yet he was keenly aware of the pragmatic and broad educational values of western education. His appreciation of the new times had made him accept the position of a professor of oriental literature at the Scotch Mission College.

Fortunately for Iqbal, Sayyid Mīr Hasan knew his father, and lived in Kucha Mīr Hisām-ud Din of Sadr Bazaar, not too far from the house of Iqbal's parents. (Sadr Bazaar was later named Iqbal Street in honor of the poet-philosopher.) Sayyid Mīr Hasan offered to tutor Iqbal, and when Iqbal graduated from high school (1892) with honor and an award of a scholarship from the Scotch Mission College, Mīr Hasan persuaded Shaikh Nūr Muhammad to let Iqbal continue his education. Consequently, on May 5, 1893, Iqbal entered the college as a first-year student, taking courses in liberal arts.

Intellectually, Iqbal blossomed at the Scotch Mission College. After attending classes at the college, Iqbal attended the discourses of Sayyid Mīr Hasan at his home. Mīr Hasan had committed to memory thousands of Arabic, Persian, and Urdu verses of great masters. He tutored his students, and particularly Iqbal, with an eye to cultivating in them a refined taste and a feeling for Persian and Arabic poetry. He never composed a verse himself, but taught Iqbal the mechanics of classical Urdu and Persian poetry.

Like all beginners, Iqbal needed the help of a master of Urdu poetry, and he found one in Nawab Mirza Khan Dāgh (1831–1905), a poet par excellence, who had the position of poetical preceptor to Nizam Mir Mahbūb Ali Khan of Hyderabad. Young Urdu poets from all over India sent him their works for his comments. In order to deal effectively with this correspondence Dāgh established in his home a secretariat of poetry, which kept track of the master's corrections. Dāgh's poetry did not bear the burden of philosophy or mysticism or great depth of thought. He was a *ghazal* writer, and his poetry was cherished for its purity of idiom, the sparkle of its simple language, and its brilliant wit.[10] Sir 'Abdūl Qādir, a life-long friend of Iqbal, has stated that Iqbal sent Dāgh his early lyrics for correction. Recognizing the poetic talent of Iqbal, Dāgh informed him after a short period of time that there was little room for improvement in his poetry. Nevertheless, both the teacher and the pupil were proud of this short-lived relationship.[11]

Iqbal was now on the road which was destined to bring him success and international fame. However, the year of his high school graduation laid the foundation for the personal anguish and unhappiness which was to mar his life during most of his remaining years. In 1892 his parents married him to Karīm Bibi, the daughter of Khan Bahadur 'Atta Muhammad Khan, an affluent physician in the city of Gujrat. Three children were born to the couple. Mi'rāj Begum, the eldest child and the exact image of her father, was born in 1895. After a prolonged illness, punctuated by eleven operations for scrofula, she died in 1914. The second child, Aftab Iqbal, was born in 1899. Like his father, Aftab studied philosophy, and obtained from the London University a bachelor of arts degree with first class honors in 1923, followed by a master's degree in philosophy two years later. He also qualified as a barrister-at-law at Lincoln's Inn, London, and is currently practicing law in Karachi as an international corporation lawyer. Iqbal's third male child, who was born in 1901, died soon after birth.

The couple lived together in relative harmony for more than two decades, but differences began to develop and finally became intolerable, especially after Iqbal's return from Europe in 1908. "My life is extremely miserable; they forced my wife upon me," confided Iqbal to a lady friend, Miss 'Atiya Begum Faizee, in 1909, adding: "I have written to my father that he had no right to arrange my marriage, especially when I had refused to enter into any alliance of that sort. I am quite willing to support her, but I am not prepared to make my life miserable by keeping her with me."[12] Iqbal's affections were largely alienated from Karīm Bibi because of his prolonged separations from her and also because of his attachment to Miss Faizee, whom he came to know in Europe. Despite her love and respect for Iqbal, Karīm Bibi preferred not to live with a husband who failed to reciprocate her feelings. Finally, in 1916 they decided to live separately, and Iqbal agreed to support her. Karīm Bibi died on February 28, 1946, but Iqbal had supported her until his death in 1938. The broken home had a telling effect on Aftab Iqbal, who grew up nurturing a resentment of the treatment accorded his mother and keenly missing the presence and affection of his father. However, in spite of the alienation of father and son, Aftab Iqbal has not allowed personal feelings to affect his wholesome respect for his father's poetic accomplishments, philosophic excellence, and political judgment.

## QUADRANGLE DAYS

IN 1895 Iqbal completed his second year at the Scotch Mission College in Sialkot. His teacher and parents recognized his talents and encouraged him to pursue higher studies. The same year Iqbal went to Lahore and entered the Government College, which was (and still is) considered to be the best institution of higher learning in the subcontinent. The subjects Iqbal studied for the bachelor of arts degree included Arabic and English literature and philosophy. He graduated *cum laude*, and was also awarded a scholarship for further study leading toward a master's degree in philosophy. Two years later (1899) he won a gold medal for the unique distinction of being the only candidate who passed the final comprehensive examination.

Iqbal's early years in Lahore opened new vistas of learning and experience. Away from the scrutiny of parents and early teachers Iqbal tasted an unknown freedom. As a young man he sowed his wild oats in the streets of Lahore, and yet had the good sense to benefit from the best of the city's intellectuals.

At age twenty-two Iqbal's poetic reputation began making its way into a more public light. In the last decade of the nineteenth century a *musha'ra* (poetical symposium) was regularly organized in the Bazaar Hakīmañ inside Bhati Gate of the walled city of Lahore. Hakīm Amīn-ud-Din, a local attorney, was the host and initiator, and Hakīm Shuja'-ud-Din often presided over the sessions of the *musha'ra*. Noted Urdu poets including Mirza Arshad Gorgani and Mīr Nazīr Husain participated in these sessions. Bhati Gate was then the center of Lahore's intellectual and cultural activities. Students of local colleges often came, sometimes to enjoy the recitation of poetry, sometimes to compete as budding poets. Iqbal, who was then the poet laureate of the quadrangle, was lured to the poetical symposia of Bhati Gate. In the presence of Gorgani, Iqbal once recited a lyric containing this famous verse:

> *Moti samjh kay shān-i karīmi nay chun li'ay*
> *Qatray jo thay mary araq-i infa'l kay.*
>
> His Grace gathered them as pearls, so shining and bright—
> The pearls of perspiration of my remorse.

Mirza Gorgani immediately exclaimed: "Iqbal! Such beautiful verse at your tender age!"

Nor was this his only early public recognition. During these years the Kashmiri families of Lahore had organized an Anjuman Kashmiri Musalmanan to implement social and educational reforms. Muhammad Din Fauq, a well-known publicist and ethnographer of the peoples of Kashmir, was the most active member of the Anjuman. Under his influence Iqbal became a supporting member and at the meetings of the Anjuman recited several poems dealing with the political and cultural problems of the Kashmiris, including *Flah-i Qawm* (Welfare of the Nation), emphasizing self-help and mutual solidarity.[13] By the time Iqbal obtained his master's degree in 1899 he was recognized as a promising young poet in the literary circles of Lahore.

By far the most pervasive influence on Iqbal's intellectual development at the Government College came from Sir Thomas Arnold, an accomplished scholar of Islam and modern philosophy. After teaching for almost ten years at the Anglo-Muhammadan College, Aligarh, Sir Thomas became professor of philosophy at the Government College in February 1898. At a farewell party in Aligarh, Maulana Muhammad Shibli Nu'mani delivered a speech highlighting Sir Thomas's personal qualities. He said: "It is not the sword of Europe alone which conquered all the nations of the world, and won their allegiance; it is their admirable moral character which has won all hearts. And Arnold is the best living example of [Europe's] virtuous conduct and praiseworthy character."[14]

Unlike most western missionaries, who presented Islam as the religion of the sword, Sir Thomas wrote at Aligarh a monumental study, *The Preaching of Islam*, emphasizing the peaceful "propagation of the Muslim faith." The study owed much, as he admitted in the preface, to the "abundance of [Shibli's] knowledge of early Muhammadan history" (p. ix). "Shibli too," maintains Sayyid Sulaiman Nadwi, "benefited from Arnold. He taught Shibli modern principles and techniques of research and acquainted him with the western criticism of old disciplines of knowledge."[15] Shibli's familiarity with western scholars of Islam and modern research techniques is visible in his well-known historical studies, including *Al-Farūq*, *Al-Mamūn*, *Al-Kalām*, and in his definitive biography of the Prophet Muhammad, *Sīrat al-Nabī*. For these Indic-Islamic studies owe much to the intellectual generosity of Sir Thomas. Such then, was the sympathy and scope of wisdom that Sir Thomas brought to his relationship with Iqbal.

At the Government College in Lahore the relationship between Sir Thomas and Iqbal was that of a disciple and a teacher. In Arnold, Iqbal found a loving teacher, who combined in himself a profound knowledge of western philosophy and a deep understanding of Islamic culture and Arabic literature. This happy melange of the East and West Arnold helped to develop in Iqbal. Also, Arnold became a bridge of friendship between Shibli Nuʿmani and Iqbal. (When Iqbal published in 1901 his technical study of economics, *Ilm-i Iqtisād*, Shibli edited his prose style.) Arnold also inspired in Iqbal the desire to pursue higher graduate studies in Europe. In 1904, when Arnold left Lahore for London, Iqbal composed a beautiful poem, *Nalā-i Firāq* (Lament of Separation), indicating the student's devotion to his teacher and his determination to follow Arnold to England in quest of knowledge.

In May 1899, a few months after Iqbal's graduation with a master's degree in philosophy, he was appointed Macleod-Punjab Reader of Arabic at the University Oriental College of Lahore. His salary was seventy-three rupees a month, and he was required to teach history and economics in addition to Arabic. Probably Sir Thomas, who was then the acting principal (president) of the Oriental College, was instrumental in his appointment, because Iqbal did not possess the requisite terminal degree in Arabic literature, even though the University Syndicate, in its proceedings of June 23, 1899, had noted that he "stood first in Arabic both at the B.A. and Intermediate examinations." From January 1901 to March 1904, when he resigned from the position of reader, Iqbal taught intermittently as assistant professor of English at Islamia College and at the Government College at Lahore. During this period he spent no more than a few months of teaching at the Oriental College. As a junior faculty member of the Punjab University he was not entitled to live in any of the comfortable and spacious houses surrounding the Punjab University and the Government College, as these houses were then reserved exclusively for the British professors. Consequently, he rented the second story of a very modest house inside Bhati Gate directly across the street from Mahala Jlotiañ. (Today, the number of this house is eleven, and the first floor is rented by a potter.)

For Iqbal, the span of time from 1900 to 1905 was filled with hopes and frustrations. The academic profession which was most congenial to his temperament had lost its luster. The social prestige of a professor ranked rather low in the hierarchy of professions (and this is still true sixty years later). Positions in the civil service and the practice of law offered greater economic and social rewards. In addition, since education was controlled by the British government, freedom of thought and expression was limited—even much more so than during the Mughal period when the private academies of eminent scholars could get generous state subsidies without loss of academic freedom.

For the ambitious Iqbal, therefore, the professorial role was constricting. (His dissatisfaction with the academic profession is vividly reflected in some of the quatrains included in the *Zarīfanā* [satirical] section of *Bāng-i-Dara* [The Call of the Highway].) In order to escape from the academic profession, he studied law simultaneously with his master's course of philosophy. His heart, however, was in philosophy rather than in law; consequently, in December 1898 he failed the preliminary examination in law because he had obtained insufficient points in jurisprudence. Two years later, when he was already Macleod Reader of Arabic at the Oriental College, Iqbal petitioned the chief justice of the Chief Court of the Punjab in Lahore to allow him to retake the law examination without repeating the schedule of lectures. A great stickler for the rules, Chief Justice Chatterji turned down his petition.[16] Probably this rebuff prompted him to study law later in England.

In 1901 Iqbal tried to enter the civil service of the Punjab and applied to take the examination for the competitive position of extra assistant commissioner (E.A.C.). This ambition also was thwarted when he was removed from the list of the candidates by the medical board. In reaction, the leading Muslim periodicals of Lahore criticized the medical board and the procedure of the examination. "The elders of the [Muslim] nation know several promising young men including Shaikh Muhammad Iqbal, M.A., who has achieved a considerable reputation for his unmatched intellectual ability," commented Muhammad Din Fauq and Maulavi Mahbūb 'Alam, "but he became a victim of the medical board of examination along with a Hindu candidate. A day before the examination the candidates are given a thorough medical checkup and for minor physical defects they are forbidden to take the examination. . . . Shaikh Muhammad Iqbal's health seems to be suffering from no defect, but one has to bow before the verdict of the doctors. Would it not be desirable if the applicants are given a medical checkup before their admittance to candidacy? After they have gone through the ordeal of preparation to compete in the examination their eleventh hour rejection on account of minor medical reasons causes them a great deal of spiritual agony."[17]

The denial of an opportunity to compete for a rewarding position was indeed a spiritual agony. Iqbal must have felt that the built-in mechanism of the sociopolitical order of colonial India provided no outlet for the fulfillment of his talents. Viewed retrospectively, however, Iqbal's early failures were proverbial blessings in disguise. As an extra assistant commissioner he would have achieved empty but glittering success and spent the remaining years of his life in the wilderness of the rural Punjab as a little czar of the British colonial administration, but he would have cheated his destiny.

The end of his frustrations was not yet in sight. In 1903 his elder brother, Shaikh 'Atta Muhammad, who was then a subdivisional officer in the Department of Military Works, was dragged into a criminal conspiracy by his jealous rivals and colleagues. In the belief that Shaikh 'Atta Muhammad would not get a fair trial, Iqbal sent a memorandum to Lord Curzon, the viceroy of India, describing in detail the facts of his brother's case. Lord Curzon ordered the Baluchistan political agency to put an end to this conspiracy.

The period of his brother's oppression, however, provided Iqbal the occasion for notable poetry. Acutely disturbed by the injustice to his brother, he gave release to his anguish in a pathetic ode, *Berg-i Gul*, to Khawja Nizām-ud Din Awliya,[18] asking the saint to intercede with Allah for His mercy. Khawja Hasan Nizāmi, the custodian of the saint's shrine and a friend of Iqbal, had the ode sung at the annual festival (*'urs*) of 1903. One of the verses of the ode was suspended from the door of the saint's mausoleum.

In 1905, on his way to Europe for advanced graduate studies, Iqbal visited the saint's mausoleum and brought another ode with him expressing his gratitude for past favors and indicating his future aspirations and quest for knowledge. In the stillness of the mausoleum sitting near the head of the saint's grave, Iqbal recited the ode, *Iltajā-i Masafer* (Request of the Traveler).[19]

Iqbal's generous compassion for his brother was met equally by Shaikh 'Atta Muhammad's generosity in love and financial help for his younger brother. No degree of frugality within a faculty salary could have sponsored his European studies; nor in fact, even allowed its consideration. Those who knew Iqbal maintained that he did manage to put aside some funds for his future educational expenses in Europe; but the remainder was paid by Shaikh 'Atta Muhammad. Iqbal never forgot his help, and in fact helped to support his brother when he retired. Later, differences in religious beliefs developed between the brothers because Shaikh 'Atta Muhammad had joined the Ahmadi movement.[20] This did not diminish Iqbal's love or respect for his elder brother, although he generally deplored the Ahmadi schism for its corrosive influence on the Muslims' national solidarity.

To his European departure (1905) Iqbal provided a fitting prelude. The recitation of his poetry at the annual sessions of Anjuman-i-Himāyat-i-Islam of Lahore catapulted him to all-India fame. The advent of the Anjuman in September 1884 was inspired by the Aligarh movement, and its annual meetings attracted the leading literary and political collaborators of Sir Sayyid Ahmad Khan. Muslims made pilgrimages to these meetings to reaffirm their social and cultural solidarity and to take part in the efforts of their national leaders. Parents often took their children to the Anjuman's annual sessions "so that they might learn the views of the national leaders in their formative years."[21]

It was at the Anjuman's annual session of 1900 that Iqbal made his national debut. While Maulana Nazīr Ahmad presided over the session of February 24, Iqbal sung his poem *Nalā'-i Yatīm* (Orphan's Cry). It had a remarkable impact, moving the audience to the depths of their souls. Many of them wept, whereas the pragmatic ones donated generously (almost three hundred rupees) to the Anjuman's funds. The printed copies of the poem designed to sell for pennies fetched four rupees each. When the meeting was over the people nearly mobbed the poet.[22] Not wanting to compliment the poet extravagantly, Maulana Nazīr Ahmad remarked: "I have heard several elegies of Anīs and Debīr, but never did I hear before such a heart-breaking poem [as that of Iqbal]."[23]

At the subsequent four annual sessions of the Anjuman, Iqbal recited *Yatīm Kā Khatāb Hilāl-i 'Id sāy* (Orphan's Plaint to the Crescent of 'Id) (1901), *Islamia College Kā Khatāb Punjab Kay Musalmānu sāy* (Islamia College's Address to the Muslims of the Punjab) and *Dīn-o-Dunyā* (Religion and World) (1902), *Abr-i Gawher Bār* (Blessed Showers) dedicated to the Prophet Muhammad (1903), and *Taswīr-i-Dard* (Portrait of Anguish) (1904). Not all of these were included in *Bāng-i-Dara* (The Call of the Highway), but like the first, they became very popular and by 1905 had endeared the poet to the hearts of his Muslim audience.

Also, during this period, Iqbal's popularity was at its peak among the Hindus. Although he was to emerge from his stay in Europe as a Muslim Nationalist, they hailed him now as a Nationalist Muslim preaching (they thought) the Congress' brand of nationalism which aspired to envelop Hindus and Muslims in an Indian nationality. There was justification for this interpretation. Iqbal composed several poems on the theme of Hindu-Muslim amity, including *Tarāna-i Hindi* (The Song of India), *Hindustani Bachoñ Kā Qawmi Gīt* (National Anthem of Indian Children) and *Nayā Shiwalā* (New Temple). In the last poem he chided both the Hindus and the Muslims for their narrow mental horizons:

> I'll tell you truth, Oh Brahmin, if I may make so bold!
> Those idols in your temples—these idols have grown old;
> To hate your fellow-mortals is all they teach you, while
> Our God too sets his preachers to scold and revile;
> Sickened, from both your temple and our shrine I have seen,
> Alike our preachers' sermons and your fond myths I shun.
> In every graven image you fancied God: I see
> In each speck of my country's poor dust, divinity.[24]

When Iqbal arrived in England in 1905, he was already well-known in India.

## THE YEAST OF THE WEST

DURING his three years of residence in Europe, Iqbal composed twenty-four small poems and lyrics, averaging eight compositions a year. Although poetry had made him famous in India, in Europe he began to doubt the usefulness of his being a poet. "I have made up my mind that I will give up poetry; instead, I would devote my time in the pursuit of something more useful," he confided to Shaikh 'Abdūl Qādir, his life-long friend and companion for two years in Europe. Qādir reasoned with him to the contrary, saying that his poetry had a magnetic quality capable of inspiring a new life in the backward Muslim nation. The final decision was left to Sir Thomas, who fortunately agreed with Qādir. Iqbal bowed to their collective judgment.

One decision which Iqbal did implement in Europe was of major poetic importance. From Urdu, he shifted to Persian as the vehicle for his poetic composition. "His host at a dinner party asked Iqbal to recite his Persian verses," narrates Qādir, "and the poet had to confess that he never composed more than a verse or two in Persian." The next morning Iqbal met Qādir and recited to him two fresh Persian lyrics. From then on, Persian became the medium of his poetic inspirations, while he used Urdu only occasionally after 1908. Seven years later, in 1915, Iqbal published his magnum opus, *Asrār-i Khudi*. He felt obliged to explain his reasons for this switch to Persian, especially in a country where very few of his audience understood Persian:

> Poetizing is not the aim of this *mathnavi*
> Beauty-worshipping and love-making is not its aim.
> I am of India: Persian is not my native tongue;
> I am like the crescent moon: my cup is not full.
> Do not seek from one charm of style in exposition,
> Do not seek from me Khansar and Isfahan.[25]
> Although the language of Hind is sweet as sugar,
> Yet sweeter is the fashion of Persian speech.
> My mind was enchanted by its loveliness.
> My pen became as a twig of the Burning Bush.
> Because of the loftiness of my thoughts,
> Persian alone is suitable to them.
> O Reader! do not find fault with the wine cup,
> But consider attentively the taste of the wine.[26]

Originally Iqbal composed 150 verses of *Asrār-i Khudi* in Urdu; subsequently, however, he destroyed these verses, feeling that he had failed adequately to convey his ideas. Some years later he made another attempt and then forsook the idea of composing *Asrār-i Khudi* in Urdu. The critics of Urdu literature do not agree with Iqbal that Urdu was unequal "to the strain put upon it by his feelings and imagination," because "some of the poems in *Bāng-i-Dara* are a standing refutation of this view."[27] Probably he wanted a wider public than the Urdu-reading Muslims of India, and Persian appeared to him as the lingua franca of the Muslim world. His contemporary, Tagore, had also sought a wider audience, through English. It won him the Nobel Prize for what Nabaneeta Sen calls, "nebulous, mystic, and sentimental verses," but Tagore made no lasting impression on the western audience. American and Indian scholars of Bengali literature agree that "Rabindranath only became a temporary craze, but never a serious literary figure in the western scene."[28]

Although Iqbal's Persian is not the contemporary Iranian *Farsi*, and modern Iranis do not read his Persian works for their beauty of expression,[29] nevertheless Iqbal's switch to Persian enabled him to win a large following in the Muslim world. There is hardly a Muslim country in the world where his original works or local translations have not appeared.

Iqbal studied in both Britain and Germany. In London he studied at Lincoln's Inn in order to qualify at the Bar, and at the Trinity College of Cambridge University he enrolled as an undergraduate student to earn a bachelor of arts degree. This enrollment was unusual, however, since he already had a master's degree in philosophy from the University of the Punjab at Lahore and was simultaneously preparing to submit a doctoral dissertation in philosophy to Munich University. The German university not only allowed him to submit his dissertation in English, but also exempted him from a mandatory stay of two terms on the campus before submitting his dissertation, "The Development of Metaphysics in Persia," to Professor F. Hommel. After his successful defense of the dissertation, Iqbal was awarded the *doctoris philosophiae gradum* on November 4, 1907. The dissertation, which was published the following year in London, was dedicated to T. W. Arnold.

Philosophy being his first love, Iqbal probably wanted to benefit from the lectures of the neo-Hegelians, John McTaggart and James Ward, who lectured then at Cambridge to the undergraduates. Moreover, two outstanding orientalists, E. G. Browne and Reynold A. Nicholson, were also at Cambridge lecturing on Persian literature. In view of this, Iqbal's admission as an undergraduate at Cambridge, though unusual, is understandable. Iqbal's intellect was sharpened, and his mental horizon widened under these eminent scholars; they also admired him and recognized his philosophic and poetic talent.

"The *Asrār-i Khudi* was first published at Lahore in 1915. I read it soon afterwards," writes Reynold Nicholson, "and thought so highly of it that I wrote to Iqbal, whom I had the pleasure of meeting at Cambridge some fifteen years ago, asking leave to prepare an English translation."[30] Iqbal's reaction to this invitation was also characteristic of a poet who was passionately involved in his people. After reading Nicholson's letter Iqbal could not control his tears; when his friend Faqīr Sayyid Najm-ud-Din asked for an explanation, Iqbal said, "that my people, whose self-hood I wanted to resurrect, neither care to appreciate it nor recognize its value. Europeans, for whom this book was not intended, want to understand my message."[31] (Even though only five hundred copies of the *Asrār-i Khudi* were first published, it raised a storm of vilification against Iqbal because of his indictment of the *Wahdat al-Wujād* [unitarian monism] school of Sufism.)[32]

Iqbal was never at home in politics, but he was invariably drawn into it. One year after Iqbal's arrival in England, the All-India Muslim League had been established in India. Two years later in London (May 1908) the British Committee of the All-India Muslim League was inaugurated under the presidency of Sayyid Amīr Ali, a former judge of the Calcutta High Court and the author of several scholarly studies on Islamic law and history, including *The Spirit of Islam* and *A History of the Saracens*. Even though Iqbal was to depart from England three months later, he was elected to the executive committee and, along with Sayyid Hassan Bilgrami and Sayyid Amīr Ali, Iqbal was nominated to a subcommittee to draft the rules and regulations of the British Committee of the Muslim League. With the exception of one brief interruption, Iqbal maintained this relationship with the All-India Muslim League throughout his life.

As to Iqbal's personal life in Europe, very little authentic information is available. Miss 'Atiya Begum Faizee, who knew Iqbal in Europe, has partially filled the gap. She said that Iqbal also studied at Heidelberg University, where he was tutored in philosophy and in the German language by Fräulein Wagnast and Fräulein Senechal. "Here at Heidelberg Iqbal acquired remarkable proficiency in German only in three months at which his German instructors were astonished; this firmly established his prestige among his professors."[33] (When he returned from Europe in July 1908, in addition to his doctorate in philosophy, he had obtained in 1907 a bachelor of arts degree from Cambridge and had also successfully qualified in July 1908 as a barrister-at-law at Lincoln's Inn, London.)

In Europe, Iqbal formed a deep and lasting friendship with Miss Faizee, an attractive and intelligent woman who personified a new spirit of awakening among Muslim women. In fact, Iqbal traveled from Cambridge to London on April 1, 1907 to meet her for the first time. "Why did you come to see me?" Miss Faizee asked Iqbal rather bluntly. "Because of your travelogue [serially published in India] you have become so famous both in India and Britain that I could not help looking you up," answered Iqbal. "I can't believe that you traveled that distance just to pay me that homage," retorted Miss Faizee.

Iqbal gave a highly embellished answer: "I am here to invite you to come to Cambridge at the Bilgramis. My mission is to escort you there. If you decline the invitation the hurt of disappointment will ever remain with me. And I have never accepted such a disappointment. Your acceptance of the invitation will truly honor your hosts." She agreed to visit the Bilgramis on April 22, 1907.

Thereafter, Iqbal saw her frequently, entertaining her sometimes at the Frascoti in London and at other times at his residence. One day at the Frascoti he told her, she tells us, that his personality contained external and internal aspects—the former was utilitarian and pragmatic, and the latter was mystic and philosophic. Under his influence Miss Faizee's interest in philosophy deepened considerably. "We agreed to study philosophy together for two hours each day on July 13, 14, 15, 1907," writes Miss Faizee. Consequently, they spent several enjoyable hours of discussion, which she says were also shared by another scholar of German philosophy.

In August, Iqbal wrote Miss Faizee a letter inviting her to visit him in Germany for three weeks. He promised to show her around in Heidelberg, Munich, and Leipzig, especially the cities' libraries and museums. On August 20, she joined him in Heidelberg and remained with him until September 4, 1907.[34] Miss Faizee's diary gives us some interesting insights into Iqbal's personality. In London and Cambridge, he was vivacious, gregarious, eager to engage in verbal duals both with his peers and superiors, and relentlessly self-assertive. For instance, at a dinner at the Arnolds in London, Miss Faizee tells us, Professor Arnold told Iqbal that some rare manuscripts had been discovered in Germany, and that he would like Iqbal to examine them. "You are my teacher, I, your pupil, what could I do for you?" answered Iqbal. "Yes, sometimes a student excels his teacher; moreover, the student should obey the teacher," Arnold thus flattered Iqbal. Heartily conceding the point, Iqbal said: "As a teacher you know better; if that is what you want, I bow my head in submission."[35]

Occasionally, Iqbal could also engage in a harmless practical joke. In order to impress his German friends with the supernatural power so often associated with the "inscrutable East," he played the lost mystic. On the eve of a picnic in Heidelberg (August 22, 1907), while friends waited outside of his room, Iqbal pretended to be in a trance. Finally, Miss Faizee entered his room and found that Iqbal's gaze was fixed on books and that his eyes had a dreadful glassy stare. Some thought that he had frozen to death overnight. Finally Miss Faizee shook him by his shoulders rather vigorously and quietly shouted at him: "Wake up, you are not in India, where an antic like this can be tolerated." Iqbal meekly mumbled an explanation for this strange act: "I was up in the heavenly spheres."[36]

Miss Faizee left for India in 1907, but she revisited Europe in 1908 for a brief period and spent some time with Iqbal. She has left no information about this short reunion except that Iqbal wrote on June 9, 1908 a few verses in the autograph album of her sister-in-law, Rufi'ah Sultan Nāzli Begum. However, when Miss Faizee went back to India Iqbal sent her a poem, *Wasāl* (Union) from Munich, which he subsequently incorporated in the *Bāng-i-Dara*. A few verses are translated here:

> *Justjū jis gul key tarpāty thi ay bulbūl mujhay*
> *Khūbi-i qismat sāy akhir mil gayā woh gul mujhay.*
>
> Hark ye Nightingale! the flower that I was restlessly
>     in search of, I fortunately got.
> My restlessness was infectious for the garden-dwellers,
> When I heard your melody, I invariably blushed.
> Like mercury my heart was in constant flux,
> Perhaps the "sin" of love made it so impatient.
> The rouge of love has radiated the mirror of my dust
>     [that is, life]
> And in this mirror is reflected the image of the old beloved.
> I gained freedom in my captivity,
> The plunder of my heart rehabilitated my home.

The poem bursts with candor of earthly emotions of man for woman. Iqbal planted a tree of joy in Europe and eventually it blossomed, but he adored it from afar and never did he permanently possess "that flower" to adorn his lapel. Reflecting on Iqbal's romantic involvements as portrayed through his poetry, Khalīfah 'Abdūl Hakīm said that unlike traditional Urdu poetry "Iqbal's poetry was not artificial. If he dedicated a poem to a beloved (*mahbūb*) the beloved was invariably a human being. In love affairs Iqbal believed in doing and getting over it rather than in never giving his heart to anyone."[37]

Miss Faizee accused Iqbal of "indifference" and "hypocrisy." However, Iqbal vigorously protested against these accusations, saying "If opportunity comes I shall certainly show you how intensely I love my friends and how deeply my heart feels for them all. People hold life dear and rightly so. I have got the strength to give it freely away. . . . No! don't call me indifferent or hypocrite, not even by implication for it hurts my soul and makes me shudder at your ignorance of my nature. I wish I could turn inside outward in order to give you better view of my soul, which you think is darkened by hypocrisy and indifference."[38]

Perhaps Miss Faizee did not understand Iqbal's nature, but she was keenly aware of his emotional problems. She knew how unhappy he was, and she also knew what made him so, especially after his return from Europe to Lahore in 1908. Writing in 1947, almost ten years after Iqbal's death, she offered a very convincing analysis:

In India [Muslim] morés are not [always] directly related to religion; but they have gained compelling significance. An individual is obligated to bow before the wishes and orders of his family. In view of this, many men and women, though endowed with extraordinary intellectual abilities, ruined their lives. Iqbal's life was indeed a cruel tragedy, which developed as a result of his family's intransigence.

Iqbal was not in India what he had been in Europe. Those who did not have the good fortune of knowing him in his early life, can never imagine the quality of his God-given intellectual brilliance, which he exercised so well. In India his genius was corroded, and with the passage of time this overwhelmed his consciousness. He felt a measure of degradation, and his life, according to him, was constricted, because he always knew what he could have become.

As of this writing, I know two Indian girls who are good and gentle, and have the mental ability to soar high in life. But they had to sacrifice themselves at the altar of their family's wishes. The family wanted them to marry men in order to gain respectability as if their own lives had no intrinsic value.

In view of Iqbal's tragedy I appeal to my *millat* (nation) to be aware of this danger, and before they interfere in the lives of the young people, they must seriously weigh its pros and cons.[39]

Iqbal yearned for personal happiness and longed for self-fulfillment; however, both were to elude him. "To disburden my soul," as he described it, Iqbal wrote often to Miss Faizee. In a letter of April 9, 1909 he wrote, "As a human being I have a right to happiness; if society or nature [culture] deny that to me I defy both. The only cure is that I should leave this wretched country for ever, or take refuge in liquor, which makes suicide easier. These dead barren leaves of books cannot yield happiness; I have got sufficient fire in my soul to burn them up and all social conventions as well. . . ."[40] Why did he not propose to Miss Faizee? In view of their previous attachment in Europe the question is intriguing; however, no definite answer can be given. Only a plausible explanation can be offered.

Because she was an avant-garde female Muslim, Miss Faizee's friendship in Europe was probably very fascinating for Iqbal, but in the more conservative and sedate Muslim cultural milieu of the Punjab she would have been completely out of place. Their different social backgrounds also presented a formidable obstacle. Iqbal was a product of the middle class, aspiring to prominence by virtue of his talents, whereas Miss Faizee belonged to an aristocratic and princely family of Bombay. (She was the first cousin of Sir Akbar Hayderi, who was then the revenue minister of Hyderabad, and her sister was married to Nawab Sayyidi Ahmad Khan.) Such a marriage would have been repugnant to Iqbal's ego.

In 1909 Iqbal's family arranged a second marriage with Sardar Begum, a charming but physically frail young lady belonging to a respectable Kashmiri family from the neighborhood of Mochi Gate in Lahore. (Here sources disagree, some maintaining that the *nikah* [a ceremony solemnizing the contract of marriage, often without the consummation of the marriage, however] was actually performed, others asserting that only the engagement ceremony was celebrated.) It is established, nevertheless, that the bride did not come to the house of the groom. Iqbal had received anonymous letters impugning the character of the young bride. (Actually this was the mischief of a local lawyer, Nabi Bakhsh, who wanted very much to marry his own son to Sardar Begum.) This situation caused no small amount of misery to Iqbal, but it seems that he did not act prudently in handling this matter. Without terminating his formal matrimonial relationship with Sardar Begum, Iqbal married another girl, Mukhtar Begum, the niece of a very wealthy business man of Ludhana. She died in 1924.

A few years after the uncompleted marriage, Sardar Begum wrote a letter to Iqbal chiding him for his injustice and lack of compassion. "I was married to you, a second marriage is now inconceivable to me," Sardar Begum wrote, adding: "I will remain in my present state til I die, and on the day of Judgment will hold you [responsible for ruining my life]."[41] Her statement indicates that the *nikah* ceremony had been performed even though the marriage was not consummated. Iqbal, however, was not sure whether his negative intentions toward Sardar Begum had not constituted a virtual divorce, according to the Hanafi school of law. In order to clarify the status of his marriage in the light of the *Shariʿa*, Iqbal sent Mirza Jalāl-ud-Din, a fellow barrister-at-law, to Hakīm Nūr-ud-Din of Qadian, to obtain his views. Hakīm Nur-ud-Din did not think that the undeclared intentions constituted divorce, but advised the performance of a second *nikah* as the best way out. Consequently, Iqbal was married to Sardar Begum for the second time in 1913. She gave Iqbal love, devotion, and peace of mind. However, she died prematurely on May 23, 1935, when she was only thirty-seven years old, and left Iqbal with a son, Javid Iqbal (born in 1924), and a daughter, Munirah (born in 1930). Following in the footsteps of his father, Javid Iqbal obtained his Ph.D. from Cambridge University, and also qualified for the Bar at Lincoln's Inn, London. (Currently, he is a practicing attorney in Lahore, Pakistan.)

## THE LAWYER AND THE POET

WHEN Iqbal came back from Europe in 1908, he started his professional career as an attorney, college professor, and poet—all at once. At length, however, the true poet won out at the expense of the professor and the attorney, but not before years of personal turmoil

The yoking of the professor to the poet might have worked if Iqbal had been able to teach in a private university or college like Harvard or Amherst. But the position of assistant professor at the Government College in Lahore promised him only a modest monthly income without guaranteeing academic freedom as it was understood at Cambridge and Oxford or Yale and Princeton. In 1909 Aligarh Muslim University offered him a professorship of history, but he declined the invitation. After deciding to resign his temporary teaching position at the college, Iqbal confided (July 17, 1909) to Miss Faizee: "The

Lieutenant-Governor was willing to recommend me to the Secretary of State for India for the vacant Professorship in the Lahore Government College, but I gave up the idea of standing as candidate, much against my personal inclination. Force of circumstances compels me to consider things from [the] financial point of view—a point of view which was revolting to me a few years ago. I have decided to continue the legal profession trusting in God's help."[42]

Iqbal so repeatedly versified the proverb "God helps those who help themselves" that today every schoolboy in Pakistan knows it by heart. Yet he did precious little to help his own law practice, which started in October 1908, and virtually ended in 1934.[43] After ten years of law practice he wrote to his father in 1918: "I have made the determination not to personally benefit from the income derived from the sale of my prose and poetry. Because [poetry] is a God-given talent, involving no physical labor, and it should be exercised in the service of mankind, but I have been compelled by need to act otherwise."[44] According to his friends and associates Iqbal hardly ever earned more than a thousand rupees a month—the income of a moderately successful attorney of the lower courts in today's Pakistan.

Iqbal never really aspired to earn more than he actually needed. Performing the role of an appellate lawyer, he confined his practice to the High Court of Judicature at Lahore. It is estimated that including the house and office rent and the salaries of his clerk and domestic servants, his fixed expenses amounted to approximately seven hundred rupees. He would be quite content when he earned enough to cover his overhead, plus a few hundred extra for incidental expenses. Consequently, any additional cases coming to him after the tenth of each month were refused or referred to other attorneys; and if the client insisted on retaining him he was advised to come before the tenth of the following month.[45]

This self-imposed limitation naturally provided him the leisure which he thought he needed for the cultivation of his friends and his own soul. In the first years of his practice, after appearing before the courts, Iqbal regularly visited his friend Mirza Jalāl-ud-Din. He and his boon companions, including Nawab Zulfiqār Ali Khan, Sir Jogendera Singh, and Sardar Umrao Singh, regularly gathered at Mirza's residence. For their entertainment they arranged private sitar concerts, exchanged witticisms with each other, and then dispersed in the evening. Iqbal often would stay overnight for more merriment. These scions of Punjabi aristocracy could very well afford this life of leisure, but Iqbal could not; his law practice never gave him the life of comfort and financial security which a man of his intelligence, had he been industrious, could have commanded.

Throughout his life he supplemented his income from the proceeds of his poetical works. He published all of his works himself and then franchised different booksellers, giving them a commission of three annas for a rupee on each copy. In the case of hard cover books the commission was considerably increased, but the bookseller had to assume the responsibility of advertising Iqbal's works.[46] His fame as a poet was also heightened by his recitation of his own poetry at the annual meetings of Anjuman-i-Himāyat-i-Islam (*Shikwah* or *Complaint* in 1911), and the specially called public meetings outside Mochi Gate (*Jawab Shikwah* or *Answer* in 1912), and the Shahi Mosque (*Fatimah binat 'Abdūllah* in 1912) in Lahore. Two years after the publication of *The Secrets of the Self* (1922), an English translation of *Asrār-i Khudi* by Reynold A. Nicholson of Cambridge University, the British government, recognizing his scholarship and poetic talent, knighted him. These were the days of the Khilafat agitation and noncooperation which had temporarily united the Hindus and the Muslims. Now that Iqbal was a Sir he was resented by the Khilafatists. It was probably Maulana Zafar Ali Khan (one of the Khilafat leaders) who satirized the occasion with these caustic verses:

> *Lo madressah-i 'ilm hu'a qaser-i hakūmat,*
> *Afsus kah Alamah say Sir ho gai'ay Iqbal.*
> *Pahlay to sir-i millat-i baydā kay thay woh tāj,*
> *Ab awr suno tāj kay Sir ho gai'ay Iqbal.*
> *Kahtā thā yah kal thandi saṛak per kowiy gustākh,*
> *Sarkar key dahlīyz peh Sir ho gai'ay Iqbal.*

Lo and behold! the seat of learning has become the
                                             Government House;
Alas! Iqbal stooped to knighthood from an Alamah [scholar]
Formerly, he was the crown of the Muslim people
Hark another news! Iqbal has become a knight
                                             of the [British] crown,
An impertinent fellow said yesterday on the Mall:
"Iqbal bowed his head low at the threshold of Sarkar
                                             [British government]."[47]

Iqbal devoted his time primarily to his legal practice and cultural activities, but when elections were introduced in the Punjab under the Montagu-Chelmsford Reforms, his friends and admirers prevailed upon him to run. In November 1926 Iqbal contested a seat from a Muslim district of Lahore. Out of the total of 12,000 registered voters, 68 per cent actually voted; Iqbal obtained 5,675, and his opponent, Malik Muhammad Din, received 2,498.⁴⁸ True to his sedentary habits, Iqbal had hardly ever ventured to campaign outside of his residence. His popularity had ensured his success. When the result was declared Iqbal's volunteers and campaigners rushed to his home and repeatedly shouted, *Iqbal zindeh bād*, "Long live Iqbal." (For a description of his legislative and political role see Chapter 4.)

In December 1928, Iqbal traveled to South India in order to deliver six lectures on Islam at the request of the Madras Muslim Association. In these addresses Iqbal stated that he was attempting to "reconstruct Muslim religious philosophy with due regard to the philosophical tradition of Islam and the more recent development in the domains of human knowledge."⁴⁹ Having taken three years to compose these lectures, Iqbal viewed them as indicative of his mature philosophic and rational approach to Islam. He expected that others would follow him in a responsible *ijtihād* (the right of interpreting the Qur'ān and the *Sunnah* or of forming a new opinion by applying analogical deduction). Once he told an admirer, Professor Yusuf Salīm Chishtī: "If this book of mine had appeared during the reign of [the 'Abbasid] Khalifah Ma'mūn al-Rashīd [813–833], it would have had profound repercussions in the entire intellectual world of Islam."⁵⁰ At least for the present age, Iqbal hoped to lay the groundwork for religion and science to "discover hitherto unsuspected mutual harmonies."

## BRIEF SOJOURNS IN EUROPE

TWENTY-THREE years after he returned from Europe in 1908, Iqbal had another occasion to visit Britain and other continental countries. The opportunity was provided by the second (September 7–December 1, 1931) and the third (November 17–December 24, 1932) London Round Table Conferences. (Iqbal had not been invited to the first conference.) The Round Table Conferences were called by the British government to consult with Indian leaders on the problems of constitutional reforms for India. (For Iqbal's role in these conferences, see Chapter 4.)

Although he remained in Europe for less than a year, European diplomacy and the political and intellectual trends which engulfed Europe in the bloodbath of the late 1930s left a deep impression on Iqbal's mind. (Most of these impressions are reflected in the verses of *Darb-i Kalīm* [The Rod of Moses], first published in July 1936.) During the second conference Iqbal was occupied with the business of the conference and had no significant opportunity to travel in Europe. In the third conference (1932) his participation was minimal. He spent four months traveling in Europe and meeting scholars and political leaders, including Henri Bergson and Louis Massignon of France and Benito Mussolini of Italy.

Accompanied by Sayyid Amjad Ali (later Pakistan's ambassador to the United States and the United Nations) and Sardar Umrao Singh Majithia, Iqbal visited Les Invalides. This visit to Napoleon's tomb brought forth a poetic expression of Iqbal's concept of activism and the role of sustained effort in the rise to power:

> The prayers of God's folk treading
>    The battlefield's red sod,
> Forged in that flame of action
>    Become the voice of God!
> But only a brief moment
>    Is granted to the brave—
> One breath or two, whose wage is
>    The long nights of the grave.
> Then since at last the valley
>    Of silence is our goal,
> Beneath this vault of heaven
>    Let our deed's echoes roll![51]

Iqbal's visit with Massignon renewed his admiration for the French orientalist's profound scholarship in Sufism. Massignon had made a significant contribution to the understanding of Mansūr Hallaj, a ninth-century Sufi, who was put to death for expounding a mystic view of reality which the contemporary Muslim world had failed to appreciate. (For a detailed discussion of this problem, see Chapter 15.) Rather directly Iqbal expressed the Muslims' grievance that many European orientalists and historians appeared to study Islam primarily with a view to maligning it. Iqbal asked Massignon whether their prejudice and enmity was decreasing. Massignon pointed out that western scholars had come to adopt a relatively neutral attitude in their treatment of Islamic movements. As a gracious host he also indicated that Europe was indebted to Islam for diffusing certain traits of its civilization into Europe, thus enriching future possibilities of progress in the West.[52]

His visit with Bergson was an intellectual treat for Iqbal. Bergson's dynamic concept of time, in Iqbal's judgment, was close to the view of the Muslim mystics. Iqbal is said to have cited the Prophet Muhammad's Tradition to Bergson, saying: "Do not speak ill of time; God says, I am time." Bergson was pleasantly surprised and repeatedly asked Iqbal if that was an authentic Tradition.[53] (For Iqbal's concept of time, see Chapter 11.)

Spain and Italy followed France on Iqbal's itinerary. In Madrid, Miguel Asín Palacios, who had earned a wide reputation for his *La Escatalogia Muslimana en la Divina Comedia* demonstrated the impact of Islamic legends on Dante, had invited Iqbal to deliver a lecture at the university. Appropriately, Iqbal highlighted the role of medieval Spain in the intellectual development of the Muslim world. However, Spanish traditions had more than intellectual interest for him. Iqbal was emotionally drawn to the culture and history of Spain. The fact that Spain had once been Muslim led Iqbal to call it "the treasure-house of Muslims' blood and the sacred land of Islam." Like a pilgrim he visited medieval Muslim monuments, which inspired three beautiful poems later included in the *Bāl-i Jibrīl* (Gabriel's Wing). At the mosque of Cordoba (which had been converted into a church in 1236) Iqbal offered a prayer of thanksgiving. When, in the traditional Muslim style, he raised his hands in supplication to Allah, tears rolled down his cheeks. In those intense moments of inspiration he composed *The Mosque of Cordoba*, a splendid poem on the cruelties of time and the immortality of love:

> All Art's wonders arise only to vanish once more;
> All things built on this earth sink as if built on sand!
> Inward and outward things, first things and last, must die;
> Things from of old or new-born find their last goal in death;

Yet, in this frame of things, gleams of immortal life
Show where some servant of God wrought into some high shape
Work whose perfection is still bright with the splendour of love—
Love, the well-spring of life; love, on which death has no claim.
Shrine of Cordoba! from love all your existence is sprung,
Love that can know no end, stranger to Then-and-Now.[54]

From Spain Iqbal went to Italy and visited with Mussolini. The visit took place before Il Duce's invasion of Ethiopia. The record of their conversation is not available; only a poem entitled *Mussolini* remains, in which Iqbal admired Il Duce's political vitality and the magnetic quality of his bright eyes. Subsequently, ill-informed critics charged that Iqbal was a Muslim Nietzsche propagandizing the worship of power. This criticism was grossly inaccurate because the poems in the *Ḍarb-i Kalīm* (first published in July 1936) contained a vigorous indictment not only of Mussolini, but also of the major powers in the League of Nations, which connived at Italian imperialism. (Jan Marek deals with this subject exhaustively in Chapter 7.)

## A VISIT TO AFGHANISTAN

IN February 1933 Iqbal was back in Lahore. Seven months later Muhammad Nādir Shah, the King of Afghanistan, invited him along with Sayyid Sulaiman Nadwi and Sir Sayyid Ross Masʿūd to visit Kabul. The Afghan king asked them to advise his government in the establishment of a new university and in utilizing the best of modern western and traditional Islamic values in the reorganization of higher education. By the end of October 1933 Iqbal and his fellow delegates reached Afghanistan and remained there for almost four weeks. Iqbal recorded the impressions of his visit in a Persian poem, *Masafer* (The Traveler). The poem lacks the vitality and freshness of ideas evident in many of his earlier works, but as a record of his travels in Afghanistan it is a useful source of information. In addition to Kabul, Iqbal visited the wilderness of Ghazni, the capital of Sultan Mahmūd's Empire. During the eleventh century the empire of Ghazni had included the province of Lahore, and was one of the most powerful and civilized states in the medieval world. The ruins of bygone glory filled Iqbal's heart with emotion, and the poet gave vent to his anguish in verse:

> Al-āman az makr-i-ayyām al-āman.
> Al-āman az suboh-o-shām al-āman.
>
> Protect us O! Lord from the treachery of time, O! Lord.
> Protect us O! Lord from the days and nights, O! Lord.

With tears in his eyes for the decline of the Muslims, Iqbal asked Allah: "Why are you so kind to the British, they have confined mankind to the house of bondage?" Unhesitatingly, the poet answered this rhetorical question. "The Muslim has lost the zest for life and his heart beats no more. He was the *israfīl* (the angel of resurrection), but his *saūr* (the trumpet of life) blows no more." Iqbal expressed similar sentiments at the mausoleums of Sultan Mahmūd and Emperor Babūr, the founder of the Mughal Empire in India. When Iqbal had an audience with Nādir Shah he presented the Afghan king with a copy of the Qur'ān, saying: "It is the beacon-light of those who follow the truth."[55]

Not much is known about the educational recommendations of Iqbal and his associates. On October 10, 1933 he issued a statement saying that "an educated Afghanistan will be the best friend of India." He decried secular education for Afghanistan, because the "complete secularization of education has not produced good results anywhere, especially in Muslim lands." Despite Afghanistan's general backwardness and the conservatism of the royal family, Iqbal complimented the Afghan regime in a statement of November 6: "All the ministers are discharging their duties. Even the orthodox party stands solidly behind these workers and consequently there is—as was stated in our presence by a leading Afghan divine—no difference between the *mullas* and the young men in the Afghanistan of today."[56]

Iqbal admired the Afghans, not because their government was progressive, but because they had escaped colonial domination. The fact that it had been the clash of Russian policy and British imperial interests which had allowed Afghanistan to survive as a buffer state was not of much significance to Iqbal. In his judgment the Afghans' love for freedom and their rugged individualism were the decisive factors. Precisely for these reasons, Iqbal's poetry exudes admiration for the Afghans.

## THE LAST FIVE YEARS

AFTER his return from Afghanistan Iqbal's health steadily deteriorated. However, his intellect remained sharp, and during this time he conceived many new projects, including proposed studies on Islamic jurisprudence and *Aids to the Study of Qur'ān*. An interpretive study, *Islam As I Understand It*, was to reconcile modern science and philosophy with Islam. In the style of *Thus Spake Zarathustra* Iqbal planned to write *The Book of an Unknown Prophet* discussing metaphysical problems. Iqbal spent considerable mental effort in determining the exact literary style for his bible. None of these studies saw the light of day; political preoccupations and indifferent health made their execution impossible.

One academic project (which was to widely influence the Muslims after the establishment of Pakistan) did materialize. Iqbal wanted to establish an Institute of Advanced Research in the Punjab, where the studies of Muslim scholars of classical Islam and of representatives of contemporary social sciences would be subsidized. These scholars were to have a tenured appointment and freedom from want, enabling them to investigate contemporary political and economic problems from the viewpoint of Islam. Iqbal hoped this would create a revolution in the intellectual climate of Indic Islam. Iqbal wrote to Shaikh Mustafa al-Maraghi, rector of al-Azhar, explaining the nature of the proposed institute and asking him to send an accomplished Egyptian scholar at the institute's expense. Shaikh al-Maraghi promised to help, but nothing came of it.

In 1937 Niyāz Ali Khan, an admirer of Iqbal, and an influential landlord in the district of Gurdaspur, offered Iqbal a vast tract of his agricultural land in Pathankot to build the institute. From Hyderabad-Deccan Iqbal invited a young scholar of thirty-five, Abul 'Alā Maudūdi, to found Adarah Darul Islam in Pathankot on the land donated by Niyāz Ali Khan. Maudūdi transferred himself to Pathankot in 1938 and founded not only his Jama'āt-i Islami, but also started to publish *Tarjmān al-Qur'ān*, which became the vehicle of his conservative Islamic and political interpretations. After 1947 Maudūdi moved to Lahore and involved himself in a struggle for power in Pakistan. His critics have charged that Maudūdi has merely used Iqbal's name without the latter's balanced emphasis on modernism.

Although Iqbal's religious and political ideas were gaining wide acceptance and his popularity was at its peak, his personal life became bleak. To Sayyid Naẕīr Niyāzī he wrote on March 27, 1935 that "for more than a year I have done nothing [that is, not practiced law] and the sources of income have dried up." In view of this he requested Niyāzī to persuade Hakīm 'Abdūl Wahab, the famous blind physician of Delhi, to examine his sick wife at Lahore for a moderate fee. On June 1, 1935 in another letter Iqbal confided to Niyāzī that "the Nawab of Bhopal has granted me a pension of Rs. 500/- monthly. He helped me out just in time."[57] His wife's health failed to improve, however, (see Chapter 3 by Javid Iqbal) and he himself succumbed to several illnesses in quick succession. He lost his voice and had to decline Oxford University's invitation to deliver the Rhodes lectures in 1935.

Iqbal went to Bhopal for medical treatment three times during 1935–1936. In Bhopal his friend, Sir Sayyid Ross Mas'ud (grandson of Sir Sayyid Ahmad Khan) was the minister of education. Although Iqbal considerably reduced his travels because of his illnesses, he managed to attend Altaf Husain Hali's centennial celebrations (October 26, 27, 1935) at Panipat. While the Nawab of Bhopal, Hamīd Allah Khan, presided over a meeting of the centennial, Iqbal recited his four Persian verses in homage of Hali, the first Muslim nationalist poet of Muslim India. Even though Iqbal, in his last years, was surrounded by admirers whose devotion he cherished, he suffered from a gnawing sense of isolation. When Mas'ūd died in July 1937 he composed an elegy which mourns not only the national loss in Mas'ūd's death, but also portrays his feeling of loneliness.

With the start of 1938 Iqbal's health sharply deteriorated. Overwhelmed by asthmatic attacks, he steadily grew weaker, but his mind suffered no disability. On April 20, only a few hours before his death, he recited a Persian quatrain to Hasan Akhtar, a young admirer. Probably it had been composed a few months earlier. The quatrain is indicative of his own significance in history:

> The departed melody may or may not come,
> The breeze from Hedjaz may or may not come.
> The days of this *Faqīr* have come to an end,
> Another wise one may or may not come!

When the news of Iqbal's death was broadcast from the Lahore

Radio Station government offices and private stores were closed as a mark of respect. The leading Muslim citizens of Lahore (including Khalifah Shuja'-ud-Din, Mian Nizām-ud-Din, Mian Amīr-ud-Din, and Ghulam Rasūl Mehr) successfully sought the permission of the Punjab governor to bury Iqbal on a spot to the left of the steps leading to the Badshahi mosque in Lahore. On the evening of April 21, 1938 Iqbal was lowered into the grave.

The construction of the present mausoleum on the grave was started in 1946, when the Mausoleum Committee accepted the plan of Nawab Zīn Yār Jung, a noted Muslim architect of Hyderabad. As a token of its admiration for Iqbal, the government of Afghanistan donated the lapis lazuli marble for the structure. On the front of the mausoleum one of Iqbal's quatrains is inscribed, reflecting the poet's sentiments about the unity of the Indic Muslims:

> Neither are we Afghans nor Turks,
> > nor yet from the lands of Central Asia
> We belong to the garden, and descend from the same ancestors.
> Forbidden unto us are the distinctions of color or race,
> Yes! we are the harvest of a new spring.

# 2

# Glimpses of the Man

## MUHAMMAD DAUD RAHBAR

MOST of the poetical works of Iqbal have been translated into English. The trends of his thought have become known in the worlds of Islam and Islamics. His political contribution has become concrete in the form of a living Pakistan. However, the quality of Iqbal's presence as a companion remains very inadequately recorded, although the wonders of his conversation have been perpetuated in a large number of essays of reminiscences written by his friends and admirers. Many of these are scattered in Urdu journals. For instance, a delightful account written by Dr. 'Ashiq Husain Batalavi tells this story: Once he spotted in the Nila Gumbad market place of Lahore a young Hindu dejected to the point of attempting suicide. Dr. Batalavi took this young man to Iqbal who, with a flash of a loving glance, a cheering eye-twinkle, and an amusing dialectic based on the doctrine of karma, pulled the young Hindu instantly from the abyss of despair. Dr. Batalavi tells in this essay how he discovered years later that this young man had grown up to become Davindar Satyarthi, the well-known Hindi writer.

Likewise, this writer recollects a delightful essay of reminiscence by Professor M. Mujīb of the Jamia'-i Milliyā-i-Islamiyā of Delhi containing a beautiful description of Iqbal's conversational style. Maulana Ghulam Ahmad Parvaiz, the well-known Ahl al-Qur'ān leader of Pakistan, has written an account of his last meeting with Iqbal in his booklet, *Iqbal aur Qur'ān*. Professor Rashīd Ahmad Siddiqi of Aligarh has included an essay on his associations and meeting with Iqbal in his *Ganjha-i-Garañmayā*. Another invaluable source of information about Iqbal is a collection of essays entitled *Malfūzat-i-Iqbal*.

The *Malfūzat* (Conversational Discourses) departs from the traditional *Malfūzat* literature in many ways. The latter, in the course of the development of Sufi literature, has been confined to reports of pious utterances of saints and divines gathered by their disciples. In the *Malfūzat* of Iqbal the authors write more as friends, and their literary training in modern biography does not restrain their disclosure of memories of all varieties. All the essays in the volume were read at the meetings of a short-lived little society called *Anjuman-i-Halqa-i-Naqd-o-Nazar* (Society of the Critics and Observers) held at the residence of Professor 'Abd al-Wahid in Lahore, with Professor Saīd Allah as chairman.

The volume contains seventeen essays in all. Of these there are four by Iqbal's friends from his own generation: (1) Sir 'Abdūl Qādir, lawyer and later judge of the Punjab High Court, and editor of *Makhzan*, the literary journal that published all the early Urdu masterpieces of Iqbal's poetry. He also wrote an illuminating introduction to Iqbal's Urdu anthology, *Bāng-i-Dara* (The Call of the Highway); (2) Hakīm Muhammad Hasan Qarshi, the personal physician of Iqbal. He was not trained as a modern allopath but adhered to the system of medicine known in the Muslim lands as *Tibbi-i-Yūnani* (greek medicine); (3) Muhammad Husain 'Arshi, a savant who turned to Iqbal for guidance in his story of Rumi and the Qur'ān; (4) Mirza Jalāl-ud-Din, who remained close to Iqbal when both practiced law at the Punjab High Court.

Among the remaining thirteen essays, there is an essay by Iqbal's beloved and loving son, Dr. Javid Iqbal, after whom the poet named his book of verse entitled *Javid-Namah* (The Book of Eternity). The rest are essays by Iqbal's younger contemporaries, mostly from the literary and academic community of Lahore.

To the same category of recollections belongs another essay published as a separate booklet under the title *Rūzgār-i Faqīr*. The author of this work is Faqīr Sayyid Wahīd al-Din, a son of Iqbal's close friend, Faqīr Sayyid Iftikhār al-Din.

Before discussing the first essay in the *Malfūzat*, written by Sir 'Abdūl Qādir, a lecture delivered by Qādir before the master's candidates of Urdu literature at the Punjab University should be recounted. He related that a certain gentleman had asked Iqbal about the circumstances of the composition of this verse:

> *Yād-i watan fusurdagi-i-be sabab banī.*
> *Dhauq-i Nazar bani Kabhi Shauq-i-Talab banī.*

> The memory of the homeland became a sadness without cause.
> Sometimes it transformed itself into a desire to look at beauty
> and sometimes into passionate pursuits.

He sought from the poet a confirmation of the conjecture that the verse indicated Iqbal's nostalgia for Lahore and Sialkot during his stay in England and Europe. Iqbal startled the enquirer by explaining that the verse actually spoke of that pre-earthly home from which all come to live in this terrestrial world.

## A SAD SOUL

IQBAL's sad temperament, though effectively balanced by his rich sense of humour, was inherited from his father, Shaikh Nūr Muhammad. In a letter to Akbar of Allahabad, Iqbal mentions how, during a period of mourning, his father wept for several hours at the thought of man's separation from his Creator.[1] In spite of a highly refined joviality and sprightliness imbibed by Iqbal from his senior contemporary, Maulana Girāmi,[2] and Maulana Mīr Hasan, his teacher,[3] Iqbal's soul remained deeply embedded in sadness. In fact, as one rambles through the *Malfūzat*, the occasional glimpses of this hidden transcendental sadness in the midst of Iqbal's vivacious conversations provide that magnetic touch of drama in his personal presence that attracted people to him. The nature of this sadness is vividly described by Sir 'Abdūl Qādir in the article ("The State of Grief") he contributed to the *Malfūzat*. In this essay, he cites a line from Iqbal's verse that is true of the poet himself:

> 'Ibadat chashm-i -'ashiq ki hai har dam ba wuḍū rehna.
> The worship of the lover's eye is to remain
> moistened by ablution every moment.

In another verse Iqbal says:

> Pīr-i-mughan farang ki mai ka nishāt hai athar.
> Is men vu kaif-i-gham nahiñ, mujh ko to khana saz de.
> O Preceptor of drinkers! The wine of the West
> gives only mirth.
> It has no state of grief to offer. So give me
> the brew of my native land.

## Glimpses of the Man

Sir 'Abdūl Qādir recalls how he noticed a resemblance between the facial expressions of Iqbal and Iqbal's father when the poet recited (in April 1911) his great poem *Shikwah* (Complaint) at the annual meeting of the Anjuman-i-Himāyat-i-Islam in Lahore. On the faces of the father and the son, says 'Abdūl Qādir, grief was visible. Whenever Iqbal recited his poetry the genuineness of the pathos in the poet's thought made his listeners sad.

Iqbal's friend of his days in Europe, Miss 'Atiya Faizee, refers to a note in her European diary that describes an occasion in Germany when the poet withdrew into an inner world of sadness, completely forgetting the company surrounding him. She had to shake him by the shoulder and say, "Wake up. This is Germany, not India."[4] Iqbal recalls in verse his longing for solitude in the midst of crowds during his youthful days in the West:

> *Kahīñ sarmaya-i-mehfil thi merī garm guftāri.*
> *Kabhi sab ko parishāñ kar gai meri kam amezi.*
> On one occasion my lively talk was the life of the assembly.
> On another my unsociable mood spoilt my joy of all around me.

In a letter to Akbar of Allahabad, Iqbal especially admires this line by Akbar:

> *Gham bara mudrik-i-haqaiq hai.*
> Grief is great in the comprehension of realities.

In another letter (to Shātir Madrasi), the poet maintains that the basic state of human soul is grief.

Instances of Iqbal's sudden lapses into sadness and withdrawals into private and silent thought are scattered throughout the pages of the *Malfūzat*. His gifts of charming physique, sense of humor, and brilliant conversation were the steel, stone, and mortar of the dam that checked the torrent of tears. However, this dam would burst now and then when certain topics were discussed. During his last years he invariably wept when listening to the recitation of the Qur'ān. His physician, Hakīm Muhammad Hasan Qarshi, recalled that while reciting the famous poem *Khizr-i-Rah* (The Guide) at a meeting of the Anjuman-i-Himayāt-i-Islam in Lahore, Iqbal's eyes had become tearful at the line:[5]

*Ho gaya manind-i-āb arzañ musalmañ ka lahū.*
The blood of Muslims became cheap like water.

The Qur'ān recitation could not have failed to arouse in him a storm of historical memories and a welter of hopes and fears about man's destiny. The extensive learning of the poet enabled him to visualize the millennia of world history; with his poetical imagination and his philosophical concern with the theme of infinity he could share the pain of divine sovereignty and purpose. The gift of sharing the responsibility of making and shaping the world and the gift of prophetic vision mellowed the poet's heart with love.

A sense of triumph in rising above worldly gain and sublimating poetical feeling, his wonder and awe at man's anguish and joy in discovering human and divine realities, and above all his gratitude for the loving admiration of millions of simple Muslims made Iqbal truly happy, while at the same time instilling in him a deep sorrow for his awesome responsibilities towards his fellow man.

The problems of the poverty-stricken Orient, of which the disunited Muslim world is a part, hurt him most. He often showed sudden changes of mood when contemplating these problems, plunging into a state of sorrow after being jovial and entertaining only a few moments before.

Iqbal recalled his visit to Spain on his way to India after the second Round Table Conference in London. He spoke of the prayer he offered inside the Mosque of Cordoba by special permission of the Spanish government. This request for permission, to him the irony of fate, injured him deeply. The prayer he had made on the occasion he later recounted with great emotion:[6] "O Lord! This is the land of thy pure people. This magnificent mosque, the Al-Hamra Palace and these grand forts are evidence of the greatness of the people who built them. Preserve these monuments, O Lord!"

On another occasion the questions of Muhammad Husain 'Arshi led the conversation to the meaning of a verse of Rumi:

*Nutq-i-āb-o nutq-i-bād-o-nutq-i-gil*
*Hast mahsus-i-hawās-i-ahl-i-dil.*

The senses of those endowed with the triumph of heart
                                           [over mind]
Can perceive the speech of waters, of the winds and of clay.

To this Iqbal replied by quoting from the Qur'ān:

> Every being knows its prayer and the glorification of Him (24:41).
> The seven heavens and the earth celebrate His praises, and all who therein are; nor is there aught, but what celebrates His praise ... (17:46).

'Arshi added that his question did not imply a denial of the reality of the speech of things and elements; rather he wanted to know if "those endowed with the triumph of heart" really had the ability to hear the speech of the elements. For did the latter verse from the Qur'ān not end with the words: "But ye cannot understand their celebration."? At this Iqbal recited the verse:

> *Har ki 'ashiq gasht husni-i-dhāt rā*
> *Gasht sayyid jumla maujūdāt rā.*

> Whoever becomes a lover of the beauty of the Essence
> Becomes a master of all things.

Here, 'Arshi reports, Iqbal's eyes became tearful.[7]

During the same meeting with Iqbal, 'Arshi consulted the poet about the meanings of other verses from Rumi. In explaining the ways of the Sufis, Iqbal recited the following verse from Rumi's *Mathnawi*:

> *Zad-i-danishmand athar-i-qalam.*
> *Zad-i-Sufi chist anwar-i-qadam.*

> The provisions of the man of intellect are the inscriptions of pen.
> The provisions of a Sufi? The illuminations of foot-steps.

Here again, recounts 'Arshi, Iqbal wept. When composed, he recited another verse by Rumi indicating that the Sufi finds the clue to the antelope in its footsteps and in the course of the quest comes upon the trail of musk which then leads him to the antelope itself. He then added: "The pedestrian who follows the route of the inscriptions of pen, too reaches the destination, but uneventfully." At this time, 'Arshi introduced a man named Rafīq who accompanied him and asked Iqbal whether he wished to listen to his own poetry sung by the sweet-voiced Rafīq. Iqbal liked the idea and a copy of his *Bāl-i Jibrīl* (Gabriel's Wing) was brought. The singer sang the *ghazal*:

> *Tirī banda parvari se mirī din guzar rahe haiñ*
> *Na gila hai dostoñ ka na shikayat -i-zamanā.*

As long as the *ghazal* was being sung, Iqbal shed tears.

On another occasion Iqbal was seized with great emotion at the thought of Haḍrat Ayyub Ansari's zeal for holy war when he was already ninety years of age. Remembering this in connection with the earliest Muslim conquest of Constantinople, Iqbal was extremely moved. The poet's emotional response to the mere mention of the prophet Muhammad was always intense, indicating his profound love for Him.

While talking to admirers one day, Sayyid Altaf Husain records, Iqbal described man-worship or hero-worship as un-Islamic. At a meeting presided over by the viceroy of India, Iqbal had refused to rise to show veneration for Mahatma Gandhi. In a conversation with the viceroy, Iqbal later explained that his ways were not Hindu ways,[8] which permitted idolatrous veneration for a fellow man.

Altaf Husain describes the rest of Iqbal's discourse, which turned to the Prophet: The Prophet always discouraged any display of special veneration toward himself by his companions. During a stroll in the desert in the company of friends, some antelopes came to kiss the feet of the Prophet. His envious companions asked why they were kept from doing the same. The Prophet replied (at this point Iqbal's voice faltered with great emotion and for a minute he was speechless, until tearfully he resumed speaking), "Prostrate before Allah alone and as for your elders, only respect them." Here, with better composure, Iqbal said that in all of world literature he had not come across a worthier sentence.

In a conversation with Muhammad Husain 'Arshi about a verse of Sarmad of Delhi on the Prophet's ascension and about a version of the childhood days of the Prophet in Rumi's *Mathnawi*, Iqbal is described as being consumed by tears.

Iqbal was very fond of listening to the stanzas in adoration of the Prophet in the *Musaddas* of Hali, which begin with the line:

*Wu nabyoñ meñ rahmat laqab pane walā.*
The one among prophets to win the title of Mercy.[9]

## A GRACIOUS HOST TO HIGH AND LOW

In the view of Maulana 'Abdūl Majīd Sālik, the fame of Iqbal's intellectual and spiritual accomplishments spread not so much because of his poetry but because of his conversational charm and style.

From morning to evening this man of renunciation sat on a plain bedstead or an armchair, wearing simple clothes, and the influx of visitors continued. The political magnates of the Punjab, lawyers, scholars, college professors, editors of newspapers, poets and *littérateurs*, students, illiterate admirers—in short men from all walks of life, came to visit him. All kinds of subjects were discussed with him, from the trivialities of people's domestics to the most intricate questions in the domain of jurisprudence, philosophy, politics, religion and science . . . . Iqbal shed light on all problems with his vast learning. Every visitor departed impressed by the depth of his learning. Educated people from all over the Punjab brought their intellectual and emotional problems to him, and he helped them. The most modest citizens could enter his house without formalities or permission and could sit there as long as they wished. The learned poet never displayed any symptom of boredom with anyone's presence. To his court of learning and reflection came innumerable magnates of the world of scholarship and politics, including Sir Fazl-i-Husain, Sir Sikandar Hayāt Khan, Jawaharlal Nehru, Quaʾid-i-Aʿzam Muhammad ʿAli Jinnah, Lord Lowthian, to benefit from his mature counsels. No doubt Iqbal had political differences with some of them, but since he was frank, selfless and transparently sincere, unpleasantness was banished from his presence.[10]

It is amazing how a poet and a thinker, whose thought was focused on the dynamics of *razm* (epic adventure) could be the very life of *bazm* (sedentary companionship). It is hard for the people in the West to appreciate the measure of Oriental leisure which allowed the full blossoming of Iqbal's faculty of conversation.

The warm gregariousness of Iqbal was a natural gift. But it was coached and reinforced by his association with Girāmi and Mīr Hasan. In his quality of frankness Iqbal was probably influenced by Ghālib, Dāgh, and Girāmi. But most of all it was probably Girāmi, coming for long stays with Iqbal as a guest, who influenced him.

Perhaps from Girāmi Iqbal imbibed also an informality in his pronunciation and accent of acquired languages. Girāmi's accent in Persian and Urdu was distinctly Punjabi and was considered delightful precisely for that quality. Iqbal's accent in Urdu, Persian, and even English, was likewise distinctly Punjabi. This annoyed some speakers of "King's Urdu" from Delhi and Lucknow with their haughtiness in the matter of accent.[11] But men with bigger spirits found the high scholarship of his Punjabized discourses in Urdu, English, and Persian at once charming and enlightening.

During his years in Lahore as an active practicing lawyer, Iqbal found relaxing diversion after the day's work in musical sessions, often at the house of his lawyer friend Mirza Jalāl-ud-din. The melody and rhythm occasionally stimulated Iqbal to compose poetry. At the first signs of the approach of his inspiration, the musicians would discontinue their piece and improvise some gentle instrumental accompaniment to suit the recitation by the poet. For singing poetry as well as for speech Iqbal was gifted with a melodious voice. His singing of his poems at symposiums of poetry actually influenced the styles of recitation of poetry for an entire generation of poets in twentieth-century India.

'Abdul Wahid, in his essay in the *Malfūzat* of Iqbal, has made some extremely penetrating comments about Iqbal the man while admiring the almost celestial qualities of Iqbal the poet. Two aspects of Iqbal the man which, he says, would remain hidden if one made acquaintance with the poet only through his poetry are highlighted by 'Abdūl Wahid: simplicity of habits and sense of humor.[12] Iqbal's poetry as a rule is ornate and sophisticated, and in his maturer poetry humor is there only as undertone. But in company Iqbal's humor and joviality were profuse and strongly contagious. 'Abdūl Wahid quite appropriately remarks that "Iqbal's company was an antidote for all the troubles and tyrannies of life. In him there was an invincible optimism which accounts for his smiling countenance till his last breath."[13]

In his heart Iqbal was more thankful for this chain of admiring visitors than for anything else. His audience came to him; what more can a performing artist of conversation want! His popularity of course was enhanced by his selflessness and his uncommon indifference to commercializing his poetic genius. Mian Bashīr Ahmad, the famous editor of *Humayūñ* and son of Iqbal's dear friend Justice Shah Din Humayūñ, once deplored the apathy of the Muslim nation toward Iqbal, asserting that an anthology like *Bāng-i-Dara* would sell millions in some Western countries whereas comparatively few copies of Iqbal's works would sell in Urdu-reading India. Iqbal disliked the remark protesting that he would not expect commercial benefits from his poor compatriots. He added, however, "When some poor man comes to visit me and kneads my arms and legs to give rest to my tired muscles, I feel that the entire world is appreciating me."

Iqbal's manner of receiving his visitors was not formal; his style of answering the *salaam* of visitors was seemingly cold. To acknowledge their greetings he would only lift his right hand, letting it drop casually. But the glow of warmth would appear on his face as soon as he plunged into conversation. When stimulated he would break his pensive silence, indicating his desire for conversation by muttering "hmm." This masterly announcement would alert his admirers to the infinite possibilities of a conversational advance. During intervals of silence, he combed his hair with his fingers and occasionally uttered aside "Ya Allah." Usually, Iqbal kept his eyes only half open when he talked, but with the rise of his enthusiasm and excitement in conversation his eyes would open fully. Iqbal talked with everyone according to the intellectual capacities of the listener (a quality the intellectuals of the West rarely display because of their general aloofness from the common people).

During the years of illness and vocal incapacity that preceded his death, Iqbal never closed the door of his residence to informal and uninvited visitors. Even in a state of physical pain, which necessitated his confinement to bed in a lying position, the lure of cherished themes would make him sit up again and again, and his merry wit was able to dominate his suffering.

His humorous comments were capable of injecting life even into the most hackneyed topics. 'Abdūl Wahid, whose essay in the *Mulfūzat* combines the spirit of a disciple and a critic, makes the thought-provoking remark that a well-integrated and well-knit faith is a prerequisite of the mature and abundant humor displayed by Iqbal.

## SENSE OF HUMOR

IN the Bar Room of the Punjab High Court, Iqbal was the center of witty conversation during the active days of his practice. To pragmatic Sir Fazl-i-Husain (founder of the Unionist party in the Punjab in 1930) the friendship of Iqbal, Sir Nawab Zulfiqār Ali Khan and Mirza Jalāl-ud-din was an entertaining feature of Bar circles, and he often referred to the three as the Trio. In those days of Iqbal's youth two other men often associated with the Trio were Mian Shah Nawaz and Sir Jogendera Singh. There is a touching account in the *Malfūzat* of a reunion of Mirza Jalāl-ud-din, Mian Shah Nawaz, and Iqbal in January 1938, only three months before the poet's death. It was an occasion that saw the renewal of Iqbal's witty fireworks. The richness of that wit is difficult to reproduce since it is not easy to reconstruct fully the informal native setting, the tonal subtleties of the Punjabi he spoke, the intimacies of friends, and the fine shades of sentiment blending harmless sarcasm and affection. The emotional elements registered in Urdu and Punjabi by consistent or spasmodic use of the plural of respect in both pronouns and verbs indicate a whole world of attitudes or dramatic discriminations in one's relation with men that is liquidated if reported in "stingy" English, which has discarded such linguistic subtlety in the name of economy (or perhaps democracy) in language. To try to reproduce Iqbal's wit in English, therefore, is a hopeless task. Yet it would be eminently unfair to go on to other aspects of his personality without a glimpse of his merry sparkle.

When Iqbal's wife Sardar Begum died (May 23, 1935), he was already quite senior and past the age of considering remarriage. Only a few days after Sardar Begum's death, some young friends, including ʿAbd al-Rashīd Tāriq, came to visit him. The conversation turned to the fair sex. Iqbal smiled and said, "When women read my poetry, they imagine that I am quite young. Since the death of Javid's mother I have received several marriage proposals. Recently one letter came from an intelligent and educated girl saying that she had enjoyed my poetry all the time and proposed marriage to me. I wrote to her, 'You'd better be contented with reading my poetry.'"[14] Here Iqbal had a hearty laugh and made the others laugh too.

One day during the month of Ramaḍan Maulana ʿAbdūl Majīd Sālik and Maulana Ghulām Rasūl Mehr visited the poet close to sunset, the hour of breaking the fast. Iqbal summoned his servant Rehma and instructed him to bring "oranges, dates, and sweet-meats and some salty items for the breaking of fast." Maulana Sālik protested, saying, "No formality is necessary. Just some dates will suffice." With a sauciness reflecting childlike innocence, Iqbal said, "Let us impress everyone by announcing a big list. Rehma will bring something after all." The reporter of the above incident in the *Malfūzat* adds, "Rehma considered a word by word fulfillment of the instructions unnecessary and contented himself with meeting the wishes of Maulana Sālik."

Once during a session at home Iqbal was being entertained by the sharp-witted jesting of a much younger lawyer, occasionally interjecting his own remarks in the same spirit. Suddenly Iqbal interrupted himself and with amusing informality addressed the young lawyer in Punjabi thus, "Pal! You should always have two hookahs around: one for yourself and one for others. When you put the hookah-tube into your mouth, there it stays and you forget that others are waiting for the same! Where did you learn that awful habit?" The jolly manner made everyone present laugh. Iqbal smiled and said to his servant 'Ali Bakhah, "Bring the second hookah for Pīr Sahib." ("Pīr Sahib" signifies that the young lawyer belonged to a family of distinguished Sufis.)

On his way to Kabul, King Nādir Khan of Afghanistan stopped in Lahore and met Iqbal for the first time. The King had imagined Iqbal's physique and face and dress as very different from what he actually discovered at this first meeting. Amazed, he said, "So you are Iqbal. I had pictured you with a beard." Iqbal retorted, "My surprise is greater than yours. You are a military general. I had pictured you as a man with the physique of a giant, but I find you without any likeness of a general. You are so lean and puny."[15]

During a visit to Iqbal, his admirer 'Abd al-Rashīd Tāriq discussed the pilgrimage of his grandfather, Haji Ahmad Bakhsh, a great friend of Iqbal. Tāriq's errand was to deliver some presents his grandfather had sent for Iqbal. Tāriq reported that his grandfather had been inquiring after Iqbal's health in every letter and had been quoting often from his poetry. With particular relish the grandfather had quoted the following verse:

> Iqbal! For the Pilgrims I have a question.
> Is Zamzam the only gift-suggestion?[16]

Iqbal, too, was amused by this quotation from his verses and laughed. Tāriq added, "Guided by this verse, my grandfather has observed the caution of sending you other gifts including the prayer-mat, the rosary and some dates. He has been particular about excluding the water of Zamzam."

Iqbal said, "How thoughtful! I certainly needed a rosary and a prayer-mat these days. The prayer-mat will be preserved with great care *inshā Allah* [God willing]. It is a gift from the home of the Beloved of God. To stand on it will be to spoil it." (Here Iqbal laughed at his own remark.)

A little later Iqbal requested Tāriq to convey his thanks to the considerate pilgrim and to add in the letter Iqbal's line:

> My heart is a veteran of sin.
> Its prayer is empty din.[17]

While avoiding vulgarity in discussing the most frivolous themes, Iqbal never refrained from participating in innocent naughtiness or harmless practical jokes. Once he discovered that a *maulawi* (a religious teacher) had surreptitiously visited the house of a song-and-dance girl in Lucknow. Iqbal teasingly threatened to expose the man and derived much enjoyment from his embarrassment. The event offered Iqbal exceptional amusement since the occasion of his visit to Lucknow was a religious conference at which he and the *maulawi* were fellow delegates.

During his very first visit to Iqbal, Sayyid Altaf Husain, a young admirer, was relieved of his uneasy awe of the poet when with childlike excitement Iqbal recounted the story of a romance in Sialkot between a *maulawi* and a much younger girl the *maulawi* had tutored.

## RELIGIOUS LIBERALISM

SEVERAL essays in the *Malfūzat* relate Iqbal's spontaneous handling of sophisticated themes regarding Muslim tradition and world civilizations. On Iqbal's methods of exegesis of the Qur'ān, the best essay in the *Malfūzat* is that of Muhammad Husain 'Arshi. In one of the discourses recorded in this essay, Iqbal said, "The world of today, with all its arts and crafts and techniques (of theoretical and applied science), is a 'creature' of the Muslims." 'Arshi expressed his surprise at Iqbal's use of the word 'creature.' Iqbal explained, "The true creator undoubtedly is Allah, the Exalted, but there can be other Creators too, as is clear from the Qur'ān's verse containing the phrase 'the best of creators' " (23:14).[18]

Original interpretations of Qur'ānic phrases came with spontaneous inspiration in the course of Iqbal's conversation. Once a friend of Iqbal was expressing pessimistic ideas about the rebirth of fallen nations. Iqbal explained why there was such a spirit of hopelessness among the people whose sacred book had proclaimed the *qiyāmat* (resurrection), the rebirth of all dead people. The comment surprised the pessimistic friend happily and the contagion of hope brought a sudden joyful flush to his face.

Very startling indeed is Iqbal's unusual interpretation of the reputed utterance of the famous mystic Mansur Hallaj: "Ānā al-Haqq." Ordinarily translated as "I am the reality," it is one of the favorite slogans of the pantheistic Sufis. As an opponent of pantheism, Iqbal gave a valid alternative translation of the slogan: "I" is the reality, signifying that egohood is the true reality. Thus this slogan became a potent counter-slogan of antipantheists.[19]

On one occasion Muhammad Husain 'Arshi inquired about the miraculous birth of Jesus Christ and his resurrection. Iqbal answered that "these two beliefs entered Muslim beliefs via the Christians who converted to Islam." 'Arshi then asked, "Is the whole of Islam comprehended by the Qur'ān?" When Iqbal requested that he be more explicit, 'Arshi clarified, "Is the store of traditions and ideas in book of Hadith and Fiqh an integral part of Islam or is the Qur'ān by itself comprehensive?" Iqbal replied, "These things (other than the Qur'ān) cover subjects of history and inter-human affairs; they too are needed. They give clues to the situations that called for them. But the substance of Islam is covered fully by the Qur'ān. We do not have to go outside the Qur'ān to discover the will of God."[20]

In another discussion with some staunch *Ahl al-Hadith*[21] who came to visit Iqbal, the talk turned to the second coming of Christ, a subject that Iqbal did not particularly favor. To him this expectation, as well as the waiting for the arrival of the *Mahdi* (messiah), were pretexts among Muslims for lethargy. The visitors supported their opinion with the appropriate Hadith. Iqbal conclusively remarked, "In fundamental matters I rely only on the Qur'ān." At this the visitors became angry, but Iqbal remained calm.

Iqbal's lawyer friend Mirza Jalāl-ud-Din pays tribute to Iqbal's liberal spirit in dealing with questions of Muslim jurisprudence, citing the poet's oft-made remark that "*ijtihād*[22] is every man's natural right." Iqbal's attitude was based on the Qur'ān's invitation to believers: "Ponder and reflect."

On one occasion Sayyid Altaf Husain drew Iqbal's attention to a remark in R. A. Nicholson's *Literary History of the Arabs* pointing to a "self-contradiction" in the Qur'ān on the subject of free will and predestination. Iqbal recollected that he had discussed the subject with Professor Nicholson personally and had reminded him that what had appeared contradictory to him was in fact true to reality. Did every man not go through moments of deeming himself free and moments of knowing himself constrained by Providence? This paradox, Iqbal said, was represented by the Qur'ān, adding that "Reality is not a single-colored thing, rather it is a variegated complex."

In spite of his tendency toward support of the Ahl al-Qur'ān purists, Iqbal does not demonstrate any fanaticism in the matter. When one of his admirers, Sayyid Altaf Husain, criticized the pedantic quibbles of exegetes over grammatical issues, Iqbal differed, saying, "Commentaries of that nature are also needed." Although Iqbal's discovery of the distinction between Hellenized Muslim theology and the Simitic world-view of the Qur'ān was not fundamentalist in motive and level, his intuition was the first step toward a fully scientific discovery of the distinction. Expounded in terms of the ultimate ego, Iqbal's understanding of the Qur'ān's Allah stops short of really disentangling Qur'ānic thought from Hellenized Muslim thought. Although open to criticism from the point of view of historical method, his semi-Hellenized exposition of Qur'ānic thought points to his liberal subjectivity which accommodates Greek elements.

Mian Bashīr Ahmad, a much younger man and a journalist, offered to Iqbal the conjecture that in his verse

> The taverns of India have been shut for three hundred years.
> Now your beneficence should abound again O Saqi.

The reference was to the Mughal Emperor Jehāngīr, the wine-loving sovereign of India. Iqbal corrected this view by explaining that he had been referring to the spiritual renewal led by Shaikh Ahmad Sarhindi.

Muhammad Husain 'Arshi once asked Iqbal what was meant by the word *nazar* (glance) in the following line in the poem entitled *Pas Cha Bayad Kard* (What Is To Be Done):

> '*Ilm-o-hikmat az kutub din az nazar.*
> Knowledge and learning from books you get.
> If faith you want, from a glance beget.

Iqbal replied, "Association with the pious."

'Arshi narrates another meaningful incident:

A member of the Red Crescent Mission [from Turkey] accompanied Iqbal to the Shahi Mosque of Lahore. This guest was an old man. The leader of the congregation prayer led a rather lengthy prayer, causing the guest to become uneasy. After leaving the Mosque, the old man, with some wonderment, asked Iqbal the reason for this protraction of the prayer. Iqbal replied, "The lengthy prayer is evidence of the Indian Muslim's purposelessness in life. You [Turks], on the contrary, have set before yourselves the task of reconstruction of your national life. Therefore you have no leisure for such empty rituals of lengthy prayer. The lazy *mullahs* and vain Muslims of India would have nothing to occupy them if they did not fill their time with religious quibbles and lengthy formulas or pious recitals and their endless repetitions."[23]

In two places in the *Malfūzat* there are very fascinating discourses by Iqbal made in the presence (1935) of Mūsa Jārullah, a Russian Muslim who made a long journey to seek wisdom from the poet. The themes touched in them are the political system of Islam, faith and irreligion, the meaning of paradise, and the significance of prayer.

## DISDAIN FOR MYSTIC COMMERCIALISM

IQBAL was pained by the commercialism of contemporary Sufi life. He expressed his misgivings, but his friends protested on such occasions saying that his criticism was based on mere hearsay. To make his point Iqbal recounted two incidents from his own experience:

When I lived in the Anarkali Bazaar, one day a Pīr [a Sufi preceptor] came in the company of some disciples. He spoke about the annual gathering of his disciples at a certain place along the border of Afghanistan and the North-Western Frontier Province, complaining that accommodation facilities for the gathering were inadequate and that food was scarce. He asked me to apply on his behalf to the Frontier government for a grant of some acres of land that might be cultivated to guarantee some income. This Pīr Sahib was my old friend and I was disillusioned and shocked. I reminded him that he was a Sayyid, a descendant of the Prophet Muhammad; that his ancestor, the Chosen One of the Two Worlds, had never spread the hand of beggary; that the proper person for his request was not the British governor but God, the true master of lands and skies. Pīr Sahib departed displeased, but my words were not wasted. Pīr Sahib returned the following day to say that in the presence of his disciples my words had offended him but upon deliberation in solitude those words sounded very true. He promised not to stoop to such beggary again. A week or so later I received a telegram from him sent from Delhi informing me that (by some Providential help) the land had now been secured.

The second incident recounted by Iqbal reflects his sense of humor in a similar situation. He narrated:

After my moving to Javid Manzil [Iqbal's residence on Mayo Road, now called Iqbal Road. It was named after Javid Iqbal], one day in summer a Pīr Sahib came to see me. The heat was at its height and the glare of the sun was too much for the eyes. A man drenched in sweat and breathless from exhaustion came and flung himself at the feet of the Pīr. This was a disciple. He said: "I heard that your Holiness had arrived. I left Mughalpura [a suburb of Lahore] quite early in the morning. I followed your trail, failing to find you at numerous places until I was directed here. Thank God I found you after all. My plight is miserable Your Holiness! I am starving and under a debt of two hundred rupees. I can find no job. Pray for my rescue from all these troubles." Here the disciple took out two rupees from his pocket and offered them to the Pīr. Pīr Sahib pocketed the money and raised his hands to pray, asking me to join him. I said to him, "You go ahead yourself. I shall pray when you conclude." Pīr Sahib shut his eyes, mumbled for a while, and concluded by covering his face with his hands, sweeping them down to the tip of his beard, and blowing his holy breath upon his disciple. The disciple was overjoyed with great hopes of the instant subsiding of the clouds of misfortune and destitution. I then said to Pīr Sahib, "Now it is my turn." So I lifted my hand and said aloud: "O God! The Pīrs of our days have gone astray. Guide them to the right path." Pīr Sahib protested, demanding an explanation for this uncalled-for supplication. I said, "Look here Pīr Sahib! I did not interrupt your prayer at all. Let me make my supplication in peace now." He became silent and I continued, "O Lord! enlighten the disciples of our times, and keep them safe from the misguidance of their Pīrs." Pīr Sahib interrupted again but I paid no heed to his protest and continued, "The poor disciple says he is under a debt of two hundred rupees, not realizing that now his debt has grown to be two hundred and two rupees." At this Pīr Sahib became more indignant, saying, "This is an insult, mind you sir." I said, "Alright. I end my prayer but on one condition: You return the two rupees to the disciple, arrange for his relief from his debts, and get him some job." Pīr Sahib was highly displeased but returned the two rupees and promised to look after the needs of the disciple. These are the ways of the Pīrs.[24]

Iqbal's attitude toward *Tasawwuf* (Sufism) is a major subject in the field of contemporary Islam. His poetry and letters are the best source for that study, but the *Malfūzat* contains some discourses that are quite revealing. One of Iqbal's important accomplishments was to exemplify a new kind of Sufi free from the concept of Sufism as a full-time vocation. He accomplished this by refusing to recruit disciples and thus discontinued the chain of formalized Sufi succession, a remarkable act, since he had taken the oath of discipleship "at his father's hands" in the Qadiriya order.

Mirza Jalāl-ud-Din, Iqbal's lawyer friend, made this remark about Iqbal's Sufism: "Iqbal was neither a dry ascetic nor a hypocritical Sufi. However, in the last years of his life he had to a great extent withdrawn himself from the world and adopted the ways of a dervish. Oblivious to the material world, Iqbal had lost himself in his own spiritual reverie. But from the halo of holiness that has encircled him one should not shut one's eyes to his true rank and drag him into the category of the great Sufi saints."[25]

Iqbal's comments on *Tasawwuf* in the *Malfūzat* have a conversational informality that makes them doubly significant. Very bold and meaningful is this remark: "Islam has nothing to do with the discussion of *wahdat* (unity) and *kathrat* (plurality). The essence of Islam is *Tawhīd* [belief in the uniqueness and singleness of God], and the opposite of the latter is not *kathrat* but *shirk* [attribution of partnership to God]."

"*Tasawwuf*" Iqbal said,

is always a sign of decline of a nation. Greek mysticism, Persian mysticism, Indian mysticism—all are signs of decline of these nations; the same is true of Islamic mysticism. The Sufis of the earliest days of Islam were ascetics. Austerity and a God-fearing piety were their real concerns. In the *Tasawwuf* of later times metaphysics and theorizing mixed. *Tasawwuf* then ceased to be mere asceticism and mingled with philosophy. *Hama Ust* [All is He], the slogan of the pantheists, is not a religious but a philosophical theme. Islam has nothing to do with *wahdat* and *kathrat*. The essence of Islam is *Tawhīd* and the opposite of the latter is not *kathrat* but *shirk*. Any philosophy or religious teaching that prevents the blossoming and maturing of the human personality is worthless. *Tasawwuf* has inflicted much damage on the scientific spirit. People run after amulets instead of consulting a physician. To shut one's ears and eyes to the material world and to emphasize only the inward perception is a sign of stagnation and degeneration. It is the search after easy ways instead of making the effort for the conquest of nature by dynamic struggle. I think the forbidden tree means *Tasawwuf*. Pure Islamic *Tasawwuf* is that in which the divine injunctions become imperatives ensuing from one's own wishes:

> The Believer isn't known by a casual look.
> Though reciter he seems, yet himself is the Book.

In view of Iqbal's opposition to pantheism, two of his remarks about Ibn al-'Arabi are noteworthy: On one occasion, Iqbal remembered reading aloud portions of the *Fuṣūṣ al-Hikām* of Ibn al-'Arabi as a regular activity at his father's store in Sialkot. (He also disclosed that Mirza Ghulam Ahmad of Quadyān had often joined the reading sessions.) On another occasion, Iqbal said, "Whoever gets caught in the snares of Ibn al-'Arabi, Mirza Bedil, or Hegel, has no easy rescue from them."[26]

A conversation recorded by Hamīd Ahmad Khan contains illuminating remarks by Iqbal on the thought of Mirza Bedil and his relation to Sufi schools:

Beidil's admiration for the Naqshbandi Order and for Haḍrat Mujaddid Alf Thani is based on this very feature of dynamism. The Naqshbandi Path is founded on dynamism and optimism, while the Chishti Path reflects pessimism and tranquility. For this reason the circle of discipleship of the Chishti Order is confined mostly to India, while outside India, in Afghanistan, Bukhara, Turkey and other Muslim countries, the Naqshbandi Order flourishes. The poets of the Naqshbandi Order such as Nāsir 'Ali Sarhindi are not imitation-minded. That is why Nāsir 'Ali is more popular among dynamic nations; in India Nāsir 'Ali is not particularly appreciated. But in the *outside* world he is highly esteemed.

Students of Muslim literature know that for hundreds of years sentiments of revolt against legalistic authority and state-imposed theologies could be expressed only in the garb of ambiguous poetic diction. A sweet impudence toward Allah is thus a feature of the Sufi lyrical poetry of several centuries. Beginning with his poem *Shikwah* (Complaint), Iqbal's grumbling under the rule of God becomes less ambiguous and indirect; he cultivates consciousness of the confrontation of his own ego and the Ultimate Ego of Allah. The element of baffled complaint about the ironies of existence is found throughout Iqbal's poetry wherever he addresses or makes supplication to Allah.

This is done with subtlety and humor very much in the traditional style. Iqbal's honest championship of the idea of egohood gave him the courage to be an exception by expressing his self-assertion in the divine presence in prose as well as in poetry. In a fascinating discourse on Muslim architecture, Iqbal spoke this way of his visit to Al-Hamra Palace in Spain: "Whichever way I looked, especially on the walls, I saw the inscription *Huwa al-Ghālib* (He is the Dominant). I said to myself, 'Here Allah is the dominant all over. It would make sense to see man, too, dominate somewhere.'"[27]

The contributors of essays in the *Malfūzat* have recorded their impressions with utmost candidness. They depict the personality of Iqbal as profoundly human and warm. The traits that rise into prominence in the essays are his renunciation, humor, frankness, robust optimism, and unusual gregariousness—aspects of Iqbal's character that do not emerge clearly from his poetry alone, nor even from his letters.

# 3

# Iqbal: My Father

## JAVID IQBAL

A YEAR or so before I was born (1924), father visited the mausoleum of Shaikh Ahmad Sarhindi, also known as Mujaddid Alf Thani. This sixteenth-century Sufi who denounced Ibn al-'Arabi's conception of *Wahdat al-Wujūd* and criticized Emperor Akbar's religious policy is regarded as one of the founders of the Muslim nationality in India. At the mausoleum, my father prayed for a child—a son—whom he could bring up in accordance with his own ideals of religion and morality. If God did grant him a son, he promised the saint that he would one day bring him to the mausoleum.

### RESPECT FOR MUJADDID ALF THANI

His prayer was heard, and later, in the summer of 1934, when I had attained an impressionable age, he took me to Sarhind. I can recollect our visit to the mausoleum of Shaikh Ahmad, for it is impressed vividly on my mind. Father took me inside the mausoleum, sat close to the grave of the saint, and recited the Qur'ān. I felt afraid of the darkness and was terrified by the grave; yet I was aware of a peculiar familiarity with my hushed and desolate surroundings. I watched father recite the Qur'ān. His sad voice vibrated through the dark dome of the mausoleum and tears streamed down his cheeks.

After staying at Sarhind for a day or two we returned to Lahore, but I could never discover the purpose for our visit to the mausoleum and the reason for the tears streaming down father's cheeks. It was the first time I had seen father weep. I well remember how these questions bothered me in my childhood.

Father rarely gave me an opportunity to judge how much affection and love he felt for me. He seldom held me close or kissed me, and because of this, I never really felt the warmth of fatherly affection. Apparently he gave the impression of being a taciturn and rather cold man. When he saw me running about the house, he would smile faintly, as if someone were forcing him to smile. But frequently I noticed him sitting alone in an easy chair with his eyes closed, absorbed in his own thoughts.

However, it would be wrong to conclude that he was incapable of loving or bestowing affection. Although his love for me was devoid of youthful vigor, it had the depth of maturity. I was, as it were, not only his son but "the younger generation of Islam personified"—the little cubs of his today who were to be trained so that they could learn to involve themselves deeply with and provide a life-giving response to the dead world in which he lived. They were to grow up to be the lions of his tomorrow and realize the new world of which he frequently dreamed, the fears and hopes which disturbed his sleep during the long wintry nights and made him appear as a stranger in his mornings.

Parents sometimes disagree as to how their children are to be brought up. I was a frequent cause of disagreement between my father and mother. Mother thought that unless she fed me with her own hands I would remain undernourished. But father maintained that she was spoiling me. His standing instructions were that I should always feed myself. The instructions were of course carried out, but sometimes mother fed me stealthily, and if father happened to discover our little conspiracy, he smiled knowingly.

Although mother was very strict and punished me if I was mischievous, father's rebuke always proved a better corrective. On very few occasions did father beat me. The reasons usually were rudeness to the servants (which he resented most) or running about barefooted in the summer sun.

One rule that father was strict about was silence in our home. Sometimes, when I played with other children on the lawn, he would order us to play elsewhere. But at other times he would join us in our games. When I was flying a kite, he occasionally appeared on the roof and took the string from my hand. Perhaps kite-flying reminded him of his own childhood.

As a child I was very fond of painting, but father was not aware of my interest. When he learned that I liked painting and saw a few of my "works of art," he encouraged me a great deal and purchased large prints by French, Italian, and Spanish masters for me. I was also very fond of music, but he had neither a gramophone nor a radio in the house. Despite this lack, father, too, enjoyed music and even played a *sitār* before he went abroad for higher studies. His love for music never died. In the later phase of his life, Faqīr Najm-ud-Din, one of his friends, occasionally played the *sitār* for him. Whenever a singer came to our house and sang some of his *ghazals*, father sent for me.

In 1931, when father went to England to attend the Round Table Conference, I was about seven years old. I wrote him a letter asking him to bring me a gramophone. The gramophone never arrived, but my letter moved him to write the following poem, *To Javid on Receiving His First Letter*:

> Build in love's empire your hearth and your home;
> Build Time anew, a new dawn, a new eve!
> Your speech, if God give you the friendship of Nature,
> From the rose and the tulip's long silence weave.
> No gifts of the Franks' clever glass-blowers ask!
> From India's own clay mould your cup and your flask.
> My songs are the grapes on the spray of my vine;
> Distil from their clusters the poppy-red wine!
> The way of the hermit, not fortune, is mine;
> Sell not your soul! in a beggar's rags shine.

## MOTHER'S DEATH IN THE NEW HOUSE

MOTHER's constant concern was that father did not do any work. I, too, used to wonder what he really did. If anyone asked me about the nature of his occupation, I felt embarrassed. Mother was anxious that we should build a house of our own. (In those days we used to live in a rented house on Macleod Road.) By May 1935, mother's wish was fulfilled, and we moved to the new house. Tragically, on the third day after our arrival in the house, mother died. I was then about eleven years old and Munīra, my sister, about five.

After Mother's death Munīra and I drew closer to father. I well remember how the two of us wept bitterly because of our mother's death, and holding each other's hands, went to our father's room. He was, as usual, lying in bed, for he was not in good health at this time. He had also lost his voice and could not speak clearly. Munīra and I stood at the door of his room not knowing what to do. He noticed us and asked us to come closer. When we came near him, he motioned for us to sit on his right and left sides. Then placing his hands affectionately on our shoulders, he said rather angrily to me: "You must not cry like this. Remember, you are a man—and men do not cry." He then kissed both of us on the forehead—probably for the first time in his life.

The following March, in 1936, father took me to Bhopal with him. In Bhopal, most of my time was spent in his company. He took a keen interest in my upbringing, being extremely particular about table manners. Since I was temperamentally shy, he told me repeatedly that I should not remain silent or self-possessed in company but should talk to people.

On our way back home in April we stayed in Delhi for a few days. There he took me on a sight-seeing trip. We visited the Red Fort, the tomb of Nizām-ud Din Awliya, and the Qutab Minār. When I asked him to take me up the Qutab Minār, father expressed his inability to climb. However, he allowed me to go up, admonishing: "Only do not look down from that height, otherwise you will feel frightened."

As the years passed father's life became very inactive because of chronic liver trouble. During the summer father slept in the courtyard at night. My bed was close to his and sometimes I woke up in the dead of night and saw him sitting up in bed with his head resting on his knees. It was during the night that he had attacks of pain. And also, when inspiration came to him, the color of his face changed, and he gave the impression of suffering from great physical discomfort.

During the late hours of the night he frequently called Ali Bakhsh, his servant, by clapping his hands, and told him to bring his pen and notebook. As he wrote verses in his notebook, his face relaxed as if he had been relieved of great pain. Soon afterward he fell fast asleep as if nothing had happened. On numerous occasions I saw father smiling or weeping without apparent cause. Alone, he recited his verses for personal stimulation, raising his hand in the air and then letting it fall.

## SOME FOND MEMORIES

He usually slept on his right side with his arm placed under the pillow. Sometimes, while lying in that position, he would shake one of his feet, indicating that he was not asleep but was thinking. When he was sound asleep, however, he would snore loudly.

He rarely missed the morning prayers, his prayer-mat was spread on a wooden divan lying in the courtyard. Extremely simple in his habits, father wore a *tahband* and a vest and covered his head with a towel when offering his prayers. His room was packed with books which were scattered all around him. He hated going out, but loved to sit on his sofa or recline in his bed reading or taking notes. Sometimes he was so absorbed in reading that he forgot whether he had eaten his meals or not. On finishing the book, he would raise his head and ask Ali Bakhsh innocently: "Well, have I had my meals?" In the evening he walked up and down the courtyard of our house. Besides this he had no other physical activity, and his life appeared static.

After mother's death, father gave up dyeing his hair. One day I called to his attention that his hair needed dyeing. He smiled and said: "I am an old man now." "But," I replied, "we want to see you young, father." He recommenced tinting his hair, but after a few months gave it up, and I never found another opportunity to ask him to begin again.

Father looked terribly disturbed whenever he learned that Munīra and I had quarreled. He could not bear to see us fighting with each other. If I were ever harsh to her, he became very upset and scolded: "You really are a stone-hearted fellow. Have you no sensitivity? Don't you realize that she is the only friend you have in this world? Your mother is already dead, and so shall I die when my time comes. What would you be left with except her? If you quarreled with her you would be the loneliest of men—and I tell you that it is not very pleasant to be lonely in this world."

Father wanted me to become a great orator. He also wished that I should learn wrestling, and for this purpose had an arena dug for me in the back-yard of the house. On 'Id-ul-adha he would insist that I be present at the time of the animal sacrifice, although he himself could not stand the sight of blood.

One of his friends, a Saudi Arab, used to visit him and occasionally recited passages from the Qur'ān for him. The Arab had a lovely voice, and whenever he recited the Qur'ān, father sent for me and made me sit close to him. Once the Arab recited *Sura al-Muzammil*, and father was extremely moved. When the Arab had finished, father raised his head and said to me: "This is how I would like you to recite the Qur'ān."

On another occasion he asked me to recite from *Musaddas-i-Hali*. Someone sitting in the room pointed out that I should recite the verses about the Prophet Muhammad, which ran thus: "The One called Mercy among the Prophets." Before the second verse could be uttered, father was moved to tears. But there were times when he, too, would recite. He narrated stories from Islamic history, frequently talking about the Caliph 'Umar and Khalid bin Walīd. He told me that the ancestors of Napoleon originally hailed from Arabia, and that the Arabs had shown Vasco de Gama the route to India.

Father was not very fond of European clothes. He always advised me to wear our national dress. Similarly, he disapproved of expensive material for clothes, and rebuked me if I spent money unnecessarily. If he was told that I had slept on the floor instead of sleeping on the bed, he felt very pleased and proud of me.

Sometime in 1937 Quaid-i-Azam Muhammad Ali Jinnah, the founder of Pakistan, came to visit father. I entered the sitting room to ask for his autograph. The Quaid-i-Azam graciously obliged. I remember his asking me if I also wrote poetry. When I answered in the negative he again asked: "Then what do you intend to do when you grow up?" I did not know what to say and therefore stood mute. He turned to father and said smilingly: "He does not answer." "He would not," replied father, "because he is waiting for the day when you would tell him what to do."

In his later years father's eyesight grew very weak; therefore, I read the newspapers to him every day. Every night I recited his own poems (or Hali's) for him. If I ever mispronounced a word, he became angry. The slightest error in recitation also irritated him. "Is it poetry or prose that you are reciting?" he would snap.

However, Munīra was his favourite. She, with her German governess whom we used to call "Āpajan," would spend hours in his room. Father spoke German fluently, and usually talked in German to Āpajan.

He also told Munīra to learn German. "German women are very brave," he explained to her.

Many friends and admirers used to call on father, usually in the evening. Chairs were placed around his bed; he loved to chat with his friends while smoking his hookah. He was not in the habit of taking evening meals, only one or two cups of Kashmiri tea.

I had strict instructions to be present when father had company, although listening to the grownups was an ordeal for me. I stole out of his room whenever I found an opportunity. This usually hurt him very much, and he would complain to his friends: "I do not know why this boy shuns my company." During this phase of his life he was haunted by a peculiar sense of loneliness, frequently lamenting: "I spend the whole of my day lying here as if I were a stranger. No one ever comes and sits with me."

## THE LAST NIGHT

ON his last night, April 20–21, 1938, he lay on a bed in the sitting room, surrounded by his friends and admirers. It was about 9 P.M. when I entered the room.

"Who is it?" he asked, since he could not recognize me. "I am Javid," I replied. He broke into a smile and said: "I would only believe it when you really become Javid" (Javid means Eternity). Then he turned to one of his friends, Chaudhari Muhammad Hussain, and asked: "Chaudhari Sahib, please see to it that he learns the prayer entitled 'Addressed to Javid' which appears towards the end of my *Javid-namah*."\*

That night there were anxious whisperings everywhere in the house, for the doctors had warned that father had only a few hours to live. He was spitting blood and his condition had suddenly taken a very dangerous turn. Although the doctors' opinion had been concealed from him, father knew that his end was near. Nevertheless, he was cheerful and full of humor, much more than he normally used to be.

I, too, was not told about the seriousness of father's illness. I retired to my room and went to sleep. At dawn I felt the hands of Ali Bakhsh

---

\*A few selected verses of this prayer, which appear at the end of this chapter, were translated by Hadi Hussain at the request of the editor.

shake me as he shouted: "Come. Get up. See what has happened to your father." I did not really believe he was dead. I got out of the bed only so that I could see what had happened to him. While proceeding to his room, I passed through the adjoining one and noticed Munīra sitting alone on a divan. She had covered her face with her hands and was crying bitterly.

As soon as she saw me going in the direction of father's room, she leapt towards me and grabbed my arm. Clinging to me, she tried to walk, but her feet staggered. We stood at the door of father's room and peeked inside. There was no one in his room. The windows were open, and he was lying straight on his bed. A white sheet covered him up to his neck. His eyes were shut and his face was turned toward the west. His moustache had turned completely gray, but the edges of the hair of his head still retained the faded blackness of the dye he had used months ago for the last time—at my request.

Still clutching my arm, her legs shaking, Munīra sobbed and cried. In spite of my best efforts, I could not weep. I was afraid that if I shed a tear, he would rise suddenly, ask us to come closer, and when I had come near him, he would make the two of us sit on his right and left sides. Then placing his hands affectionately on our shoulders, he would say rather angrily to me: "You must not cry like this. Remember, you are a man—and men do not weep."

The passing of one's father is a dreadful loss. But at the age of fourteen I was too young to realize the value of what was lost.

Under the leadership of Quaid-i-Azam Muhammad Ali Jinnah, the Muslims of India had already started moving in the direction of carving out a separate Muslim homeland in the subcontinent. This meant that the time for the realization of father's dream was fast approaching. In March 1940, the Pakistan resolution was adopted by the Muslim League, and within seven years Pakistan actually came into being as an independent state.

I came to know and love father as I grew up—like many others of my generation. He infused a new spirit in the Muslims by constantly goading them to passionate action instead of scholastic quibbling. Today he is a living force in the minds of sensitive Pakistanis—inspiring, directing, and sustaining us in our struggle to reconstruct our national life.

## FATHER'S PRAYER

If God grants you the gift of eyes that see,
Look at the auguries of things to be,
Intelligences bold, hearts passionless and cold,
Eyes shamelessly to fiction-worship sold.
Religion, politics, science, and art,
At Matter's altar laying head and heart.
The Orient, that birthplace of the sun,
Other-oriented, to itself alien.
Its heart devoid of new experience;
Its self-expression all sound and no sense.
Its life a relic, dead and glacial,
Without the joy of motion, frozen, still.
Its thought a lame and wounded deer at bay,
To autocrats and *mullas* easy prey.
Its intellect, religion, honor, pride,
All to the Western hunters' saddlestraps tied.
I've wandered far and wide on its thought's trail
And torn apart its every secret's veil.
My heart has bled profusely at its plight,
And with its blood has dyed the prospect's bright.
You learn a thousand books from learned men;
A better teacher than your eyes is none.
The wine that bubbles forth out of the eyes
Intoxicates men in such various ways.
Death to the candle's flame is the breath of morn;
It fills the tulip's cup with rich, red wine.
Humanity involves respect for man;
Learn well what is man's place in Nature's plan.
Humanity binds men together in fraternity;
So keep your feet fixed on the path of amity.
The man of love, who sees men with God's eye,
Loves heathen and believer equally.
Give both of them a warm place in your heart.
Woe to the heart, if heart from heart should part.
The heart, a captive in a frame of clay,
Has this world under its immortal sway.
Among the Muslims you will seek in vain
The faith, the ecstasy of days bygone.

## Iqbal: My Father

The scholars are without Qur'ānic lore;
The Sufis, long-haired beasts and nothing more.
The frenzy at the saints' tombs is a fraud:
Show me a single man who is drunk with God.
As for the Muslims dazzled by the West,
A mirage is the object of their quest.
These men cannot at all appreciate
Religion: they are gospellers of hate.
The privileged possess no charity;
But in the masses there's sincerity.
"Distinguish men of faith from men of hate.
Seek out a man of God for your soul mate."

# II
# POLITICS

# 4

# The Man of Thought and the Man of Action

## HAFEEZ MALIK

IQBAL'S political career, professionally speaking, started with his membership (November 1926–1930) in the Punjab Legislative Council; this council and the principle of election itself was introduced by the Montagu-Chelmsford Reforms in 1919. However, his participation in India's politics, and especially in that of the Muslim League, considerably antedated the Montagu-Chelmsford Reforms, going back, in fact, to his student days in London. Iqbal therefore exercised the role of a political leader at the provincial and national levels. His role was significant both for the contemporary period and for what it portended for future generations. (This subject is so involved and the sources so meager that only its salient features are highlighted here.)

What kind of political leader was Iqbal? The appraisal of course would vary, but probably most scholars of recent Indic-Muslim history would agree that, despite the criticism of his opponents that he was a leader in an "ivory tower," his political judgment was sound. His aloofness and his incapacity to relish the rough-and-tumble of party politics was his weakness as well as his strength. Without involving himself in party intrigues, he could evolve a comprehensive view of the political and cultural problems of the Muslims. To his debit, however, he did not have the control and support of political machines, and therefore failed to achieve the position of president (speaker) in the Punjab Legislative Council, although it was generally agreed that he was the most suitable candidate. The reason for this failure was his blunt but justifiable attack on the policies of the Punjab National Unionist party (to which he then belonged), which were causing a split between the rural and urban Muslims.

If politics can be defined as a struggle for power among competing groups, or as (in Harold Laswell's words) "who gets what and how,"[1] then Iqbal could not be considered an actor on the political scene of the Punjab, or of India. In a Laswellian sense, the true politicians of the Punjab were Mian Muhammad Shafi, Fazl-i Husain, Chandhary Shahāb-ud-Din, and the sole survivor of that era, Zafarullah Khan. In practical politics, Iqbal played second fiddle to these "pros." But if politics is viewed as a milieu "in which the actor strives for the attainment of various values for which power is a necessary (and perhaps also sufficient) condition,"[2] then Iqbal was a statesman par excellence and surpassed all of his contemporaries. For Iqbal the highest moral and political value was the preservation of Indic Muslims' cultural entity and their eventual self-determination. The fact that the Muslims were a nation in their own right and not just a religious minority was realized and enunciated by him gradually. An understanding of this intellectual transformation is necessary for any evaluation of his political participation.

## FROM UNITARIAN MONISM TO ECOLOGICAL STRUGGLE

SINCE their arrival in the eighth century, the Muslims had faced a dilemma in the Indian environment: Could they isolate themselves from the Hindu cultural influences, and if not, then to what extent should they welcome the diffusion of cultural traits? The significance of this issue is central to the understanding of the Muslims' political behavior in the subcontinent.

Hindu civilization has shown a remarkable capacity for the assimilation of foreign races (that is, Persians, Greeks, Scythians, Kushans, the white Huns, etc.) and their cultures. Throughout Indian history a four-stage process is generally evident: foreign races invaded India; they became amalgamated with the native Indian population; the foreign and indigenous cultures were synthesized; and the invaders eventually disappeared as a separate cultural entity. Would this assimilation be the fate of the Muslims? The patterns of the Muslim history indicate their extreme preoccupation with this fear. It affected their politics as well as spiritual and cultural movements.

During the period of the Delhi Sultanate and the Mughal Empire, the Sufis, who most influenced the foreign-born and Indian Muslims, came to be divided among the followers of the Hispanic-Arab Sufi Muhy al-Din Ibn al-'Arabi (1165–1240), and those of his opponents, including Ibn Taimiyya (1263–1328) and 'Alā al-Daulah Simnani (1261–1336). Al-'Arabi's disciples subscribed to his innovated doctrine of *Wahdat al-Wajūd* (unitarian monism), believing that "all Being is essentially one, as it all is a manifestation of the divine substance. The different religions were, thus, in his [al-'Arabi's] opinion identical."[3] The followers of Simnani's school of Sufism came to believe in *Wahdat al-Shahūd* (phenomenological monism), asserting that the Qur'ān should be interpreted in accordance with the view-point of the *'ulamā'* (scholars), and that deviation from the *Shari'a* should not be tolerated. The aim of union with reality (*fanā fil haq*), renunciation of the world, and asceticism, generally practiced by the Sufis of al-'Arabi school, were *bida'* (impious innovations) and un-Islamic practices.[4]

In the fifteenth century the Indic disciples of al-'Arabi sought to reconcile the symbols of the Vaishnavite poetry and other devotional Hindu songs with Muslim beliefs. For instance, Mīr 'Abdūl Wāhid Bilgrami wrote a treatise, *Haqāiq-i Hind*, (in 1566) in which he endeavored to reconcile and integrate "more than fifty symbols of the Vaishnavites" and several other terms and expressions of Hindu devotional songs into Muslim religious conceptions. For example,

Krishna and other names used for him sometimes symbolized Prophet Muhammad, sometimes "Man," and sometimes the reality of human beings (*Haqiqat-i Insān*) . . . *Gopis* (cow herd's wives) sometimes symbolized angels, sometimes the human race, and sometimes its reality in relation to the *wahidiyyā* (relative unity, that is, unity in plurality) of the Divine attributes . . . *Gobra* (cow dung) symbolized the faults and follies of human beings. Udhu (a friend of Krishna) sometimes represented Prophet Muhammad himself, and sometimes his followers . . . Braj of Gokul (a town of Mathura) sometimes symbolized *'Alam-i Nasūt* (the human world), sometimes *'Alam-i Malkūt* (the invisible world) and sometimes *'Alam-i Jabrūt* (the highest world). Jumana and Ganga sometimes indicated the sea of *Wahdat* (unity), and at other [times] *Marifat* (gnosis) . . .[5]

In order to meet the *Wahdat al-Wujūd* brand of Islam half way, the Hindus also wrote the *Alo (Allah) Upanishad* during the Mughal period. Critics of the *Wahdat al-Wujūd* believed that if this trend continued unabated Islam as a culture-making force would have disappeared from India. The potential synthesis of Muslim and Hindu cultures was shattered by the endeavors of the *'ulamā'* and the *Wahdat al-Shahūd* school of mystics led by Shaikh Ahmad Mujaddid Alf Thani[6] (born 1564), and by the policies of Emperor Aurangzeb 'Alamgīr (d. 1707).

There is a consensus that Iqbal also subscribed to the doctrine of *Wahdat al-Wujūd* until at least 1907, the year in which he submitted his doctoral dissertation. (In the introduction Iqbal has paid a glowing tribute to Ibn al-'Arabi.)[7] Iqbal's admiration for al-'Arabi was not the outcome of his two years of research for his dissertation, but was the product of the philosophical orientation he inherited from his parents and from his early teachers. Probably he had completed the better part of his doctoral research before he arrived in Europe; it would have been almost impossible for him to complete his work in two years, especially since he was working for two other degrees. Iqbal's subsequent studies carried him farther away from al-'Arabi. Writing in 1915 his foreword to the first edition of *Asrār-i Khudi* (The Secrets of the Self), Iqbal repudiated Ibn al-'Arabi and *Wahdat al-Wujūd*. He complimented Ibn Taimiyya and Wāhid Mahmūd for raising their voices high against the life-negating impact of al-'Arabi. Also, he advised his readers to look to the western nations of Europe in order to learn the meaning of life. "By virtue of their will to action, the western nations are preeminent among the nations of the world. For this reason, and in order to appreciate the secret of life, their literatures and ideas are the best guides for the nations of the East."[8]

Among the western nations he singled out Britain.

The world is indebted to the British for their pragmatism. Their ability to comprehend situations is sharper and more developed than that of other nations. For this reason, no high-flown philosophic systems, which fail to stand up in the light of facts, have gained popularity in England. Therefore, the works of British thinkers have a place of their own in the world literature. After benefiting from them [that is, British ideas], the mind and the heart [philosophy and literature] of the East must revise their intellectual legacy.[9]

It is here maintained that Iqbal graduated from the *Wahdat al-Wujūd* of Ibn al-'Arabi to the concept of the ecological struggle. He was aided in this evolutionary thinking by the ideas of Ibn Taimiyya, Wāhid Mahmūd, and Majaddid Alf Thani, and also more significantly by

# The Man of Thought and of Action

Darwin and the European ecologists, including Ernest Haeckel (the German biologist who, in *History of Creation* [1868] first used the term ecology) and their followers. In 1904, a year before he went to Europe, Iqbal demonstrated a sharp awareness of the ecological struggle even though he still subscribed to the theory of *Wahdat al-Wujūd*. (It is, however, not suggested that Iqbal's system of philosophy was basically Darwinian; although he was influenced by the concept of the ecological struggle, it was only one of the strands of thought which helped him formulate his own philosophic system.)

## THE CONCEPT OF ECOLOGY

THE basis of modern ecology lies in the work of the biologists Darwin and Wallace. In particular, Darwin's *Origin of Species* (1859) and *Descent of Man* (1871) set the stage for a new era in biological research. Attention shifted from a preoccupation with cosmological problems, such as the ultimate meaning of each form of life for every other which followed from the assumption of the inscrutability of species, to a search for specific causes for the existence of species, based upon accumulated evidence of change in the organic world. Final causes were forsaken in favor of necessary and sufficient conditions.

Darwin formulated the basic ideas which were later brought together to constitute the theoretical understructure, the frame of reference, of modern ecology. All life was his province and he perceived it as a moving system of vital relationships in which were implicated every organism and species of life. (This general conception he described metaphorically as the *web of life*.) Organisms are related to one another in the web, Darwin pointed out, on the basis of a struggle for existence. The phrase "struggle for existence" includes in its meaning the competition among forms of life as well as the cooperation and mutual aid that develop among organisms. Through the struggle for existence order develops and the web of life unfolds as organisms become adjusted to one another and to the physical environment.[10]

Writing in 1904 an article on the theme of national life, Iqbal adopted the ecological concept for the rise and fall of nations. "After observing the phenomena of nature, scholars have reached a conclusion," maintained Iqbal, "that among all organic beings (including *homo sapiens* and varieties of animal and plant life), constant war is waged. . . . In this struggle for existence all forms of life are engaged, final victory being achieved by those who have the ability to survive and who can adjust themselves to the changed circumstances. . . . The modern progeny of *homo sapiens* is a memorial to the long-gone national civilizations and cultures, which suffered death and destruction in their struggle for survival."[11]

This law of natural selection, contended Iqbal, was equally applicable to religions and to national languages. "Hundreds of religions came into being in this world. They flourished and then eventually decayed. Why? The answer is obvious. The intellectual development of man gave rise to new needs and wants, which these religions could not satisfy." Similar was the case with languages. "At one time Latin, Greek, and Sanskrit were living languages; they are now almost defunct. They lapsed into disuse because of the law of natural selection. . . ."

Complimenting the Chinese, Hindus, Jews, and Zoroastrians for their ability to survive the ravages of time, Iqbal deplored what he thought was the critical situation of the Muslims in India. He feared that they were on the precipice of extinction and needed to reform their entire national life. The modern struggle, Iqbal believed, was conditioned by trade and industry. "Among the Asian nations, the Japanese were the first to comprehend the secret of the revolution. They dedicated themselves to industrializing their national economy. Today, they are recognized as one of the civilized nations of the world. They have achieved this distinction because of their highly industrialized economy and not because of the contributions of any national philosopher, poet, or *littérateur*."

His advice was unequivocal: Muslims must take to industry and *craftsmanship*. "In my eyes," declared Iqbal, "the hands of a carpenter, rough and coarse due to the constant use of the saw, are far more attractive and useful compared to the soft and delicate hands of a scholar, which never carry more than the weight of a pen."

Since the Muslims were outnumbered four to one in India, Iqbal came to believe that their culture did not have an even chance to survive. This realization became the motive force for the formulation of his doctrine of *khudi* (ego), the main arch of his philosophic system. *Khudi*, or self-affirmation, became the frame of reference for the analysis

## The Man of Thought and of Action 75

of Indian history. Political forces or persons who strengthened collective Muslim *khudi* became heroes because they strengthened the Muslims' ability to survive in their ecological struggle. Hence, Iqbal's lack of appreciation for the Mughal Emperor Akbar's *Din-i Ilahi* and its concomittant cultural syncreticism, and his approbation of Shaikh Ahmad Mujaddid Alf Thani, who spent his life combating the legacy of *Din-i Ilahi* during the reign of Akbar's son, Emperor Jehangīr (1605–1628). In an elegant Urdu poem Iqbal extolled the deeds of Shaikh Ahmad, saying that Allah sent him to India "to keep watch over the treasure-house of Islam":

> I stood by the Reformer's tomb: that dust
> Whence here below an orient splendour breaks,
> Dust at whose least speck stars hang their heads,
> Dust shrouding that high knower of things unknown
> Who to Jehangīr would not bend his neck,
> Whose ardent breath fans every free heart's ardour,
> Whom Allah sent in season to keep watch
> In India on the treasure-house of Islam.

By the same token, Aurangzeb was the builder of *khudi* to Iqbal, because in Iqbal's judgment he understood the reality of the ecological struggle in India. "The political genius of Aurangzeb was extremely comprehensive," wrote Iqbal in his private notebook, which he started keeping in 1910.

His [Aurangzeb's] one aim of life was, as it were, to subsume the various communities of this country under the notion of one universal empire. . . . Ignoring the factor of time in the political evolution of his contemplated empire, he started an endless struggle [a reference to his fifty years' wars against the Sikhs, Rajputs, and Marathas] in the hope that he would be able to unify the discordant political units of India in his own life-time. He failed to Islamise (not in the religious sense) India just as Alexander had failed to Hellenise Asia.

The history of the preceding Muslim dynasties had taught Aurangzeb that the strength of Islam in India did not depend, as his ancestor Akbar had thought, so much on the goodwill of the people of this land as on the strength of the ruling race. With all his keen political perception, however, he could not undo the doings of his forefather. Sevaji[12] [Shivaji, the Maratha leader] was not the product of Aurangzeb's reign; the Maharatta owed his existence to social and political forces called into being by the policy of Akbar.

Aurangzeb's political perception, though true, was too late. Yet considering the significance of this perception, he must be looked upon as the founder of *Musalman* [Muslim] nationality in India. I am sure posterity will one day recognize the truth of what I say.[13]

Discussing in *Ramūz-i-Bekhudi* (The Mysteries of Selflessness) the personal fulfillment of the individual in society, Iqbal described Aurangzeb as:

> He the last arrow in our quiver left
> In the affray of faith with unbelief.

and

> An Abraham in India's idol-house.[14]

Iqbal had thus come firmly to believe that in the post-Aurangzeb era Indian Muslims as a self-conscious nationality had appeared on the political horizon. Parenthetically, it may be added that the Hindus and the Sikhs started developing a similar political consciousness in this period. Consequently, his orientation in practical politics led him to advocate the separation of Muslim India from Hindu India. Whereas Jinnah (until at least 1930s) sought compromise and *modus vivendi* with the All-India National Congress, Iqbal stood for separate electorates, other constitutional safeguards to protect the cultural identity of the Muslims, and their eventual self-determination.

## THE POLITICAL LIFE OF THE PUNJAB
(1900–1940)

IQBAL's political arena was the Punjab. He had to deal with the political and economic equations as they then existed. These conditions must be understood in order to perceive the significance of Iqbal's policies and actions and evaluate them accurately in historical perspective. The economic life of the province had been determined by the British government through the implementation of the Land Alienation Act of 1900. Its political life had been shaped by the All-India National Congress and the All-India Muslim League through the Lucknow Pact of 1916. The significance of these factors and their relationships must be understood in order to develop a comprehensive view of Iqbal's role.

## THE LAND ALIENATION ACT: ITS BACKGROUND

The mutually suspicious and often antagonistic elements in the population of the Punjab were the Muslims (who constituted 55 per cent of the total population), and the Hindus (who formed 35 per cent), who were located mainly in the eastern districts. The Sikhs, constituting 10 to 13 per cent of the total population, comprised a third factor. They were scattered all over the province and retained vivid memories of their recent rule in the Punjab. The Muslims made up almost 57 per cent of the rural population, and even under the Sikh rule had owned the majority of the agricultural acreage in the province. The commercial and financial interests before and after the advent of the British remained the exclusive monopoly of the Hindu moneylenders.

Historical evidence suggests that Hindu moneylenders existed even under Mughal and Sikh rule. In fact, many modern economists maintain that in an agricultural country like India their existence was essential and useful. However, the pre-British governments limited their power, forestalling the extortion which became widespread after the establishment of British rule in the Punjab. After the British defeated the Sikhs in 1849, the Pax Britannica in the province ushered in an economic laissez-faire policy removing all the social and legal restraints from the business transactions of the three Hindu subcastes: the Bania or Aggarwal, the Khatri, and the Arora, who had a monopoly on moneylending in the Punjab. Actually, the newly created British civil courts started to help these moneylenders to recover their debts, thus putting the peasants entirely at the mercy of the creditors.

The economic ascendency of the moneylenders dated from the 1870s, and characteristically it began with a series of famines. Mortgages, which had been rare in the days of the Sikhs, appeared in every village, and by 1878 7 per cent of the province was pledged. In Amritsar, for example, there were 798 mortgages in 1880 against only 23 recorded before 1865. In Jullunder, over Rs. 1,400,000 were raised by mortgage in 1871–1881 against only Rs. 40,000 in the 1850s. The number of mortgages, which in the early 1870s had averaged only 15,000 a year, averaged over 50,000 twenty years later (1883–1893); in ten years the annual increase in the area under mortgage rose from 165,000 acres (1875–1878) to 385,000 (1884–1888). Encouraged by the economic laissez-faire policy of the British government the number of moneylenders, including their dependents, increased from 53,263 in 1868 to 193,890 in 1911.[15]

Eventually, the British government realized the nature of this silent economic revolution. The initiative was taken by an accomplished administrator, S. S. Thorburn, who published a remarkable book, *Mussalmans and Money-lenders in the Punjab* (London, 1886), demonstrating with statistics the Hindu moneylenders' dominance over the majority of Muslim peasant proprietors. As the new century opened the British government took the first steps of correction and passed the Land Alienation Act of 1900, which came into force a year later.

### SOCIAL AND ECONOMIC CONSEQUENCES OF THE LAND ALIENATION ACT

The act saved the Muslim peasant proprietors, who constituted the majority of Punjabi rural society. Hindu and Sikh peasant proprietors, although not very numerous, were also beneficiaries, since the main object of the act was to prevent the expropriation of the land of the small peasant proprietor by the village moneylender. Also, the act legally disqualified the nonagricultural classes from owning land. Even if the owner wanted to sell his land to a nonagricultural buyer he was not allowed to do so. The nonagricultural classes could not even keep the agricultural land in mortgage for more than twenty years. The act emancipated the peasant proprietors, but it divided both the Hindu and Muslim societies into opposing rural and urban classes. To the British, this policy delivered handsome dividends: the peasant proprietor became the bulwark of political conservatism and also an inexhaustible source of manpower for the British army.

The act by no means eliminated debts. At the beginning of the twentieth century, tenants and farm servants' families who were dependent upon agriculture but owned no land numbered about $1\frac{1}{4}$ million. Their average debt in 1930 was estimated at 20 crors (Rs. 200,000,000). Adding this to the 120 crors (1 cror = 10,000,000) for peasant proprietors, the total agricultural debt in the province amounted to 140 crors, or £105 million according to the then current rate of exchange. Sir Malcolm Darling stated that the Muslim peasant proprietors' debt exceeded 80 crors. The debt of £105 million represented $26\frac{1}{2}$ times the land revenue charged by the British government.[16]

The only class which was free from debt was that of the landlords. Although the Punjab was a province of small proprietors, along the Indus River the landlords were paramount. About 40 per cent of the cultivated area was in the hands of landlords who owned over 50 acres. In Multan, for instance, the holdings were well over 50 acres. In the districts of Mianwali, Muzaffargarh, Dera Ghazi Khan, and Rawalpindi, Sayyid, Jat, Pathan, and Baluch landlords dominated. They received rents from the tiller, while doing nothing or little for the tenants. The tenants' exploitation knew no limits when some of their landlords also assumed the role of *pīr* (spiritual leader). Mostly uneducated, and parochial in outlook, the landlords traveled no further than their local 'Idgah (mosque for 'Id prayers). *The Multan Gazetteer* (1901, p. 107), for instance, says that the big landlords were "as bewildered and as unhappy in Lahore [the capital of the Punjab] as Highlanders of the eighteenth century in London."

A comparatively small number of Hindu landlords hailed mainly from Rohtak, Hisar, and Anbala. During the last two decades of the nineteenth century the British government constructed a network of canals to facilitate agriculture in the barren districts of Shahpur, Lyallpur, and Montgomery. In these districts the prospects of profitable farming attracted enterprising but loyal Sikh landlords and some Muslims. In the twentieth century, however, as a counterweight to the influence of the newly emerging educated[17] urban middle and higher classes the British bolstered up the landed gentry in rural areas by giving them title[18] and grants of land in these new canal colonies. All the Maliks, Khans, Tiwanas, Noons, Mamdots, and Daultanas, members of the landed aristocracy, became pillars of the British rule in the Punjab. Although smaller in number, they also had their counterparts among the Hindus and the Sikhs.

Reserving the Punjab as the main supplier of infantrymen for the British Indian Army and in order to isolate the province from the whirlwind of politics, the British delayed the introduction of the constitutional reforms. The Indian Councils Act of 1861 established legislative councils in Bombay and Madras and authorized the creation of similar councils in other provinces. In Bengal and the United Provinces these councils were constituted in 1863 and 1866 respectively, but in the Punjab a council was not created until 1897. The Indian Councils Act of 1892 authorized an increase in the membership of the councils and allowed reserved seats to be filled by indirect elections from public associations and municipal bodies.

These provisions were applied in all provinces except the Punjab, where the strength of the council (established in 1897) was fixed at nine, and all the seats were filled by nomination of the lieutenant-governor.

The Minto-Morley Reforms (1909) also maintained the discrimination against the Punjab. Like Assam, the Punjab was given a thirty-member legislative council despite the fact that the Punjab's population was 20 million and that of Assam only 7 million. Also, until 1920 the lieutenant-governor of the Punjab functioned without an executive council.

Under the Montagu-Chelmsford Reforms of 1919, the first Punjab Legislative Council came into being in 1921. It consisted of 71 elected members (besides 23 nominated officials and nonofficials), of whom 35 were Muslims, 15 Sikhs, and the rest Hindus and others. The Muslim population had an overall majority of 55 per cent in the province, but they had been alloted only 50 per cent of the seats in the legislative council. Since the council had seven representatives from special constituencies and nominated seats, the Muslims wound up a minority of 45.56 per cent.[19] This situation, the result of the Lucknow Pact, remained stable throughout the Montagu-Chelmsford Reform era.

### THE LUCKNOW PACT OF 1916

The Minto-Morley Reforms (1909) had accepted the principle of separate electorates at the request of the All-India Muslim League. The principle of separate electorates guaranteed representation of Muslims by the Muslims elected from clearly designated constituencies; it also provided the same arrangement for Hindus, Sikhs, and Christians. In 1916 the League and the All-India National Congress held a joint session at Lucknow and a scheme of reforms for India was adopted unanimously. The scheme, however, was the product of major concessions and compromises by both sides, and like most compromises, failed in the long run to satisfy both parties.

Despite her ideological objections to the separate electorates, the Congress accepted them at this time without any reservations. The League also made a major concession, which according to some participants and competent political observers,[20] sowed the seeds of

Muslim frustrations, intensified the fears of Hindu domination in the Muslim majority provinces, and nurtured the eventual partition of India. This was the acceptance of the principal of weightage for minorities. In Bengal, the Muslims agreed to forgo a quarter of their seats in the provincial legislature to which they would have been otherwise entitled on the basis of their population. In the Punjab, they agreed to surrender one-tenth of the seats. In return, they were given 33 per cent representation in Bombay although it had a Muslim population of only 20 per cent; 30 per cent in Uttar Pradesh with but a population of 14 per cent; 29 per cent in Bihar with a population of 13 per cent; 15 per cent in Madras with a population of 6.15 per cent; and 15 per cent in C.P. with a population of 4 per cent.[21]

Despite these illusory gains achieved through the artificial device of the weightage, the Muslims in general held on to the principle of separate electorates. Also, to the Punjab Muslim peasant proprietors the Land Alienation Act of 1900 had acquired a certain sanctity even though it splintered the Muslims into urban and rural classes.

IQBAL IN THE LEGISLATIVE COUNCIL (NOVEMBER 1926–1930)

All three legislative councils (1921, 1923, 1926–1930) of the Montagu-Chelmsford Reforms era were dominated by the landed gentry. Politically ultraconservative but shrewd in practical matters, these country squires were concerned primarily with protecting and promoting the vested interests of the land-owning class, if necessary, at the expense of the townsmen.

A group of urban Muslim leaders headed by Mian Fazl-i Husain (a former classmate of Iqbal's at the Government College) realized that the power in the councils must rest ultimately with rural Muslim members. Consequently, Fazl-i Husain created the Rural party in the first council, which in the second council was renamed the Punjab National Unionist party. All the landlords, Hindu, Sikh, and Muslim, joined this party and elected Sir Fazl-i Husain as their leader. The party adopted a sixteen-point[22] program, which with impressive rhetorical phrases attempted to conceal the real purpose of this alliance—the maintenance of the economic status quo. The Unionist party did not exist outside of the legislative chambers, nor did it ever make an attempt to establish contacts with the people. Mass political parties such as the Congress and the League hardly existed in the Punjab.

A branch of the Congress was formed in the Punjab in 1885, but it did not have much influence, even among the Hindus, until the late 1930s; no more than a handful of Muslims ever supported the Congress in the Punjab. The only Hindu movement in the Punjab of any significance was the Arya Samaj, which by 1889 had developed an attitude of hostility towards the Congress.[23] When the Land Alienation Act of 1900 was passed, the Arya Samaj expected the Congress to oppose it. Realizing that the Congress did not want to antagonize the peasant proprietors of the Punjab, the Samaj withheld its support.

Iqbal's sympathies were with the Muslim League, and he wanted to see it organized as a truly mass party. However, the League fell victim to a power struggle between Mian Muhammad Shafi and Mian Fazl-i Husain. By 1906 two rival League organizations in the Punjab had sprung up—one headed by Mian Muhammad Shafi, and the other by Mian Fazl-i Husain. The Karachi session (December 1907) of the All-India Muslim League recognized the Shafi League as the bona-fide provincial organization, and, as the result of a compromise, Mian Fazl-i Husain became its joint secretary. Mian Shafi continued to be the head of the League until 1916, and Iqbal remained his ardent supporter. This compromise proved to be disastrous for the League. After founding the Unionist party in the legislative council, Mian Fazl-i Husain maintained only nominal membership in the League and did not help it to flourish or function.

When Iqbal was elected to the Punjab Legislative Council in November 1926, the Muslim League existed only on paper. In the council the Unionist party headed by Fazl-i Husain dominated. Also represented were the Sawarj party, consisting of a few members, and a handful of die-hard Khilafatists. The Sawarj party was more urban and pro-Hindu than nationalist, and was opposed to rural interests. The Hindu Sabha had returned a sizable number of representatives who preferred to remain in the opposition rather than join other parties or alliances within the legislative council. Looking upon the Unionist alliance as a lesser evil, Iqbal joined it. He knew that the Unionist party was a marriage of convenience between the majority of Muslim and the minority of Hindu landlords, and that he was only an odd man in their alliance. Actually, for Iqbal and other like-minded urban Muslims the alternative was equally unpleasant. By forming a separate bloc in the council, they would have reduced the Unionist strength, making

## The Man of Thought and of Action

the rule of the Hindu Sabha and the Congress group a distinct possibility. The latter were publicly committed to annul the separate electorates in all shapes and forms, and to repeal the Land Alienation Act. To Iqbal both were necessary for the protection of the Muslims' interest.

During his term of office as a legislator (November 1926–1930), Iqbal maintained a nominal membership among the Unionists, simultaneously subjecting them to his relentless criticism. To the chagrin of the ruling landlords, he also attacked the provincial revenue system which favored the big landowners, and the primary and secondary educational system which he thought had failed to benefit private Muslim institutions.

### CRITICISM OF THE REVENUE AND EDUCATIONAL SYSTEMS

After the overthrow of Mughal rule, the British had adopted a revenue system for agricultural land on the assumption that the land belonged to the crown. The British justification for this policy lay in the precedents established during the Muslim and the Hindu eras. The British interpretation of the previous systems led them to declare that in India the concept of the ownership of land in the juridical sense of the word never existed: if a subject occupied land, he was required to pay a share of its gross produce to the sovereign in return for the protection he was entitled to receive. The question of the ownership of land did not arise.[24] This theory was assiduously cultivated during the viceroyalty of Lord Curzon (1899–1905), who was the classic prototype of an English proconsul.

In the Punjab the Unionist landlords adhered to the British theory of the crown's ownership of land. For instance, in the spring 1928 legislative session Lala Mohan Lal (representative from Simla) supported the assessment of the Punjab government's revenue member, Mian Fazl-i Husain, regarding the principle of state ownership of agricultural land. "This offers a fitting occasion for the application of that humorous Punjabi proverb," retorted Iqbal in the council on February 23, 1928, " 'Chor nāloñ pand Kalhi,' that is to say, the property stolen is readier to run away than the thief," implying that the Unionists were more royalist than the king.

The proposition that all land belonged to the crown, Iqbal said, "was the barbarous theory," and that "neither in ancient India nor even in the days of the Mughals had the sovereign ever claimed universal ownership. . . . We are told that the Mughals claimed such rights; but the people of the Punjab owned and possessed the land of this country long before the race of Babur [the founder of the Mughal Empire] entered into history—the unmistakable lesson of which is that crowns come and go; the people alone are immortal."[25] To clinch his argument, Iqbal then recited two of his Persian verses:

> Alexander is dead and gone, and so are his sword and the imperial flag;
> Gone are also the cities and the mines which yielded him the tribute.
> Why don't you regard the nations as more lasting than the kings;
> Can you not see: Iran lives, but her Emperors have gone.

Tested on the anvil of history, the government's theory of the state ownership of land proved to be spurious. Citing the French scholar Perron (1777), and the English scholar Briggs (1830), Iqbal pointed out that the latter particularly "gives in his book an accurate description of the laws of Manu, of Muslim law and practices prevailing in the various parts of India—Bengal, Malwa, the Punjab, etc., and arrives at the conclusion that in no period in the history of India the state ever claimed the proprietorship of land."[26]

In view of this Iqbal insisted that the land revenue system was unjust also because it recognized no distinction between a small landowner and an absentee landlord. Iqbal suggested that land revenue be treated as a graduated income tax. The Unionists did not tax a person who earned "from sources other than land less than 2,000 rupees a year," whereas they assessed the peasant proprietor who made much less than this amount. The minimum economically viable land holding in the Punjab was considered to be eight acres. Iqbal therefore pleaded that land holdings not exceeding five *bighas* (acres) be declared revenue-free. The Unionist's chief, Mian Fazl-i Husain, argued to the contrary, saying that the minimum economical land holding was about ten or eleven *bighas*; the remission of five acres would provide no relief to the peasant, but would cause a deficit of Rs. 25,000,000 in the budget. To Fazl-i Husain this amounted to committing a fruitless sin. It might be, reasoned Iqbal, but it would show "that there is at least some sense of justice in you."[27]

On March 4, 1929, and a year later on March 7, 1930, Iqbal made some provocative suggestions to balance the budget. He concluded that "we spend more than any other country in the world on the present system of administration. . . . We pay much more than our revenues justify." This statement immediately evoked a protest from the British officials present in the legislative council, and Iqbal's implicit suggestion that large cuts be made in the salaries of the bureaucrats was dismissed. Iqbal then proposed the imposition of inheritance tax for those who would inherit property to the value of twenty or thirty thousand rupees. He described it as "death duties." Quickly, Mian Fazl-i Husain retorted: "Living duties would be more appropriate." Not twitted by the remark, Iqbal said: "It is the living who would have to pay."[28] The legislative council, composed largely of landlords, was obviously not receptive to these proposals.

It was against this background that Iqbal came to realize that in a just polity the land as a means of production should not be owned, in large or small acreage, by individuals. Land should be collectively owned by the society for the benefit of all. *Al-Arḍ l-Allah* (The Earth Is God's), a poem in *Bāl-i Jibrīl* (Gabriel's Wing), succinctly sums up the idea of collective ownership of land and openly challenges the landlords:

> Landlord! this earth is not thine, is not thine,
> Nor yet thy father's; no, not thine, nor mine.[29]

Iqbal also turned his attention to the educational system of the province. In the heat of debates he tended to be impatient and at times overlooked the progress made by the Punjab. Because only 2.4 per cent of the population of $20\frac{3}{8}$ million, until 1920, were receiving education in the Punjab, Iqbal asserted that "the disinterested foreign Government in this country wants to keep the people ignorant."[30] However, under the Montagu-Chelmsford Reforms, Mian Fazl-i Husain, the education minister, had initiated a wholesome program to diffuse educational facilities. The Compulsory Education Act of 1919 was partially implemented, and by 1926 the number of students had increased to 6.71 per cent of the potential student population. Also, by 1926, twelve intermediate (junior) colleges had been established.[31]

Before the reforms, the Muslims, as compared to the Hindus and the Sikhs, were considered to be backward in education. Therefore, a sizable number of scholarships were awarded to them after the reforms were instituted. In order to overcome the opposition of Muslim parents, Muslim head teachers were appointed to the schools in Muslim neighborhoods. Consequently, in two years the Muslim student population in public and private institutions increased by 42.3 per cent, whereas the increase among the Hindus was 19.6 per cent.[32]

Iqbal's attack was, however, mainly directed at the Punjab government's policy of grants-in-aid to private schools. The government graded private schools according to their financial position; those who spent more, received more aid. Under this system municipal and privately chartered institutions received government grants to cover 50 to 90 per cent of their expenditures. Although the Muslims composed a majority of the province, they formed the bulk of the lower economic classes, and therefore the Muslims' institutions failed to compete with those of the Hindus.

Delivering a speech (March 4, 1929) on the budget of 1929–1930 in the Punjab Legislative Council, Iqbal reviewed the government's grants-in-aid to various private schools, pointing out the disparity between their need and the financial support they were actually receiving. In 1922–1923 fifty-five new schools were given grants-in-aid, of which sixteen were Islamic schools. The total amount of the grants was Rs. 121,906, of which Rs. 29,214 were granted to Muslim schools. In 1926–1927 the total amount of grants was Rs. 122,287; Muslim schools received Rs. 29,214 or 23 per cent of the total amount. In 1927–1928 the grants-in-aid amounted to Rs. 1,013,154, and the share of Muslim schools was Rs. 204,330. In the budget speech of March 7, 1930 Iqbal revealed that during 1928–1929 twenty-one schools had received grants-in-aid; these included thirteen Hindu, six Sikh, and two Muslim institutions. The Hindu schools received Rs. 16,973, the Sikh schools Rs. 9,908, and the Muslim schools Rs. 2,200.

Iqbal questioned the equity of the principle of matching the grant-in-aid with privately raised funds. He wanted the government to distribute funds equally, especially in "places where people are backward and too poor to pay for education."[33] There was some merit in Iqbal's criticism, because the distribution of educational funds reflected the relative political strength of the Hindus, the Muslims, and the Sikhs in the provincial council. The Lucknow Pact had taken away the Muslims' numerical majority in the Punjab Legislative Council. Consequently, the Unionist Muslim landlords were dependent on the support of a handful of Hindu legislators, and Hindu ministers including Dr. Gokal Chand Narang and Monohar Lal, the minister of education.[34]

In these circumstances, Iqbal began to voice serious doubts about the possibility of a secular Indian nationalism and about India's future territorial unity. The political atmosphere of the Punjab largely contributed to his profound misgivings. During 1922–1927 fourteen bloody riots erupted in the Punjab between the Hindus, the Muslims, and the Sikhs. In desperation, Iqbal stated on July 18, 1927 in the legislative council that "we are actually living in a state of civil war." The following day he challenged the concept of Indian nationalism, saying: "In this country one community is always aiming at the destruction of the other community. . . . Well, I do not know whether it is desirable to become a nation."[35]

Commenting (July 19, 1937) on Sardar Ujjal Singh's proposal for filling government positions by open competitive examination, Iqbal highlighted the mutual lack of communication and trust between Hindu and Muslim. In the Punjab University's final examination students were assigned anonymous roll numbers to conceal their identity. This system was adopted, Iqbal pointed out, because the Hindu examiners might fail Muslim candidates, and the Muslims might do the same to the Hindus. In order to gain the sympathy of the examiners shrewd students started writing symbols on their papers revealing their identity. "Only the other day, I was reading the L.L.B. examination papers," Iqbal informed the Council, "[and] I found the number 786 which is the numerical value of an Arabic formula, and on others I found *Om* meant [by the Hindu student] to invoke the blessings of God."[36]

Then Iqbal described another incident in which he was a participant. During the riot in Lahore he accompanied the Muslims' deputations to the deputy commissioner. The English administrator told them: "Before the Reforms Scheme came into operation, there were 120 British officers in the Police department, but there are only 68 now [that is, in 1927]. . . . Both communities want European officers." Accepting the need for impartial British police officers, Iqbal unequivocally stated: "The talk of a united nationalism is futile and will perhaps remain so for a long time to come."[37]

### IQBAL'S OPPOSITION TO JINNAH

At the All-India level Iqbal also consistently endeavored to establish a separate Muslim political identity. To the British and the Congress he would extend tactical cooperation in order to gain political rights for the Muslims. In the late 1920s this policy pitted him against Jinnah, who was then willing to compromise with the Congress by abolishing separate electorates for the Muslims.

At the Unity Conference held on March 20, 1927 at Delhi, Jinnah, as the president of the League, and Srinivasa Iyengar, president of the Congress, achieved an agreement for the future constitutional development of India. They agreed to accept joint electorates provided Sindh was separated from the Bombay province and reforms were introduced in the North-West Frontier Province and Baluchistan. Also, they agreed to reserve seats for all communities in all provinces, and in Bengal and the Punjab the allocation of seats was to be in proportion to population, which abrogated the Lucknow Pact. In the central legislature Muslim seats were to be no less than one-third of the total seats. This initial agreement came to be known as the Delhi Proposals.[38]

In May 1927 the All-India Congress Committee passed a resolution "substantially accepting the Muslim proposals."[39] Consequently, in December 1927 the League and the Congress appointed subcommittees to finalize their negotiations on the basis of the Delhi Proposals in order to draft a *swaraj* (self-government) constitution for India.[40] However, the Punjab Muslim League, under the leadership of Mian Muhammad Shafi, Mian Fazl-i Husain, and Iqbal denounced the Delhi Proposals, and this seriously weakened Jinnah's bargaining position with the Congress. Undaunted by this repudiation, Jinnah participated in the All-Parties Conference (February 12 to March 15, 1928), which produced the Nehru Report.[41]

The Nehru Report agreed to the separation of Sindh and the elevation of the Frontier Province and Baluchistan to the status of the constitutional provinces, but it did not concede reservation of seats in the Punjab and Bengal. Also, it insisted that the central government retain residuary powers and that Muslims compose only 25 per cent of the central legislature. The Congress adopted the Nehru Report and decided to initiate a policy of nonviolent noncooperation with the British if they did not accept it by December 31, 1929. This was the Congress' way of defying the British for not including an Indian in the Simon Commission, which was set up to make recommendations for future constitutional reforms. The commission visited India in February and March 1928 and again in October 1928 to April 1929.

The appointment of the Simon Commission split the League into two sections: one was led by Jinnah (president) and Dr. Kitchlew (secretary), and the other by Mian Muhammad Shafi (president) and Iqbal (secretary). The Shafi League met in 1928 at Lahore; it rejected the Delhi Proposals and offered to cooperate with the Simon Commission. At Calcutta (1928) the Jinnah League disavowed the Punjab Muslim League, adopted the Delhi Proposals, and accepted the Nehru Report subject to four amendments.[42] Jinnah was authorized to get these amendments accepted by the Congress. The Jinnah League also declared noncooperation with the Simon Commission. However, all four of its proposed amendments were rejected by the Congress. The Jinnah League was thus in the position of being repudiated by the Congress while it was simultaneously alienated from significant Muslim public opinion.

In the Shafi League the thinking element was led by Iqbal. On December 15, 1927 Iqbal, Nawab Zulfiqār Ali Khan, and Maulana Muhammad Ali (head of the Lahore branch of the Ahmadi movement) had issued a joint statement accepting with regret Lord Birkenhead's contention that Indians could not be included in the Simon Commission because of their wide differences of opinion. The statement urged Indians in general and Muslims in particular to cooperate with the Commission.[43]

In order to draft the memorandum for the Simon Commission, the Draft Committee of the Shafi League held a preliminary session in May 1928 at the president's house. Here, Iqbal vigorously advocated the concept of provincial autonomy. A tentative draft was adopted with a view to eliciting opinions from other leaders of the League. However, Mian Shafi adopted a very conservative position which appalled Iqbal. Before the final draft was adopted Iqbal went to Delhi for a few weeks for medical treatment. During his absence the final draft appeared in the press. Considering it a reactionary approach to contemporary constitutional problems, Iqbal resigned as League's secretary, releasing his letter of resignation to the press on June 24, 1928. "I now find that the extract of the League memorandum as published in the press," wrote Iqbal to Mian Shafi, "makes no demand for full provincial autonomy and suggests a unitary form of provincial government in which law, order and justice should be placed under the direct charge of the governor. . . . This suggestion is only a veiled form of diarchy and means no constitutional advance at all. . . . I ought not in the circumstances remain secretary of the All-India Muslim League."⁴⁴

Immediately Mian Shafi reversed himself and adopted Iqbal's proposals. Iqbal withdrew his resignation and signed the final draft of the memorandum. Consequently, when on November 5, 1928 the League's deputation appeared before the Simon Commission for testimony, Iqbal assisted Mian Shafi in answering the Commission's interrogatories.

The Muslim leadership soon realized the need of political union for effective bargaining with the Congress and the British government. In order to achieve unity the All-Parties' Muslim Conference (later transformed into All-India Muslim Conference) was scheduled on December 31, 1928 and January 1, 1929 at Delhi, under the presidency of the Aga Khan. Iqbal along with Mian Fazl-i Husain had initiated the idea of this conference. The Jinnah-Kitchlew and the Shafi-Iqbal factions of the League attended the conference along with other Muslim leaders. The conference adopted a manifesto of Muslim claims "of which the most important were that the future constitution must be federal with the maximum of autonomy and the residual powers vested in the provinces; that the separate electorates and weightage must be retained; and that Muslims must have their due share in the Central and Provincial Cabinets."⁴⁵ Highlighting the significance of the conference the Aga Khan stated that "it marked the return—long delayed and for the moment private and with no public avowal of his change of mind —of Mr. M. A. Jinnah to agreement with his fellow-Muslims."⁴⁶

The change in Jinnah's political ideas was overstated. His agreement with fellow Muslims was only in regard to constitutional safeguards for the Muslims; the ideology of separation was still alien to Jinnah's thinking. The split in the ranks of the Muslim League did not end until 1934, when Jinnah was finally elected president of the united League. In the interim (1930–1934), Iqbal provided the ideological leadership, spearheading the Muslims' demand for a separate Muslim state. In 1930, he was elected to preside over the annual session of the Muslim League at Allahabad. In his presidential address, Iqbal rejected the notion that India was socially unified; he then suggested that "I would like to see the Punjab, North-west Frontier Province, Sindh and Baluchistan amalgamated into a single state. Self-government within the British Empire or without the British Empire, the formation of a consolidated North-west Indian Muslim state appears to me to be the final destiny of the Muslims, at least of North-west India."

The formation of a separate Muslim state was justified by Iqbal on the principle of one nation, one state: "We are seventy millions and far more homogeneous than any other people in India. Indeed the Muslims of India are the only Indian people who can fitly be described as a nation in the modern sense of the word." (Using identical language ten years later, Jinnah restated Iqbal's two-nation theory, and asked the League to officially adopt the so-called Pakistan Resolution.)

It should be noted that the Allahabad address did not propose a separate and sovereign Muslim state; Iqbal only formulated the two-nation theory. The view that a sovereign Muslim state was the sole solution to Hindu-Muslim conflict was emphatically stated by Iqbal only in his correspondence with Jinnah between May 1936 and November 1937. (For the text of the two most important letters see the appendix.)

In order to break the constitutional deadlock for the progress of India, the British government decided to hold three Round Table Conferences in London. On November 12, 1930 the first session of the conference opened. All Indian political parties were represented except those of the Congress, whose leaders were in jail, having launched the civil disobedience campaign a year earlier. Prominent representatives of the Muslim League included the Aga Khan, Mian Muhammad Shafi, Maulana Muhammad Ali, and M. A. Jinnah; Iqbal was not invited. The first conference made some progress; there was agreement that the new constitution should be federal. However, it was believed that "general agreement had been reached only because of the absence of the Congress Party."[47]

The second Round Table Conference lasted from September 7 to December 1, 1931. The Congress was represented by Mahatma Gandhi alone; the Muslim delegation now included Iqbal. During the Muslim delegates' discussions with Mahatma Gandhi, the Aga Khan indicated that "always the argument returned to certain basic points of difference: was India a nation or two nations?"[48] The Muslim delegates contended that the British Raj had created an artificial and transient territorial unity in India, while profound religious, cultural, and racial differences among different groups remained. Mahatma Gandhi held fast to the one-nation theory of the Congress. However close the negotiators might come to agreement on points of detail, "this ultimate disagreement on point of principle could not be bridged."[49]

At the conference Iqbal made his contribution in the subcommittee on minorities. In this committee, Iqbal later declared, Mahatma Gandhi challenged the representative character of the Muslim delegation, and also insisted that he and the Congress represented all the Indian people.[50] Failing to achieve an agreement with Mahatma Gandhi, the minorities, with the exception of the Sikhs, signed an Indian Minorities Pact and gave it to the British prime minister. With this accomplishment the last meeting of the Minorities Committee ended on November 13.

In the counsels within the Muslim delegation itself, Iqbal had taken the position that the British government be advised to accept provincial autonomy before introducing the principle of central responsibility in the government of India. Iqbal opined that a great deal of spadework was needed at the provincial level before India could effectively utilize a modern federal constitution. This view did prevail in the delegation and on November 15 the Muslim delegates decided not to participate in the discussions of the Federal Structure Committee. Disregarding its earlier decision, the Muslim delegation agreed on November 26 in the Federal Committee to the simultaneous introduction of provincial autonomy and central responsibility. Iqbal suspected that the Muslim "spokesmen were badly advised by certain English politicians in rejecting the immediate introduction of responsible government in the provinces of British India."[51] Protesting against this policy of the Muslim delegates, which would hinder the struggle for provincial autonomy, Iqbal dissociated himself from the delegation.

After the second Round Table Conference the British government published the Communal Award (August 17, 1932), which retained separate electorates for the Muslims and other minorities. Weightage was given to the Muslims in the Hindu majority provinces and to the Sikhs and the Hindus in the Punjab. But the Muslim majorities in the Punjab and Bengal were reduced to minorities.[52]

After attending the Round Table Conference, but prior to the publication of Communal Award, Iqbal returned to Lahore (December 20, 1931). Although the Congress flatly rejected the Communal Award, Iqbal was ready to compromise. "The communal issues which have been settled," opined Iqbal, "should not be reopened. The separation of Sindh from Bombay, the introduction of constitutional reforms in the Frontier Province, and the separate electorates for the Muslims are now finally determined. The securing of majority for the Muslims in the Punjab and Bengal is the only unresolved problem requiring solution."[53]

Iqbal anticipated a new group of constitutional reforms as the result of the London Round Table Conferences and believed that the Muslims had to organize themselves in order to take full advantage of them. On the other side the Congress and several militant Hindu organizations started a wide campaign against the Communal Award, especially against the provision for separate electorates. This drove Iqbal more headlong into the whirlwind of the Punjab politics than ever before. In order to reinforce Muslim solidarity, Iqbal addressed the annual session of the All-India Muslim Conference at Lahore on March 21, 1932. The address contained a popular version of his vitalist philosophy of *khudi* (ego) as well as some practical suggestions: "Concentrate your whole ego on yourself alone, and ripen your clay into real manhood if you wish to see your aspirations realized," Iqbal exhorted his Muslim audience. "Be hard and work hard. This is the whole secret of individual and collective life. Our ideal is well defined. It is to win in the coming constitution a position for Islam which may bring her opportunities to fulfill her destiny in this country."

How was this objective to be realized? The course of action, reasoned Iqbal, "should be partly political, partly cultural." First, the Muslims should join "one political organization with provincial and district branches all over the country." The constitution of this party should have built-in resiliance "to make it possible for any school of political thought to come into power, and to guide the community according to its own ideas and methods." This would make ruptures between diverse views "impossible," and would also "reintegrate and discipline our scattered forces to the best interests of Islam in India."

Second, Iqbal recommended that the conference should raise "a national fund of 50 lakhs [5,000,000] of rupees." These funds were to be spent to organize the Muslims' political organization.

Iqbal's third plank envisaged "the formation of youth leagues and well-equipped volunteer corps throughout the country under the control and guidance of the central organization." The youth leagues were to devote themselves to social service, cultural reform, and commercial organization of the Muslims. Referring to the perennial indebtedness of the Muslim peasant to the Hindu moneylender Iqbal remarked that they "have reached the breaking point as in China in 1925, when peasant leagues came into being in that country." Iqbal therefore advised that "Muslim agriculturists cannot be allowed to wait for the drastic remedies provided by agrarian upheavals." The future of Islam in India, maintained Iqbal, "largely depends on the freedom of Muslim peasants in the Punjab." The youth leagues must help "the peasantry in escaping from its present bondage."

Discussing the Muslims' cultural problems, Iqbal suggested the creation of "male and female cultural institutes in all the big towns of India." Those institutes should completely eschew politics and should make the younger generation realize "what Islam has already achieved and what it has still to achieve in the religious and cultural history of mankind." The cultural institutes were advised to maintain an intellectual liaison with old and new Muslim educational centers "to secure the ultimate convergence of all the lines of educational endeavor on a single purpose."

Last, Iqbal suggested the creation of "an assembly of '*ulamā*,'" including also "Muslim lawyers who have received education in modern jurisprudence." The proposed body was "to protect, expand and, if necessary, to reinterpret the laws of Islam in the light of modern conditions." Iqbal recommended a legally recognized position for the proposed assembly of '*ulamā*'. "No bill affecting the personal law of Muslims," demanded Iqbal, "may be put on the legislative anvil before it has passed through the crucible of this assembly."[54]

REORGANIZATION OF THE MUSLIM LEAGUE IN THE PUNJAB

Iqbal did not live to see all of his program implemented, although he set in motion political forces which subsequently brought his ideas to fruition.[55] From 1932 to the last day of his life in 1938, Iqbal concentrated his energy in reorganizing the Muslim League in the Punjab. In public statements he urged the Muslims to sever relations with other Muslim and non-Muslim parties in order to create a united front. This policy pitted him against the power structure in the Punjab, which was constituted by the landlords and their leaders, including Fazl-i Husain, and after his death in 1936 his successor, Sir Sikander Hayāt Khan.

In order to implement the constitutional provisions of the Government of India Act, 1935, the British government decided to hold elections in the provinces during January–February 1937. This was a signal for the Muslim League and the National Congress to lubricate their weapons for combat. In response to the Congress, the League also decided in May 1936 to nominate a parliamentary board. The board was charged to draft a platform and to organize election campaigns in the provinces.

In the first half of 1936, the Punjab political scene was primarily dominated by Fazl-i Husain and to a lesser degree by Iqbal. Fazl-i Husain had just returned from Delhi after completing his term as a member of the viceroy's executive council. Realizing that the Muslim Unionist landlords could not form their own ministry without the help of the Hindus, he was busy revitalizing the Unionist party. Iqbal, on the other hand, was the president of the Punjab Muslim League and wanted the League to become a mass party. The arrival of Jinnah to Lahore in May brought the political activity to a climax. Iqbal taught Jinnah the significant difference between the power derived from the support of the common man and that derived from constitutional hairsplitting and party alliances.

True to his background of parliamentary leadership, Jinnah first turned to Fazl-i Husain, urging him to accept the discipline of the League's Parliamentary Board, which Jinnah was to constitute. Fazl-i Husain balked, advancing the arguments of a typical machine politician: (1) provincial autonomy means decentralization; therefore, it is wrong to centralize provincial elections; (2) conditions in each province vary; it is impossible to have a uniform principle; (3) in the Punjab it is impossible to secure a Muslim majority through separate control of elections; (4) in many provinces Muslims may find it necessary to have noncommunal organizations, and in that case a central Muslim agency would obviously be out of the question.

To clinch his argument, Fazl-i Husain pleaded the need for "elasticity and initiative," and then said rather bluntly that it "should not be sacrificed for the sake of an All-India leader's aspirations."[56] Like a patient lawyer, Jinnah suggested that Fazl-i Husain could enter into alliances with other political parties and politicians within the Assembly, but that his party should contest elections in the name of the League. As to the noncommunal character of the Unionists, Jinnah's subtle retort was biting: "Why, the Congress is more progressive and non-communal than the Unionist Party. Why not join the Congress?" This dialogue between Jinnah and Fazl-i Husain was futile and led to nothing; rebuffed by the political boss of the Punjab, Jinnah then turned to Iqbal.

When Jinnah visited Iqbal at his residence on Macleod Road, he did not find a contentious man, as he had at the time of the League's split (1928), but a leader who was now willing to be led. For Iqbal, this was not a defeat, but a victory—he had won over a leader whose integrity he had never doubted. Broken in health, Iqbal was content to see the League slowly but surely inching toward his ideal under Jinnah's stewardship.

On May 8, 1936 Iqbal, along with his supporters (among whom were Khalifah Shuja'-ud-Din and Malik Barkat Ali), issued a statement complimenting Jinnah's political acumen and sagacity. "Our nation has full confidence in Jinnah's integrity and political judgment," said the statement, "it is for this reason that now reactionary circles are flustered. Jinnah's organizational endeavors would shatter illusory leadership of the selfish leaders, because the Muslims would now elect their true representatives in the forthcoming elections."[57]

Four days later the Punjab Muslim League held a special meeting outside Yakki Gate in Lahore, electing Iqbal president, Malik Barkat Ali and Khalifah Shuja'-ud-Din vice-presidents, Ghulam Rasūl Khan secretary, Miam 'Abdūl Majīd and 'Ashaq Husain Batalvi joint secretaries. The meeting also pledged that the Punjab Muslim League would support the Central Parliamentary Board and its policies. Unexpectedly, Jinnah also won over the leaders of the local militant Muslim parties, Majlis-i Ahrār and Ittahād-i Millat, although both parties had been at loggerheads with each other over the Shahidganj mosque. When on May 21 Jinnah announced the names of the members of the Central Parliamentary Board, he included Iqbal at the top of the list, but out of the eleven seats reserved for the Punjab he allocated three to Ittahād-i Millat, and four each to the Ahrār and the League. The Ahrār joined with Jinnah hoping to receive handsome subsidies for their election campaigns. However, they discovered before long that their hopes had been misplaced, and they consequently severed relations with the League. In a few weeks, Maulana Zafar Ali Khan, the president of Ittahād-i Millat, defected because his group had failed to achieve parity with the Ahrār. Subsequently, both of these erstwhile allies of the League fought against her in the elections.

On July 9, 1936 Fazl-i Husain died. His place was occupied by Sir Sikander Hayat Khan, who resigned his position as the governor of the Reserve Bank of India after winning the leadership of the Unionist party. The death of Fazl-i Husain, however, occasioned the significant defection of Malik Zamān Mahdi Khan to the League. Iqbal had a high regard for Malik Zamān's organizational ability and soon had him co-opted as one of the vice-presidents of the League and a member of the Parliamentary Board.

In order to popularize the League in the Punjab, Iqbal constituted two subcommittees: the Draft Committee for the Election Platform and the Propaganda Committee. The first committee consisted of such notable individuals as Khalifah Shujaʻ-ud-Din, Sayyid Tasaddaq Husain, Shaikh Muhammad Hasan, Muhammad ʻAzīm Khan, Malik Barkat Ali, Malik Zamān Mahdi, Ghulam Rasūl Khan, ʻAshaq Husain Batalvi, and Muzaffar Ali Khan Qizilbash, who was later to defect the League (and after the creation of Pakistan to become a minister in the cabinet of the Republican party). The Propaganda Committee was staffed by relatively younger men including Raja Ghazanfar Ali Khan, Pīr Tāj-ud-Din, and Mian Muhammad Shafi, who was also the secretary of Inter-Collegiate Muslim Brotherhood of Lahore.[58]

Before the election campaign started, Iqbal invited Jinnah to visit Lahore in order to inaugurate the League's campaign. Jinnah arrived there on October 9, 1936; the Punjab League had had considerable difficulty in arranging an enthusiastic welcome since, unlike the other parties, the League had no uniformed volunteers. Finally, the volunteers of Anjuman-i Islamia were mustered to appear at the station to welcome the leader. Jinnah stayed in Lahore for two weeks, politicking in the province.

On October 11, the League's campaign was scheduled to start with a public meeting outside Delhi Gate of walled Lahore. Iqbal was to preside, and Jinnah was scheduled to be the main speaker. To the dismay of the party, Iqbal became ill and could not attend. Instead, Malik Zamān Mahdi Khan presided and Jinnah declared the League's war against the Unionists. Calling the Unionist party an organization of vested interests and fortune-seekers, Jinnah challenged Sir Sikander Hayāt Khan: "If you were so anxious to serve the Punjab on a non-communal basis, then where were you 'yesterday'?" The implications of this rhetorical question were obvious: Until July 22, 1936 Sir Sikander was the governor of the Reserve Bank of India. But what about Jinnah's audience, did they grasp his message? Jinnah's campaign speeches had practically no impact on the election fortunes of the League, since his refined English was completely unintelligible to the unlettered citizens of Lahore. In fact, not many of them had bothered to come when the news of Iqbal's sickness circulated in the bazaars. The meeting was brief and colorless; not more than fifteen hundred Lahoris attended it. However, during these weeks Jinnah acquired a wide personal exposure which subsequently helped him to build his image in the Punjab.

During the first week of November only eight individuals applied for the League's nomination.[59] One of the candidates, Muzaffar Ali Khan Qizilbash, when denied the League's nomination, managed to secure the nomination of the Unionist party and then defeated the League's nominee. When the election results were tabulated only two candidates of the League had been elected: Malik Barkat Ali, who defeated his Unionist rival by ninety votes, and Raja Ghazanfar Ali Khan, who defected to the Unionist party on the day of his victory. In the Punjab Legislature, the electoral rolls stood as follows:

| | |
|---|---|
| Congress | 18 |
| Muslim League | 1 |
| Other Muslims | 4 |
| Akali (Sikhs) | 10 |
| Khalsa Nationalist (Sikhs) | 13 |
| Non-Congress Hindus (Sikhs) | 13 |
| Unionists | 89 |
| Independents | 27 |
| Total | 175 |

After forging a tripartite coalition between the Unionists, the Khalsa Nationalist party, and the Hindu Election Board party, Sir Sikander Hayat Khan formed the Punjab ministry. Among the Hindu landlords ten legislators, led by Sir Chhotu Ram, were members of the Unionist party. However, the backbone of the alliance was constituted by the Muslim landlords of the Unionist party. This coalition remained in

## The Man of Thought and of Action

power until 1945 when the legislature was dissolved in order to hold new elections. In addition to protecting their landed interests, these parties were determined to stunt the growth of the Muslim League in the Punjab. They were very forceful and might have succeeded had it not been for the policy of the All-India National Congress.

To the National Congress the election of 1936 gave a great victory, greater than its leaders had expected. Of the 1,585 seats in all the provincial lower houses the Congress won 711 seats. However, six of the seven provinces (Madras, Uttar Pradesh, the Central Province, Bihar, Orissa, Bombay) in which the Congress achieved a clear majority or proved the strongest party were Hindu-majority provinces. In the three Muslim-majority provinces, the Congress fared badly. In Bengal it secured 60 seats out of 250, in the Punjab 18 out of 175, in Sindh 8 out of 60. Almost all of these seats were Hindu constituencies. In the 482 Muslim constituencies in British India Congress Muslims contested 58 seats and won 26.[60]

As the result of this victory the Congress adopted a two-pronged policy: (1) to form exclusively Congress ministries in the provinces; (2) and to wean the Muslim masses away from the "communal" parties. The latter policy came to be known as the Muslim mass-contact campaign.[61] A special office for this campaign was established in the central office of the All-India Congress Committee at Allahabad; Dr. Muhammad Ashraf, a noted Communist leader, was given charge of this office. Nehru offered a revealing interpretation for this campaign.[62] Power was bipolarized, according to Nehru, in "two opposing ranks and we have in India today two dominating powers—Congress India, representing Indian nationalism, and British imperialism." Discussing the place of the Muslims in the Congress, he admitted: "It is true that Muslim masses have been largely neglected by us in recent years." He wanted "to repair that omission," and to bring the Muslim masses to the fold of the Congress.[63] In view of this policy the provincial Congress committees were advised to establish branch offices to foster mass contact with the Muslims and to carry the campaign to the villages.

In the Punjab the Muslim mass-contact campaign threatened the power structure which the Unionist party had carefully constructed. Sir Sikander was worried about the impact of the campaign: if the Hindu and Sikh members joined with the Congress, the Unionist party would crumble; and if the Muslims deserted them for the Congress, that would be equally disastrous for the Unionist party. The League had nothing to lose by the extinction of the Unionists; on the other hand, an alliance with the League could save the Unionist party from the political deluge of the Congress. The Unionist leaders adopted a shrewd policy. To Jinnah they dangled the prospect of cooperation for "All-India problems," if he would not disturb the Punjab's power structure. Within the province they would ally with the League and appoint their trusted men to key positions. In this way they would remain the Unionists as well as members of the Muslim League. The implementation of this policy was very largely thwarted by Iqbal.

Iqbal did not believe that Jinnah could profitably enter into a covenant with Sir Sikander which would benefit the League in the Punjab. He wanted Jinnah to concentrate the League's energy "on the North-West Indian Musalmans," in order to win over the common man. The wooing of the Muslims in the minority provinces appeared to Iqbal a futile attempt, which would make the League in the eyes of her opponents a party of scared Muslims. As the president of the Punjab League, Iqbal invited (August 11, 1937) Jinnah to hold the League's annual session "in Lahore in the middle or end of October."[64] Iqbal assured Jinnah that "the enthusiasm for the League is rapidly increasing in the Punjab, and I have no doubt that the holding of the session in Lahore will be a turning point in the history of the League and an important step towards mass contact."[65]

Disregarding Iqbal's advice, Jinnah held the League's session at Lucknow on October 15, 1937, and especially invited Sir Sikander. Iqbal could not travel because of ill-health, but on October 7 he wrote to Jinnah, advising him to expel twenty-eight Punjabi members of the League's Council, who were actually staunch Unionists. To the chagrin of the Punjab League and its president, Jinnah retained these twenty-eight members in the new Council.[66] He was anxious to strike a bargain with the Unionist chief, Sir Sikander.

On the evening of October 16, while the League session was being presided over by Nawab Isma'īl Khan, negotiations proceeded between Sir Sikander and Jinnah in the latter's suite. 'Ashaq Husain Batalvi, an eyewitness, has described the scene:

"Malik Barkat Ali drafted a declaration and then handed it over to Sir Sikander." The declaration averred: "The Unionist Party, which had been reorganized by Sir Fazl-i Husain in April, 1936, and which

## The Man of Thought and of Action

subsequently contested the election of 1937, has ceased to exist. And the Muslim members of this Party, after pledging the membership, have become the members of the Muslim League."[67]

Indignantly, Sir Sikander answered: "Malik Sahib is determined to wreck our ministry." After some amendments a draft declaration was agreed upon. Then Jinnah and Sir Sikander joined the League's session, where Jinnah welcomed the Punjab premier to the League and the latter, after acknowledging Jinnah as his leader, stated that he would join the Muslim League.

Sir Sikander's declaration of intention has been erroneously described as the Sikander-Jinnah Pact; in reality, it contained obligations which were unliaterally assumed by the Unionist chief. The four-point declaration contained the following:

(a) That on his return to the Punjab, Sir Sikander Hayat Khan will convene a special meeting of his party and advise all members of the party who are not members of the Muslim League already to sign its creed and join it. As such they will be subject to the rules and regulations of the Central and Provincial Boards of the All-India Muslim League. This will not affect the continuance of the present coalition of the Unionist Party.

(b) That in future elections and by-elections for the Legislature after the adoption of this arrangement, the groups constituting the present Unionist Party will jointly support candidates put up by their respective groups.

(c) That the Muslim members of the Legislature, who are elected on or accept the League Ticket [nomination], will constitute the Muslim League Party within the Legislature. It shall be open to the Muslim League Party so formed to maintain or enter into a coalition or alliance with any other party consistently with the fundamental principles of the policy and Program of the League. Such alliances may be evolved before or after the elections. The existing combination shall maintain its present name, the Unionist Party.

(d) In view of the aforesaid arrangement, the Provincial League Parliamentary Board shall be reconstituted.

Similar declarations of support were made by Fazl-ul-Haq, premier of Bengal, and Sir Sa'adullah, premier of Assam.[68]

This declaration was ambiguous, and was probably deliberately so designed, allowing both parties temporary advantages. But subsequent developments in the Punjab proved to be disastrous for the growth of the League. Iqbal and his colleagues in the Punjab Muslim League construed the declaration as terminating the independent existence of the Unionist party. The Unionist party, in their eyes, was the name of the parliamentary coalition, and nothing more. They expected Sir Sikander and his Muslim colleagues to accept the discipline of the provincial League, headed by Iqbal. The Unionists, on the other hand, viewed their chief's role at Lucknow as a theatrical performance, which made no fundamental change in their power structure. For them the Unionist party continued to exist; the Muslim League simply became its handmaiden. Jinnah adopted a laissez-faire policy toward these developments in the Punjab and thus failed to make the League a truly mass party throughout the 1930s and early 1940s.

From the end of October 1937 to April 1938 a battle for political survival was fought between Iqbal and Sir Sikander. First the latter temporized, then defiantly refused to sign the pledge of membership in the League.[69] Whereas Iqbal demanded full compliance with the Lucknow declaration, Sir Sikander contended that in addition to the written "pact" between him and Jinnah, there was also a certain verbal understanding, which gave him considerable flexibility of action. Consequently, Sir Sikander insisted that his party have a majority on the League's Provincial Parliamentary Board. Frustrated by these developments, Iqbal wrote to Jinnah on November 1, saying: "Sir Sikander Hayat Khan with some of the members of his party saw me yesterday and we had a long talk about the differences between the League and the Unionist Party. . . . I further want to ask you whether you agreed to the Provincial Parliamentary Board being controlled by the Unionist Party. Sir Sikander tells me that you agreed to this and therefore he claims that the Unionist Party must have their majority in the Board. This as far as I know does not appear in the Jinnah-Sikander agreement."[70] (The record shows that Jinnah did not answer Iqbal's letter.)

Simultaneously Iqbal intensified the League's mass-contact movement in the Punjab. He sent political workers to the rural areas, who in a short period of time established thirty-four branch offices. In order to bolster his position in the rural Punjab, Sir Sikander launched a new political party of his own, the Punjab Zamindara League.[71] Despite its claim to be the protector of the Punjabi peasant proprietors, the Zamindara League was conceived for the purpose of minimizing the influence of the Muslim League in the rural areas. Although officially the Unionists claimed to be League members, in their actions they continued to undermine the League, saying that "the Sikander-Jinnah

## The Man of Thought and of Action

Pact" had absorbed the Punjab's Muslim League into the Unionist party.

Sir Sikander also increased his political demands on Iqbal. Not only did he want a Unionist majority on the Parliamentary Board, but he also demanded, Iqbal informed Jinnah in his letter of November 10, "that the finances of the League should be controlled by his men." Iqbal indicated that he might be inclined to give the Unionists a majority on the Parliamentary Board, but he could not agree to "a complete change in the office-holders of the League, especially the Secretary [Ghulam Rasūl Khan], who has done so much for the League." Finally, Iqbal warned Jinnah: "All this to my mind amounts to capturing of the League and then killing it. Knowing the opinion of the province as I do I cannot take the responsibility of handing over the League to Sir Sikander and his friends. . . . In these circumstances please let me know what we should do."[72] Despite Iqbal's solicitations, Jinnah remained silent.

To Iqbal the national poet and philosopher, Sir Sikander held out an olive branch. On December 4, he sent a message to the Inter-Collegiate Muslim Brotherhood of Lahore regarding their plans for Iqbal Day celebrations, which were scheduled to be held on December 26. "Today, after years of deep slumber, Muslims are awake; this is largely due to the message of Iqbal. . . . It is an obligation of every Indian to participate in the Iqbal Day celebrations. I would propose that in the cities where Iqbal Day is celebrated, the citizens should collect money and present it to the great poet. The Iqbal committee should immediately open an Iqbal Day account in the Imperial Bank of India, and his followers and admirers should directly make contributions to this fund."[73]

Although Iqbal was in dire financial straits, he was not lacking in self-respect. Commenting on Sir Sikander's proposal, Iqbal replied: "I feel that the needs of the people as a whole are far more pressing than the needs of a private individual even though his work may have been a source of inspiration to most people. The individual and his needs pass away: the people and their needs remain." If people wanted to honor him, they should, Iqbal suggested, establish "a chair for Islamic research on modern lines in the local Islamia College." This was the real need of the people. Referring to the exploitation of the Unionist landlords, some of whom masqueraded as *pīrs* (spiritual mentors) Iqbal said: "Nowhere in India has the ignorance of Islamic history, theology, jurisprudence and Sufism been so successfully exploited as in the Punjab."[74] Then, addressing Sir Sikander, Iqbal remarked that he hoped that his proposal "will meet the Premier's approval and his influence will make this proposal a success. I offer a humble contribution of one hundred rupees to the fund."[75]

Sir Sikander (d. December 1942) survived Iqbal for three years and eight months. He could have implemented Iqbal's proposal, if he had wanted to. That was not to be, because Sir Sikander's statement was no more than a propaganda gimmick.

The year 1937 ended in a stalemate between the Unionist chief and Iqbal. During the remaining four months of Iqbal's life Sir Sikander managed to infiltrate the Punjab Muslim League and finally succeeded in smothering it. The League's basic weakness was its lack of funds; Iqbal made several attempts to persuade well-to-do Muslims to make generous donations. Initially, they agreed out of respect for Iqbal, but then backed down, saying that they could not afford to antagonize Sir Sikander.

Finally, Malik Barkat Ali persuaded Iqbal to accept the rich Nawab of Mamdot (Shah Nawaz Khan) as his successor, since the former was physically unable to cope with the duties of presidency. Nawab Mamdot was known to be a trusted confidant of Sir Sikander. Why the Punjab League voluntarily installed this Trojan horse in its organization is inexplicable. The matter is completely shrouded in mystery upon which the available sources shed no ray of light. Probably, Iqbal and Ali hoped that the lure of leadership might drive a wedge between Nawab Mamdot and Sir Sikander, and that Nawab Mamdot would then spend money on the League in order to bolster his position. On the contrary, however, Iqbal and Ali's serious error of judgment created sharp dissension in their own ranks.

For instance, on the instructions of Iqbal, the Provincial League's secretary (Ghulam Rasūl Khan) wrote on March 2, 1938 a letter to Jinnah, inviting him to hold the All-India League's annual session in Lahore during the Easter holidays. Almost on the same day Nawab Mamdot wrote to Jinnah: "Probably you know that I have been elected the President of the Punjab Muslim League. In deference to the wishes of Sir Muhammad Iqbal, I have accepted this office. In a meeting, where I was not present, the decision was made to invite you to hold the special session of the All-India Muslim League at Lahore. It is my duty to inform you that in order to protect the League's interest and that of Shahidganj mosque, the League's session should not be held in Lahore. . . ."[76] To the utter mortification of Malik Barkat Ali, Malik Zamān Mahdi, 'Ashaq Husain Batalvi, and Ghulam Rasūl Khan, Jinnah read them Mamdot's letter, at which time they verbally renewed the Punjab League's invitation to Jinnah on March 19 at Delhi. In order to strengthen the Zamindara League and also to protect it from the competing propaganda of the Muslim League, Sir Sikander wanted to keep the national leaders of the League out of the Punjab. The League leaders then realized that their divided house would fall in time, since their president was playing the game of their opponent—Sir Sikander.

Sir Sikander made one final bid to capture the Punjab League. This was done in a very subtle manner when the Provincial Leagues applied in 1938 for affiliation to the central office of the Muslim League. In a session on March 2, the All-India Muslim League Council had appointed a five-man committee, consisting of Nawab Isma'īl Khan (president), Liaquat Ali Khan (secretary), and three other members to examine the credentials of the Provincial Leagues. On March 11, the Punjab League applied for affiliation, and on the same day elected ninety members of the Provincial Council. Since the Unionists had not signed the membership blanks, they were excluded from the council.

On April 5, Liaquat Ali Khan informed the Punjab Muslim League that its application for affiliation had been rejected for the following reasons: First, the Punjab League's rules contravened the constitution of the All-India Muslim League. For instance, Liaquat pointed out, article 33 of the Punjab League's constitution permitted this body's alliance with other Muslim parties. According to the old constitution of the All-India Muslim League this was permitted, but it was not permitted by the new one. Now the All-India Muslim League was a comprehensive and representative body of all Muslims, and it could not allow its affiliates to ally with other organizations.

The second reason, according to Liaquat Ali Khan, was the membership clauses (5, 6, 7) of the Punjab League's constitution. They envisaged membership of the League at the provincial level, whereas the All-India Muslim League's constitution decreed membership at the primary level, that is, district or city leagues.[77]

These explanations for their rejection outraged the leaders of the Punjab Muslim League, especially when they knew that numerous provincial leagues, which existed only on paper, had been affiliated. Iqbal advised them to carry the fight for their organization to the special session of the League, which was scheduled to be held on April 17, 18, and 19, 1938 at Calcutta. Consequently, Malik Barkat Ali, Khalifah Shuja'-ud-Din, Pīr Tāj-ud-Din, Malik Zamān Mahdi, and 'Ashaq Husain Batalvi departed for Calcutta on April 14. At Saharanpur railroad station, Nawab Isma'īl Khan, president of the Affiliation Committee, boarded the train. The Punjab leaders won him over to their cause and succeeded in obtaining his unqualified recommendation for their affiliation.

To cope with the opposition of Liaquat Ali Khan, who had been approached by Sir Sikander's lieutenants, the Punjab leaders devised a strategy of relentlessly interrupting the meetings unless they were heard. On April 17, the session of the All-India Muslim League Council started, and Liaquat explained the actions of his committee. Rising instantly from the front rows, Batalvi demanded an explanation for the rejection of their application.

"Sit down," growled Liaquat Ali Khan.

"I am not a high school student, nor you a teacher, that I should be addressed like this," retorted Batalvi.

"Did you come to insult us like this from Lahore," Liaquat wanted to know.

"I did not come to insult you, nor come here to be insulted by you," Batalvi thus persisted in his demands.

With a smile on his face, Jinnah watched this encounter, and then intervened: "What do you want"?

"The affiliation of the Punjab Muslim League to the parent body" was the collective answer of the Punjab delegates.[78]

Finally Malik Barkat Ali was invited to present the case. Noted for his forensic talent Ali won over the council. Jinnah asked the council to postpone the decision for another twenty-four hours to await the arrival of Sir Sikander. Completely disregarding the issue of the Punjab League's affiliation, Jinnah gave his verdict the following day in the presence of Sir Sikander, his ministers, and Parliamentary secretaries, including Nawab Mamdot. In order to reorganize the Punjab League, Jinnah said, a thirty-five-man organizing committee would be nominated, of which 50 per cent would be Unionists. The same evening, in clear disregard of this public commitment, Liaquat announced the membership list of the committee in which Iqbal and his followers in the Punjab League numbered twenty-six to thirty-five. Twenty-five seats had been given to the Unionists, and Sir Sikander had been made the president of the committee, his name heading the list.[79] On April 21, two days after the Calcutta session, Iqbal died; with his departure the domination of the League by the Unionists was ensured.

An assessment of Iqbal's and Jinnah's policies might be in order. Stung by the criticism that the League represented a minority view, Jinnah was anxious to demonstrate, particularly in the Punjab, that the Congress' Muslim mass-contact movement had failed. That impression could be created by quick and dramatic political shifts. The idea of the Unionists joining the Muslim League en masse was too tempting and intriguing to be forsaken for Iqbal's strategy of patiently building the League at the grass-roots level. Jinnah paid a price for this policy. Under Sir Sikander, and since 1942 under his successor, Khizer Hayat Khan, the Muslim League existed in the Punjab only in paper, at least until 1946.

In 1940, "the Pakistan Resolution" was passed in Lahore. Supporting the resolution, Jinnah reiterated Iqbal's two-nation theory, and coined the slogan of "unity, discipline, and faith." The Unionists, however, made their distaste for subordination clear to Jinnah, who then realized that he had better depend on the common man for support. When, in early 1946, elections were held to ascertain the relative strength of Indian political parties, the Unionists forged an alliance with the Congress, and harassed the League in the Punjab. Reciting Iqbal's verses in the streets, and repeating almost verbatim the language of Iqbal, the League workers galvanized the masses and defeated the Unionists.[80] The League's landslide of 1946 was very much the victory of Iqbal's strategy, which he had urged on Jinnah ten years earlier.

# 5

# Ideology of Muslim Nationalism

## L. R. GORDON-POLONSKAYA

THE name of Muhammad Iqbal is connected with an important stage in the development of Muslim social thought on the Indo-Pakistan subcontinent—the formative stage of the ideology of Muslim nationalism. Iqbal's religio-philosophical and sociopolitical views fully reflected the complexity and contradictoriness of the social nature of the Muslim social strata that were taking part in the national liberation movement for the independence of the peoples of colonial India. To a significant extent this explains Iqbal's tremendous influence on the development of the social thought of the Muslims of colonial India and modern Pakistan.

The formation of a new national ideology among the bourgeoisie and the middle strata everywhere in the countries of the colonial world was linked inseparably with the reformation of religion.

Iqbal was the first reformer of Islam who endeavored to find in it not only the spiritual expression of the anticolonial nationalist aspirations of the Muslim bourgeoisie and middle strata of colonial India but also the basis of a path of social development such as would be distinct from the capitalist path of the West. His sociopolitical ideals also reflected to a certain degree utopian concepts of the social equality of the popular masses. Herein lay the primary reason for his importance as a religious reformer and Muslim ideologist.

(The present chapter is devoted to a characterization of these features of Iqbal's sociopolitical ideology, but it in no way pretends to be a comprehensive analysis of his religio-philosophical system as a whole.)

## DIALECTICAL CONTRADICTIONS

IQBAL'S sociopolitical and philosophical views and his poetic mastery took shape during a period of turbulent growth in the national

## Ideology of Muslim Nationalism

self-consciousness of the Indian intelligentsia. The world view of the latter was marked by a profound duality. At that time it was almost the sole channel of expression for the striving of the peoples of the Indo-Pakistan subcontinent toward independence and the struggle against the foreign yoke. It reflected the endeavor of the rising classes to put an end to feudal backwardness, to create their own industry, and to set the country on a course of independent capitalistic development. Also manifested in its ideology was the striving of the masses toward reforms; utopian socialist ideas often characterized it. At the same time it often idealized the precolonial past and endeavored to safeguard from Europeans encroachment the religion and traditions of the past as institutions determining the distinctiveness of the way of life and culture of its people and as symbolic of past independence. The philosophical and sociopolitical views of various representatives of the intelligentsia were influenced by the contradictory and dualist psychology of the peasants and urban underprivileged classes: patriotic anticolonialist feelings and utopian striving toward social equality on the one hand, and conservatism and adherence to a religious world view on the other.

The Indian intelligentsia was extremely heterogeneous in its composition. But the combination of peace-loving ideals and the contradictions and weaknesses noted above was to some degree characteristic of the majority of its representatives, including Muhammad Iqbal.

The seeds of Iqbal's greatness and weakness were already being planted in the early period of his work (end of the nineteenth, beginning of the twentieth century). In this period Iqbal was closely connected with the Anjuman-i-Himāyat-i-Islam (Society for the Support of Islam)—a Punjabi educational organization created with the direct participation of the Muhammadan Educational Conference, headed by Sayyid Ahmad Khan, India's first Muslim educator. At the annual session of the Society for the Support of Islam in 1899 Iqbal made his debut as a poet, trying to express in poetic form the doubts and aspirations of Punjabi Muslim intelligentsia. His poetry immediately assumed a civic ring.

Sayyid Ahmad Khan's ideas, the activity of the educational societies he created, and the Aligarh College exerted a direct influence on the formation of Iqbal's views. This influence was just as complex and contradictory as the first Muslim educator's world view itself.

Sayyid Ahmad Khan's educational activity reflected two trends in the social thought of Muslims in colonial India: the anti-imperialist ideology of Muslim nationalists and the pro-British "communalist" ideology of the elite of the Muslim community.

Hafeez Malik, a prominent researcher on the problems of Muslim nationalism in India and Pakistan, has noted that

> the Muslims of the Punjab were in a particularly receptive frame of mind for his [Khan's] program of reformation and national advancement. They had considered the establishment of British rule in 1849 as an act of providence designed to liberate them from the Sikhs. Unlike other people in India they had not yet suffered humiliation at the hands of the British. The Wars of 1857 had not engendered bitterness and hatred of everything western. Therefore, the Muslims of the Punjab welcomed Sayyid Ahmad Khan as a genuine social, political and religious reformer without resenting his pro-British policies.[1]

This statement is completely applicable to the leaders of the Muslim community in the Punjab. As for the attitudes of the greater part of the Punjabi Muslim intelligentsia, including Iqbal, toward the teaching of Sayyid Ahmad Khan, it was considerably more complex.

Iqbal knew and understood the opinions of Sayyid Ahmad Khan on the patriotic unity of Hindus and Muslims, which belonged to the first period of his educational activity. Sayyid Ahmad Khan's teachings on "national self-help" had a great influence on him. Iqbal accepted the idea, fundamental to these teachings, of the necessity of vigorous activity by man in the name of the social good, by which Sayyid Ahmad Khan meant primarily the good of the Muslims.

But Iqbal did not share his pro-British orientation or his desire to isolate the Muslims from the all-Indian movement on the grounds that the representatives of the various religious communities in India allegedly "had no common national interests."[2] Iqbal's patriotic speeches on the eve of the first upsurge of the national liberation movement of the peoples of India in 1905–1909 served as lucid testimony to this. At this time it seemed that the country's air was suffused with liberation ideas. However, the participation of the elite of the Punjabi Muslim community in the political awakening was comparatively insignificant.

As before, the leadership of the Anjuman-i-Himāyat-i-Islam, with a bourgeois landowner class composition, occupied itself primarily

## Ideology of Muslim Nationalism

with problems of education and the development of the Urdu language, and also with the spreading of English education and English literature among the Muslims. Loyal to the colonial authorities, it stood aside from the political questions that disturbed progressive people in India. And then, at the Anjuman's annual session in 1904, a forum from which only well-intentioned speeches had previously been delivered, a poem full of anguish and anger about the sufferings of an enslaved India was sung, lamenting the lack of unity within the ranks of Indian patriots. It was also a poetic appeal to Muslims, urging them to awaken from their political somnolence and unite in the name of the liberation of the homeland. The author of the poem *Taswīr-i-Dard* (Portrait of Anguish) was Muhammad Iqbal, then a young teacher at the Government College in Lahore.

On the eve of the first revolutionary uprising in colonial India his song of anger merged with the voices of all the progressive people in the country. Political apathy, as indicated in the poem *Khuftagān-i Khāk Say Istafsār* (A Land Asleep), and the absence of the unity necessary to oppose foreign domination were, in Iqbal's opinion, the basic reasons for the sufferings of the Indian people.

From the very beginning young Iqbal saw that the basic task of the poet, religious reformer, and political figure was above all to awaken the people's patriotic feelings and to show how pernicious was foreign domination for the entire population of colonial India, regardless of religious, ethnic, and social affiliation. He created the beautiful image of the poet as the "all-seeing eye of the people," but, like many other representatives of the Indian intelligentsia, saw in the working people only the "hands and feet" of the people and regarded the members of the higher, socially elect strata as their natural leaders—their "face." However, this did not prevent Iqbal from constantly emphasizing that the strength of the poet is his unbreakable tie with his "body"—the people.[3]

Until 1905, when he went to Europe for the first time to continue his education, Iqbal had devoted his main attention to the passionate preaching of national unity, without which it was impossible, in his words, to realize the wonderful ideals of freedom and independence for India. Iqbal's poetic metaphors (for example, the metaphor of the captive bird India in the poem *Parinde ke Faryād* (The Bird's Lament) were widely disseminated far beyond the borders of the Punjab. For multilingual India, where differences had been preserved between upper and lower castes and between Hindus and Muslims, Iqbal's poems about the necessity of overcoming these internal differences and strengthening unity among Indians took on a special patriotic ring.

It is enough to recall *Sadā'-i Dard* (A Cry of Pain) which literally burst forth from the poet after one of the Hindu-Muslim clashes on the eve of the revolutionary uprising of 1905–1909. In those years the colonial authorities were preparing a law on separate political representation for the Muslims and the Hindus, a law that ultimately led to a split in the country's national forces. And at this time Iqbal was calling on his compatriots to create a *nayā shiwalā* (new temple) in which religious barriers would disappear and love for mother India would prevail. He created an inspiring poetic image of Hindu-Muslim unity: "We shall erase the boundary of blind hostility in order that we may again walk along the same path."[4]

In the first of his poetic and philosophical statements, Iqbal still took positions not of Muslim but of all-Indian nationalism and did not call for the isolation of the Muslims. However, the contradictoriness of his world view was manifested in the fact that while fighting to overcome religious barriers, he remained above all a Muslim. In many respects this circumstance determined the future evolution of his views.

Early in life Iqbal sought substantiation for his nationalist ideals in the religious traditions of Islam. As a philosopher and religious reformer he was under the strong influence of the ideas of the pantheistic school of Sufism. The religio-philosophical teachings of the Sufis on the role of intuition in the cognition process and on the interrelation between man and God, as well as the poetry of these great mystics of the East, had a great effect on Iqbal's works. Before his trip to Europe he came under the influence of pantheistic concepts about man's path to unity with God. In accordance with these concepts, the man who desires to achieve this unity must lapse into a state of ecstasy, experience moments of renunciation of everything earthly, and be interested in nothing. However, Iqbal was far from accepting the Sufi philosophy as a whole.

From the very beginning he had a strong desire to interpret anew the religious traditions of Islam. He was attracted not so much by the religio-philosophical conceptions themselves, which were limited (in his own words) by the conditions under which they were created, as by the approach of the creators of these conceptions to the possibility

## Ideology of Muslim Nationalism 113

of a new interpretation of Islamic dogma in connection with the change in historical conditions and in man's concepts of nature and society. It is for this reason that Iqbal linked his "reconstruction of Islam" primarily with the names of those Muslim ideologists who recognized not the letter but the spirit of the Qur'ān and the *Sharīʿa* (Islamic laws), endeavoring to reinterpret the traditions of Islam as applied to their country and their times and to prove their right to such a reinterpretation. The fact that the religio-philosophical conceptions and political positions of these predecessors frequently differed substantially from each other had no decisive significance for Iqbal.

Iqbal's trip to Europe (1905–1908) intensified his commitment to Islam as the chief means of achieving his national ideals. At the same time it led him to break with Sufism and contributed to the growth of his striving toward a reconstruction of Islam that would take into consideration the achievements of modern science and the philosophy of the West.

Kant, Leibnitz, Fichte, Bergson, and several other Western philosophers had a serious influence on Iqbal. However, he borrowed from them mostly the concepts that had points of contact with traditional philosophy. Hegel's dialectics were an important element in shaping the ideas that became the basis of Iqbal's reconstruction of Islam. (For a detailed discussion of the impact of Western philosophers on Iqbal, see B. A. Dar's Chapter 9.)

Although using Western sources, Iqbal borrowed not so much the philosophical conceptions and definitions as such, but rather the method of research, the approach to the various phenomena of nature and society. Iqbal's attitude toward Nietzsche's philosophy is of great interest in this connection. As with Nietzsche, the man-personality "ego" is at the center of Iqbal's philosophical conception, despite its religious nature. As with Nietzsche's superman, a characteristic of the ego was the striving toward constant action. However, Iqbal evaluated the relationship of man to God and to society from positions contrary to those of Nietzsche, and Nietzscheism as a whole was unacceptable to him.

From the very first steps along the path of the reconstruction of Islam Iqbal opposed following blindly the ideas of the West. "This new wine will weaken our minds, this light will only intensify the darkness,"[5] he wrote about the bourgeois civilization of the West, constantly contrasting it to the "great reforming role of Islam."

Iqbal's philosophical credo was reflected not only in his religio-philosophical tracts and political speeches but also in his poetry. Iqbal himself considered poetry the "halo of true philosophy and genuine knowledge," and his contemporaries called him a poet-philosopher.

After Iqbal's return from his trip to Europe (1909) the ideology of Muslim nationalism found ever clearer expression in his religio-philosophical, didactic, and poetic work. At its base was the idea that spiritual unity founded on Islam was the most important integral feature of the national society. Islam emerges in this ideology as a form of national unity and (in essence) absorbs political thought.

The shaping of the ideology of Muslim nationalism preceded the spread of the ideas of pan-Islamism, which asserted the necessity of uniting on the basis of Islam irrespective of state, territorial, ethnic, and national differences. The contrast contained in pan-Islamism, of religious unity to national community based on territorial, ethnic, and economic bonds, was unacceptable to the bourgeois society evolving in the East. Therefore the ideology of Muslim nationalism, which reflected the interests of the Muslim bourgeois strata, proceeded from the necessity of reforming Islam in accordance with the historical, ethnic, and economic features of the development of individual Muslim peoples and from the existence of several Muslim nations inhabiting different territory.

This was the feature of Muslim nationalism, clearly reflected in Iqbal's philosophy, that ensured its comparatively wide dissemination in the period of the rise of the national liberation movement of the oppressed peoples of the East. Religious motivation in philosophical and sociopolitical ideas was not characteristic of the ideology of Muslim nationalism alone. To some extent it was also a trait of other nationalist trends in the social thought of the rising bourgeois society of the colonial East. This was a way of reacting to colonial oppression, since in the eyes of the colonial peoples religion was a symbol of past independence, a guarantee of the possibility and the necessity of preserving their own distinctive path of development. In India, where the ideology of Muslim nationalism was the ideology of a religious and cultural minority, it inevitably harbored from the very beginning the seeds of political separatism.

Ideas of the existence in India of two nations became widespread among the Indian intelligentsia after the First World War. Some ideologists acknowledged the existence of both of these nations, others, like Iqbal, only of one of them. Attempting to refute certain Western theories that only British domination ensured unity in India, many representatives of the intelligentsia regarded Hinduism and Islam as the basic manifestation of a community of Indians, antedating the British conquest and independent of foreign domination. They saw community consolidation as one form of national consolidation. Hence also arose the tendency to endow the religious community with features of a national community. However, the preaching of community consolidation inevitably came into conflict with the ideology of the all-Indian national liberation movement, with the ideas of patriotic unity of the entire population of colonial India. It was used extensively by the colonial authorities in India to split the national liberation movement. As a result, some former advocates of an uncompromising struggle against foreign domination turned at the end of the 1920s into ideologists for national separations which inevitably led to the establishment of Pakistan.

In many ways this path was characteristic of Iqbal.

## PAN-ISLAMISM: INFLUENCE OF JAMAL-UD-DIN AFGHANI

ON the eve of the First World War, like many other representatives of the Muslim middle strata in India, Iqbal began to be influenced by the teachings of Jamal-ud-Din Afghani, the first important ideologist of pan-Islamism. He was attracted most of all by Jamal-ud-Din Afghani's endeavor to find in Islam a means of unity for resisting the domination of the West and substantiation for the necessity of the social progress and independent development of the peoples of the East. At the same time, Iqbal essentially shared the desire of Afghani and other ideologists of pan-Islamism to express unity on the religious basis of Muslims as a supraclass and a supranational unity, which contributed to the appearance in his political philosophy of the motif of religious isolation of the Muslim community, as well as the blending of the concepts of religious and national unity.

In a letter of March 28, 1909, he wrote: "I myself have been of the view that religious differences should disappear from this country

[India], and even now, act on this principle, in my private life. But now, I think that the preservation of their separate national entities is desirable for the Hindus and Muslims. The vision of the common nationhood in India is a beautiful ideal, and has a poetic appeal, but looking to the present conditions, and the unconscious trends of the two, appears incapable of fulfillment."[6] This statement attests to the inception in Iqbal's world view of the idea of an antithesis between Hindus and Muslims as two nations.

Although he affirmed the existence of a separate nation of Muslims of India, Iqbal did not lose his pan-Islamic sympathies. Muslim nationalism has always had a pan-Islamic tinge and has envisaged the necessity of a close bond among Muslim nations and the establishment of definite supranational pan-Islamic forms of unity. On the eve of and during the First World War, Iqbal directly tied his hopes for liberation from colonial dependency to pan-Islamic "solidarity" and the caliphate forms of the liberation movement. This was reflected, in particular, in his poem *Shamā'Awr Shā'ir* (The Candle and the Poet), written in 1912. However, it should be remembered that Iqbal never regarded the Muslim community as only a religious community. According to his interpretation, Islam was a philosophy of life, the embodiment of definite historical and cultural traditions, social and legal institutions, and way of living. He never equated Muslim nationalism with religious intolerance on the one hand, and narrow communal outlook on the other. While upholding Muslim nationalism, he remained an ardent preacher of patriotic unity in the struggle against foreign domination. In no period of his activity did he deem it possible to set an alliance of Muslims with British colonialists against the Hindus.

On the eve of the First World War, Iqbal cooperated closely with Abul Kalam Azad, Muhammad Ali, and other Muslim nationalists who at that time were simultaneously members of both the National Congress and the Muslim League and their left wings. His activity was aimed, in his own words, at prompting Muslims to become involved in the political struggle. This was incompatible with government service, and in 1909 Iqbal was forced to give up his well-paid job as a professor at the Government College in Lahore and to engage in private law practice. It was in these years that he came forth with his "message to the people." This message included an exhortation to the people, expressed in verse as well as in essay form, to free themselves from

## Ideology of Muslim Nationalism    117

political apathy and to become involved in the all-Indian liberation movement. The ideas of this message found reflection particularly in his poem *Tulbā'-i Aligarh College Kay Nām* (To the Students of Aligarh College).

Among the students and teachers at Aligarh College, which despite its pro-British orientation promoted the political awakening of the Muslims, were representatives of various political trends. However, the leaders of the college, who belonged at that time to the right wing of the Muslim leadership, endeavored to insulate young people against the spread of revolutionary ideas and anti-British sentiments. From the college faculties came appeals for prudence and support of the British authorities, for the isolation of the Muslim community from the activity of the National Congress. Iqbal's message was sharply distinct from these speeches for its political orientation:

> *Awrūñ kā hay payām awr mayrā payām awr hay.*
> *'Ishaq kay dardmand kā tarz-i kalām awr hay.*
> *Tā'ir-i zyr-i dām kay nalay tu sūn chukay ho tūm*
> *Yah be sūno kah nalā-i tā'ir-i bām awr hay.*
> *Badah hay nīm ras abhi showq hay na-rasā abhi*
> *Rahnay dow Khum Kay Sir pay tum Khisht-i Kalysiyā abhi.*[7]

People are sending many messages; mine is different.
When one loves [the fatherland] his words have a different ring.
You have been hearing the impotent murmur
                                    of fluttering birds in snares,
Listen to a free bird—its wail is different.
For the time being leave the brick of tradition
In the neck of the pitcher!
When the wine has fermented, another consciousness
Will come!

The poet exhorted students to vigorous action, to participation in the all-Indian movement. However, at the same time he recognized that they still could not free themselves from the traditions of the past, that they were still not ready for the struggle for self-administration. He realized that the hour of liberation had not yet struck, that the time to cast down the "brick of tradition" had not yet come. He wrote, too, of the preservation of the rule of past tradition and the consequent unpreparedness of Indians for revolutionary methods of struggle in many other poetic, philosophical and didactic works. Nevertheless, his constant refrain that another consciousness would inevitably come, the consciousness of the necessity of liberation, left no doubt as to his own desire to cast down this "brick" more quickly.

Iqbal was never a consistent supporter of mass revolutionary methods of struggle. In politics, as in philosophy, he turned primarily to the reforming role of Islam. The complexity and contradictoriness of his world view was also clearly reflected in his first philosophical poems, *Asrār-i Khudi* (The Secrets of the Self, 1915) and *Ramūz-i-Bekhudi* (The Mysteries of Selflessness, 1918). In these poems he presented, actually for the first time, substantiation of the necessity of combining the traditions of Islam and their reformation in the spirit of the times with an expostulation of the moral and ethical conceptions of Muslim nationalism and his philosophy of the man-activist.

During and after the First World War these philosophical poems enjoyed tremendous success among the Muslims of India. They were written not in Urdu but in Persian, since Iqbal was appealing not only to his compatriots but also to the Muslims of all the oppressed countries of Asia. At first these poems roused the Muslim intelligentsia of colonial India. This was attested, in particular, by the utterances of Muhammad Ali, to whom Iqbal's poems were brought in prison, where he was confined for anti-British activity. "We soon realized, however," he wrote in his autobiography, "that this was even greater and more enduring than what Iqbal had so far written." The Muslim intelligentsia was attracted above all by the appeals in these works to Muslim traditions in the name of solidarity among Muslims in the liberation struggle and the reformation of Islam in the spirit of the times, a spirit of libertarian ideals and utopian concepts of freedom for the human personality and social equality. "He was the poet of Islam reawakening in India in the twentieth century, and to no man does Muslim India owe a greater debt than to this modest, and retiring barrister of the Punjab," Muhammad Ali wrote.[9] Iqbal became a ruler of the minds of the Muslim intelligentsia of colonial India.

## THE INFLUENCE OF SOCIALIST RUSSIA

THE October Socialist Revolution in Russia had a great influence on the national liberation movement of the peoples of the Indo-Pakistan subcontinent and on the sociopolitical views of the Indian intelligentsia, including Iqbal. The first major political acts of the Indian proletariat convinced the intelligentsia that the working people could play an independent role in the general national liberation movement. This intensified the aspiration of the nationalistically inclined intelligentsia to find support among the masses and furthered the spread of socialistic ideas in its midst.

Many of the intelligentsia derived from religious teachings images and concepts close to the masses in order to awaken their national self-consciousness and draw them into active opposition to colonial oppression. They endeavored to bring their social and national ideals nearer to those understood by the broad strata of the population. Anticapitalist tendencies appeared in the teachings of many of them. At the same time they believed in the possibility of the development of the peoples of the East in their own original way, distinct from capitalism and from scientific socialism, and they sought substantiation for this way in religion. All of this was reflected in Iqbal's ideology and his reformation of Islam.

Iqbal was one of the first to welcome the Great October Socialist Revolution. In his words this revolution opened a new era, "the era of the workers." He called on his compatriots to heed the voice of the worker, in whose mouth he put the call to unite and overthrow the old principles:

> *Maghān-o-dayr-i maghañ ra nazām-i tazā dhaȳm*
> *Banā'i maykadah hāy-i kuhan ber andāzyam.*
> Let us give new regulations to the magicians and their temple,
> Let us overturn the foundation stones of old taverns.

Thus wrote Iqbal in his *Nawa'i Mazdūr* (Song of the Worker).[10] (In the united efforts of all Indians lie the key to the desired freedom—this thought runs through all of Iqbal's work in the years 1918–1923.)

The revolution in Russia demonstrated, in his words, the inevitability of the destruction of old systems:

> *Dil ōn meiñ walwala' inqalāb hay pay-dā*
> *Qarib aā ga'eȳ shayad jehan-i pīr key mot.*
> Rage is growing in the hearts, strength is growing in the hands
> Old rotten world! Your time has obviously come![11]

Many of his poetic works tell of this. He created poetic images of the crown forcibly wrested away and of the stonemason (*kuhkan*) demanding "the estate of Pervaiz" (that is, the rule). These served as symbols of the changes and the birth of a new world that had taken place in Russia.

Iqbal endeavored to express in poetic form his deep conviction that after the great changes occurring in Russia, the peoples of the East could no longer live in the old way. In one of his best poems on this subject—*Payām-i Mashriq* (Message of the East)—he wrote:

> *Waqt ān ast kah ā'īn-i diger taza kunaym*
> *Loh-i dil pāk bashwaym wa-z sir taza kunaym*
> *Afsar-i padshahi raft wa ba yaghma'i raft*
> *Nay-i Askanderi wa naghma'i Dara'i raft*
> *Kuhkan taysha badast āmad wa Pervaizi Khwast*
> *'Ishrat-i Khawjgi wa mahnat-i la la'i raft*
> *Chashm bakushāy agar chashm-i tū sahib-i nazr ast*
> *Zindgi der pay'i ta'mȳr-i Jehan-i diger ast.*

Now is a time for establishing new orders,
Let us wipe the heart's slate clean and begin everything anew,
The imperial crown is tarnished, it has been cast away,
Kuhkan came with a chipping hammer
                        in his hands and demanded
For himself (the estate of) Pervaiz.
Gone is the time of luxury for the masters,
                        of service by the lowly.
If thine eyes know how to see, open them;
Life is marching to the creation of another world![12]

To the end of his days, Iqbal admired the Russian revolution, which had put an end to man's oppression by man. However, he remained first of all a Muslim ideologist and considered the path of revolutionary Russia unacceptable for the peoples of colonial India.

In the foreword to his first lyrical anthology, *Payām-i Mashriq*, which came out in 1923 and brought together poems written before and during the First World War, the October Socialist Revolution in Russia, and the upsurge caused by this revolution in the liberation movements of the colonial East, Iqbal wrote that "the East, especially the Muslim East, finally, after a long slumber of many centuries, opened its eyes."[13] It was here, however, that he made the reservation that no new world could appear until the very nature of man changed.

## THE REFORMATION OF ISLAM

IQBAL believed that profound socioeconomic changes were necessary for the establishment of social justice. At the same time he made the implementation of these changes dependent on the moral perfection of man, in which Islam must have a deciding role.

Iqbal's moral and ethical ideals, sociopolitical ideals, and philosophical views were embodied in his teachings on the reformation of Islam. The basic ideas of these teachings, which sounded forth for the first time in Iqbal's philosophical poems *Asrār-i Khudi* and *Ramūz-i-Bekhudi* (already mentioned), achieved their ultimate formulation at the end of the 1920s in his lectures on Islam, *The Reconstruction of Religious Thought in Islam*, as well as in the philosophical poem *Javid-Namah* (The Book of Eternity), which Iqbal himself called his swan song. Moreover, whether Iqbal spoke as a philosopher, as an ideologist of Muslim nationalism, or as a politician, the moral and ethical, and the human side of any problem was always of paramount significance for him.

Iqbal explained the need to reform Islam by citing the progress of the development of social thought, science, and experience. This reformation was to play, in his words, the same role in the development of progressive thought in the East as did Protestantism in the West at a certain stage in history. It was called upon to liberate reason and at the same time to replace, as did Protestantism, a system of universal ethics with "national systems of ethics."[14] "It is the duty of the leaders of the world of Islam today to understand the real meaning of what has happened in Europe and then to move forward with self-control and a clear insight into the ultimate aims of Islam as a social policy" Iqbal wrote in his lecture, "The Principles of Movement in the Structure of Islam."[15]

Thus, Iqbal openly acknowledged that the reformation of Islam would serve sociopolitical ends. He strove to demonstrate the need to preserve religion and religious forms of world view for substantiation of the true meaning of the existence of the human personality and the ideal society, as well as for the disclosure of objective truths that cannot be penetrated with the aid of scientific analysis.

Iqbal separated philosophy from religion but awarded the palm of superiority to the latter:

> Philosophy, no doubt, has jurisdiction to judge religion, but what is to be judged is of such a nature that it will not submit to the jurisdiction of philosophy except on its own terms. . . . While sitting in judgment on religion, philosophy cannot give religion an inferior place among its data. Religion is not a departmental affair; it is neither mere thought, nor mere feeling, nor mere action; it is an expression of the whole man. Thus, in the evaluation of religion, philosophy must recognize the central position of religion and has no other alternative but to admit it as something focal in the process of reflective synthesis.[16]

This was one of the reasons why Iqbal presented his philosophical and sociopolitical ideas as part of his doctrine for the reformation of Islam.

The basis of his religio-philosophical views was the opposition of the idea of "God as a personality—a higher 'I' to the classical Greek philosophical idea of 'God as substance.' "[17] From the idealistic thesis of an eternally living and eternally creating God, Iqbal draws a dialectic conclusion on nature and society, which are in perpetual spasmodic development.

Borrowing from the Ash'arite school the so-called atomistic theory, according to which the universe consists of tiny particles—*jawahir*—and modernizing it in the light of the teachings of Leibnitz, Iqbal reaches the conclusion that God created not the things themselves existing in reality but the atoms of which they consist. Creative activity does not cease. "Fresh atoms are coming into being every moment, the universe is therefore constantly growing. . . . The essence of the atom is independent of its existence. . . . Existence is a quality with which God has endowed atoms. What we call a thing then, is in its essential nature a combination of atomic acts." Iqbal also says: "The atoms possess inseparable or negative qualities. They exist in opposed couples as life and death, motion and rest—and possess particularly no duration. . . . Nothing is a stable nature."[18]

Iqbal himself called nature "the clothing of God" and his own philosophy "really pure monotheism," but according to the just observation of the Italian scholar, Alessandro Bausani, one of the outstanding scholars of Iqbal's religious and philosophical views "this pure monotheism completely deprives the forces of nature of their divine character."[19] Iqbal in fact arrives through teleology at an understanding of dialectic movement.

This is also characteristic of his theory of cognition. He criticizes ideas of the world's unknowability. Citing the Qur'ān, he distinguishes three sources of cognition—inner experience, history, and nature. Knowledge is "a marriage of reason and experience." Iqbal acknowledged that individual knowledge of the universe (the ultimate ego) is always relative, but knowledge, in the sense of discursive knowledge, however infinite, cannot therefore be predicted of an ego who knows and at the same time forms the ground of the object known.[20] Despite his idealistic conception, Iqbal arrived spontaneously at a dialectic posing the question of relative and absolute truth. His theory of cognition prompted an endeavor by man to know surrounding nature and himself.

## BREAK WITH SUFISM

IQBAL borrowed from the Sufis their critical attitude toward the thesis (widespread among Muslim dogmatists) of the impossibility of man's knowledge of God, the surrounding world, and himself. He reshaped, in the spirit of his own philosophy of action, the teachings of the Sufis on the role of intuition in the process of cognition and their conception of the perfect man. At the same time he completely rejected the negative attitude of the Sufis toward reason and rationalistic philosophy on the whole, as well as their preaching of man's estrangement from the real world. "The mystics' condemnation of the intellect as the source of cognition finds no justification in the history of religion," he wrote.[21] Iqbal's break with Sufism began (as already stated) during his stay in Europe (1905–1908). It was during this period that he switched from pantheism and mysticism to consistent monotheism.

In his poetry the break with Sufism manifested itself as a change in the poetic interpretation of many traditional Sufi images (for example, the traditional images of the moth and the candle). In contrast to the Sufi ascetic, a striving for earthly delights was characteristic of Iqbal's hero. In "The Development of Metaphysics in Persia," his doctoral dissertation, Iqbal reached the conclusion that the mysticism of the Sufis hindered the comprehensive development of the human personality.

(This thought found further development in his lectures on the reconstruction of Islam.) The criticism of the ideas of the mystical possibility of man's spiritual communion with God as the source of cognition and of the passivity of the human personality doubtless had positive significance, although Iqbal derived it from idealistic positions.

## THE IMPACT OF SHAH WALIULLAH AND SAYYID AHMAD KHAN

IQBAL sought in the reformation of Islam a way to harmonize religion and the natural laws of the development of nature and society. Here he drew heavily upon the teachings of Shah Waliullah on the essence and form of religion, the "philosophy of nature" of Sayyid Ahmad Khan, and the ideas of Jamul-ud-Din Afghani on the creative nature of Islam, which stimulates social progress and connects the traditions of the past with the tasks of modern society. They attracted Iqbal above all as attempts to reshape Islam in line with the development of one's own people and the conditions of one's own time. That is why he linked the reconstruction of Islam to the names of these three ideologists.

According to the teachings of Shah Waliullah, the concrete expressions of religion—its forms (the interpretation of basic dogmas, ceremonies, religious prescriptions relating to specific events, etc.)—can and do differ among separate peoples at definite periods of time depending upon the various specific conditions of their lives. Therefore, many statements by the Prophet Muhammad concerning Arabia are inapplicable to India. But the essence of religion, which is based on consistent monotheism, is the same for all peoples and applicable to all eras. "The prophetic method of teaching, according to Shah Waiullah," Iqbal noted, "is that generally speaking, the law revealed by a prophet takes special notice of the habits, ways, and peculiarities of the people to whom he is specifically sent." "The *shariat* values (*ahkām*) resulting from this application [for example, rules relating to penalties for crimes]," Iqbal wrote further, "are in a sense specific to that people, and since their observance is not an end in itself, they cannot be strictly enforced in the case of future generations."[22]

Iqbal developed the teachings of Shah Waliullah on the form and substance of religion. He called special attention to the fact that rebirth was possible only for the spiritual principles of Islam, which respond to the interests of all of society, and not for Muslim social institutions, fashioned during a definite social era in the interests of the dominant strata of the individual peoples.

Iqbal attached great importance to Shah Waliullah's teachings on "independent judgment" (*ijtihād*). Shah Waliullah opposed the viewpoint, prevalent in his time, that the final words on questions of theology were spoken in the tenth century, and that since then no one has had the right to independent judgment on religious questions (the right of *ijtihād*). Shah Waliullah supported the restoration of the Muslims' right to *ijtihād* in order to separate the authentic text of the Qur'ān (*Nass*) and the prescriptions of the *Sunna* concerning "common phenomena" (*'Am*) from the literal interpretation (*Zāhir*) of the Qur'ān and the *Sunna* concerning particular phenomena (*Khāṣ*).[23] Such a demarcation, in his opinion, was necessary for deciding the basic question of whether this or that religious prescription is applicable to given specific historic conditions. It was this part of his teachings on *ijtihād* that Iqbal used.

The right of independent judgment, as interpreted by Iqbal, excluded any rigid dogma and was to serve, in his words, as the basis for the development of social thought. On this point, Iqbal constantly stressed that only collective *ijtihād* could be true *ijtihād*, that is, an interpretation of the principles of Islam, a judgment that instead of reflecting the opinion of one man, will meet the interests of society.

The interpretation Iqbal gave to *ijtihād* attests to his endeavor to rid himself of outdated dogmas and to put forth, in religious form, new ideas that, in his own words, meet the interests of social development.

"Perhaps the first Muslim who felt the urge of a new spirit in him was Shah Waliullah of Delhi," Iqbal emphasized.[24] He called special attention to the fact that the interpretation of *ijtihād* given by Shah Waliullah excluded the simple "rebirth" of the dogmas of Islam, which had belonged to the period of the Arab caliphate, and made possible a new interpretation of its principles, applicable to the national conditions of separate Muslim peoples in the modern stage of their development. At the same time Iqbal could not help but see that Shah Waliullah. who lived and was active during the period of the crisis of the Mughal Empire and who was closely tied to a class of feudalists already doomed by history, was not yet able to work out a philosophy of Islam to meet the interests of the society of Iqbal's time, that is, a bourgeois society. Shah Waliullah, in Iqbal's words, could only feel the necessity of a new orientation in Islam: "The man, however, who fully realized the importance and immensity of the task, and whose deep insight into inner meaning of the history of Muslim thought and life, combined with a broad vision engendered by his wide experience of man and manners, would have made him a living link between the past and future, was Jamal-ud-Din Afghani," Iqbal wrote. "If his indefatigable but divided energy could have devoted itself entirely to Islam as a system of human belief and conduct, the world of Islam, intellectually speaking, would have been on much more solid ground today."[25]

However, Jamal-ud-Din Afghani, according to Iqbal's just assertion, also failed to offer an expanded philosophical and political conception of an Islam reshaped to meet the social conditions of Iqbal's time. In Iqbal's opinion, Sayyid Ahmad Khan took a great step forward in this respect. His philosophy of nature (*nacharia*), called upon to substantiate the "correspondence" of Islam to the laws of nature, was especially attractive to Iqbal.

In developing Shah Waliullah's teachings on the essence and form of religion, Sayyid Ahmad Khan maintained that the essence of religion was in the correspondence of religious dogmas to phenomena of nature. He also believed that life exists in accordance with these laws, and that the causal relationship among phenomena exists objectively and does not depend on the will of people. Many critics of Sayyid Ahmad Khan's philosophy of nature observed that a consistent interpretation of this conception left no room for God. However, Sayyid Ahmad Khan himself regarded the objective causality existing in nature as imposed by God.

## DIALECTICAL MOVEMENT IN SOCIETY

IQBAL had a high estimation of Sayyid Ahmad Khan's philosophy of nature, which offered, in his words, "a new orientation of Islam." At the same time he went beyond him. Thus, Sayyid Ahmad Khan, resting on the theory of *nacharia*, acknowledged the possibility of man's knowing the world, studying the laws of nature, and utilizing them for social good. However, he denied the possibility of man's changing the world and often wrote of the "insignificance and impotence of man before God."

Iqbal, on the contrary, brought man in his activity nearer to God the Creator and endowed him in a number of instances with the right to change the world. From an understanding of the dialectic movement in nature he essentially arrived at an understanding of dialectic movement in society. Iqbal considered nature, society, and man to be in constant motion, development, and formation. It is no accident that he himself admitted that he could not be completely satisfied by the steps taken by his predecessors in the reshaping of Islam. "Thus the problems facing the modern generation of Muslims are tremendous," he wrote. "The only course open to us is to approach modern knowledge with a respectful but independent attitude and to appreciate the teachings of Islam in the light of that knowledge, even though we may be led to differ from those who have gone before us."[26]

Iqbal's teachings on nature and society were based on his philosophy of the man-activist. It rests on two basic principles: the first likens man the creator, to God the Creator; the second principle asserts an unbreakable tie between man's activity and society.

In Iqbal's first philosophical poem, *Asrār-i Khudi*, the human personality came forth as the result of the self-development of the divine individuality embodied in man at various stages on his path to God. Iqbal's philosophy appealed more to emotions than to cold logic; it was a philosophy of love for man, preaching humanity and active struggle for the happiness of the individual human personality and of all mankind.

*Asrār-i Khudi* was also a poetic affirmation of the inexhaustible creative possibilities of the human personality. Iqbal believed that the reason for the decline of Muslim society lay in the human personality's loss of self-consciousness (*nafī-i-Khudi*). He saw in man's consciousness of his own creative possibilities (*iṣbāt-i-Khudi*) and in an active love for life the only means of progress among Muslims in India. In *Asrār-i Khudi* Iqbal maintained:

> The pith of life is contained in action,
> To delight in creation is the life of life.[27]

The poet-philosopher glorified not obedience and submission but firmness, daring, and persistence in the struggle against evil. Only in this struggle did he see the path to perfecting the human personality, the way to its immortality. Between the lines of the famous dialogue of the coal and the diamond from the poem *Ramūz-i-Bekhudi* (The Mysteries of Selflessness) lay the opposition of the man who reconciles himself to his slave position (the spineless coal) to the personality tempered in battle and striving to eliminate the evil and violence not in the beyond but in the real, earthly world (the diamond, which possesses the "glory of light").

In Iqbal's poem the coal utters the following words:

> Everyone puts the sole of his foot on my head
> And covers my stock of existence with ashes
> My fate must needs be deplored;
> Dost thou know what is the gist of my being?[28]

Only struggle, Iqbal said, can grind down the soft edges of the coal and turn it into a diamond. The diamond's answer to the coal is Iqbal's answer for the Muslim intelligentsia to the questions sharply put to it by life:

> Be void of fear, grief, and anxiety,
> Be hard as a stone, be a diamond!
> Whosoever strives hard and grips tight,
> The two worlds are illumined by him.[29]

In *Ramūz-i-Bekhudi*, which is a thematic continuation of *Asrār-i Khudi*, Iqbal considered the problem of interrelations between the personality and society. Only man's vigorous activity in the name of social progress turns him, in Iqbal's words, from a biological individual whose life is limited in time into a personality that acquires immortality. This idea received final philosophical substantiation in the lectures on the reconstruction of Islam:

The ultimate aim of the ego is not to see something, but to be something. It is in the ego's effort to be something that he (man) discovers his final opportunity to sharpen his objectivity and acquire a more fundamental "I am," which finds evidence of its reality not in the Cartesian "I think" but in the Kantian "I can." . . . The final act is not an intellectual act, but a vital act which deepens the whole being of the ego, and sharpens his will with the creative assurance that the world is not something to be merely seen or known through concepts, but something to be made and re-made by continuous action.[30]

To the Cartesian concept of true existence—"I think, therefore I am" —Iqbal contrasted his "I act, therefore I am." Considering man's activity the manifestation of his free will, Iqbal strove to bring Kant's "free will" into agreement with the Sufi "perfect man."

At the same time he also went farther than his predecessors, the philosopher-mystics, and Kant. He shared neither Kant's agnosticism nor his judgment that it was sufficient to carry out the will inherent in man—"I can"—in the other world. Iqbal made the possibility of the "activity of the soul" (so-called immortality) dependent on the behavior of man in life. However, Iqbal saw sense not in any activity of man but only in activity aimed at serving God and society.

He was not free of the metaphysical opposition of the personality and society. For example, he regarded the endeavor of society to subordinate the human personality and the endeavor of the personality to preserve its free will as one of the contradictions basic to all social systems. He saw the solution to this question primarily in the service to God.

However, by service to God he meant following the moral and ethical principles of Islam. In his interpretation, "man's submission to God" meant first of all man's renunciation of his egoistic inclinations and desires. He opposed blind fanaticism and the idea of man's helplessness before God. While acknowledging, in accordance with his religio-idealistic conception, that the world was created by God and that God blew the breath of life into man, Iqbal constantly stressed that a change in this world depended only on the labor and activity of man.

In developing Sayyid Ahmad Khan's idea of national self-help Iqbal emphasized that activity for the good of society consists in establishing social justice. His teachings on nature and society were based on the opposition of the principles of good and evil, light and darkness. Utilizing the Sufi interpretation of evil as unrealized potential for good, Iqbal created a dialectic conception of good and evil. According to his philosophy, only the unity of these two principles, which under the influence of man's constant activity and the appropriate conditions could be reincarnated in one another, constituted a basis for social progress. These ideas had something directly in common with the thesis of dialectic philosophy on the unity and struggle of opposites. According to Iqbal's teachings, whether or not good or evil triumphed in the world depended upon man's activity. The poet's doctrine that the activity of man is creative and reshapes the world doubtless had progressive significance.

Iqbal's poetic œuvre presents, parallel to the contrast of good and evil, a contrast of modern political phenomena: the West, whose civilization, in his opinion, was on the road to ruin, and the East, which was awaiting its renovation and seeking its special path of historical progress. In considering the historical changes that were going on in the world, Iqbal proceeded from the inevitability of historical progress. Only Muslims, in his words, see in history the "continuous collective movement, a real, inevitable development in time."[31]

Iqbal had no specific notion of the nature of the socioeconomic structure and political system of the future "ideal society." In his philosophical and didactic works he often spoke of an ideal theocratic state. However, by theocratic he meant, in his own words, the ideal form of democracy and by no means implied the participation of the Muslim *mullās* and *'ulamā'* in the administration of the country. Thus, when criticizing the Iranian constitution, which gave a committee of *'ulamā'* the right to determine the conformity of one law or other to the dogma of Islam, Iqbal spoke up against the interference of the *'ulamā'* in affairs of state. In the Muslim state, he constantly stressed, there can be neither opposition between secular and spiritual authority nor assumption by the clergy of state functions, since Islam, in Iqbal's words, has no clergy at all.

Although he connected his social ideals with Islam, Iqbal was innocent of religious intolerance in his interpretation of social justice and the ideal state. A society could be just only if it protected equally the interests of the orthodox Muslim and of the man who professes another religion. Iqbal's entire sociopolitical philosophy was permeated with profound humanism. "Humaneness consists in respecting man, therefore, imbue yourselves with the grandeur of man." The humane man receives instructions from God, therefore he is "humane to the believer and the non-believer alike," Iqbal appealed to his contemporaries.

The man in Iqbal's poem *Javid-Namah* who sets out on a journey to the other world in search of truth becomes all-powerful and approaches God through constant activity; he incorporates all the best created by mankind before him through tolerance; he frees himself from dependence on more powerful men and gains the opportunity to exercise his free will through service to God and society.

## Ideology of Muslim Nationalism

Despite his rejection of theocracy as the ideal society, Iqbal nevertheless linked to religion his sociopolitical norms, which were based, in his words, on the consistent application of the principle of monotheism (*Tawhīd*). At the same time Iqbal offered his own interpretation of the social meaning of *Tawhīd* as the realization of "equality, solidarity, and freedom."[32] By equality Iqbal meant above all the equality of all men before God. He also argued for the just distribution of social blessings and often expressed his liking for the socialist reforms being carried out in the Soviet Union. By solidarity Iqbal meant primarily solidarity among Muslims, and he linked his ideal of freedom inseparably with the struggle of the peoples of the East against colonial domination.

For all the ambiguity and contradictoriness of his world view, as an opponent of all forms of human oppression Iqbal ranked with the most progressive men in India. He opposed the oppression of the peoples of the East by capitalist Europe, of peasants by landowners, of workers by capitalists. He scoffed at Western democracy and indignantly questioned the right of the capitalist in his own country to appropriate the fruits of the worker's labor, or the landowners to drink the blood of the peasant. He derided the attempts of the rich to distract the workers from the struggle for their rights with promises of blessings in the other world. The contrast between the patriot actively fighting against evil and the indifferent and submissive man, as well as condemnation of exploiters and compassion for the exploited, formed the undercurrent of many of Iqbal's philosophical poems and satirical works that reflected his political sympathies. He sympathized with the mass struggle of the peoples of the East for their independence. He often emphasized in his political speeches and letters that only the politician and party that relied on the masses could count on success.

In his poetic works he compared the activist torn away from the people to a branch broken from a tree:

> *Millat kāy sāth rabta ūstwār rakh*
> *Paywastah rah shajer say ūmȳd-i bahār rakh.*[33]
> Hold on to the tree, the ever-living trunk,
> And believe in your spring, your great people.

At the same time, in his political philosophy he proceeded from the promise that the people of India were not ready for the mass revolutionary action and the mass methods of struggle that had brought victory to the peoples of Russia. Although welcoming revolutionary reforms in the countries of the East fighting for their independence, he often expressed his liking for an evolutionary form of development. He had, for example, a high regard for the activity of Mustafa Kemal and acknowledged his right to religious reforms.

"The truth," said Iqbal, "is that among the Muslim nations of today, Turkey alone has shaken off its dogmatic slumber, and attained to self-consciousness." Moweover, he did not hide his sympathies for the reformist party, which tied Turkey's future development directly to religion. He openly expressed disagreement with Kemal Ataturk's position on the caliphate. "Personally, I think it is a mistake to suppose that the idea of state is more dominant and rules all other ideas embodied in the system of Islam," Iqbal wrote.[34]

Iqbal considered even a Kemal-style revolution unacceptable for India. He wrote that the peoples of the Indo-Pakistan subcontinent had not yet found their own path in the struggle for the creation of an independent state. He constantly emphasized the difficulty of solving internal problems and, having gradually reached the conclusion that self-determination was necessary for the Muslims of India, regarded Pakistan as the best path for realizing independence from foreign domination.

## SELF-DETERMINATION FOR THE MUSLIMS OF INDIA

IQBAL's philosophical conceptions led him to the conclusion that his ideals of equality and freedom could be embodied only in an Islamic state, and that consequently the Muslims of India had no other course but self-determination and the creation of Pakistan. The idea of Pakistan was a logical outgrowth of his concept of Muslim nationalism. It was most fully reflected in the political speeches, letters, and political tracts of his last period of activity (the 1930s).

In the middle of the 1930s many representatives of the radically inclined Muslim intelligentsia set their course toward the creation of a special Muslim state in India. As a consequence of the peculiarities of historical development in colonial India, and also because of the influence of British policy, the national aspirations of many representatives of the Bengali, Punjabi, and Sindhi bourgeoisie and middle strata, the rivalries among individual groups of the bourgeoisie and among the various groups of the civil-service intelligentsia, and the social contradictions between peasants and landowners and between commercial-financial elements and the farming classes of Northern India, all ended up along the line of Hindu-Muslim contradictions.

One part of the Muslim intelligentsia continued to struggle for the independence of a united India and bound its fate with the National Congress, whereas another part shared a belief in the necessity of Muslim self-determination and supported the Muslim League, the political party heading the movement for the creation of an independent Pakistani state. On the eve of the First World War Abul Kalam Azad and Muhammad Iqbal, the two most important ideologists of the Muslims of India, were in one camp of ardent patriots of India—bards and ideologists of the struggle against foreign enslavement; but at the end of the 1930s Azad took the path of the National Congress, and Iqbal chose the separate Muslim path of struggle for independence and supported the political movement headed by the Muslim League.

Nevertheless, it is impossible not to see definite differences between Iqbal's sociopolitical views and the views of the leadership of the Muslim League. Unlike the leadership of the League, Iqbal always supported a closer tie between the Muslim intelligentsia and the masses, and he always put the struggle for independence first. In many ways he reflected the doubts and aspirations of the Muslim intelligentsia and all the Muslim middle strata, who at the end of the 1930s saw no clear way of solving the problems of the anti-imperialist struggle and realizing their hopes for social justice.

Iqbal the philosopher never had a clear concept of the differences between the religious community and the national community. Although he did try to distinguish between the concepts of national community (*qawm*) and religious community (*millat*), he was not always consistent here. For example, he considered Indian Muslims a nation. "Indeed the Muslims of India are the only people who can fully be described as a nation in the modern sense of the word," he stated in his famous presidential address at the 1930 session of the Muslim League in Allahabad. However, in his opinion this did not mean that any religious community constituted a nation. Thus, the

Hindus, in his words, "are not a nation, although this is what they are striving for."

The definition of the Muslims of India as a separate nation did not mean, however, that Iqbal acknowledged the complete coincidence of national and religious community. He did not discount the fact that in other countries where Muslims did not constitute a minority, as they did in India, they were able to achieve greater progress by developing "along national, i.e., territorial lines."

At the same time, Iqbal constantly emphasized that the desire to consolidate on a religious basis was characteristic of the peoples professing Islam. This desire was intensified under the influence of the colonial invasions. "Today it is being gradually realized in the countries of Islam and in the shape of what is called Muslim nationalism," he noted. Thus Iqbal himself defined "Muslim nationalism" as the consciousness of a national-religious community characteristic of the stage of the national liberation movement of colonial peoples in his time. Recognizing the emergence of this consciousness as logical, he endeavored on this basis to substantiate the necessity of state self-determination for the Muslims of the Indian subcontinent. "I would like to see the Punjab, North-West Frontier Province, Sindh and Baluchistan amalgamated into a single state. Self-government within the British Empire or without the British Empire, and the formation of a consolidated North-West Indian Muslim state appears to me to be the final destiny of the Muslims, at least of North-West India," he stated at the above-mentioned session of the Muslim League.

Iqbal's statements did not give a clear idea of what Pakistan's political status and interrelations with India should be. "The Muslim demand for the creation of a Muslim India within India is . . . perfectly justified," he said in the 1930 presidential address. It was there that he called for strengthening of unity on a federal basis, basing the formation of autonomous regions on "linguistic and economic community and religious unity." These statements make it possible to suggest that Iqbal considered complete division between the Hindu and Muslim states expedient.

Iqbal emphasized many times that he would recognize only an ideology of religio-communal unity that was based on respect for the interests of other communities. The endeavor to reconcile communalism with nationalism was as characteristic of his sociopolitical views as it was of the social thought of the Muslim intelligentsia as a whole.

"Nationalism in the sense of love of one's country and even readiness to die for its honor is a part of the Muslim faith; it comes into conflict with Islam only when it begins to play the role of a political concept, and claims to be a principle of human solidarity demanding that Islam should recede to the background of a mere private opinion and cease to be a living factor in the national life," Iqbal stressed in a famous letter to Jawaharlal Nehru. "Nationalism was an independent problem for Muslims only in those countries where they were in the minority. . . ." he wrote in the same letter. "In countries with a Muslim majority, nationalism and Islam are practically identical, but in countries where Muslims are in the minority, their demand for self-determination as cultural unification is completely justified."[35]

Thus, in Iqbal's interpretation, Muslim nationalism retained a clearly expressed anticolonialist trend, was permeated with ideas of social justice clothed in religious form, and did not rule out unification of the representatives of various religious communities and varying state formation based on national-religious unity, in the name of common goals.

Despite the inner weaknesses and contradictory nature of Iqbal's world view, he remained, at all stages of his religio-philosophical and political activity and poetic work, the spokesman for the hopes and aspirations of the Muslim intelligentsia of India, a ruler of its thoughts, an ardent patriot of his homeland, an impassioned fighter against colonialism and any form of man's oppression of man, and a champion of freedom and humanism.

# 6

# The Development of Political Philosophy

## RIFFAT HASSAN

IQBAL'S eminence as a poet has been acknowledged; however, his status as a philosopher is a controversial matter. An important reason for this controversy is that Iqbal's thought has been studied in parts but not as a whole. In order to appreciate a work, whether political or philosophical, it is necessary to analyze the elements that compose the whole; moreover, one must consider the relation of the parts to each other and to the whole. Iqbal's ideas have been divided into fragments but the elements have not been synthesized.

This has resulted in the general impression that Iqbal had certain ideas of philosophical significance, but that these ideas do not form a system. It is important to understand the underlying pattern of Iqbal's thinking and the nature of his vision, for only then is one able to understand the true significance of his ideas.

Concerning his political philosophy, Iqbal is often accused of inconsistencies and contradictions. This accusation is largely the result either of regarding Iqbal's general philosophy as arising from his political philosophy or of studying his political philosophy in isolation from his general philosophy. Actually, Iqbal's political philosophy is an integral part of his general philosophy and is best understood if studied with reference to the wider whole.

What is known as Iqbal's political philosophy is usually based on his writings from 1908 to 1938. However, in order to understand the continuity of his thinking it is necessary to pay considerable attention to the two earlier phases of Iqbal's poetic career, that is, from 1895 to 1905 and from 1905 to 1908. (Most of the poems written during these two periods are found in Parts I and II of *Bāng-i-Dara* [The Call of the

## DISTINCTION BETWEEN PATRIOTIC AND NATIONALISTIC POETRY

IQBAL's pre-1905 poetry is often described as nationalistic. It is necessary, however, to differentiate between patriotic and nationalistic verses because the latter implies an awareness of, and an involvement with, political theory or practice which may be entirely absent from the former. "Patriotism is a perfectly natural virtue and has a place in the moral life of man,"[1] wrote Iqbal, and he himself never lacked this virtue. *Himalā*, the first poem in *Bāng-i-Dara* and a hymn of the magnificence and grandeur of the tallest mountain range in the world, is patriotic: it was inspired by the beauty of the land of his birth. Like *Himalā* (The Home of Snow), Iqbal's other "patriotic" poems are buoyant and heart-lifting. The fire that raged within him left on his poetry the stamp of Miltonic restlessness. There are, amongst the vast bulk of Iqbal's writings, only a few poems which impart a feeling of peace and joy. These poems reflect those moments when the poet sought an escape from the ravages of his soul in thoughts of love and sensuous beauty.

That Iqbal the poet was a patriot there is no doubt. That he remained a patriot is sometimes forgotten. H. L. Chopra, an Indian scholar, has truly said: "Iqbal sprang up in the realm of Indian poetry as a bard of India and even after so many vicissitudes in his career when he left this earth on 21st April, 1938 he remained a truly patriotic poet of India."[2] But it must be kept in mind that patriotism is not the same thing as nationalism.

## PRE-1905 POLITICAL POETRY: THE TEMPLE OF LOVE

THE two things which stand foremost in Iqbal's pre-1905 political poetry are: (1) his desire to see a self-governing and united India—a country free of both alien domination and inner dissension, in particular the Hindu-Muslim conflict; and (2) his constant endeavor to draw attention to those factors of decadence which caused the decline of the Muslims in India.

The political poems in the first part of *Bāng-i-Dara* indicate that Iqbal suffered more on account of the factions which divided the Indian people than the imperialistic yoke imposed on his countrymen. One reason for this was, no doubt, the feeling that until the people of India could resolve their differences and come to terms with each other, the ideal of sovereign rule for India would remain a dream. But as will be explained later, there was another reason—one far more fundamental —for Iqbal's passionate nationalism, which found its expression in poetic outbursts that resounded throughout India.

Iqbal the young poet was deeply disturbed by the discord and distrust between Hindus and Muslims which he saw all around him. With his usual eloquence he cried out against the forces of disruption. No one was spared; the *Mulla* and the *Brahman* were criticized equally. He maintained that from their gods they learned only hatred and hostility ("You think in idols carved of stone there is divinity") and professed allegiance to a faith other than theirs ("Each particle of my country's dust is as a god to me").

The poet adored his country, but its places of worship were defiled by hatred; hence he believed a new temple, a sanctuary of love, had to be built wherein all could worship. In *Nayā Shiwalā* (New Temple) the poet addresses the keepers of the temple and the mosque:

> Come, let us lift the curtain of Apartness once again,
> Unite once more the parted ones, erase duality's stain.
> Since a long time heart's habitat has been so desolate,
> O Come, a temple new, in this land, let us elevate.[3]

Although the theme of this poem recurs in Iqbal's early verses, it is unique because it gives a message of universal love not in general terms as it appears elsewhere in Iqbal's poetry, but in specifically Hindu vocabulary. This poem was a direct appeal to the Hindus, and its terminology indicates the poet's sincere desire to establish intellectual communication and spiritual rapport between Hindus and Muslims.

In *Taswīr-i-Dard* (Portrait of Anguish), the poet cries for Hindustan whose people are lost "in tales of ancient days" and do not indulge even in "the joys of complaint." The poet expresses his own determination "to string together the separated beads of the rosary," the religious association of the image making it more effective. In the name of an all-embracing principle of human love, the poet urges his compatriots to transcend cultural and religious boundaries, attaining true freedom:

> In Love is hidden Liberty, if only you could see
> And bondage is discrimination between you and me.[4]

Iqbal did not minimize the difficulty of eliminating bias. He admired natural phenomena for their "impartiality"; nature's beauty entertained one and all. The poet was conscious, however, of his own limitations. To the *shamā'* (the candle), he said wistfully:

> In the Ka'bah and the house of idols, your glow is the same,
> But in differences of mosque and temple lost I am.

And to his compatriots he said unequivocally:

> People of India, if you do not learn, you'll be no more.[5]

The message of the poet for the people of India was that of love and faith. Many years later, when discussing the problems of India, Iqbal wrote: "It is, and has always been, a question of faith. Our faith too depends on affection and understanding. What we need for a swift solution of the political problem of India is faith."[6] This message of love and faith must be kept in mind because Iqbal's political philosophy is an integral part of his total commitment, and to regard his words as possessing merely political significance is to elude the core of his thought.

A number of poems for children were obviously written with India's political situation in mind. *Parinde ke Faryād* (The Bird's Lament), the longing of a caged bird for the freedom of the skies and its nest, bears reference to the greater bondage and deeper yearnings for liberty of a whole subcontinent. The vision of *Hindustani Bachoñ Ka Qawmi Gīt* (National Anthem of Indian Children) is again one of universal love, peace, and good will. The poet wished to create in little children the feeling that to live in India was to lead "a heavenly life," and that they must "adorn my country as a flower adorns a garden." Iqbal's *Tārānā-i Hindi* (The Song of India) became the unofficial national anthem of India.[7] According to one Indian writer, it "remains to this day the best patriotic poem written by any Indian poet in modern times. It comes nearest, in fact, to a truly non-communal national anthem of India."[8]

The message it contained said nothing new, but perhaps the words were more explicit than they had been before:

> Religion does not teach us mutual belligerency,
> We are the people of India, and India is our country.

Perhaps it was the tragedy of Iqbal's youth that the India-mother-of-all myth exploded before the children who sang his songs and grew to manhood. Disillusionment came, as it must when the idealism of youth is touched by the coldness of reality. But, as Keats had clung to the principle of beauty even as sickness and sorrow consumed his mortal self, although the tune of his melody became more solemn as the ease of the first fresh notes of his singing became burdened with experience.

Iqbal, so concerned about the fate of India, was, naturally enough, concerned about the plight of his coreligionists. He participated in the activities of the Anjuman-i-Himāyat-i-Islam (Society for the Support of Islam), an organization in Lahore which did much to disseminate modern Western education among the Muslims. At the annual meetings of the Anjuman Iqbal read several poems expressing eloquently the sorrows and aspirations of the Muslims.* It is important to keep this in mind because it is sometimes assumed that in the first phase of his poetic career Iqbal's thought was exclusively nationalistic and that he was not particularly concerned about the Muslims. Even in this phase, however, Iqbal shared with the Indian Muslims their feelings of desolation at finding themselves faced both with political bondage and spiritual and economic poverty. He felt very deeply that Islam as he saw it practiced was not as it was meant to be. He protested against those who failed to understand or deliberately distorted the true spirit of Islam. His protest was to continue all his life.

It is difficult to say that before 1905 Iqbal had a definite philosophy. But an analysis of his early poems reveals in embryo most of the ideas which later played a prominent part in the system of his thought. For instance, one finds the idea that the development of the individual depends on his capacity for purposeful action. The destiny of a nation too depends on action:

> 'Tis Divinity's decree and Creation's mode—
> Who walks along the path of Action is by Nature loved.[9]

---

*For detailed information about these poems, see pages 16–17.

## Development of Political Philosophy

"Action is the highest form of contemplation,"[10] Iqbal wrote in 1925, but he knew this truth a long time before. He knew it, in fact, before the active West had sharpened his awareness of the consequences of unpreparedness and unwillingness or inability to act when action was required. Perhaps he learned to believe in action from the Qur'ān, which "emphasizes 'deed' rather than 'idea'."[11] But it is more likely that his love for action sprang from his particular disposition and that it was strengthened rather than induced by his religious faith.

Another interesting idea in Iqbal's early verse is that religion does not demand that a man neglect his material needs. In *Dīn-o-Dunyā* (Religion and World) Iqbal states that in fact "religion is the guardian of the material world." In another poem, the spirit of Sir Sayyid Ahmad Khan tells the poet:

> To teach religion in the world, if this be your aim,
> Do not teach your nation that the world they should disclaim.[12]

This is the foreshadowing of the idea which later became one of the pivots of his political philosophy—that the spiritual and temporal aspects of human life, far from being mutually exclusive, were organically related to each other, and that there was no need to bifurcate the unity of individual and collective life into the domains of church and state.

*The Temple of Love* may be said to symbolize the first phase of Iqbal's poetic career. E. M. Forster has misunderstood the vision enshrined in this symbol. He described the new temple as "the Temple of India" and observed: "The glory of the courtyard from Mecca shall inhabit that temple; the image on its shrine shall be gold, inscribed Hindustan, shall wear both the Brahman thread and the Muslim rosary, and the *Muezzin* shall call worshippers to prayer upon a horn."[13] The new temple is in India, but it is not of India. Nor is it conceived by Iqbal as heralding the advent of a new faith containing elements of Hinduism and Islam. Such a faith could not create an organic unity and might very well have destroyed the distinct identity of either faith. The temple is raised to love, which transcends the images in which it is expressed.

### 1905–1908: SOJOURN IN EUROPE

ALSO, it is asserted that Iqbal's thinking was completely changed by his contact with Western civilization. This is hardly true; Europe crystallized rather than fundamentally altered his thinking. Coming face to face with a society so different from his own, he had the opportunity to compare the modes of living and the systems of values he saw in the East and the West. No longer was it sufficient for him to believe instinctively or vaguely in the reality or validity of a certain world order. He had to develop a rational basis for his beliefs. The spontaneous outpourings of his verse had to give way to poetry based on considered judgments. In his future work he was to guard against what T. S. Eliot has called the "dissociation of sensibility."

Iqbal, who had sung so many hymns to love, felt nothing more acutely in the West than its lack of love. The heart (regarded by the mystic tradition to be the repository of love and the source of true knowledge) had been displaced in the West by the mind. Iqbal was not anti-intellectual; for him, thought (the source of which is the mind) and intuition (the source of which is the heart) both occupy a necessary place in the life of man. However, the problem of the place of the head and the heart in the scale of values had also stirred the imagination of Western thinkers and poets.

Tennyson, faced with the problem of reconciling science and faith, wrote about the respective ranks of knowledge and wisdom:

> Who loves not knowledge? Who shall rail
> Against her beauty? May she mix
> With men and prosper!

but

> Let her know her place;
> She is the second, not the first.
> A higher hand must make her mild,
> If all be not in vain; and guide
> Her footsteps, moving side by side
> With wisdom, like a younger child:
> For she is earthly of the mind,
> But wisdom heavenly of the soul.

Iqbal, confronted with a similar problem, believed in almost the same thing. He saw reason and revelation, intellect and intuition, as part of the same plan but differing in function and in importance.*

*For detailed discussion on Iqbal's concept of intellect and intuition, see pages 188–90; 238–39; 278–80; 303–306.

## Development of Political Philosophy 143

Nearly all the poems written during the second phase of Iqbal's career (1905-1908) are concerned with love. This is no accident; Iqbal believed in love as a principle of eternity, which in a world of flux gave meaning and stability to human life. In Western society Iqbal saw that love meant weakness and surrender, if anything. But for him love was to be the informing vision giving unity to his poetical as well as philosophical concepts.

It is also misleading to assert that Iqbal was anti-intellectual "essentially as a revolt against modern capitalism."[14] First of all, there was no necessary connection between intellect as Iqbal conceived it and capitalism. Intellect was a gift of God which gave man the power to form concepts and thus raised him above the angels.[15] Second, even if it is assumed that in Iqbal's mind there was a link between intellect and capitalism, it still does not follow that Iqbal's philosophy became anti-intellectual as a result of his revolt against capitalism. Iqbal's conception of intellect is of prime importance in his philosophic system and it was evolved carefully, the chief influences which moulded it being religious and philosophical, not political. The European political scene did strengthen Iqbal's belief that intellect alone was not enough, but he did not arrive at that belief because of what he observed.

The poems Iqbal composed during his three-year stay in Europe revealed a few new contours of his developing ideas. First, his recoil from the glamorous and materially prosperous West, which intoxicates rather than enlightens:

> The European tavern-keeper's wine brings jubilee,
> It has not sorrow's ecstasy: give home-brewed wine to me.

Second, Iqbal started thinking philosophically about the nature of the Islamic community. With the widening of his intellectual horizon, India and its problems no longer loomed so large before him. Away from the scene of turmoil he could think more clearly about fundamental issues which had been obscured by the dust of constant controversy. In 1908 he wrote:

> The life of the individual is contingent,
>        the life of the community is real,
> Sacrifice yourself for your community,
>        burn the magic of the illusory.[16]

(In the latter part of this essay an attempt will be made to present an outline of Iqbal's ideas regarding the place of the individual in society. Here it is sufficient to draw attention to the first appearance of this subject.)

Perhaps the most important political idea in the second part of *Bāng-i-Dara* is that in Islam "nationality . . . is a pure idea; it has no geographical basis." The Prophet of Islam, says Iqbal, taught: "What determines the bounds of our nation is not oneness of state."[17] This is not a rejection of nationalism, but a glimpse of a wider concept. Earlier Iqbal had visualized a particular fulfillment of his universal vision of love and good will in a unified India. It seems that now he had begun to realize that unity, in order to be real and lasting, must spring from within; that is, it must be organic. Even if it were possible to impose some kind of unity on the naturally ill-adjusted nationalities of India, such a unity would not fulfill Iqbal's ideal. In his search for a group with an inner cohesion, Iqbal began to concentrate more and more on the Muslims. He then wrote:

> The creators of sects in India are acting like Azar;
> Protecting yourself from idols,
>     become the dust of the way to Hejaz.[18]

## 1908–1938: THE VISION UNVEILED

During the next thirty years Iqbal wrote his major poetical works and his *Lectures on the Reconstruction of Religious Thought in Islam*. When Iqbal returned from Europe, a number of his most significant ideas had already emerged, but these had yet to be developed into a consistent and dynamic philosophy of life, a philosophy which satisfied the intellect and also gave sustenance to the spirit and an impetus to action. The most burning questions of the day in India were concerned, directly or indirectly, with politics, and a man of Iqbal's wide sympathies and interests could not remain indifferent or aloof. Writing in 1920 on Iqbal's poetry, E. M. Forster had observed: "Poets in India cannot be parted from politics. Would that they could! But there is no hope in the present circumstances, one could as easily part Dante from Florence."[19] It is true that Iqbal cannot be separated from

## Development of Political Philosophy 145

politics, but this is so because politics cannot be isolated from human activity. Owing to Iqbal's great influence on the political history of his country, it is easy enough to think of him as a political poet, sometimes even as a politician. He was a political thinker, but it is misleading to stress this too much, for it may lead one to think that he was only, or even primarily, a political philosopher.

It would not be true to say that on his return from Europe Iqbal ceased entirely to try to unify India and began to concentrate exclusively on the effort to present in practicable shape his moral and political ideal to the Muslims. He still considered unity a good thing even though he realized that conditions being what they were, his ideal of unity could not be achieved in India. In 1927 Iqbal said in the Punjab Legislative Assembly: "I do not know whether it is desirable to become a nation."[20] Iqbal was concerned with the fate of India as a whole, and especially with the place of the Muslims in India, till the end of his days. Although he wished to see peace and good will between the various peoples in India, he could no longer think of an Indian nation, "in view of India's infinite variety in climates, races, languages, creeds and social systems."[21]

Soon after his return to India, Iqbal wrote:

Islam is something more than a creed, it is also a community, a nation. The membership of Islam as a community is not determined by birth, locality or naturalisation. The expression "Indian Muhammedan," however convenient it may be, is a contradiction in terms; since Islam in its essence is above all conditions of time and space. Nationality with us is a pure idea, it has no geographical basis. But in as much as the average man demands a material center of nationality, the Muslim looks for it in the holy town of Mecca, so that the basis of Muslim nationality combines the real and the ideal, the concrete and the abstract.[22]

The transition from India to Hejaz has been made, and Iqbal has arrived, quite conclusively, at what is perhaps the most significant idea in his political philosophy—the extraterritorial, supranational character of the Islamic community.

The first corollary of this idea is the rejection of a social order which is subject to the limitations of territory or is nationalistic in outlook. But Iqbal was loath to reject anything outright. He recognized that "the idea of nationality is certainly a healthy factor in the growth of communities."[23] He also believed that it was not always necessary to reject nationalism, for it was not always inconsistent or incompatible with Islam.

It comes into conflict with Islam only when it begins to play the role of a political concept and claims to be a principle of human solidarity demanding that Islam should recede to the background of a mere private opinion and cease to be a living factor in the national life. In Turkey, Persia, Egypt and other Muslim countries it will never become a problem. In these countries the Muslims constitute an overwhelming majority and their minorities, i.e., Jews, Christians, and Zoroastrians, according to the law of Islam, are either "People of the Book" or "like the People of the Book," with whom the law of Islam allows free alliances. It becomes a problem for the Muslims only in countries where they happen to be in a minority, and nationalism demands their complete self-effacement. In majority countries, Islam accommodates nationalism, for there Islam and nationalism are practically identical, in minority countries it is justified in seeking self-determination as a cultural unit. In either case, it is thoroughly consistent with itself.[24]

Why did Iqbal move away from nationalism? Certainly the ravages of fierce nationalism he had witnessed in the West influenced his judgment. Nationalism was considered by Iqbal to be a "subtle form of idolatry; a deification of a material object," and consequently, "what was to be demolished by Islam could not be made the very principle of its structure as a political community."[25]

Iqbal also saw nationalism as a weapon of European imperialism: "I have been repudiating the concept of nationalism since the time when it was well-known in India and the Muslim world. At the very start it had become clear to me from the writings of European authors that the imperialistic designs of Europe were in great need of this effective weapon—the propagation of the European conception of nationalism in Muslim countries—to shatter the religious unity of Islam in pieces."[26] It is suggested sometimes that Iqbal repudiated nationalism because nationalism was a Western concept, and that he was opposed to all things Western. This is palpably untrue; he has given many reasons for his attitude, and there is no reason to doubt them.

The narrowness of the political concept of nationalism was Iqbal's greatest difficulty in accepting it. "From nationalism thoughts naturally turn more towards the idea that mankind has been so sharply divided into nations that it is impossible to bring about unity among them."[27]

## Development of Political Philosophy

Such a concept could not but be opposed to the universal nature of his vision.

Why did Iqbal move away from nationalism and toward the conception of the Islamic community? The psychological and religious orientation of Iqbal's early education offers a partial explanation,* but there are other, perhaps far more important, reasons to be taken into account.

In order to appreciate Iqbal's dedication to the Islamic community, one must first grasp the concept of the *millat* (Islamic community). Iqbal repeatedly stressed that it was not a narrow concept:

It is not the unity of language or country or the identity of economic interest that constitutes the basic principles of our nationality. It is because we all believe in a certain view of the universe and participate in the same historical tradition that we are members of the society founded by the Prophet of Islam. Islam abhors all material limitations, and bases its nationality on a purely abstract idea objectified in a potentially expansive group of concrete personalities. It is not dependent for its life principle on the character and genius of a particular people. In its essence, it is non-temporal, non-spatial.[28]

The second characteristic of the *millat* was its homogeneity. Ideally, Islam was a great unifying force; the unity it could achieve would be a "true and living" unity.

The law of Islam does not recognise the apparent natural differences of race, nor the historical differences of nationality. The political ideal of Islam consists in the creation of a people born of a free fusion of all races and nationalities. Nationality with Islam is not the highest limit of political development; for the general principles of the law of Islam rest on human nature, not on the peculiarities of particular people. The inner cohesion of such a nation would consist not in ethnic or geographic unity, not in the unity of language or social tradition, but in the unity of the religious and political ideal; or in the psychological fact of "like-mindedness."[29]

For Iqbal, "like-mindedness" was a necessary condition for the fulfillment of his ideal. The lack of this "like-mindedness," implying the absence of unanimity of aims and purposes, as well as of mutual faith and good will, made Iqbal doubt the ideal of a nationhood for India. In 1909, he had written: "I have myself been of the view that

---

*For this aspect of Iqbal's life, see pages 6–8.

religious differences should disappear from this country [India], and even now act on this principle in my private life. But now I think that the preservation of their separate national entities is desirable for both the Hindus and Muslims. The vision of a common nationhood for India has a poetic appeal, but looking to the present conditions and the unconscious trends of the two communities, appears incapable of fulfillment."[30] In 1927 he repeated the same thought: "The talk of a united nationalism is futile and will perhaps remain so for a long time to come. The word has existed on the lips of the people of this country for the last fifty years, and like a hen it has cackled a great deal without laying a single egg . . . in this country one community is always aiming at the destruction of the other community. . . . the present state of things is such that the communities do not trust each other; they have no faith in each other."[31]

Consequently, Iqbal asked himself an important rhetorical question: "Look at the history of mankind, it is an unending succession of deadly combats, blood feuds, and internecine wars. Now the question arises as to whether in these circumstances it is possible to bring forth a community, the basis of whose collective life will be peace and goodwill."[32] Iqbal had come to believe that the Islamic *millat* was such a political community.

Iqbal adopted the conception of the Islamic community as a gradual unveiling of his vision because "the ideal territory for this nation would be the whole earth," but some critics believed it made his philosophy narrower in scope. For instance, Dickinson, in reviewing Iqbal's *Asrār-i Khudi* (The Secrets of the Self), said: "Thus, while Mr. Iqbal's philosophy is universal, his application of it is particular and exclusive. Only Muslims are worthy of the Kingdom. The rest of the world is either to be absorbed or excluded."[33]

Iqbal answered thus:

The humanitarian ideal is always universal in poetry and philosophy, but if you make it an effective ideal and work it out in actual life you must start, not with poets and philosophers, but with a society exclusive in the sense of having a creed and well defined outline, but ever enlarging its limits by example and persuasion. Such a society according to my belief is Islam. This society has so far proved itself a more successful opponent of the race-idea which is probably the hardest barrier in the way of the humanitarian ideal . . . it is in view of practical and not patriotic considerations . . . that I am compelled to start with a specific society [e.g., Islam] which, among the societies of the world, happens to be the only one suitable to my purpose. All men and not Muslims alone, are meant for the Kingdom of God on earth, provided they say goodbye to their idols of race and nationality and treat one another as personalities. The object of my Persian poems is not to make out a case for Islam: my aim is simply to discover a universal social reconstruction, and in this endeavour, I find it philosophically impossible to ignore a social system which exists with the express object of doing away with all the distinctions of caste, rank and race, and which, while keeping a watchful eye on the affairs of the world, fosters a spirit of unworldliness so absolutely essential to man in his relation with his neighbours.[34]

Iqbal referred repeatedly to the universality of his ideal. The question then arises: If Islam is extraterritorial and supranational, why was it not sufficient for Iqbal to have exposed the limitations of the political concept of nationalism? Why did he work so hard to win points of material political importance for the Indian Muslims? Did his policy differ from his theory? How, in the final analysis, is it possible for his antinationalism to be compatible with the nationalist movement—of which he was a pioneer—which resulted in Pakistan? In view of Iqbal's ideal it would not be difficult to answer these questions. In a word: having willed the end, he had to will the means to achieve the end.

In practical terms Iqbal interpreted the unity of man's spiritual and material life as a double-edged intellectual weapon. He asserted that the *Mullas* who considered themselves responsible for the Muslims' spiritual welfare could not justifiably condemn material progress as profane. And those who were concerned with the temporal side of life could not isolate it from the spiritual aspect. Material progress, although necessary, could not be regarded as sufficient in itself. Standing between the two world views, Iqbal maintained:

> Body lives and spirit lives
> By the life their union gives.[35]

If it had been possible to separate the spirit from the body, then it would have been possible to separate the church from the state. A British Catholic, for example, could owe spiritual allegiance to the Pope and temporal allegiance to the Queen of England. But in Islam the religious order could not be separated from the temporal order. To believe that "religion is the private affair of the individual, and has nothing to do with what is called man's temporal life," was to deny that "spirit and matter, Church and State, are organic to each other."[36] Islam as an extraterritorial and supranational polity was concerned with the total life of man and could not confine itself to its spiritual aspect alone. In Iqbal's words, it was an "individual experience creative of a social order. Its immediate outcome is the fundamentals of a policy with implicit legal concepts whose civic significance cannot be belittled merely because their origin is revelational. The religious ideal of Islam, therefore, is organically related to the social order in which it was created. The rejection of one will eventually involve the rejection of the other."[37]

For Iqbal, "the ideal nation does already exist in germ," but the germ had to grow. The incipient nation needed political guidance and intellectual direction. Iqbal provided this leadership, employing the philosophic concept of the individual ego and the collective ego of the Muslims. "Just as in the individual life the acquisition of gain, protection against injury, determination for action, and appreciation of higher values, are all dependent upon the gradual development of the ego-consciousness, its continuity, enhancement and consolidation, similarly the secret of the life of nations and people depends on the same process, which can be described as the development, preservation and consolidation of the communal ego."[38]

Under what political and psychological conditions could the collective ego flourish? Iqbal explained that "Muslim society, with its remarkable homogeneity and inner unity, has grown to be what it is under the pressure of the laws and institutions associated with the culture of Islam." In an environment in which the Islamic culture could not develop, the individual would not become "a living member of the Muslim community." In order to internalize the values of Islam the individual

> must thoroughly assimilate the culture of Islam. The object of the assimilation is to create a uniform mental outlook, a peculiar way of looking at the world, a certain standpoint from where to judge the value of things which sharply defines our community, and transforms it into a corporate individual giving it a definite purpose and ideal of its own . . . . the mental outfit of the individual belonging to the Muslim community must be mainly formed out of the material which the intellectual energy of his forefather has

produced, so that he may be made to feel the continuity of the present with the past and the future.[39]

Obviously, Iqbal felt strongly about preservation of Muslims' cultural identity. He stated unequivocally: "That which really matters is a man's faith, his culture, his historical tradition. These are the things which, in my eyes, are worth living for and dying for, and not the piece of earth with which the spirit of man happens to be temporarily associated." Referring to Nehru's concept of organic nationalism, Iqbal asserted that if Nehru stood for "the fusion of the communities in a biological sense," he could not subscribe to such a notion. This would have destroyed the entity of Muslim collective life in India, completely thwarting the realization of Iqbal's ideal.

In order to create the intellectual climate for the development of the Muslims' collective ego in India, it was necessary to achieve "self-determination as a cultural unit."[40] Political and territorial separation explicit in the concept of self-determination may be sought as an end in itself, or it may be only a means to an end. Political power for Iqbal was a means to an end (the end being the preservation of Muslim identity), not an end in itself. To M. A. Jinnah, he wrote: "It is absolutely necessary to tell the world both inside and outside India, that the economic problem is not the only problem in the country. From the Muslim point of view, the cultural problem is of much greater consequence to most Indian Muslims."[41]

Iqbal stressed that "the Indian Muslim is entitled to full and free development on the lines of his own culture and tradition in his own Indian homeland." Did he believe this right could be exercised in India? On March 20, 1937, less than a year before his death, Iqbal again wrote to Jinnah: "The enforcement and development of the *Sharia't* of Islam is impossible in this country without a free Muslim State or states."[42] Actually, he had publicly stated this idea in the presidential address to the annual session of the Muslim League in 1930: "The life of Islam as a cultural force in this country very largely depends on its centralization in a specified territory." To Iqbal a "consolidated North-West Indian Muslim State" appeared "to be the final destiny of Muslims, at least of North-West India." This state was to be part of a confederation as a "Muslim India within India."[43]

Would Iqbal have supported the idea of Pakistan as a sovereign state? It is almost certain that he would have done so. The question for him (had he been alive in 1947) would not have been to choose between nationalism or antinationalism. It would have been the preservation of Islamic culture in India. In 1930 he had put forward a suggestion for a Muslim state in India, believing that this end could be achieved. But if his suggestion had proved unworkable or unacceptable he would have accepted any alternative means of achieving the desired goal. If the territorial unity of India had appeared detrimental to the cultural identity of the Muslims, undermining their solidarity, Iqbal would have emphatically rejected it. However, the creation of Pakistan would have been for Iqbal only a means to achieving a universal brotherhood of man baptized with love.

Although this interpretation of his ideas sounds hypothetical, even a casual reading of his published views leads one to believe that they are in accord with the overall pattern of his thought. Only four and one-half months before his death Iqbal reiterated these ideas in a New Year message broadcast on January 1, 1938 from the Lahore radio station:

National unity is not a very durable force. Only one unity is dependable and that unity is brotherhood of man, which is above race, nationality, colour or language, and so long as this so-called democracy, this accursed nationalism and this degraded imperialism are not shattered; so long as men do not demonstrate by their actions that they believe that the whole world is the family of God; so long as distinctions of race, colour and geographical nationalities are not wiped out completely they will never be able to lead a happy and contented life, and the beautiful ideals of liberty, equality and fraternity will never materialize.[44]

## IQBAL AND SOCIALISM

IN recent years, Iqbal's attitude toward socialism has been the subject of growing interest. Iqbal was sympathetic to the socialist movement because he regarded it "as a storm that sweeps away all the foul airs in the atmosphere." Khalifah 'Abdūl Hakīm explains the factors which might have determined Iqbal's attitude toward socialism:

The *laissez-faire* capitalism of the industrial West had pulverised humanity into hostile national groups, and within every nation too there was class war because the classes of haves and have-nots were at loggerheads. His [Iqbal's] own country was predominantly an agricultural country where no industrial proletariat had developed but the conflict of the landlord and the tenant was becoming an acute socio-economic problem. The usurious money-lender was even more callous than the landlord. Through usury and the judicial support of the system set up by British in complete disregard of local traditions, the ownership of land was rapidly passing into the hands of money-lending owners who did nothing to improve the soil or the condition of the tiller. Iqbal would welcome a revolution in which the do-nothing absentee landlord, or the usurious money-lender, is swept away.[45]

However, the revolution of Iqbal's choice was not along the lines of communistic socialism with its ideal of absolute equality, representing "an unlimited extension of the ideal of the family to the State" and finding its expression in the maxim "from each according to his capacity, to each according to his needs." It was more along the lines of the socialism which has as its ideal "not a mechanical equality of all members of society, but rather a potential equality in the sense of the maxim of Saint-Simon's followers: 'From each according to his capacity, to each according to his merit,' which has as its fundamental tenet not common ownership, but the elimination of all unearned increment."[46]

Iqbal's sympathy for socialism flowed out of his passionate dislike for injustice and despotism. Economic injustice had starved and depraved the body and religious despotism had shackled the spirit. As demonstrated in his poem *Lenin Khudā Kay Hadhūr Mein* (Lenin before God), he was one with Lenin when the latter protested against Western civilization:

> What they call commerce is a game of dice:
> For one, profit, for millions swooping death.
> There science, philosophy, scholarship, government
> Preach man's equality and drink man's blood.[47]

Iqbal was also relieved to see the house of God purged of idols:

> Unsearchably God's edicts move; who knows
> What thoughts are stirring deep in the world-mind!
> Those are appointed to pull down, who lately
> Held it salvation to protect, the priests;
> On godless Russia the command descends:
> Smite all the Baal and Dagons of the Church![48]

That Russia was godless, Iqbal knew. That she would remain godless he did not anticipate, as he wrote to Sir Francis Younghusband: "The present negative state of Russian mind will not last indefinitely, for no system of society can rest on an atheistic basis."[49] Iqbal attacked "Atheist Socialism" but never socialism, for to him "Bolshevism plus God is almost identical."[50] In a letter to Jinnah he wrote: "If Hinduism accepts social democracy, it must necessarily cease to be Hinduism. For Islam the acceptance of social democracy in some suitable form is not a revolution but a return to the original purity of Islam."[51]

It is sometimes asserted that Iqbal did not know what socialism was. There are of course several interpretations of the doctrine of socialism. Marxist interpretation describes dialectical materialism as scientific socialism. To be a dialectic materialist is "to regard nature as primary, to hold that matter is independently real and that the mental develops out of the material and must be explained in physical terms. This view has to be understood as negation of the Hegelian idealism. The reality of thought and other mental phenomena is not denied, only their primacy. Idealism and materialism are treated as being the only possible philosophical positions."[52] There is no indication in Iqbal's ideas, however, "that there is a dichotomony of matter and spirit,"[53] as has been maintained by Professor W. C. Smith. To say that man has spiritual as well as physical needs is not necessarily to admit the duality of spirit and matter. Had Iqbal admitted such a duality, he could not logically have claimed that the union of religion with socialism would amount to Islam. (Here Islam is a symbol of man's material and spiritual unity and development.) Obviously such a statement assumes an organic relationship between matter and spirit. Denying the primacy of the material phenomena over the spiritual, Iqbal rejected the Marxist determination of dialectical materialism. Does this rejection amount to lack of knowledge or understanding? It has never been explained.

Smith has rather naïvely maintained that Iqbal's writings are "throughout tinged socialistically,"[54] while saying at the same time that Iqbal did not know what socialism was. Should it be inferred that Iqbal wrote socialistically without any understanding of this doctrine? Since Iqbal wrote on socialistic themes he obviously adopted a brand of socialism. According to *The Encyclopaedia of the Social Sciences*, the six characteristics common to all socialistic ideologies throughout history are: "First, a condemnation of the existing political and social order as unjust; second, an advocacy of a new order consistent with moral values; third, a belief that this ideal is realizable; fourth, a conviction that the immorality of the established order is traceable not to a fixed world order or to the changing nature of man but to corrupt institutions; fifth, a programme of action leading to the ideal through a fundamental remoulding of human nature or of institutions or both; and sixth, a revolutionary will to carry out this programme."[55] All these characteristics are present in Iqbal's sociopolitical thought.

## DEMOCRACY OR DEMOCRACY OF THE WEST

It is often asserted that Iqbal did not believe in democracy. Iqbal did indeed write against democracy, but criticism is not rejection, and it should be remembered that he wrote much in favor of it as well.

It was not democracy itself but "democracy of the West" that Iqbal had difficulty in accepting. Western democracy, in his view, was a cover for far too many injustices. It was, for instance, a weapon in the hands of imperialism and capitalism:

> The democracy of the West is the same old organ,
> Which strikes the selfsame note of Imperialism;
> That which thou regard'st as the fairy Queen of Freedom
> In reality is the demon of autocracy clothed in the garb
> of deception.
> Legislation, reforms, concessions, rights and privileges
> In the materia medica of the West are but sweet narcotics.
> The heated discussions of assemblies
> Are the camouflage of capitalists.[56]

Iqbal was outraged because Western democracies used individuals and nations as means to an end, not as ends in themselves. Other aspects of democracy did not particularly appeal to Iqbal, and he pointed them out forthrightly: "Democracy means rows," he said, referring to the endless debate and controversy, not always very constructive, that seemed prevalent in democracies; "it lets loose all sorts of aspirations and grievances," which may have an anarchic tendency; "it arouses hope and ambitions often quite impractical."[57] Iqbal also indicated some misgivings about democracy's addiction to excessive legalism:

"Democracy has a tendency to foster the spirit of legality. This is not in itself bad; but unfortunately it tends to displace the purely moral standpoint, and to make the illegal and wrong identical in meaning." Although Iqbal was apprehensive of the difficulties created by democratic processes, he did not despair of this form of government. "Democratic government," he said, "has attendant difficulties but these are difficulties which human experience elsewhere has shown to be surmountable."[58]

The common assumption of Iqbal's disbelief in democracy rests largely on his satirical view that democracy "counts" rather than "weighs" people:

> Run away from the democratic form [of government],
> Be a slave to a wise man,
> For even the brains of two hundred donkeys
> Do not produce the thought of a man.

In order to appreciate Iqbal's satire one must grasp his total philosophy and his distinction between "individuality" and "personality," which has been so admirably highlighted by J. J. Houben:

The notion of personality . . . does not refer to matter as individuality does. It refers to the highest and deepest dimension of being. Personality is rooted in the spirit and it constitutes the secret depth of an ontological structure, a source of dynamic unity and inner unification. The spirit forms personality, enlightens and transfigures the biological individual and makes it the concrete fulness of life . . . . The community too readily recognizes what belongs to the world of matter, meanwhile being blind to the reality of the spirit. It sees in men only the shadow of real personality, namely the material individuality. The consequence is that the person is enslaved to the social body.[59]

Iqbal's criticism that in a democracy persons are "counted" not "weighed" must be interpreted as an assertion that society takes note of "individuality"—which is a material fact, but not of "personality" —which is a spiritual fact. To "run away from the democratic form of government" is not to become enslaved to the body politic. The wise man is the symbol of a fully developed personality, who gives inspiration for the development of personality.

One writer has observed: "Iqbal's 'Kingdom of God on Earth' means the democracy of the more or less most unique individuals possible. The rule of one Wise Man is better than that of an assembly of asses. . . . This superior man with his moral and intellectual forces is the most suitable person to guide the human society. The possibility of such development in a single individual is much more than in many. The decision of a group of people represents average intellect. Thus Iqbal's concept is Nietzschean through and through."⁶⁰

Iqbal's "Kingdom of God on Earth" is, however, a moral not a political ideal, and has no relationship to Nietzsche's "Aristocracy of Supermen" as seen from the moral standpoint. Explaining the concept of Islamic democracy, Iqbal himself outlined his differences with the ideas of Nietzsche:

Nietzsche . . . abhors the "rule of the herd" and, hopeless of the plebeian, he bases all higher culture on the cultivation and growth of an Aristocracy of Supermen. But is the plebeian so absolutely hopeless? The Democracy of Islam did not grow out of the extension of economic opportunity, it is a spiritual principle based on the assumption that every human being is a center of latent power, the possibilities of which can be developed by cultivating a certain type of character. Out of the plebeian material Islam has formed men of the noblest type of life and power. Is not, then, the Democracy of early Islam an experimental refutation of the ideas of Nietzsche?⁶¹

In an essay entitled "Islam as a Moral and Political Ideal" Iqbal said plainly: "Democracy . . . is the most important aspect of Islam regarded as a political ideal." For him, the two basic principles underlying Muslim political constitution were:

(1) The law of God is absolutely supreme. Authority, except as an interpreter of the law, has no place in the social structure of Islam. Islam has a horror of personal authority. We regard it as inimical to the unfoldment of human individuality . . . ..

(2) The absolute equality of all the members of the community . . . ..⁶²

In view of these ideas, expressed with such clarity, it is difficult to see how Iqbal could be accused of being opposed to democracy and the rights of the individual.

The idea that "the individual's truest self in the community alone achieves fulfillment" is scattered throughout Iqbal's writings.

> The community is like an ocean and
> the individual like a drop
> Which, seeking to expand,

> Becomes an ocean. It is strong and rich
> In ancient ways, a mirror to the Past
> As to the Future, and the link between
> What is to come, and what has gone before,
> So that its moments are as infinite
> As in eternity
> Since the Individual
> Alone, is heedless of high purposes;
> His strength is apt to dissipate itself.

He must learn discipline through his interaction with his fellow man. In society he also finds "security and preservation."[63] The individual's needs are not as important as that of the society, for "the individual and his needs pass away: the people and their needs remain." The individual, important as he is, must sacrifice his interests for the sake of social solidarity. "When it is said," Iqbal pointed out, "that the interests of Islam are superior to those of the Muslim, it is meant that the interests of the individual as a unit are subordinate to the interests of the community as an external symbol of the Islamic principle. This is the only principle which limits the liberty of the individual, who is otherwise absolutely free."[64]

If the society as a whole is more important than the individual, then what is the relationship of the individual to the social aggregate? Is the former of greater importance than the latter, or vice versa? The answer lies in the distinction already referred to between "individuality" and "personality." "In so far as the human person entering society is a material individuality, he enters as a part whose good is inferior to the good of the whole." Human personality, on the other hand, "is worth more than the whole Universe of bodies and material goods. There is nothing above the human person except God. In regard, therefore, to the eternal destiny of the soul and its supra-temporal goods, society exists for each person and is subordinate to it."[65]

This brief outline of Iqbal's political philosophy demonstrates that his ideas are not unsystemized, and are by no means strung together like the patchwork of a quilt. If studied as a whole, with a view to their evolution, his ideas reveal an organized system including political, philosophical, and ethical strands. Their rigid separation for an analytical exercise has led several well-meaning scholars to a blind alley and endless personal frustrations.

# 7

# Perceptions of International Politics

## JAN MAREK

IQBAL composed *Ḍarb-i Kalīm* (The Rod of Moses) in 1934–1935 and published it in May 1936. In this collection Iqbal turned from sweet and sublime Persian to pithier and (in India) more intelligible Urdu. Otherwise, his poetry continued in classical Persian form, although he tried hard to use less formal embellishments and metaphors. Nevertheless, his expression became more complex and difficult to understand and was addressed primarily to the intellectual.

### POLITICAL AND SOCIAL THEMES

*Ḍarb-i Kalīm* is Iqbal's only poetic collection devoted to topical, political, and social themes. This is apparent from the subtitle of the volume—*A'lān-i Jang Dawr-i Hāḍir Ke Khilāf* (A Call to War against the Present Times). Iqbal did not incorporate in the volume one long lyric (*ghazal*) but only short poems (*nazm*), each with its own caption.[1] Like an undertone there runs through all the verses a new variation on Iqbal's everlasting theme, the philosophy of the *khudi* (ego) and its development, as well as the need for an active and creative life in accord with the doctrines of the Qur'ān.[2]

What were the circumstances which led Iqbal to a deep interest in world affairs and to a spontaneous reaction to them? First of all, he was stirred by the turbulent political situation in India in the mid-thirties. The strengthening of the freedom movement intensified hatred toward Great Britain and her colonial rule of India. Zealous liberal leaders agitated against capitalism and imperialism, and their moral fervor affected Iqbal and lesser Indian poets of the time.

Iqbal's dislike for the politics of the Western European powers and his scorn of them were further intensified by the unprovoked attack of fascist Italy (August 18, 1936) on defenseless Abyssinia (Ethiopia). Earlier, he had expressed his deep indignation against the actions of fascist Italy in a short collection of Persian verses: *Pas Chā Bayad Kard Ay Aqwām-i Sharq?* (What Is to Be Done, O Nations of the East?). In several passages Iqbal voiced the conviction that it was necessary to put an end to the social order which allows such infamous crimes to go unpunished. He condemned also the dilatory tactics of the European powers regarding the attack on Abyssinia, pointing out that the great powers did not counteract the attack on Abyssinia but only invoked trifling economic sanctions against Italy in the League of Nations. Iqbal recognized that this measure was not prompted by the noble motive of helping the victim, but was an attempt to defend particular interests in Abyssinia. The Western European powers were well aware that the Italian aggression was directed not only against Abyssinia but also against England and her maritime routes from Europe to India and eastward. The policy of England to prevent Italy from establishing herself in Abyssinia was unsuccessful. The Western European states in the League of Nations preferred to temporize until Italy had humiliated Abyssinia in order to share in the spoils. Having sufficient political acumen to grasp the significance of these events, Iqbal challenged Indian Muslims to draw a lesson from the case of Abyssinia. He told them that they could not rely on the League of Nations and the representatives of its member states, who in Iqbal's own words were only "coffin pillagers":

> Fate incessantly brings struggle,
> We must draw a lesson from the plight of Abyssinia.
> The law of Europe placidly and without contest,
> Allows wolves to devour lambs.
> A new order must be established in the world,
> A solution cannot be hoped for
>           from those who pillage coffins.[3]

The attack on Abyssinia led Iqbal to scrutinize more carefully existing world divisions. He suspected that the policy of gaining new colonies and markets was one of the causes of sharpening antagonism among Western European countries. His sense of justice was outraged by the colonial system, which permitted developed nations to subjugate the less developed. Condemnation of the exploitative aspects of European civilization frequently appears in his poetry during this period. In 1934 he wrote:

> One nation pastures on the other,
> One sows the grain which another harvests.
> Philosophy teaches that bread is to be
> pilfered from the hand of the weak,
> And his soul rent from his body.
> Extortion of one's fellowman is the law
> of the new civilization,
> And it conceals itself behind the veil of commerce.[4]

Iqbal's indignation over the case of Abyssinia was so strong that he returned to this subject time and again. In *Darb-i Kalīm* several poems are devoted to it. In the poem *Abyssinia* Iqbal expressed his conviction that the struggle of the European powers over new markets and new divisions of the world must necessarily unleash a second world war. He regarded symbolically the Abyssinian "corpse" infested with poison, which he believed the European powers wished to divide as carrions do their spoil:

> The European vultures still do not know how
> poisonous is the corpse of Abyssinia,
> At any moment this old carcass is likely to fall to pieces,
> With civilization at its peak there is a
> bankruptcy of noblemindedness,
> The nations of the world behave themselves as free-booters,
> Each wolf seeks an innocent lamb.[5]

Iqbal's religious feelings were deeply stirred by the fact that the attack on Abyssinia was made by the country in whose capital city the supreme authority of the Catholic Church is situated. The attack seemed to him to be an insult and an offense to the entire Catholic Church, which professes the doctrine of love and peace among nations. Iqbal was grieved that the Pope remained silent during the military operation against the weak Abyssinians and that he failed publicly to dissociate the Church from the policy of the Italian state:

> Alas, Rome has publicly shattered the adored
> mirror of the Church into bits,
> O Pope, it breaks the heart that this could have
> taken place!

When Iqbal learned of the sanctions the League of Nations had invoked against Italy he wrote a poem, *Mussolini*, which at first glance gives the impression that Iqbal supported Mussolini's invasion of Abyssinia. A more careful examination of the verses reveals that Iqbal instead wished to condemn the European colonial powers which had embarked on colonialism prior to Mussolini, as well as the Italian dictator himself. He referred to England, France, Holland, and Belgium, each of which in the preceding century had reaped great wealth from its colonies; Italy's Il Duce had merely followed in the footsteps of his European predecessors. Iqbal even found Mussolini slightly better than they since his regime did not conceal its motives under the guise of democracy, thus misleading the world. He indicated that parliamentary democracy and fascism have a common goal, namely, the shedding of the blood of innocent nations in Asia and Africa and their enslavement:

> Is then Mussolini's crime unique in the world?
> Exasperation ill befits the European innocents.
> You are kicking into the longings for empire,
> Have you not shattered the goblets of weak nations?
> You have mercilessly despoiled the tents of nomads,
> You plundered the lands of the peasantry and
>     pilfered thrones and crowns.
> Under the pretext of spreading civilization,
> You pillaged and murdered yesterday; so do I today.[6]

### IMPERIALISM

With the intensification of international tensions, Iqbal began to realize the growing danger of a new world war. Even though he was unable to see the menace to European safety in the rise of Hitler, he believed that Italy and Germany had set out on a feverish armaments race. However, he saw the situation in Asia more clearly, noticing, for example, that Japan's longing for Manchuria, which would bring her to the borders of the Soviet Union, was the reason she had attacked China. He condemned each outrage of the imperialist states, busy manufacturing weapons to flood the world with blood:

> If war is to be abandoned it is necessary
>     to educate him [the leaders of Europe]
> Whose bloodthirsty talons endanger the world.
> Europe is wholly immersed in armaments,
> For the protection of false splendor and might.[7]

Iqbal was well aware of the horrors another world war would unleash. In a bitter satire on the First World War written in 1924 he had warned of the prospect of wholesale killing and the bombardment of the people. He realized that a defense against the expansion of the imperialistic states was necessary. Resignation and pacifism were contrary to the spirit of his philosophy; instead he believed in an armed struggle against evil. Since he was accustomed to express his thoughts in the religious terminology of Islam, his call to action was in the name of *jihād* (the struggle for faith against infidelity). He did not think that any European state should be left with the power of warlike expansion:

> We ask the Shaikh, most solicitous about the church,
> Is war evil in the East? It is also evil in the West.
> If such is the law, then is war forbidden
> In Islam and permitted in Europe.[8]

His belief in the necessity of armed resistance to imperialism is associated with consideration of absolute power in general. He pointed out that empires are built with the flesh and bones of innocent people. In order to dramatize this thought Iqbal chose the form of a dialogue between a pirate and Emperor Alexander the Great. In this poem (*Ayk Bahrī Qazzāq Awr Sikander*), Alexander seizes the seafaring marauder and is weighing the nature of the punishment for his crimes. The pirate, however, objects that the emperor with his judgment implicates himself and all his peers, and declares:[9]

> We shed blood alike, robbers are we—
> you on the land and I on the sea.

This abhorrence of brute power led Iqbal to believe that no government based on force can long endure; several poems in *Ḍarb-i Kalīm* depict the meteoric rise and fall of the empire builders.

> Alexander stormed like lightning,
> And we all know that suddenly he died.

or:

> Nadir Shah robbed Delhi of its treasures and a single stroke
> of the sword put an end to his short history.

or:

> There is no longer the Empire of Parvaiz in the world.[10]

Iqbal believed that the common feature of the colonial politics of all imperialist states was the self-assumed role of civilizing the so-called backward countries of Asia and Africa. This, in his mind, was only a welcome pretext for economic supremacy of the European states.

> Where a guardian of civilization is needed,
> The issue, today, is not difficult.
> It is simply that where there are no dice
>     or women in tight-fitting dresses,
> Where it is held an offense to drink wine.

He devoted several poems to the affairs of the countries in the Near East, and supported the idea of the free development of Islamic nations. His poetry opposed the policy of Great Britain, which after a victorious war with Turkey was guaranteed (in the Treaty of Sèvres, August 20, 1920) rule over Syria, Iraq, Palestine, and Arabia. The English had assured the Arabs that after eliminating Turkish rule from the Near East they would modernize their country.[11] Iqbal indicated that the liberation of Arabia from Turkish rule was a mere pretext for colonial domination. He objected also to the British policy of establishing a Jewish state in Palestine because Jews had lived there during the course of history. He believed that the Arabs had a similar claim to Spain, since their ancestors had governed there.[12] Iqbal stated that the purpose of the annexation of Palestine was not associated with trade considerations but rather with dividing the Arabs, and this would be a serious obstacle to Islam's future world ascendancy.

> If the Jews have a right to the land of Palestine,
> Why have not the Arabs a right to Spain?
> The aim of British imperialism is somewhat other
> Than a question of oranges, honey or dates.[13]

Iqbal noted how imperialist politics dealt with different classes and men in order to break their resistance and subordinate their opinions to its aims. He believed that Islam was a powerful dam against social abuse and a protection against bondage. In the poem *Iblīs Kā Farmān Apany Siyasiy Farzanduñ Kay Nām* (Injunction of the Devil to His Political Offspring), Iqbal's devil tells the statesmen of the colonial powers that they should annihilate Islam in the lands they wish to subjugate, that they should drive the spirit of Muhammad from the body of the intrepid Muslim and instill European beliefs in place of the religious sentiments of the Arabs. The Muslim Afghans were adduced as an example of resistance against colonial expansion. Never having known British domination, they resolutely fought for their independence and remained free, presumably because they remained loyal to the teachings of the Qur'ān.

> The man who famine-racked still fears no death—
> Muhammad's spirit from his breast expel!
> With Frankish daydreams fill Arabia's brain—
> Islam from Yemen and Hejaz expel!
> Tear from the true believers their traditions—
> From Khutan's meadows the musk-dear expel!
> Iqbal's breath fans the poppy into flame—
> Such minstrels from the flower-garden expel![14]

### DEMOCRACY

In criticizing European civilization Iqbal often voiced his rejection of the system of parliamentary democracy; he believed that the republican systems of some states merely go by the name of governments of the people. In his first collection, *Bāng-i-Dara* (The Call of the Highway), he wrote:

> The demon Exploitation dances in the garb of
>                                     republicanism,
> And you imagine that it is a nymph of freedom.
> Institutions, reforms, privileges and rights
> Are the saccharin soporifics of Western medicine.

In the 1930s, reasoning from the mistakes of bourgeois democracy, he condemned democracy as such. The chief flaw in a democratic system he believed to be a failure to place value upon the ability and quality of the people and to value instead only their quantity. Inspired by a statement of Stendhal he wrote:

> A certain European revealed a secret, although
>     the wise do not reveal the core of the matter,
> Democracy is a certain form of government in
>     which men are counted but not weighed.

Similarly, Iqbal rejected the ideas of the Indian nationalists and the All-India National Congress. His opposition intensified after proclamation of the new constitution in 1935. This constitution gave only provincial autonomy to the Indian provinces, although Britain looked upon it as the fulfillment of Indian self-government. It is not surprising that Indian public opinion rejected it. Iqbal repudiated it wholly because of its federal provisions.[15] They crippled the national movement and discredited the union of India for which Iqbal at one time longed. He believed that with proclamation of the new constitution the colonial situation in India in no way changed, and he dissociated himself from those who overrated its significance:

> Render lip-service to the ministers of the Government!
> The constitution is new and new times are now here.
> I do not know if it is adulation or truth,
> If someone calls an owl a night eagle.[16]

Detecting sterile constitutional reforms, he compared India to a bird held captive in a cage, which the new constitution did not release to freedom but merely sought to comfort in confinement:

> The pity is the pitiless fowlers mask;
> All the fresh notes I sang—of no avail.
> Now he drops withered flowers in our cage, as though
> To reconcile his jailbirds to their jail.[17]

In the thirties Iqbal's ideal of a free, unrestrained, and active life became perhaps clearer than before. He detested any sort of bondage or enslavement; freedom was for him the basic condition for development of the human personality. He was convinced that without freedom all human capability for goodness is dwarfed. Again and again he emphasized that a free man has courage for all undertakings and an enslaved man for none.

> The thought of a free man is illuminated by truth,
> The thought of the enslaved is captive to absurdity.
> The subjugated are deluded by the wonders of *Pīrs*,
> While a free man is a living miracle in himself.[18]

The greatest misfortune which can befall a man, Iqbal supposed, is to become habituated to bondage. Therefore he complained about India, passively continuing with the glittering serpents in the British imperial crown, and compared its people to a lifeless corpse removed from its grave. It grieved him that India was soul and body sold out to foreigners:

> Your fate, poor hapless India, there's no telling—
> Always the brightest jewel in someone's crown;
> Your peasant a carcass spewed up from the grave,
> Whose coffin is mouldering still beneath the sod.
> Mortgaged to the alien, soul and body too,
> Alas—the dweller vanished with the dwelling—
> Enslaved to Britain you have kissed the rod:
> It is not Britain I reproach, but you.[19]

Iqbal realized that slavery wrests from man the possibility to freely develop his capabilities. The incapacity of slaves for independent and creative action was shown in an allegorical poem, *Ghulāmuñ Key Nimāz* (Prayer of the Slaves), written in 1935 in Lahore at the time of a visit of the delegation of the Turkish Red Crescent.[20] The delegates were invited to the royal mosque for congregational prayer. The prayer lasted a very long time, especially the prostration (*sajdā*) and recitation from the Qur'ān (*qira'ā*), which went on endlessly. In a conversation with Iqbal, the head of the Turkish delegation expressed his surprise at the unusual length of the service. Iqbal commented in the poem:

> The Turkish warrior for the faith said to me after prayer,
> Why are your *Imams* so tedious in the service?
> This simple warrior for the faith and free worshipper
> Did not understand the prayer of the enslaved.
> Free people have a thousand tasks to perform,
> Their longing for activity gives the laws to the nations.
> The body of the enslaved is deprived of the ardor of activity,
> For him days follow nights unbrokenly.
> What is there strange about the service being tedious?
> What have the slaves to do when they are not at the service?[21]

## NATIONALISM

Iqbal's message also contained an element of hate—hate for the foreign domination of Muslims. In a way his hatred was religious in character rather than political; namely, a hatred for the supremacy of the unbelieving English over the Muslim. The Muslims of India, he believed, could not serve Allah and the English simultaneously. He grieved that the Muslim nations of the East had found no one to lead them to freedom. He did not consider either Mustafa Kemal Pasha or Reza Shah[22] to be proper leaders, believing that both sovereigns ruled absolutely:

> The poppy heard my song and tore her mantle;
> The morning breeze is still in search of a garden.
> Ill lodged in Ataturk or Reza Shah,
> The soul of the East is still in search of a body.
> This thing I am may merit chastisement;
> Only—the world is still in search of a gibbet.[23]

Iqbal championed the life of creative endeavor; ceaseless activity is a characteristic theme in his poetry from the beginning of his career until his death. After his return to India from Europe he continued to voice the need for an active life, the lack of which he saw everywhere around him. He did not, however, clarify the goals of activity. He called only for striving in general, for effort as the antithesis of apathy, convinced that the struggle for existence in itself brings out the good qualities of mankind. He taught that men should never desist from activity and that every moment should be turned to account. This necessity for activity is a prerequisite not only for the development of the individual but also for the development of the nation as well. On several occasions Iqbal expressed the thought that a nation which, without striving, awaits gifts from on high will not realize its objectives:

> They have no claim to the sorrows and
>                             delights of tomorrow
> Who today do not bestir themselves and
>                             whose hearts do not burn.
> A nation which is nothing today
> Cannot expect a fullsome tomorrow.[24]

### ART FOR LIFE

In the fourth section of *Ḍarb-i Kalīm* Iqbal expressed his opinions on literature and art. Although he was not a member of the All-India Progressive Writers Association, his opinions nonetheless were similar in certain respects. Iqbal had from the outset of his creative life condemned the theory of "Art for Art's sake."[25]

He saw for poetry the role of encouraging man to noble deeds, spurring him to activity, and calling him to battle against all untruth.

His opinions about literature were merely a practical extension of his philosophical doctrines about the necessity of continuous activity. "For Iqbal, language is only the means for expressing the thought," wrote 'Ali Sardār Ja'ffrī. "What he really emphasizes is the content. For him, the best form was such a form as could in the best way express the content."[26] In the matter of content, Iqbal brought into Urdu poetry new themes and subject matter. No other Urdu writer of the time employed such remote or unusual themes. Although he was to a considerable extent influenced by works of foreign (mainly European) authors, he nonetheless theoretically opposed the imitation of foreign literature, requiring from all true artists original and independent creation. He criticized artists who merely imitated others, maintaining that neither their soul nor their real life was visible in their poetry. He declared that the soul of an artist who did not independently create was dead and that such an artist had nothing to say to his contemporaries:

> In his work there is neither a soul
>                               nor the revolution of the earth,
> It is an escape from the hard struggle of life,
> O that poor unbeliever venerates the shattered pagan
>                               goddesses of bygone days.[27]

Iqbal required originality not only from the writer but also from other artists as well. He deplored imitation of modern European trends in Indian painting because it resulted in loss of individuality:

> How common has the death of imagination here become!
> The Indian as well as the Persian imitates the European.
> I deplore that the contemporary Bihzād
> Lost all of the delights of the East.[28]

During the years between the first and second world wars there began to appear in Urdu the works of several young authors who, influenced by Lawrence's sexual ardor, depicted the intimate erotic experiences of their heros. Iqbal did not like erotic themes in literature because he was convinced they did not serve any useful purpose. He opposed them on the grounds that they encouraged low instincts, destroyed spiritual values, and harmed the nation. In the poem *Hunerwarān-i Hind* (The Indian Artist) he condemned those who in their work overemphasized the erotic motif:

Their opinions bury love and enthusiasm,
In their dark ideas is the tomb of nations.
In their temples they carve symbols of death,
The art of such Brahmins is disgusted with life.
They conceal high goals from view;
They put the spirit to slumber and awaken the body.
The senses of the poor Indian poets, painters
And literary writers are obsessed by woman.[29]

### SOCIALISM

A new factor in the political life of India which arose first in the mid-twenties and influenced the character of the struggle for freedom was the emergence of a class of industrial workers. Simultaneously, there began to arise a new ideology of the working class which became for the first time in India a political factor in the true sense. The influence of socialistic ideas permeated by degrees the youth and leftist groups of the Indian national movement and opened new horizons for them. Reflections of the movement led by this ideology appeared in Iqbal's poetry in the thirties and influenced somewhat his unchanged religious conceptions. He developed a fresh interest in socialism and in the problems of the workers. The achievements of the young Soviet state were already known in India, and in 1933 the Communist Party of India, uniting former Communist groups in the different provinces, was established. It was proclaimed illegal in July 1934, however, and thus could not widely influence the Indian working class.

Iqbal's admiration for Lenin, leader of the October Revolution, is evident in a well-known and often cited poem, *Lenin Khudā Kay Hadhūr Mein* (Lenin before God), from the collection *Bāl-i Jibrīl* (Gabriel's Wing). Iqbal in this poem has Lenin express all the grief and wrath of the working people and their indignation over the injustice that rules in the world. In a subsequent poem Allah charges the angels to destroy the homes of the rich, devastate their fields, and improve the lot of godly serfs throughout the world. Lenin's speech before God and Allah's mandate to the angels certainly cannot be described as an appeal for the overthrow of the capitalistic order. But the fact that Lenin, as a representative of a socialistic state in Iqbal's poetry, defends the rights of workers and condemns the deficiencies of capitalism turns the attention of the reader to the doctrine of socialism.

In the collection *Ḍarb-i Kalīm* Iqbal invokes the spirit of Marx and Lenin to voice disapproval of the exploitative order of Western Europe. In the well-known poem *Karl Marx Key Awāz* (The Voice of Karl Marx), he has Marx assail European economists who intentionally conceal the predatory structure of capitalism and exploit science to serve only the interests of the ruling classes.

> Your chessmatch of research and erudition—
> Your comedy of debate and disputation!—
> The world has no more patience left to watch
> This comedy of threadbare speculation.
> What, after all, sapient economists,
> Is to be found in your biblification?
> A comedy of nicely-flowing curves,
> A sort of Barmecidal invitation.
> In the idolatrous shrines of the Occident,
> Its pulpits and its seat of education,
> Greed and its murderous crimes are masked under,
> Your knavish comedy of cerebration.[30]

Although in the mid-thirties he devoted regular attention to socialism, his interest remained centered in his ingrained religious conviction that the economic basis of socialism was identical with the teaching of the Qur'ān. Similarly, he believed that Islam and socialism had the same aim; to safeguard the sustenance of all people. His opinions never substantially changed. However, he confused a scientific social system with a religious charitable activity initially prescribed by Islam but incapable of removing the roots of inequality. In the poem *Ishtrakīyat* (Socialism) he again disclaimed the oft-cited passage from the Qur'ān: "They will ask thee what they shall expend in alms; say 'the surplus.'"

> From the behaviour of the nations it appears
> That the rapid progress of Russia is not without gain.
> Perhaps it demonstrates at this time the truth
> That is hidden in the words, "Say the surplus."[31]

Iqbal demanded for Muslims a special Muslim socialism. His ideas on this subject greatly resembled the ideas of the Gandhists who wished to show that India had its peculiar culture and who found in Gandhism a peculiarly Indian national socialism. He described atheism as the chief flaw in the socialistic order of Russia, although he conceded that the

Soviet Union had unwittingly accomplished, to a certain extent, the work of God. Iqbal believed that Soviet antireligion derived merely from the failure and corruption of the Russian Orthodox Church. In the poem *Balshewīyk Rūs* (Bolshevik Russia) he declared:

> Those who assumed that the protection of the church
> would bring salvation to them
> Were predestined to be the instruments of the
> destruction of the church.
> Russian atheism was inspired from on high
> To disrupt the old heathen idols of the bigots.[32]

Iqbal conceded that he did not know the economic and social features of the better society for which he longed. In reality he knew neither its details nor its most general features. He simply called for a society which would rest on a foundation of social justice. It did not have to be entirely Islamic. He did not consider whether or not Islam would be capable of becoming a uniting force for a world society nor whether another doctrine would have greater success. Once he said: "If I should become ruler of a Muslim state, I would first and foremost create in it a socialist state."[33]

This wishful pronouncement is long way from social revolution and establishment of the rule of the proletariat. Iqbal was not satisfied with the existing state of society and longed for a change, but despite his frequent invocations of revolution he did not know how it should come about. The well-known Iqbalian discrepancy between thought and deed showed itself here too. He thought of revolution as an obscure mystic force which emanates from hidden sources and, with a stroke, changes the world for the better. He always spoke of it symbolically. Nowhere is there found the suggestion that revolution is a necessary ingredient of social evolution, nowhere does he explain which social class should bring it about. He anticipated only its approach:

> A happy life exists neither in Europe nor in Asia,
> There the spirit is beaten to death, here the heart.
> Within the hearts an impassioned revolution is born,
> The death of the old world already approaches.[34]

With a view to purging Islamic society of all foreign elements, he objected to any kind of progress originating in Europe and continuously fought against imitation of the European way of life. He opposed even English instruction in Indian middle and high schools, saying that it restricted the creative capabilities of the students, killing their individuality. Iqbal was not able to recognize what was good in European culture, what advances society and what is harmful. Because he considered European civilization in general, he repudiated all its components and was prone to believe that its end inevitably approached. Rejecting it for insufficient spirituality and too great an emphasis on the material aspects of life, he explained its ineluctable end on moral grounds:

> The culture of Europe pits heart and intuition
>                               against one another,
> The soul of such a culture cannot remain virtuous.
> What is not clean in spirit cannot achieve
> A clear conscience, lofty thoughts or good taste.[35]

# 8

# View of Democracy and the West

## FREELAND ABBOTT

IT was Iqbal's talent for persuasion that marked him as the founding father of Pakistan. His mission was to persuade the Muslims of the world that their past had been glorious, and that there was no reason why their future should not be as well.

Iqbal appealed to the emotions of men, and to their pride. This is aptly illustrated by a short quotation from one of his most beautiful poems, *Masjid-i Qirtabāh* (The Mosque of Cordoba):

> In the soul of Islam, too, is seen the restlessness of old . . .
> Strangely, divinely; its meaning cannot be told by the tongue.
> Watch! from this ocean-floor—what new portents shall burst!
> Watch! in this azure vault—what new colors shall spring!

Or more directly:

> Wake up, my friend, and defile no more with chains
> The supreme Divine Gift of thy nature born free . . ..[1]

This plea by Iqbal that slumbering Islam wake up, this emphasis on dynamism, on the ability—and the urgency—of the individual continually to develop is the heart of his message. He pictures no run-down, pessimistic, degenerate universe, but one in which the future holds undreamed-of possibilities.

> Art thou alive? [He has God ask man in one of
>     his poems]. Be eager, be creative, be the
>     conqueror of the entire Universe, like me.
> Shatter into pieces what is unworthy of thee;
>     fashion a new world out of the depths of
>     thine own being . . ..[2]

To Americans all this should have a familiar ring. Here is man battling for new worlds—"Come, be a builder . . .," he cried; here

## View of Democracy and the West

is a man urging self-confidence—"You are ordained to be the breeze of spring, to give life again to the dying embers of the East." This could come from more than one American poet.

Much of what Iqbal says has an American "tang" to it. Whether or not he ever read much of Ralph Waldo Emerson's works is not readily known; but if he did, he must have found a great deal with which he was in perfect agreement. The fact that each of these men was sternly unitarian enhances the agreement.

> He that does not command himself
> Becomes the receiver of commands from others.

Is this Emerson or Iqbal speaking?

> On this road halt is out of place;
> A static condition means death . . ..

Who is this? Iqbal? Emerson?

> Do the thing, and you shall have the power;
> But they who do not the thing have not the power.

Is this from Emerson's *Essays*, or from Iqbal's *Bāng-i Darā* (The Call of the Highway)? To try to guess is confusing, for both Iqbal and Emerson, although in somewhat different ways, were nonconformists; both appealed to action; both emphasized change; both were heavily imbued with mysticism; and if Iqbal borrowed from the West, so did Emerson borrow from the East. Each was a poet of a strongly intellectual type, and naturally enough—in view of all this—each on his lyre struck similar chords.

There is another way, too, in which these two great authors are similar. Neither was especially outspoken for democracy—Emerson tended to ignore it and Iqbal to criticize it and sometimes confuse it with other things—but each was in fundamental agreement with the bases of modern democratic philosophy. In *Payāmni Mashriq* (Message of the East) Iqbal observes:

> Do you seek the wealth of meaning from low-natured men?
> From the ants cannot proceed the brilliance of a Solomon.
> Flee from the methods of democracy because human thinking
> Cannot issue out of the brains of two hundred asses.[3]

He has also said that "democracy is a form of government in which men are counted and not weighed." It is not surprising that Iqbal viewed with alarm the concept of political democracy. One must bear in mind that he knew the Europe of 1905 to 1908, not a period in which democracy, as we envision it today, had made a great deal of progress. Although he visited England again in 1931 to attend the Round Table Conference, this was too brief a visit for any significant impressions to have been formed—and the depths of the Depression was not a period in which Europe could show itself to its best advantage.

What really worried Iqbal, however, was not democracy as it is thought of in the West today—a vast complex involving every aspect of man's life and organization while at the same time preserving his individual liberty. He was worried about an institution so completely political that it ignored the other elements of human personality. His picture of democracy, as he used and understood the word, was imperfect, even for his time—although it must be admitted that the meaning of democracy was imperfectly understood by many Westerners and scorned by many others during that period. Iqbal's view of the West was also imperfect. He had not lived in the West long enough really to understand it. He was unable to picture the West apart from imperialism, and he apparently accepted the old shibboleth that the West primarily fosters materialistic qualities, whereas the East primarily fosters spiritualistic qualities—an idea based on the belief that technology supplants religion.

"The conscience of the West is commercial, that of the East monkish," Iqbal wrote in *Armaghān-i Hijaz* (The Gift of Hijaz). Again and again he berated the West for lacking heart, sometimes directing his anger at the Western scientist:

> All that God has marked him by
> Is the speculative eye.
> Love he knows not, and the Brain
> Snakelike bites into his vein,
> Even though his golden cup
> Flowing ruby filleth up.

He also wrote:

> The scientists embellish the outer form of the dead body,
> They possess not the Hand of Moses nor the Breath of Jesus.
> My heart sees nothing [of value] in this knowledge,
> And it yearns for wisdom of another sort.

## View of Democracy and the West

Concerning Western philosophers, Iqbal had this to say:

> Love is dead in the West, because thought has become irreligious.

Of course, Iqbal's indictment of the West, in all its particulars, had been made many times before by Western poets and critics.

> O Trade! O Trade! would thou wert dead.
> The time needs heart—'tis tired of head.
> We're all for love. . . .

wrote the American, Sidney Lanier, just two years after Iqbal was born. And Walt Whitman's comments on science, so similar in thought to those expressed by Iqbal in the lines quoted above, were written eight years before Iqbal was born in Sialkot, at the foot of the Himalayas:

> When I heard the learn'd astronomer,
> When the proofs, the figures, were ranged in columns before me
> When I sitting heard the astronomer where he lectured
>     with much applause in the lecture room,
> How soon unaccountable I became tired and sick,
> Till rising and gliding out I wandered off by myself,
> In the mystical moist night-air, and from time to time
> Look'd up in perfect silence at the stars.

Iqbal's indictment of Western philosophers involved ignoring half of the intellectual life of the West—such as that upon which the entire intellectual awakening of New England was based. Only a superficial glance at the writers whose work marked the flowering of New England will demonstrate this—Thoreau, whose own philosophy of the individual later influenced India; Melville, whose greatest work is a philosophical study of the consuming passion of pride and evil; and Hawthorne. None of these writers, in fact, reflects the qualities that led to Iqbal's blanket indictment.

This is not to condemn Iqbal; it is only to observe that his knowledge of the West was far from perfect, and that his vision of the West was, naturally enough, affected by his position, that of a proud Muslim remembering a proud past, and by his times, those of domination by Western powers.

Sharp as Iqbal was in his protests against the West, only a cursory survey would be needed to point out the parallels between Iqbal's idea that every person's goal in life is to achieve a closer and closer relationship with God and Emerson's idea that the whole man was he who was most involved in the Over-Soul, or the similar idea of Walt Whitman, expressed in one of his more ecstatic moments as follows:

> And I know that the hand of God is the promise
> of my own
> And I know that the spirit of God is the brother
> of my own. . . .

Nevertheless, while Iqbal chastised the Western scientist for being all reason and no love, he also chastised the Muslim Sufi—the Muslim mystic—for being all love and no reason.

> You are looking up to the world of miracles
> [he says to the Sufi]
> While I have an eye on [daily] events.
> There is nothing strange if your eye may change it,
> This world of possibilities is inviting you.

Iqbal believed that man could achieve a closer relationship with God only by developing himself. "Man," he said, "must create his own world." Yet man can develop his highest nature only with love—and this is the reason why Iqbal looked with so baleful an eye on the Western scientist. He saw the scientist as the epitome of a materialistic world—a world without love. What he didn't seem to realize was that both the scientist's modern automobile and the Punjab peasant's bullock cart are tangible, material objects; each is simply a device, like the camel saddle, to improve transportation. Love, in Iqbal's sense of a regenerating spirit, can go into the making of either an automobile or a bullock cart. Science, Robert Frost once said, is a "great enterprise of the spirit into matter."

In the medieval West, when such a concept was not accepted, all kinds of seemingly useless antics were performed in the name of religion. The behavior of such pillar saints as Simeon Stylites, who existed for thirty years on a small platform sixty feet above the ground, or Saint Abraham, an eastern hermit, who did not wash for decades and whose biographer unwittingly wrote "His face reflected the purity of his soul," became almost the hallmark of the devout man of religion. These are instances of the spirit trying to ignore the material, and thus denying part of its birthright. Muhammad knew better. This is what he most of all wished to avoid; his religious genius recognized that religion without humanity was artifice, and humanity without material things is impossible. It is not so much that Iqbal did not recognize this, as that he realized extreme spirituality was as easy to achieve as extreme materialism. He had the example of the Kharidjites of Islam before him —the oldest Muslim sect, fanatical, puritanical, and terrorist—as well as that of the twentieth-century Communists.

The erroneous picture of the scientist described above is somewhat akin to another error, commonly found in both the East and the West —an error represented by the loud lamentations one sometimes hears about the disappearance of craftsmen; people who, living in a world in which machines are regularly designed to tolerances of a millionth of an inch—or less—bemoan the loss of the craftsman of the past who worked to a tolerance of a fiftieth of an inch—or more. Today's navigators send rockets with split-second precision to the moon or around Venus, when only two centuries ago the sailor brought his ship home across a few thousand miles of ocean by dead reckoning—a not very cultivated bit of guesswork. There is something in all men that makes the past seem more attractive, but before one accepts this hypothesis he must make sure that the present has really been viewed in its proper light.

Even if Iqbal did exaggerate in emphasizing the materialism of the West, he was doing no more than some Western poets themselves had done. And he was fulfilling the primary role of every great poet: insisting that men look upon the present in its own light. He was attacking false standards—*all* false standards—not only what he saw as the excessive materialism (and that phrase really means irreligiousness) of the West, but apathy, timidity, passivity, and obscurantism in all its forms. Iqbal attacked these just as he supported individual action, courage, confidence, and respect. His assault on false standards was carried out on essentially religious grounds; his criticism was based on Islam as he understood it. And among those whom he felt were guilty of false standards were many of the religious leaders within Islam. One of the significant things about Iqbal's fight to bring true standards to the fore (so far as the West is concerned), is how this Muslim poet, speaking out of his devoutly Muslim background, paralleled the finest thinking that has appeared in the West.

The democracy that Iqbal assailed, to translate his terms into the Western idiom, was incomplete democracy. The institutions of government are not enough, he said, and the world isn't going to change merely by the adoption of some new voting device.

> These democratic
> Institutions of the West
> Are but the old wine
> In bottles new:
> Except there be a
> Corresponding Reality behind,
> There is very little
> In names: . . .
> There are edifying
> Dissertations of the Right
> Of Man; and impassioned
> Speeches from the Forum
> On the sacred Duties of
> Citizenship; and stormy
> Debates in the Houses:
> But all these are no more
> Than so many subterfuges to
> Get hold of the world's wealth . . .

What is the value of democratic elements of government if they only serve to promote the old conditions, if they bring no relief to the poverty and suffering of many? What Iqbal opposed was not democracy, but any society geared to privileged nations. He cried out against individuals who did not fight to improve their society, who resigned themselves to what was and stopped trying to realize their dreams. He spoke out against those who, afraid of a new order, clung rigidly to the old.

> The life of this world consists in movement;
> This is the established law of the world.
> On this road halt is out of place;
> A static condition means death.
> Those on the move have gone ahead,
> Those who tarried only a little while got crushed.

Iqbal opposed, too, any society that seemed to him without a religious foundation, and all his life searched for some way by which the benefits of science might be gained without adopting the purely materialistic conception of the universe he associated with science and scientists. In a sense, within his own realm, Iqbal was posing very much the same kind of questions concerning the role of science and the scientist, and the control of science, that has so recently occupied the attention of C. P. Snow.

In his sixth lecture on the reconstruction of religious thought in Islam, Iqbal warned that "the ultimate fate of a people does not depend so much on organization as on the worth and power of individual man."[4] He had no liking for monarchy, and in this same lecture proposed a republican form of government; his objection to democracy was not, therefore, based on a dislike for its political institutions, but because:

> Colossal oppression
> Masquerades in the robes
> Of Democracy, and with iron
> Feet it tramples down the
> Weak without remorse.

Such oppression needs to be obliterated, and this can only be done with the appearance of good men.

What is a good man? Said Muhammad Iqbal, it is a religious man who acts; it is a man of right principles who believes in them and in himself. He would agree with Thomas Carlyle who said that the good man is he who unconsciously walks continually in well-doing. Iqbal's universal theme is strongly humanistic; his concept of the self involves a plea for respect for one's self and respect for one's fellow man, too. Reduced to its barest essentials, this is about as good a definition of democracy, as it is understood in much of the West today, as one is likely to find: that form of government and society based upon man's respect for man and upon man's confidence in himself. Even today, the forms are occasionally confused, and the institutionalized patterns are taken for the thing itself. The secret ballot, for example, does not insure democracy, although it makes its achievement easier. Nor does the party system insure democracy—America's history of recurring reform administrations testifies to that. Unless people will trust each other, tolerate each other, no mere political device can assure a working democracy. In this respect Iqbal has a message that is pertinent for these times, when men often seem reduced to numbers, and statistical analysis by itself often seems an open-sesame to the solution of all the problems of human society.

The basis of Iqbal's thought is religious. There are some who would pose this as his major difference with the idea of secular democracy. But this is a difference more apparent than real. Secularism as it is conceived in the West—or, at least, in much of the West—is not a denial of religion; historically, it is an extension of religion: religious precepts are taken from those who claim a monopoly over them and spread throughout the population. What people can exist—except, perhaps, temporarily—without a spiritual foundation? The so-called secular state of the United States is alive with spiritual values; is this secularism? Religious principles, in the comprehensive sense of *dīn*, are taught children all day long. The concept has been phrased this way: "We teach it in arithmetic by accuracy. In language by learning to say what we mean. In history by humanity. In geography by breadth of mind. In handicraft by thoroughness. In astronomy by reverence. On the playground by fair play."[5] Both Iqbal and Emerson would have thoroughly agreed.

Secularism does not mean an aloofness from spiritual values; it means the acceptance of universal spiritual values coupled with a respect for the right of each religious group to indoctrinate its followers and to care for their spiritual needs. Thus democracy, too, has a religious base —no less real and no less important because it is accepted naturally and no one, ordinarily, shouts about it.

The vision of Muhammad Iqbal is not very different from the ideal of democracy as understood in the West. Sometimes different words are used to express the same meaning; sometimes the dead ends of western life appear to be interpreted as its real significance; but the idea and the spirit seem to be similar.

Was it not Iqbal who said:

It is here and now that men and women must learn to live justly, decently, sincerely; it is here that they must ceaselessly cultivate their manifold inner powers and try to control the tremendous forces of Nature; it is here that they must learn to utilize them, not for domination, but for service, nor for repression and destruction but for creation and enrichment; it is here that, by devotion to the highest ideals, they can become co-partners in God's creative activity and can help in the establishment of "God's Kingdom on Earth."

## View of Democracy and the West

Muhammad Iqbal recreated the self-respect of the Indian Muslims—and on this Muhammad Ali Jinnah was able to build. But Iqbal never decided what the good days to come would be like; he merely urged a new awareness on the part of the individual which could only result in new days, brighter days.

On these shores Walt Whitman performed a rather similar service, and the spirit that moved Muhammad Iqbal must certainly have been moving Walt Whitman when he wrote:

> One's self I sing, a simple separate person, . . .
> Of Life immense in passion, pulse and power,
> Cheerful, for freest action form'd under the laws divine,
> The Modern Man I sing.

This, too, was the man of which Iqbal, from his own vantage point, sang.

# III
# PHILOSOPHY

# 9

# Inspiration from the West

## B. A. DAR

THE main source of Iqbal's thought is Islamic philosophy, as he himself claimed, but in developing his ideas he drew upon the wealth of thought available to him from Western thinkers, especially those who developed a particular trend or school of thought —Kant, Fichte, Schopenhauer, Bergson, and Nietzsche.

Kant (1724–1804) and Iqbal encountered similar problems: antagonistic claims of reason and will, science and religion, materialism and spiritualism in an age when man could no longer reconcile his spiritual aspirations with scientific facts. Science in Kant's time asserted that nature explained itself; its events were necessary and machine like. Had it been correct, there would have been no place for free will and a sense of responsibility, no meaning attached to moral endeavors and altruism; and no chance for any transutilitarian ideal in the corporate life of men. Above all, God would have been banished from the world.

### KANT: THE LIMIT OF REASON

KANT faced these problems by probing deeply into the roots and genesis of scientific knowledge. After examining the claims of rationalism and empiricism, he refused to follow the dogmatic method and employed instead the transcendental and critical method, a study of the nature of reason itself. He found that the world of experience obeys the dictates of mind, because it is the creation of mind. The so-called laws of nature are man made; they are not the laws of absolute reality, but are in fact the laws of human interpretation of reality. The first activity of mind is the view of the world in the forms of perception. The experience of the external world conveys only a formless stuff which is apprehended in different forms, as a result of which objects appear to exist in space and time. They are necessary presuppositions to which every experience must conform. The second activity of mind is the view of the world in forms of understanding or categories. It is due to these categories that everything we know possesses certain universal attributes. This function of understanding supplements that of sense; a mere sensation would be a mere isolated occurrence in consciousness. This activity of mind gives meaning and significance to the view of nature.

According to Iqbal, the act of knowledge is a constitutive element in the perception of the world of nature. Discussing the nature of knowledge, he says:

> It (that is, the external world) is independent
>             and yet intimately related to us:
> The ego bound them all by its one glance.
> If anybody sees, it becomes mountain and oceans.
> The world has significance through our seeing it—
> Its tree grows by our growth.
> Ego is the hunter, the sun and moon are its prey;
> They are chained to the strings of his intellectual efforts.[1]

Kant maintains that thinking implies the unity of consciousness: transcendental unity is never realized in the empirical consciousness. This unity of the self is an idea of reason and if we hypostatize our ideal and make it the basis and goal of knowledge, we get paralogism or false reasonings of rational psychology. On the other side of the objective, judgments imply a system in which objects have determined places. The ideal of such a comprehensive and all-inclusive system governs the process of judging. If this ideal is hypostatized, only antinomies of pure reason follow. Uniting both these ideals is the ideal of complete unity, including in itself both subject and object, the complete whole of existence. This is the ideal of pure reason par excellence, the idea of God. Thus, the idea of God is to Kant the expression of the need of reason for a perfect unity.

But, what is not the object of experience cannot be known or proved to exist. This is the limit of reason. Iqbal agrees with Kant that human reason has its utility within the sphere of the natural world, but as soon as it oversteps the limits, contradictions follow, throwing man into the abyss of skepticism. Iqbal's condemnation of reason is not directed against this important faculty of man but against that particular use which European thought made of it, undermining moral and religious values. According to him, the purely intellectual approach when stretched beyond its proper limit leads to the recreation of a veritable hell, the fire of Nimrod. The only safety for modern society lies in what he calls a "wisdom of another sort" or the staff of Moses.[2]

> *Tazah phir dānish-i haḍir nay kiyā sahir-i qadim*
> *Guzar iss dowr meiñ mumkin nhyñ bey chob-i Kalīm.*
>
> Modern science has once again revived the old magic,
> It is not possible to pass life in this epoch without
> the staff of Moses.

What is this wisdom or staff of Moses? To Kant, whose purpose was similar to Iqbal's, this new wisdom lay in asserting that the moral nature of man is as real as the physical, and that the laws governing the latter have no application in the moral sphere. The moral law reveals a life independent of animal nature and of all the world of the senses. In the world of nature, causation and logical necessity reign; in the world of will, man is free and spontaneous. Its regulative ideas are autonomy, immortality, and God, by virtue of which it issues in universal and unconditional imperatives or moral laws.

By following the dictates of the good will man escapes the determinism of the world of nature and enters into the blissful kingdom of ends. In this way Kant tried to save the world of spirit from the encroachment of naturalism. But in the final estimate, his solution, based on the division of the scopes of will and reason, reality and phenomenon, moral law and natural law, marred his view of the ultimate destiny of man. He could not visualize the higher unity where this phenomenal world is seen not as a sphere hostile to man's spiritual progress but as a steppingstone to the realization of the infinite possibilities of man when God becomes his copartner.

Iqbal's approach is more thorough than Kant's. For him the true corrective to overemphasis on the use of scientific reason is faith based on religious experience, which he calls by different names: *'ishq, nazar, 'irfān*, etc. To Iqbal, the "staff of Moses" or "wisdom of another sort" is not faith in moral law, but faith in divine presence. It is only when man is convinced of the existence of God, whom he can trust and rely on, that he realizes the infinite possibility of his spiritual life. The logical limitations of theoretical reason are resolved in the unfathomable potentiality of the intuitive vision. In the interest of securing a complete vision of reality, therefore, sense perception must be supplemented by the perception of what the Qur'ān describes as *fu'ad* or *qālb* (heart). The heart is a kind of inner intuition or insight which, in the beautiful words of Rumī, feeds on the rays of the sun and brings man into contact with aspects of reality other than those open to sense perception.³

Iqbal does not recommend that science should be eschewed. For the progress of society science is indispensable; but the material orientation of science should not allow man to lose sight of the ultimate spiritual reality:

> *Chun nihāl az khak-i aȳn gulzār khyz*
> *Dil ba ghā'ib band wa bā haḍir stayz.*
> Rise from the soil of this garden like a tree
> Be attached to the unseen and struggle with the present.

Undoubtedly, Kant's *Critiques* paved the way for looking into the nature of will as the ultimate nature of reality. This development made it possible for Iqbal to overcome Kantian dualism. Iqbal's more developed idea contains in its all-inclusive intuitive apprehension the categories of pure reason as partial manifestations of the spiritual reality.

## FICHTE: THE MYSTERY OF SELF-CONSCIOUSNESS

AMONG the successors of Kant, Fichte (1762–1814) started his speculation with self-consciousness as the ground of all experience. To him, this self-consciousness was the key to the most baffling problem of reconciling the world of nature, where necessity and mechanism reign supreme, and the world of will, where freedom is the reality.

Fichte divided all philosophical systems into two broad categories: dogmatic and idealistic. If we explain experience as the product of non-ego, we have dogmatism; if we explain it as the product of the ego, we have idealism. According to him, from the pure thing, that is, the object of thought, we can never deduce an idea, a consciousness of the thing and being. On the other hand, if we start from thought, we can deduce both the subject and the object. But an imperfect idealism, says Fichte, regards the ego as merely subject, and from it the attempt is made to deduce the multiplicity of experience. In vain shall we look "for a link or connection between subject and object, if they are not first and simply apprehended as a unity. . . . The Ego is not to be regarded as subject merely, but at once as subject and object."4

This unity of subject and object, thought and being, ideal and real, that is, the ego, is the starting point both of Fichte and Iqbal. According to Iqbal, it is possible to look upon thought "not as a principle which organizes and integrates its material from the outside, but as a potency which is formative of the very being of its material. Thus regarded, thought or idea is not alien to the nature of things; it is their ultimate ground and constitutes the very essence of their being."5

Iqbal thinks that it is possible to show that thought and being are ultimately one only if we carefully examine and interpret experience following the clue furnished by the Qur'ān, which regards experience within and without as symbolic of a reality it describes as "the First and the Last, the Visible and the Invisible."6

According to Fichte, a fundamental datum of all thought is self-consciousness; it is not a fact, but an act. Fichte calls it positing of the ego, which at the same time posits a non-ego. This non-ego is not something outside an individual, existing per se, as Kant's thing-in-itself. It is implicit in the free activity of the self-positing of an ego. Iqbal has incorporated this point of view in the following verses of *Asrār-i Khudi* (The Secrets of the Self):

> The form of existence is an effect of the Self,
> Whatsoever thou seest is a secret of the Self,
> When the Self awoke to consciousness,
> It revealed the universe of Thought.
> A hundred worlds are hidden in its essence;
> Self-affirmation brings No-self to light.
> By the Self the seed of opposition is sown in the world;
> It imagines itself to be other than itself.7

The non-ego thus postulated is not alien to the knowing ego; it is intimately related to it. The world of objects of which we are immediately aware is part and parcel of ourselves. Iqbal expresses this idea in *Gulshan-i Rāz-i Jadīd* (A Rose Garden of a New Secret):

> You look upon the world as existing outside you;
> These mountains and deserts, oceans and mines.
> This world of color and smell is our nosegay;
> It is independent and yet intimately related to us.
> The ego bound them all by its one glance:
> The earth and the sky, the moon and the sun.
> The world is nothing but the manifestation of ours,
> For without us there would be no scenes of
>                          lights and sound.[8]

According to Iqbal, ordinary thought cannot appreciate this unity. It is due to this defect that we are forced to regard the object that confronts the self as something existing in its own right, external to and independent of the self whose act of knowledge makes no difference to the object known. But the life of the ego consists in taking into itself that outside world which it first posits as foreign or external. This is development of self-consciousness.

In Fichte's view, this development unfolds itself in definite thrusts, which he called *Anstoss*. The first thrust creates mere unreflective sensation; the second differentiates the self from its perception; the third transforms perception into a world of objects; the fourth and the fifth thrusts are logico-conceptual assimilation of the world of objects. The last thrust is a break-through, which in one sweep reveals that the ego is the originator of the laws governing its thinking in all the thrusts, from inarticulate sensation to the development of the world of objects. If I could accomplish that step, Fichte remarks, I should know the whole truth about the universe; it would entirely lie within my experience, and I, the finite ego, would become the absolute ego. But in that case, "I" and "the world" would have disappeared, since all are dependent on the opposition of the ego and non-ego. Disappearance of non-ego in the thrusts of the ego means that the ego also vanishes. But the ego is perpetual activity, in which it posits itself, and in positing itself posits the non-ego. Consequently, the life of the ego consists in the eternal struggle to realize the ideal of absolute freedom (from non-ego) and the equally eternal failure to do so. At every step one meets non-ego, opposition, obstacle, antagonism, that is, something to overcome. Iqbal says in *Asrār-i Khudi*:

> It [the Self] makes from itself the forms of others
> In order to multiply the pleasure of strife.
> It is slaying by the strength of its arm
> That it may become conscious of its own strength.
> Subject, object, means and causes—
> All these are forms which it assumes for the purpose of action.
> The self rises, kindles, falls, glows, breathes,
> Burns, shines, walks and flies.[9]

The actual world of experience, with all its things, is the material for the activity of the ego. The ego wills freely the deterministic order that limits it. The moment it does that, it becomes aware that the activities of the deterministic order originated in itself and thus succeeds in overcoming the conflict between freedom and necessity in a consciousness of self-determination. The ego then feels thoroughly at home in the world. This is thus the final problem of morality: to remake our actual world into a new world which is to our liking and suits our aspirations, where the ideal and the real become one; to remodel our environment after a pattern of an ideal spiritual kingdom of ends. Iqbal says, "It is moulding the stimuli to ideal ends and purposes that the total self of man realizes itself as one of the greatest energies of nature. In great action alone the self of man becomes united with God without losing its own identity and transcends the limits of space and time. Action is the highest form of contemplation."[10]

## SCHOPENHAUER: THE TRAGEDY OF WILL

THE world as Will is the reality, says Schopenhauer, while the world as Idea, as represented in the categories of our reason, is an appearance. The world process is one of endless strife and conflict. It is a will to be, no matter how. It is therefore blind, irrational, and amoral.

The pessimistic philosophy of Schopenhauer was determined very largely by his family experience and the political and social conditions of Europe in the first decade of the nineteenth century. The scion of a merchant family, Schopenhauer was born in Danzig on February 22, 1788 and died in 1860. His father apparently committed suicide in 1805, and his grandmother had died insane. Worse still, his relations with his mother were bitter, verging on active hostility.

"The character of will," says Schopenhauer, "is inherited from the father; the intellect from the mother."[11] His mother had the intellect. She was a very popular novelist of her day. Unhappy in her married life, she took to free love when her husband died. Young Schopenhauer reacted to his mother's amours as Hamlet did to his mother's remarriage. Probably this accounts for the half-truths about women which abound in his works. One of Mrs. Schopenhauer's letters to her son sheds light on their affairs: "You are unbearable and burdensome, and very hard to live with; all your good qualities are overshadowed by your conceit, and made useless to the world simply because you cannot restrain your propensity to pick holes in other people."[12] No wonder they arranged to live apart and to visit each other only occasionally like strangers.

Goethe, who liked Mrs. Schopenhauer, made matters worse between the mother and the son by telling her that Schopenhauer would become a very famous man. The mother could not tolerate a rival, not even a son. Finally, in a quarrel, the mother pushed her son and rival down the stairs of her house. Schopenhauer then bitterly told her that she would be known to posterity only through him. Thereafter he never saw her again, although she lived twenty-four years longer.

The great work of woe, *The World as Will and Idea*, appeared in 1818. It was the age of the Holy Alliance. Waterloo had been fought, the French revolution was dead, and the child of the revolution had been confined to the pathetic little island of St. Helena. Will had been defeated, and dark death, the only victor of all the wars, reigned supreme over devasted Europe. Schopenhauer, traveling through France and Austria in 1804, was appalled by the chaos and ugliness of the villages and the poverty of the farmers. The life seemed to have gone out of the soul of Europe.

Schopenhauer was doomed by his circumstances to pessimism. He had no mother, no wife, no child, no family, no country; he had no reason to be in harmony with the world. Small wonder that life was evil in his eyes. Everywhere in nature, declared the philosopher of gloom, we see strife, competition, conflict, and a suicidal alternation of

## Inspiration from the West 195

victory and defeat. Every species fights for the matter, space, and time of the others:

> The young hydra, which grows like a bud out of the old one, and afterward separates itself from it, fights, while it is still joined to the old one, for the prey that offers itself, so that the one snatches it out of the mouth of the other. But the bull-dog ant of Australia affords us the most extraordinary example of this kind; for if it is cut in two, a battle begins between the head and tail. The head seizes the tail with its teeth, and the tail defends itself bravely by stinging the head; the battle may last for half an hour, until they die or are dragged away by other ants. This contest takes place every time the experiment is tried. Yunghahn relates that he saw in Java a plain, as far as the eye could reach, entirely covered with skeletons, and took it for a battle-field; they were, however, merely the skeletons of large turtles . . . which come this way out of the sea to lay their eggs, and are then attacked by wild dogs who with their united strength lay them on their backs, strip off the small shell from the stomach, and devour them alive. But often then a tiger pounces upon the dogs. . . . For this these turtles are born! . . . Thus the will to live everywhere preys upon itself, and in different forms is its own nourishment, till finally the human race, because it subdues all the others, regards nature as a manufactory for its own use. Yet even the human race . . . reveals in itself with most terrible distinctness this conflict, the variance of the will with itself; and we find *homo homini lupus* [man is a wolf to man].[13]

Although Schopenhauer visualized the deliverance of knowledge from servitude to the will in art, his solution to man's woes was greatly influenced by the Vedanta philosophy expounded in the *Upanishads*. (The *Upanishads* formed the concluding portion of the revealed Vedic literature and were thus called the *Vedanta*.)

Ancient Hindu sages required first the study of the *Samhitas* (four Vedas); the *Brahmanas* (treatises encouraging performance of the Vedic rituals) were studied next so that the rituals mandatory for a householder might be carried out correctly. The *Upanishads* were studied last of all; they were to help a householder to retire from the world to a secluded life in forests so that he could understand the meaning of life and the mystery of the universe. (Probably for this reason, some of the *Upanishads* were also known as *aranyakas*, forest treatises.)[14] Although there is a considerable divergence of views among the Hindu philosophers regarding the systems of thought expounded in the *Upanishads*, they generally agree on some fundamental principles: (1)

the theory of *karma* and rebirth; (2) the doctrine of *mukti*; (3) and the doctrine of soul, a permanent entity variously called *atman, purusa,* or *jiva*. In addition to these, the belief that the world is full of sorrow is also shared by all Hindu philosophers.[15] (This note of pessimism runs through all the *Upanishads*.)

In the *Upanishads* the name for reality is sometimes *Brahman* (God), sometimes *atman* (self), and sometimes simply *sat* (being). Realization of the self (*atma-vidya*) is regarded as the highest of all knowledge. Self-realization can be achieved through the control of the lower self, its deep-rooted interests and impulses, and through study, reasoning, and intensive meditation. It is a difficult process—difficult to complete unless one is sufficiently strong and wise to reject what is pleasant (*preyas*) for what is good (*seeyas*). Man is duped when he seeks pleasures, for they are sure to lead him to pain. All worldly experiences are essentially sorrowful and ultimately sorrow-begetting. Dasgupta sums up the pessimistic message of the *Upanishads*: "The greater the knowledge the higher is the sensitiveness to sorrow, and dissatisfaction with world experiences. . . . The only way to get rid of it [sorrow] is by the culmination of moral greatness and true knowledge which uproot sorrow once for all. . . . Through the highest moral elevation a man may attain absolute dispassion towards world experiences and retire in body, mind and speech from all worldly concerns."[16]

So enamored was Schopenhauer with the Vedanta philosophy that he wrote in the preface of his *Welt als Wille und Vorstellung*: "It has been the solace of my life, it will be the solace of my death."[17] It would be misleading to assert that the *Upanishads* determined the direction of Schopenhauer's philosophy; it is true, however, that their pessimism found a very receptive and congenial mind in the philosopher of gloom. Regarding the degree of their impact, Schopenhauer says: "I might express the opinion that each of the individual and disconnected aphorisms which make up the Upanishads may be deduced as a consequence from the thought I am going to impart, though the converse, that my thought is to be found in the Upanishads is by no means the case."[18]

The ultimate wisdom, according to Schopenhauer, lies in reducing one's self to a minimum of desire and will. "The world is stronger than we are, let us yield at once—the less the will is excited, the less we suffer."[19]

# Inspiration from the West

How did Schopenhauer become acquainted with the *Upanishads*? The story itself is a romance of scholarship. In 1640 Dara Shikoh, the ill-fated eldest son of the Mughal emperor Shah Jehan, heard of the *Upanishads* during a stay in Kashmir. He invited several pundits from Benares to Delhi and commissioned them to translate the *Upanishads* into Persian. In 1775 Monsieur Anquitil Duperron (the discoverer of the *Zend-Avesta*) received a manuscript of it from his friend Monsieur Le Gentil, the French resident at the court of Nawab Shuja'-ud-Daulah in Faizabad. Duperron translated it into Latin and published it in 1801–1802. This translation, although not perfect, was read by Schopenhauer with enthusiasm.

## THE JOY OF STRUGGLE

IQBAL's philosophy, on the other hand, is diametrically opposed to Schopenhauer's ideas and the Vedantic doctrines. His message is succinctly summed up in this line of his famous Persian verse:

> *Agar khāhi hayāt under khater zi.*
> Dost thou want life? Then live dangerously.

Like Schopenhauer, Iqbal was the product of his environment and education. He was brought up in a stable lower middle class family aspiring for vertical mobility. The brothers and sisters were not only close to each other but also had every reason to love their parents. It was Iqbal's elder brother, Shaikh 'Attā Muhammad, who financed his education in Europe—a debt Iqbal never failed to acknowledge. When his mother died in 1915, Iqbal expressed his grief in an elegy, *Walidāh Marhūmā key yād Meiñ* (In Memory of My Blessed Mother). Four years earlier (1911) Iqbal had started composing his masterpiece, the famous *mathnavi Asrār-i Khudi*, because the suggestion for this *mathnavi* after the style of Bū 'Ali Qālander was made by his father.

In India the nineteenth century witnessed the beginning of the Muslim Renaissance. Led by Sayyid Ahmad Kan's Aligarh movement, it stood for life and action, faith in the future, and self-confidence. Iqbal fully imbibed this optimistic spirit and participated in the drama of India's political life, not merely as a spectator, but as a dynamic intellectual leader. He agrees with the philosophic premises of Schopenhauer that the process of life demonstrates an unending struggle, and conflict between man and man and between man and the resources of nature. Referring to the Qur'ānic legend of Adam's advent, Iqbal says: "The emergence and multiplication of individualities, each fixing its gaze on the revelation of its possibilities, and seeking its own dominion, inevitably brings in its wake the awful struggle of ages—'Descend ye as enemies of one another'—says the Qur'ān. The mutual conflict of opposing individualities is the world pain which both illuminates and darkens the temporal career of life."[20] Nevertheless, to Iqbal this struggle and strife is not without purpose; reality is not blind, insane, and amoral. Reality, for Iqbal, is a pure duration in which thought, life, and purpose interpenetrate to form an organic unity. It is a rationally directed force:

> The excuse for this wastefulness and cruelty
> Is the shaping and perfecting of spiritual beauty.
> The loveliness of Shirīn justifies the anguish of Farhād,
> One fragrant navel justifies a hundred musk-deer,
> The pencil of the self limned a hundred todays,
> In order to achieve the dawn of a single morrow.
> Its flames burned a hundred Abrahams,
> That the lamp of one Muhammad might be lit.[21]

Whereas Schopenhauer wants to escape from the recurring struggle of life, seeking refuge in "artistic contemplation" and the denial of will, Iqbal accepts this conflict, seeing the development of *insān-i kāmil* (the perfect man) as its underlying purpose. (The perfect man for Iqbal is the Prophet Muhammad.) "True manhood, according to the Qur'ān," counsels Iqbal, "consists in patience under ills and hardships."[22] In *Payām-i Mashriq* (Message of the East), Iqbal has beautifully described Schopenhauer's correct analysis and wrong inference:

> A bird flew from his nest to the garden;
> A thorn from a rose ran into his delicate body.
> He spoke ill of the nature of the garden,
> He bewailed his own as well as others' griefs.
> Said he: "In this world
>     whose foundation has been laid amiss,
> There is no morning which is not followed by evening."
> He, bewailing, reached Hoopoe,

> He removed the thorn from his beak.
> He said: "Get your pain from the pocket of loss;
> The rose became pure gold from the opening of his breast.
> If you are grief-stricken, get cured of your miseries;
> Get acquainted with thorns so as to blossom into a flower."[23]

## BERGSON: THE CREATIVE EVOLUTION

IQBAL owes more to Bergson (1859-1941) than is generally realized. To Bergson, reality in its fundamental nature is a creative evolution.

This philosophy not only obviates the nihilistic and amoral conclusions which follow from Schopenhauer's concept of blind will, but also dignifies the life impulse by transforming it into an infinitely realizing, creating, and progressing movement. Bergson's original contribution lies in his rejection of the various mechanistic explanations of life. Darwinian evolutionism explains life by reference to the origin of new organs and functions, new organisms and species, and the natural selection of favorable variations. Bergson, opposing Darwinism, asserts that there is a vital urge behind this process of evolution. Earlier thinkers had been concerned only with the outer crust of change in the body of the living organism, but Bergson penetrated to the core of the evolutionary process itself and discovered a life impulse, an *élan vital*, determining the tortuous course of evolution. This original and vital impulse operates in such a way that its activities cannot be predicted. The universe grows at every moment, and the gates of the future are always open. Life produces novelties, makes fresh creations, and advances on uncharted seas. In Iqbal's system of thought this principle is axiomatic: all is constant mobility, an unceasing flux of states, a perpetual flow in which there is no stoppage and no resting place:

> Rest and immobility are mere illusions.
> Every particle of the universe pulsates with life.
> The Caravan of life never stops;
> At every stage it manifests itself in a new form.
> You think life is a mystery (No!)
> It is nothing but a continuous flow.[24]

This flow of life is continuously moving forward, growing and developing; it is this ever-changing, continuously developing aspect of life which Bergson calls "duration." Everything in the universe manifests the durational aspect of the life principle.

But are the rest and immobility—reality—illusions? For Bergson and Iqbal, it depends on how one looks at the universe. The common-sense view that the world consists of static and immobile things is meaningful, especially in view of man's biological needs. But if we are in search of the ultimate reality, this point of view projects us into an intricate maze of antinomies out of which it becomes impossible to extricate ourselves. The necessities of our daily life weave a sort of mask over the fundamental reality and, instead of continuous change and becoming, we find distinct, static objects, time divided into past, present, and future, and events happening as if in a line of succession. This view is intellectual; on the genesis of intelligence Iqbal holds:

> Thought, imagination, feeling, memory and understanding—
> All these are weapons devised by life for self-preservation
> In its ceaseless struggle.[25]

But this intellectual way of making the world our own must be surpassed; we must outgrow its utility, for it becomes a hindrance in our infinite progress. Iqbal says:

> Infinity is not amenable to our intellect,
> "One" in its hand becomes a thousand,
> As it is lame, it likes rest [immobility];
> It does not see the kernel; therefore
>         looks towards the shell,
> As we divide Reality into several spheres,
> We make a distinction of change and rest.[26]

To Bergson, fundamental reality is amenable to intuition, which penetrates deeply and becomes one with the life impulse. As we watch ourselves, he shows, we see a tendency toward reciprocal interpretation; our knowing, living self is no longer divided into distinct states; they fuse and interpenetrate achieving simply a continuity, an indivisible perpetual becoming. In this ceaseless change no one moment is the same; there is a complete qualitative heterogeneity and incommensurability between past and present. No sensation, no feeling can repeat itself. The present is forever unforeseeable and new, although organized with the past and so animated by a common life that the whole self may express itself in one state. This indivisible continuity of change is what characterizes true life. Following Rumī and Bergson, Iqbal maintains:

> Free yourself from the snare of night and day,
> Reach within yourself and retire from this noisy world,
> Throw yourself into the inner recesses of your heart.[27]

A probe into the stream of consciousness reveals the continuous flow of life in its exuberance, which is pure time, duration. Iqbal says, "To exist in real time is not to be bound by the fetters of serial time, but to create it from moment to moment and to be absolutely free and original in creation. In fact all creative activity is free activity."[28] Iqbal calls it the vital mode of appropriating the universe. He adds:

A slave is one who, engrossed in the activities necessitated by his being born in the material environment, lacks the necessary initiative to pass beyond intellect to love . . . He becomes naught within the limits of day and night, while for a free man, who, in a single jump, has crossed into the frontiers of love, days and nights themselves become naught. A slave deals in imitations and second-hand material, and his self-experience lacks originality. A free man is constantly engaged in creating and singing new songs at every moment of his life. For a slave time becomes his fetters, and he sings of *taqdīr*, the inevitable fate which awaits him. A free man, on the other hand, is a coworker with fate and new events take shape at his hand.[29]

But Iqbal does not agree with Bergson that this process is goalless and undirected; it would then be identical with Schopenhauer's blind, incessant will. If *élan vital* is blind, unconscious, and aimless, then Schopenhauer is correct in concluding that man should run away from this reality, which not only produces evil but also is evil itself. In order to save the spontaneity and creativity of fundamental reality, Bergson rejected mechanism as well as teleology. According to Iqbal, Bergson's mistake arose from his defective analysis of our living experience. "He regards conscious experiences," says Iqbal, "as the past moving along with and operating in the present. He ignores that the unity of consciousness has a forward aspect also. Life is only a series of the acts of attention and an act of attention is inexplicable without reference to a purpose, conscious and unconscious. Even our acts of perception are determined by our immediate interests and purposes." Elaborating on this point, he says:

Thus ends and purposes whether they exist as conscious or sub-conscious tendencies form the warp and woof of our conscious experience. And the notion of purpose cannot be understood except in reference to the future. The past no doubt abides and operates in the present, but this operation of the past in the present is not the whole of consciousness. The element of purpose discloses a kind of forward look in consciousness. Purpose color not only our present states of consciousness but also reveal their future direction. In fact, they constitute the forward push of our life, and thus in a way anticipate and influence the states that are yet to be. To be determined by an end is to be determined by what ought to be.[30]

Thus Iqbal provides a firm basis for moral order in the evolution of the life impulse. Without the existence of purpose, in his view, life cannot be free and creative. Mere activity without an end is no more than an uncontrollable impulse. All creative activity can be understood only in relation to an ideal.

> Life is preserved by purpose:
> Because of the goal its caravan-bell tinkles.
> Life is latent in seeking and striving,
> Its origin is hidden in desire.
> Desire is a noose for hunting ideals,
> A binder of the book of deeds.[31]

Social organization, customs, laws, science, and art—all cultural achievements—are the result of this purpose.

> What are social organization, customs and laws?
> What is the secret of the novelties of science?
> A desire which realized itself by its own strength
> And burst forth from the heart and took shape.[32]

Iqbal agrees with Bergson that the idea of a teleological causation working from without fixes the whole process of evolutionary development, and therefore deserves to be discarded. But teleology, according to Iqbal, can have a different sense altogether. There is no distant set goal which man is striving for. At every stage of our life, reasons Iqbal, we are working, developing, and shaping ourselves in the light of new aspirations. There is a sort of hormic drive in us which does not let us rest at any moment. We act as if pushed forward and backward from within ourselves. "To live is to shape and change ends and purposes and to be governed by them." The Kantian categorical imperative had its basis in the assumption "I can," this experience of inner freedom and realization of an internal hormic push which moves us at every moment to be something.

Iqbal is thus led to view ultimate reality as a pure duration in which life and purpose interpenetrate to form an organic unity. It is of the nature of a vital impulse which is constantly changing, developing, and creating. But he goes a step further and calls this reality ego—an all-embracing self—which is the ultimate source of all individual life and thought. It is not a blind and aimless drive, but a rationally directed will whose creative activity has no limit. However, to call the ultimate reality an ego does not mean that we are fashioning God after the image of man. Intuition, says Iqbal, reveals life as a centralizing ego. "It is only to accept the simple fact of experience that life is not a formless fluid, but an organizing principle of unity, a synthetic activity which holds together and focalizes the dispersing disposition of the living organism for a constructive purpose."[33] In this way Iqbal goes beyond Schopenhauer and Bergson.

The intellectual approach leads man only to see the attributes (*sifāt*) of the ultimate ego, while the vital approach brings him face to face with the ego himself (*Dhāt*, the Divine Being). This vital aspect deepens the whole being of the searching ego and sharpens will with the creative assurance that the world is not something merely to be seen or known through concepts, but an object amenable to human actions. This manipulating and vital act is born of love; it is capable of creating new values and standards to change the lines of individuals and nations.

It is the perfect man who, according to Iqbal, is capable of this vital act and is the supreme goal of evolution. He is the completest ego, the acme of life both in mind and body; in him the discord of our mental life becomes harmony. In his life, thought and action, instinct and reason become one. He is the last fruit of the tree of humanity, and the trials and tribulations of existence are justified by his appearance at the end of the evolutionary process.[34] This concept of the perfect man or the ideal type envisaged by Iqbal brings to the forefront his relation to Nietzsche.

## NIETZSCHE'S SUPERMAN AND IQBAL'S PERFECT MAN

FRIEDRICH NIETZSCHE (1844-1900) lived in Germany when Europe was at the height of its economic and political ascendancy in the world. Endowed with unique and penetrating spiritual insight, he could see through the superficial veneer of European civilization and feel acutely the inner disharmonies and turmoils of its soul. The problem of the validity of a priori synthetic judgment did not so much disturb him as the moral problem of the categorical imperative. Like Buddha, he was aware of certain intellectual dislocations in the lives of his contemporaries. Passing the stage of metaphysics, he entered the sphere of deeper psychology where one wants to experience within one's self the ultimate reality. In the words of Iqbal: "It is a vital fact, an attitude consequent on inner biological transformation which cannot be captured in the net of logical categories."[35] He looked upon the material prosperity of the time in the same light as did the prophets of Israel. Nietzsche's contemporaries believed in and claimed to follow Christianity, yet Nietzsche proclaimed that God had died and it was the people who had killed him. Thus Nietzsche says through Zoroaster, the sage of ancient Iran:

For the old Gods came to an end long ago. And verily it was a good and joyful end of God!
They did not die lingering in the twilight—although that lie is told! On the contrary, they once upon a time—laughed themselves to death!
That came to pass when, by a God himself, the most ungodly word was uttered, the word: "there is but one God! Thou shalt have no other Gods before me."
Whoever hath ears let him hear.
Thus spake Zarathustra.[36]

The phrase "God is dead" signifies that something that sustained man for centuries has vanished, thereby ringing the knell of civilization. As an escape from the nihilism which resulted from the death of God, Nietzsche placed before his contemporaries the ideal of the superman who would be a god for the common man, his source of inspiration, his lawgiver, and his ruler—in short, the embodiment of all those qualities which people once claimed were possessed by God:

Dead are all Gods; now we will that Superman live. . . .

I teach you Superman. Man is a something that shall be surpassed. What have you done to surpass him? . . .

What is great in man is that he is a bridge and a goal: what can be loved in man is that he is a transition and a destruction.

I love those who do not know how to live except in perishing, for they are those going beyond.

I love those who do not seek beyond the stars for a reason to perish and be sacrificed, but who sacrifice themselves to earth in order the earth may some day become Superman's. . . .

It is time for man to mark his goal. It is time for man to plant the germ of his highest hope. . . .

Tell me, my brethren, if the goal be lacking to humanity, is not humanity itself lacking? . . .

Feeling dissatisfied with the Christian way of life, Nietzsche tried the secular philosophies of the day—democracy, humanitarianism, socialism—but found them wanting. To him, such philosophies were but temporary veils over an ultimate conviction of the worthlessness of existence. (The spirit of optimism that seems to characterize them does not and perhaps cannot hide from the discerning mind the basic pessimism about the future of human life on this earth.) "Man has lost dignity incredibly in his own eyes," says Nietzsche. "Since Copernicus man seems to have got upon an inclined plane—he is now rolling faster away from the centre—whither? into Nothingness? into the overwhelming feeling of his nothingness."[38] Nietzsche's diagnosis of the crisis of the modern age was almost correct. It was perhaps for this reason that Iqbal called him Hallaj and a *majdhūb*. It is worth mentioning here that according to Iqbal the famous slogan "Āna'l-Haqq" was a protest against those movements of thought which were trying to undermine the dignity and worth of man.

> Once again this uncrucified Hallaj
> Delivered the same old message in a new way.
> His language is outspoken, his ideas magnificent.
> The West is torn asunder by the sword of his oratory;
> His contemporaries could not appreciate
>             the significance of his experience,
> He was a *majdhūb*, but was regarded as mad.[39]

The basic concept of Nietzsche's thought is expressed in the following passage:

I have the good fortune . . . to have rediscovered the way that leads to a yes and a no. I teach no to all that weakens—that exhausts.
I teach yes to all that strengthens, that stores up power, that justifies the feeling of power.[40]

By power Nietzsche does not mean mere physical and brute strength; it includes control of nature, intellectual and moral strength. True will to power expresses itself in self-overcoming. "Every country and people have their own valuation of good and bad, yet there is something which is found in all these different tables of values and that is: self-overcoming."[41] In man, he says, there is both creator and creature, and Nietzsche's superman is the ideal whereby one can develop the creator in oneself. Unlike Carlyle's hero, who has only instrumental value, Nietzsche's *Übermensch* is a value in himself; he embodies the state of being for which all of us yearn. He is the passionate man who controls his passion, the highest type of free human being.

In *Thus Spake Zarathustra*, while discussing the characteristics of the superman, Nietzsche deliberately uses provocative language. Opposed to the Christian emphasis on benevolence, pity, and asceticism in the character of a good man, the superman possesses what Nietzsche calls three "evil" things: voluptuousness, passion for power, and selfishness. Voluptuousness he regards as a bridge between the present and future. To its despisers (such as the Christian ascetics) the body is a sting and stake, whereas to free hearts, it is a thing innocent and free, the earth's garden of happiness. Passion for power (which is a normal phenomenon of life) is appreciated only by a superman, who knows how to exercise power most beneficially. This passion for power enables the superman to forgo self-sufficient solitude in order to exercise power over lower humanity. Selfishness, the wholesome, healthy selfishness, according to Nietzsche, springs from the powerful soul possessing a handsome, triumphant, and refreshing body. (His ideal of selfishness can best be illustrated in pregnancy: self-nurture for the sake of something growing within, which we hope will be greater than we are.) Thus, this selfishness which he praises is not the mean selfishness condemned by the moralists; Nietzsche himself calls the latter the "selfishness of the sick" and a characteristic of the degenerate. Nietzsche's criticism of altruism in favor of egoism is therefore not an advocacy of mean selfishness but an advocacy of self-perfection, self-overcoming, and self-realization.

The third characteristic of the superman is that he is an enemy of pity and the embodiment of suffering and hardness. The preachers of pity, he thinks, look only to the "creature" side of man; they show no respect for man's spiritual side, the "creator" in him. To pity others or to be pitied by others means to defeat the wholesome effect of suffering; it is the denial of life itself. "The discipline of suffering, of great suffering—know you not that only this suffering has produced all enhancements of man."[42]

Five years after the death of Nietzsche, Iqbal went to Europe and found that his philosophy had taken the whole continent by storm. Nietzsche had predicted the fall of Western culture and suggested ways and means not to prevent it, because, to him, it possessed nothing worth protection. He wished to see the reconstruction of a healthier culture on its debris. His teachings opened Iqbal's eyes to the hollowness of Western civilization.

Actually, Nietzsche's polemics against Christianity and his concept of the superman were known to Iqbal before he went to Europe. Especially regarding the superman, it should be pointed out that classical Muslim thinkers and Sufis had evolved a similar concept, that of *insān-i kāmil*, the perfect man. However, Nietzsche's ideas roused Iqbal to the realization that the panacea he was seeking for the regeneration of Muslim society was not to be found anywhere else except in Islam. As the days passed, this conviction grew stronger; in a poem composed during his stay in Europe, he expressed this new yearning:

> Rise! for darkness has spread on the horizon of the East;
> Let us illumine it by our fiery speech.
> Let us preach the lesson of the principle
>                  of progressive evolution,
> Transform the worthless drop of dew into a river;
> Let the wine be of old and so hot
> That it may melt the heart of the glass.[43]

Iqbal agrees with Nietzsche that Christianity's view of the sharp dualism between body and mind, and its contempt of the body in the interest of the spirit (which Christians inherited from Manicheanism), was greatly responsible for decadence. It was exactly this criticism which the Qur'ān had urged against the Christian hermits. The spiritual life of man can be developed not by renouncing the world of body and matter but by proper adjustment of man's relation to these material forces in the light of inner illumination. Other-worldly mysticism is based on an erroneous belief that the world is a sort of prison house of pain and misery, human instincts and passions, tying man's pure soul to his earthly abode. Salvation, according to this doctrine, lies in flight from this world, in suppressing desires, will, and passion. Iqbal's criticism of this ascetic morality, diverting attention away from this world to the world beyond, is a restatement of the moral code of Islam, which engenders a positive attitude toward both worlds. Unfortunately, according to Iqbal, Muslim mysticism under alien influences adopted the ascetic ideal and called it *faqr*. Iqbal gave this worn-out term a dynamic orientation. In the following verses he contrasts the passive, withdrawing variety of asceticism with the more active kind acceptable to Islam:

> The *Faqr* of an unbeliever is privacy in mountains,
> The *Faqr* of a believer produces commotion in land and sea.
> Life for one is quietitude in caves and mountains,
> Life for the other is honorable death.
> One seeks God by mortification of the flesh,
> The other sharpens his ego on the whetstone of God.
> One kills the ego and burns it out.
> The other illumines the ego like a lamp.
> When *faqr* becomes "naked" under the sun:
> The sun and moon tremble at its sight.
> It was this naked *faqr* which fought at Badr and Hunain
> It was this *faqr* which was manifest in the cry of Hussain.

In another place Iqbal says:

> The boat of a *faqr* is always tossing on the stormy waves.[44]

Iqbal suggests three stages in the development of the ego, symbolized by the load-bearing camel; the rebellious, no-saying lion; and the innocent, incessantly active child who says yes to life. The load-bearing animal symbolizes the basic truth that discipline born of obedience to a particular code of behavior is indispensable for the development of self. In the first stage of ego development man must submit to law as the camel bears his burden, without any complaint. Only nihilistic creeds try to dispense with law. According to Nietzsche, the nihilistic character of Christianity is due to Paul who, as Nietzsche puts it, being by nature unfit to follow the Jewish law, became the apostle of the annihilation of law. Rousseau's advocacy of the state of nature was an anathema to Nietzsche, who characterized it as wild, arbitrary, and disorderly; he wanted the individual to transform this brute nature by a rigorous discipline. "It is only the weak who have no power over themselves and who hate being bounded by style," says Nietzsche.

In the second stage of self-control, the camel in man dies a natural death. Self-control, according to Iqbal, helps man in saying nay to everything that hinders self-development. Thus he negates fears, anxieties, and inner conflicts. He feels free, no longer subdued by weakening impulses or threatening challenges; all false ideas vanish at one stroke; man becomes free of all limitations; Caesar and Khusros are dethroned.[45]

But this nay-saying is only a transitory stage to be surpassed by a new stage in which new structures are raised on the ruins of the old. Where no is separated from yes a false view of life develops, and the society nurtures in itself the seeds of its own destruction. In order to be effective, negation must be supplemented by affirmation. Iqbal epitomizes this important point by referring to the Islamic doctrine of *Tawhīd* (the unity of God; *la ilāha illa-l-lāh*, no God whatsoever but Allah), which negates and affirms in the same breath. It negates what is incompatible with the principle of affirmation. Iqbal's criticism of modern civilization is that it has accomplished the negative without affirming the ideal reality at the same time. He boldly declares that civilization based only on no will go down as others before it have gone:

> In life we begin with no and end with yes;
> When no is divorced from yes it becomes destructive.
> A nation which does not pass from no to yes
> Is undoubtedly on the brink of death.[46]

For Nietzsche, the stage of yes dawns with the joyous innocence of a child, who is all activity, pure creativity, exuberance, and life affirmation—beyond good and evil. To Iqbal, the last stage of man is what he calls *al-abduhū* (divine vice-regent). Nietzsche could not realize this stage, Iqbal believes, because his vision was completely blurred. He could not see the spiritual basis of life, and thus failed to realize the possibility of negations and affirmations unfolding in "there is no God but God":

> '*Abduhū* is the fashioner of Destiny,
> Who constructs buildings out of ruins.
> '*Abduhū* has a beginning but no end,
> His morning and evening are not like ours;
> He is why and wherefore of the universe,
> He is its inner mystery;
> He belongs neither to Arabia nor to Persia,
> He is Adam and also prior to Adam;
> *La ilāha* is a sword and '*Abduhū* is its edge.
> If you wish to know it plainly,
> *Hu* '*Abduhū*, '*Abduhū* is divine.[47]

Iqbal's *al-'abduhū* is his *insān-i kāmil*, the perfect man, who achieves this position by fulfilling the divine will. Among human beings, according to Iqbal, the Prophet Muhammad presented in himself the picture of the perfect man. By emulating him one sees the possibility of becoming divine vice-regent.

Obviously, Iqbal's *insān-i kāmil* and Nietzsche's *Übermensch* are very divergent concepts.

# 10

# The Heritage of Islamic Thought

## A. H. KAMALI

IQBAL'S message was a call of revolt against what he had pronounced as "the Persian encrustation of Islam." He led the most powerful attack on "the state of intoxication" accepted as the supreme ideal under the impact of the Persian mysticism. These two elements in the second decade of the twentieth century distinguished Iqbal's philosophical outlook from that of the rest of the Sufis of the Indian subcontinent. Iqbal was interested in the revival of Islam and in the restoration of its life-sustaining ideals as against its emotional, sentimental, and resigning spiritualism, whose origin he attributed to the development of Persian spirit in the intellectual history of Islam.

Regarding the Persian impact on Islam, Iqbal remarked:

The search for inner meanings or perception of hidden meanings in the code of a religion or way of life of a nation amounts to its nullification. This is a very subtle method of abrogation adopted by those who are sheep-like in their fundamental nature. Most of the Persian poets, by their very inherent tendency had an inclination towards the doctrine of the unity of existence. This tendency was present in Persia before the rise of Islam. The latter was, however, able to hold it back for some time, but Persia's dormant or natural instinct was bound to make its appearance at the first available opportunity with ever more vigor, and there started pouring into Islam a literature which was based on the doctrine of the unity of existence. The Persian poets tried to undermine the way of Islam, by a very round-about, though apparently, heart alluring manner. They denounced every good thing of Islam; if Islam looked upon poverty as an evil, Sanai admired it as an excellence; struggle in the way of Allah is deemed necessary in Islam; the Persian poets attempted to interpret it with new meanings, and made contemplation in a monastery the highest crusade in the way of God.[1]

About the ideal of intoxication considered to be the product of the Persian spiritualism, Iqbal wrote, "The Sufis have smuggled, without any hesitation, Persian and Greek ideas into the body of Islam. The first poet of Sufism is Iraqi, who has versified the teachings of Ibn al-'Arabi, and the last poet is Hāfiz; it is surprising that the whole poetry of Sufism in Islam was produced in the period of political decline. The nation which exhausts its fund of energy and power, as was the case with the Muslims after the Tartarian invasions, undergoes a change of outlook. Then weakness becomes for it an object of beauty and appreciation; and resignation from the world a source of satisfaction."[2]

Discussing contemporary Muslim society, Iqbal remarked in 1917 that

the present-day Muslim prefers to roam about aimlessly in the valley of Hellenic-Persian mysticism, which teaches us to shut our eyes to the hard reality around, and to fix our gaze on what is described as "illumination"— blue, red, and yellow reality springing from the cells of an over-worked brain. To me this self-mystification, this nihilism, i.e., seeking reality where it does not exist, is a physiological symptom, giving me a clue to the decadence of the Muslim world. The intellectual history of the ancient world reveals this most significant fact that the decadents in all ages tried to seek shelter behind self-mysticism and nihilism. Having lost the vitality to grapple with the temporal, these prophets of decay apply themselves to the quest of a supposed eternal, and gradually complete the spiritual impoverishment and physical degeneration of their society by evolving a seemingly charming ideal of life which reduces the healthy and powerful to death.[3]

Maintaining its historical continuity with the main core of Muslim culture and its basic ideology, Iqbal's thought made a significant advance. Iqbal is therefore not just a mirror of Bergson, Nietzsche, Schopenhauer, and Berkeley; he is truly a successor of Ghālib, Beidil, Sarhindi, Rumi, and al-Junayd, synthesizing their ideas for the modern age. "I claim that the philosophy of the *Asrār* [*-i Khudi*]," wrote Iqbal in a letter to R. A. Nicholson, "is a direct development out of the experiences and speculation of old Muslim Sufis and thinkers. . . . It is unfortunate that the history of Muslim thought is so little known in the West." "What I have written," he explained to Akbar Allahabadi, "is not a new thing; Ala-al-Daulah Sanjani and Junayd Baghdadi have written on this theme before me." He also wrote to Sayyid Sulaiman Nadwi: "Objection against syllogism was probably first raised by Razi; al-Ghazzali, Ibn Taimiyya, and perhaps Shaikh Suhurwardi al-Maqtul have also dealt with this problem. The latter arrived at conclusions which are in their nature very close to modern researches. I have made some studies of Time and Space and (in this connection) have come to realize that the Muslims of India thought over great problems, and a history of their thought and contribution must be attempted."[4]

Although Iqbal's philosophy is considerably influenced by Western thinkers, it remains directly linked with the main currents of Muslim thought. In substance Iqbal contradicts the world view of the Great Decadence which had swept the Muslim world after the Mongol invasions, causing the political disintegration of Muslim society and destroying the nerve centers of Muslim civilization. The decadence produced a new type of mentality, new forms of perception, and a new affirmation of world experience, gradually working itself out in *mathnavis*, quatrains, lyrics, and other literary genres, including the epistles of the mystics, anecdotes of the wise, and letters of the spiritual guides. This period also brought into use new metaphors, similies, and idioms which gradually shaped the outlook of the Muslims around the ideal of spiritual renunciation. Utilizing these new literary techniques, the mystics presented God as the Beloved and men as the lovers, and painted the world as a display of the Beloved or as a wail of the lovers in separation. All categories of thought and experience, nature and being, appearance and reality, were modified and utilized to create this *prime image*, coloring the lives and the tastes of the Muslim and the development of their social and political institutions.[5]

The metaphors of the moth and the candle, so frequently used in Sufi poetry, represented the beloved as murderous, unmerciful, reckless, contemptuous, conscious of his own appeal, and inconsiderate to the lovers who waited patiently for a smile or two. Absorbed, suspended, and self-effacing, the lovers in their trance eventually overstep the ring of existence. This view was—in a nutshell—religion, morality, and the acme of responsibility. Quietude, inaction, passive contemplation, and self-annihilation became the supreme religious values. In a word this was pantheism or the idea of unity of existence, a spiritual creed for which Ibn al-'Arabi served as chief. From Damascus to Delhi and Gulberga, the spell of Ibn al-'Arabi captured the Muslims, and in due course scores of commentaries were written by the Indian scholars of Ibn al-'Arabi's *Fuṣūṣ al-Hikām*. The most famous commentaries were by Mīr Ali Hamādani (d. 1384), Sayyid Muhammad Gasū

Darāz (d. 1422), Shaikh Ali Mahayāni (d. 1431), and 'Abdūl Qadūs of Gangoh (d. 1537).[6]

The literature of this period reiterates such mystical themes as these: "Thine existence is a sin with which no other sin can be compared" (attributed to Rabiha al-Adawiyyāh, d. 801); "Between me and thee is an 'I am' which tormenteth me; O take, by thine own 'I am,' mine from between us." Muslim epistemology, metaphysics, ethics, arts, aesthetics, and social theory were stamped by this negative outlook. Bayazīd of Bistam, Ibn-al-Farīd, Mahmūd of Shabister, and Jami had the widest possible appeal, and represented the "Persian encrustation of Islam." In India, Hamādani, Gasū Darāz, and Gangohi represented in turn the main tradition of this opiating philosophy of self-negation. Iqbal was also a captive of this mystic tradition until after his spiritual revolution, which occurred around 1905–1908. But after 1912 he emerged an iconoclast, zealously eroding the Persian encrustation of Islam in order to develop the *Weltanschauung* of Islam, succinctly expressed in the idea of *Tawhīd* (unity of God).

## THE IMPACT OF GHĀLIB

IN the realm of Indo-Persian literature, Iqbal had two noted precursors: Asadūllah Khan Ghālib (d. 1869) and Mirza 'Abdūl Qādir Beidil (d. 1722). Both influenced him profoundly.

The scion of Muslim aristocracy in Delhi, Ghālib was born in 1797. The post-Aurangzeb (d. 1707) century in India was that of anarchy and agonizingly slow disintegration of the Mughal empire. Ghālib saw all this, including the tragedy of 1857, which finally gave a *coup de grâce* to Muslim power in India.

Ghālib was not only a highly sensitive poet, but also an acknowledged literary genius, leaving to posterity more than a dozen Urdu and Persian works of prose and poetry. He was also a philologist of the Persian language and a pioneer of modern Urdu prose. Iqbal described him as the Goethe of the East. By recasting the image of the lover in his *Diwān*, Ghālib created a revolution in the decadent *Weltanschauung* of his contemporaries.

Ghālib's lover is self-conscious, self-respecting, and self-affirming; he possesses honor in his own right and responds to the beloved in his own style. This ideal of love shook the accepted literary values to their foundations. Without disrupting the lovers' concept of beauty and reality, Ghālib created an altogether new personality of the lover. (This personality is further embellished in Iqbal's poetry.) Ghālib's lover is not an object of contempt; he is doomed to be annihilated but expects companionship with the Beloved. He is not light-headed nor lost to trances at the sight of the beloved. Made of an entirely different mettle from most men, Ghālib's lover is heroic, yet devoted. Instead of humiliating him, the reticence of the beloved strengthens his resolve and character.

Ghālib's penetrating poetic consciousness rediscovered those values which for ages had gone unnoticed. Representing these positive values, his lover heralds the birth of a new man. "When heart is presented to someone, why should one harp on the sad tunes? If the heart is not within the breast, then what business has the tongue to be in the mouth?" Manly grace and control are the most cherished ideals of the lover, according to Ghālib. "If, the burns of the heart are not visible," says Ghālib, "the smell (of the roasted heart) is also not felt." His self-oblivion is not without significance: "Self-forgetting is not without reason," says Ghālib, "there is something that the heart confides to itself."

Ghālib elevated the position of the lover from that of an object of loathing and contempt, to whom the very consciousness of being something is a sin, to lofty heights. "How long," says he, "would one think of the feather cap of Laila? The world is saturated with the dust of the unbridled madness of Majnūn." The poet here presents a new spectacle of the world. The powerful sway of the lover is carried to unknown heights when he says, "Who says that the laments of the nightingale are wasted. Under the illusory shroud of a flower, millions of hearts (petals of the flower) are torn to pieces." His concept of power lends beauty to love. "The one who was not equal to the task breathed his last at one threatening gesture [of the Beloved]. Love, whose profession is to test the mettle, sought a [real] man. The pain I suffered was not indebted to any remedy. It was all to the good that the pain was not cured."

Self-respect and perseverance are the substance of a lover. Ghālib would not stoop to rambling in the streets to steal a glance of the beloved; it would injure his ego. Also, his beloved was not likely to invite him to her presence because of "pride of exalted position and magnificence." Thus, self-regard and pride kept them apart. "Why should we become light-headed [show lack of self-respect]," says Ghālib, "and inquire why the beloved is so hard-hearted [indifferent]. The one who cannot withstand the hammers of grief is unfit to be a keeper of my secrets."

Thus, Ghālib was a creator of new values, new to the litterateurs of decadence, who sought refuge in life-negating values. Here a quatrain of Omar Khayyam would contrast with the bold new literary values of Ghālib:

> Depart I will not, the cupbearer, from thy door
> Wert thou to kill me, I would like it more;
> My head may lie in dust, thou need not lift,
> On me thy trampling feet would blessings pour.

Ghālib, on the contrary, declares:

> In servitude, too, we are so much independent,
> Instead of kissing the door,
> We came back, were not the door of Ka'aba open.

Ghālib advises the lover, "Tear not thy heart without the blooming days of flowers. Some gesture from the precinct of the beloved is essential." (The poet conceives of the flowers as gestures of the beloved.) Without the flowers, he says, there is no sense in being distraught. His sense of self-esteem gives him bold optimism. "It is not necessary that everybody should get the same answer. Come! let us go to Mount Sinai." In another place he says:

> You are true to remark that I am self-eulogizing;
> Why not! the mercury-like idol is before me.

The vision of the radiant beloved and his audience is not a source of forgetfulness; it is an unfathomable fount of pride and joy. Ghālib questioned the very fundamentals of Neo-Platonism, which served as the rational superstructure of decadent thought:

> If knowledge, subject and object, are identical,
> Then I am puzzled as to which account I should
>                     put [the fact of] experience?

Openly he asks:

> If that Beauty, the thriller of heart, like the meridian sun,
> Himself emblazes every spectacle, then why does
> He hide His face in veils?

If Neo-Platonic doctrine is true, then there is no sense in the multiplicity beyond the One. Either there is multiplicity, or there is Neo-Platonism which negates everything in Him, but not both. If none can withstand His spectacle, none would exist, and if that is so, how is it that there are both, lovers and experience. This dilemma tears to pieces the whole gamut of spiritual monism.

Ghālib's conflict with Neo-Platonism came to the forefront on the issue of *imtenae' al-Nazir* (the impossibility of replica). Fazl al-Haq Khairabadi wanted him to compose a poem highlighting the idea that logically the "essence" of the Seal of the Prophets [Muhammad] cannot be repeated in any other person. But in the context of Neo-Platonism this belief has a specific connotation derived from the doctrine of Logos. Based on the axiom *La yaṣdur an al-wāhid illa al-wāhid* (Nothing emanates from the One except the One), the Logos in new Platonism becomes the foundation of the world order. Philo passed the Logos theory to Hebrew thought. In this transplantation the Logos was personified into the Demiurge (behind the effluence of the cosmos), which by logical necessity should lie between the One and the many. In subsequent developments the essential beings of Moses, Isaiah, and Muhammad were identified with this "universal eternal intermediary" by their respective followers. Under the spell of this concept the Muslim Neo-Platonists looked upon Muhammad, the Apostle of God, as the *raison d'être* of the universe, eternal in essence, pole of the objective world, and *actus purus* of the One, and the universal opposite of the divine subjectivity.[7] Despite his faith in the Prophet Muhammad as the Seal of the Prophets, and his acceptance of Islam as a message of peace for mankind, Ghālib did not accept the Neo-Platonic connotations of the prophets' title of the "mercy unto the worlds." He rejected the axiom that *"out of the One, only One emanates,"* thereby refusing to adhere to the doctrine of the light of Muhammad. On the contrary he declared, "It is possible for God to create many worlds, each having its own [prophets and the Last of the prophets and] mercy-upon-the-world."

Inspired by this bold thought, Iqbal gave it a prominent place in his *Javid-Namah* (The Book of Eternity). In the celestial world of *Javid-Namah*, Iqbal (who adopted the pseudonym Zinda Rud, the living stream), asks Ghālib:

> This Azur vault contains a hundred worlds
> Doth each one have its prophets and saints?

Replies Ghālib:

> The order of what is and what is not
> See carefully: each moment many worlds
> Burst into life. Each throbbing, striving world
> Is crowned by the Mercy of the worlds.

Zinda Rud wants an explicit answer; Ghālib is evasive, but at last remarks:

> Creation, order, guidance mark the birth;
> The ultimate is the Mercy of the worlds.

Zinda Rud submits that he does not yet appreciate his argument. Ghālib explains:

> Like me thou dost the reach of poesy
> Know well its string, this thought may strain and break,
> Like Moses are the children of the Muse, . . .
> Parnassus yet is not Sinai; they lack
> The shining hand: What thou demandst of me
> Is heresy—beyond all word verse.

That the world does not need a mediator between man and God and that the institution of prophethood has its rationale in divine mercy was no doubt a heresy within the framework of the Neo-Platonic theology. Ghālib redeemed the issue by transforming it into a moral problem. In his *Mathnavi Dar Beyān-i-Shān-i Nabūwat* (Splendor of Prophethood) Ghālib says:

> The intent behind the creation of every world is one.
> If there are two hundred worlds, the *seal* is one.
> Mercy-upon-the world is there, wherever there is
> A commotion of existence.[8]

The term "mercy" has a special meaning in Islamic thought. Jami (d. 1492), despite the essentialistic content of his thought, says: "When one of the contingent substances, through the concurrence of the requisite and the absence of opposing conditions, becomes capable of receiving the very being, the Mercy of the Merciful takes possession of it, and the *Being* is infused into it. . . ." However, it should be emphasized that it is due to divine mercy that a seed blossoms into a tree; divine mercy sustains the world, and nourishes it for its fulfillment. Devoid of its Neo-Platonic colors, this divine law, according to Ghālib crowns the universe. There is no logical limit to divine original creation. Divinity wants the blooming of existence, and it has no design beyond this purpose.

A story is told that a non-Muslim having heard the verse of the Qur'ān that the extent of paradise is the entire universe asked the Prophet: "Where then is hell situated?" The Prophet gave him a philosophic answer in the form of a rhetorical question, "Where is the night when the day dawns?" implying that heaven and earth are states and not geographical locations. In another place the Qur'ān has proclaimed that the *rahmat*, the love and mercy of God, cover the entire creation (VII, 156).[9] This is precisely the meaning of the mercy-upon-the-world, and paradise is the state of its fullest realization.

## BEIDIL: MAN, THE ULTIMATE PURPOSE

BEIDIL's emphasis on the principle of abundance in the nature of reality, his strong feeling for the element of activism in the universe, and his concept of self-affirmation, including his sublime view of the dignity of man, makes him distinct in the company of his contemporary poets and philosophers.

Born in Azimabad (Patna) during the reign of the Mughal emperor Shah Jehan (1628–1658), Mirza 'Abdūl Qādir Beidil lived through the reign of Emperor Aurangzeb (d. 1707), and died in 1722. The style of Indo-Persian mystic and philosophical poetry achieved its zenith in Beidil's *mathnavis*, including *'Irfān, Tilasm-i Hairet*, and *Tūr-i Ma'rifah*. Azīz Ahmad appropriately remarks that "the intensity of his subjective assessment is so acute and factual that genuine poetry emerges in all its splendor, achieving a unity of metaphysical theme, and highly conceptual image."[10]

Transforming the Sufi categories of "poverty" and "abundance" into metaphysical symbols, he communicated through them his notion of reality. According to Beidil, poverty without abundance is nakedness, a mere "isness" of no consequence; and abundance without poverty is an empty carcass, an outer husk of being without content. (Poverty [*faqr*] in mystic terminology meant a salty land, yielding no produce; hence it symbolizes an affirmable isness of no importance.)

Beidil asks: "If poverty is adequate to the fundamental essence of existence, then why is there an outburst beyond nothingness? Visible exuberance and abundance in Nature means that the nakedness of the *ḍhat* (the existential essence) requires the wraps of colors and forms. Devoid of its attributes the *ḍhat* is entirely overlooked; consequently its *faqr* (that is, its isness) is fulfilled in abundance":

> Without the wealth of attributes, the *ḍhat* is fictitious, a phantom.
> Accordingly, abundance characterizes its poverty.

Beidil thus breaks away from Sanai, Jami, and Iraqi, for whom the abundance or the many is simply a stream of ideas in the universal consciousness. For Beidil abundance is not ideal but real, a genuine fruition of reality, a luxuriant growth on the soil of isness, and a lavish effluence of the being itself.

Existence seeks richness; the poverty of being is at once a striving after abundance. Reality is richness in poverty and poverty in richness. It is being in becoming and becoming in being. Consequently, it is the isness of being, which unfolds itself in the profound richness of shapes, colors, and forms. Addressing his readers, Beidil proclaims: "Don't be indifferent to this order of opulence, don't try to withdraw from it in contempt. Undoubtedly, striving after the acquisition of wealth provided by Nature is not without pain and hardship; nothing is achieved without labor":

> The meaning of my existence is this very pain.
> Otherwise there is much soothing
>       in the chamber of nothingness

Work and activity embrace the essence of being, because to be means to abound. Passivity and inactivity are proper attributes of nonbeing.

Beidil perceives dynamism as the heart of being, which cannot remain comforted in impoverishment, sterility, and nakedness.

Grasping the principle of objectivity or exteriorization, growth and opulence, Beidil realizes the significance of existence pervading every form of being. Therefore the essence of man should not be sought in poverty. His nature is enrichment. Iqbal explains this principle in the concept of desire:

> Life is latent in seeking,
> Its origin is hidden in desire,
> Keep desire alive in thine heart
> Lest thy little dust become a tomb.
> Negation of desire is death to the living.
> Even an absence of heat extinguishes the flame.

Beidil analyzes the nature of human existence (his "I-amness") in a *ghazal* (lyric): "I am that longing which is seeking itself in the dust of its own being; I keep on going my own way to reach the goal." Man is a dynamic being; his essence is striving. His I-amness is unique in so far as it seeks its own being in the "dust" of its own existence. This leads him to strive constantly and to engage in perpetual activity. Beidil explains this principle of locomotion in his autobiography, *Chahār Enātir*, which is rich in philosophical analysis of the mystic experience and the problems of knowledge: "Sometimes I become so small that even a particle of dust may contain me; but at times my longings so expand me that I cannot remain within my own self."

Thus, Beidil revolutionized the concept of man. Monistic philosophy thrives on the metaphors of ocean and waves, river and bubbles, indicating the nature of man as a transient expression of one universal activity. Beidil modified these metaphors by introducing the imagery of river and pearl. "Just like a pearl, which though hardened in the bosom of a river, is thrown ashore, I am thrown out, because I could not be absorbed, melted, or dissolved." Beidil says in his *mathnavi 'Irfān*:

Man is the assembling point of creation, fountain of figures, center of gnosis, and the origin of action. He is the pinnacle of creation, the shaper and the maker, the knower and the doer. The Worlds are razed to dust, till the shape of man is come. O spring of "notness" realize thou thine own worth. [According to Beidil, the worlds are razed and undone till the figure of man is chiseled out.] This spring of *nothingness*, its bloom and sway, is justified in the name of man.

Man is not an instrument, he is not a means to an end, and there is no divine intent beyond him for which man is created. Beidil addresses man in his *mathnavi*, *Mohīt-i 'Azam*:

If you know the secret [you will realize that] you are your own pole [center of gravity]. If you do a little thinking [you will know] that you are the niche of your own self. Inside this doorless dome of the sky, no trace of a stranger is detectable. Since there is no door or window in this heavenly vault, it contains no exit and no entrance. If anyone exists within it, it is you. Whatever you perceive, you perceive none but your own image. Whatever you hear is nothing but your own voice.

The spectre of "notness' and the whim of "existence" are due to you. Intoxication is by you, upsurge of ecstasy is by you. Peep a little into your breast, behold the storm wrought in your own self, like the one raised in a vine jar. This assembly [world] has warmth and zest by your uproar. Your silence makes the whole world still. In the mirror of your self, your own face is the image. In the world mirror of color and form, only your portrait is presented. The good and evil that you observe is nothing but your glance of good and evil eye. If for an instant you are with you, you are the one who is the maker of both the worlds.

Beidil's conception of man presents him as a uniquely existing being whose destiny lies unto himself. His existence is the ultimate purpose. He is therefore not doomed to destruction. The relentless process of decay and destruction is consummated in his perfection; he has come to stay.

Beidil's philosophical vision did not accept the frame of reference of medieval thought, which rested on final causes. By declaring that God [the perfect being] is not in need of the world, he salvaged man from the position of an instrumental existence. The concept of man is not to be approached by reference to a higher purpose than man himself. This new approach does not sever man's relation with God, but elevates him to the dignity of a companion to Him.

How refreshingly contrasting are Beidil's views to the brand of Sufism advocated by Ibn al-'Arabi, Jalāl al-Din al Sūyūti (d. 1445), and 'Abdūl Wahhab al-Sharani (d. 1545). To them the world is merely a form in reality; the human self is also a mere form in which the real actor is the unmultiplying divine self. Out of his sheer ignorance man takes this form for a real life, proclaiming that "I exist." The "I" that makes this affirmation is a mere illusion which soon disappears as the seeker moves upward tearing the veils of separation. The ultimate gnosis is a realization that only one active agent is immanent in all the manifestations of forms. Human self is only a medium, although potentially a more perfect medium, of the active agent. "Man," says Lahiji, "is the eye of the world, whereby God sees His own works." But Beidil's thought delivers man from the snares of this static and mystic instrumentalism. Human ego is real, not a mere form but a true entity in its own right, both in essence and existence.

The radical elements of Beidil's thought came to full bloom in Iqbal's philosophy of self. Realization of human self constitutes the major point of departure for Iqbal from the traditions of emanationism and idealism, which reduce human existence to a phenomenal shape in the development of the absolute.

## AL-JUNAYD: EGO AND THE DIVINE VISION

ACCORDING to Western idealism human ego is self-contradictory in nature; it is phenomenal, and therefore it must be negated. In the common legacy of Western and Muslim thought these ideas are remnants of Neo-Platonic mysticism and emanationistic metaphysics. According to Iqbal, the idea of negation or oblivion has a place in the life of an ego, but its connotations are different. It does not weed out ego, but strengthens it, preparing man for the divine vision. This capacity of divine vision enables man to be God's vice-regent on earth. The emanationists and absolutists do not conceive of the possibility of divine vision, which would enable the self to achieve the divine audience without being shattered. Being close to the spirit of Islam, early Sufism visualized this possibility.

Al-Junayd (d. 910) describes the highest *ma'rifat* or *Tawhīd* as consisting of "existence without *shabah* (frame) before God with no third person as intermediary between them."[11] Al-Junayd, the celebrated Sufi of Baghdad, left a great deal of authentic gnostic literature. Through his efforts Islamic mysticism received its first comprehensive theoretical treatment. In establishing the limits of the Islamic gnostic approach, al-Junayd attempted to harmonize them with the rules of the *Shari'a*. His theories have had profound impact on the development of subsequent Sufi thought, including that of Ali Makhadūm Hujwari's *Kashf al-Mahjūb*. According to Hujwari, man completely loses his *shabah* before God, and returns to his early existence. This loss of the present frame and form amounts to *fanā* (abnegation or oblivion). Thus man's existence is not negated in the universal unity of God's existence, since he is not merged with the universal essence. He simply returns to his original existence—the existence in which he has made his covenant with God (that is, the pure I-amness of man, with which he undertakes his most earnest responsibility).

In his final state the worshiper, according to al-Junayd, is not a non-being. To make this point he quotes the Qur'ān: "And when your Lord drew forth their descendants from the reigns of the children of Adam and took them to witness concerning themselves, 'Am I not,' said He, 'your Lord?' They answered, 'But certainly you are.'" The former existence in al-Junayd's thought refers to the existence in which man witnessed the divinity of his lord and made a covenant with Him concerning His Lordship. (This leads to the particular theory of *fanā* on which Iqbal's *Ramūz-i-Bekhudi* [The Mysteries of Selflessness] is based.)

For al-Junayd, in order to be completely obedient to the commands of God and to be exclusively His man (removing the need even for an intermediary contact) the elimination of all ulterior motives is a prerequisite, to be followed immediately by the obliteration of pains and sensuous pleasures. The higher stage is the loss of "the consciousness of having attained the vision of God." The saint who is conscious of his saintliness, the scholar who is aware of his scholarship, and the patriot who is ever enumerating his services to the country lack finer sentiments. The true devotee is not conscious of his sacrifices. This is the stage of *fanā*, the act of living with God.

Referring to this stage, al-Junayd remarks that "this state—the final state of *fanā* includes *baqā*, abiding and continuously dwelling with God." This is a return to one's original existence in which the covenant was made. Al-Junayd maintains that "even in this divine state it is not possible for man to approach the ultimate reality which now possesses him. Only in this state God can be seen in His exalted nature and His beautific names can be appreciated." Thus, the ultimate experience is that of vision, not of mergence. The self is not lost; man overcomes its worldly frame (*shabah*, that is, unbridled motives) and gathers strength in the process of becoming one with his real ego with which he originally made the covenant with God and received his trust. The divine will superordinates his will, and he thus fulfills the divine purpose.

Al-Junayd asserts that even when God has complete possession of man, *balā* (trial and affliction) overtakes him because of his persisting human qualities, and also because of his capacity for the enjoyment of physical pleasures. This is the veil of the secret; man remains conquered by God, awaiting his commands.

Briefly stated, the mystical theory of al-Junayd does not contain any Neo-Platonic orientation. The ultimate truth is the "divine audience" which a soul may attain. The divine presence is a test required of a soul containing all the moments of longing and suffering. Yet God gives the soul the strength to endure its *balā* and receive His grace and knowledge and thus fulfill His mission. Iqbal has recaptured this theme in the beautiful verses of *Javid-Namah*:

> No one can stand unshaken in His presence;
> And he who can, verily, he is pure gold,
> Art thou a mere particle of dust,
> Tighten the knot of thy ego;
> And hold fast to thy tiny being!
> How glorious to burnish one's ego
> And test its lustre in the presence of the sun!
> Rechisel, then, thine ancient frame;
> And build up a new being.
> Such being is real being;
> Or else thy ego is a mere ring of smoke.[12]

*Balā*, the trial and affliction, in al-Junayd's view is a veil between men and God, "so that they may retain a measure of their individuality and use both their physical and spiritual faculties in this environment of glory" (*Risalā*: 6). In a small poem al-Junayd says:

> Though from my gaze profound
> Deep awe hath hid thy face
> In wonderous and ecstatic grace,
> I feel thee touch my inmost ground.[13]

The pursuit of knowledge of God is now the constant preoccupation of the soul; it is entirely devoted to submerging its frame in the attainment of intimacy with God. "The soul accepts the spiritual burden with its implications of suffering, seeks for its cure, and is preoccupied with the divine revelation vouchsafed to it." Iqbal in his lectures refers to this phenomenon: "As the Qur'ān says of the Prophet's vision of the ultimate ego, 'His eye turned not aside, nor did it wander' (53:17). This is the ideal of perfect manhood in Islam."

## SUHURWARDI: *ISHRAQI* THEORY OF KNOWLEDGE

IQBAL's philosophical view of human self, his ontological pluralism, and his concept of world history as a stage of creative development presume an unorthodox epistemology as against the conventional logic of Aristotle. In this respect Iqbal received his orientation from the anti-Graecianism of Shahab-al-Din Suhurwardi the Slain (d. 1191), whose exceptionally original approach to the problem of knowledge is a precursor of some of the basic tenets of modern realism.

Born (1153) in Persia, Shahab-al-Din Suhurwardi was executed at the age of thirty-eight "as a heretic" at Aleppo by order of the viceroy al-Malik al-Zāhir and his well-known father, Salah-al-Din, the ruler of Egypt. He left to posterity several large and small treatises on mysticism including *Taliwīhāt, Muqawwamat, Mutarahat,* and *Hikmat al-Ishrāq*, all ranking among the classics of Muslim philosophy, the last work being most important of all.

By rigorous logical analysis, Suhurwardi refuted the reification of ideas and demonstrated that predicables, universals, and abstract qualities are devoid of objective reality.[14] They are intelligibles and no claim of their externality, immune from logical difficulties, could be vindicated. If they were conceived of as objective entities, their fundamental logical essence would be forced to undergo a drastic change and they would not remain general, thus becoming particulars like other particulars. As rational entities, the intelligibles are consequently shorn of "true" existence.

Suhurwardi analyzes existence and propounds that every existing entity enjoys a singular determination, an inalienable identity and specific unity of its being which rebounds against every intrusion into its givenness. The intelligibles are denotative in their character, without being capable of participating in the constitution of a thing which exists in its own individuality. The very nature of a thing, its concreteness and singularity, belie every permeation. Consequently no universal enters into it and becomes an element of its composition.

To Suhurwardi, things, therefore, are not collections and aggregates of universals. They are unique beings dwelling in themselves, whereas universals are either their mental representations or rational entities. Suhurwardi's notion of existence is one of the fundamental elements of Iqbal's philosophy of the nature of things. The *dhat* (the existential essence) of a thing, its substance, is its own. As it is not made of universals, it is not dependent on their togetherness. It exists in its own right, endowed with its own concreteness, and particularity.[15] Even these predicates: essence, particularity, existence, are mental constructs. There can be no distinction between the essence and existence in the nature of a thing. A black thing is a black thing, indivisibly so; blackness as a general entity does not reside in it, nor does a universal like "thinghood."[16]

These ideas have profoundly influenced the development of Iqbal's philosophy. His emphasis on the concrete individuality of a truly existing ego stems from Suhurwardi's *Ishraqīyah*. (In the contemporary period these views have been revived in the movements of logical positivism and existentialism.) The system of concepts which the intellect weaves with dexterity are merely intellectual scaffoldings for the epistemic representation of reality. This thesis produces a chasm between idea and thing, thought and reality. Aristotelian rationalism moves from one to other on the basis of a metaphysical proposition that ideas, universals, and ultimately predicables are exemplified in the external world and participate in the nature of the things in existence. Refuting this proposition, Suhurwardi erased the whole structure of rationalism and thus enthroned the *Ishraqi* theory of knowledge, the intuitive apprehension of reality.[17]

Suhurwardi also attacked the epistemology of Neo-Platonic Aristotelians. (The well-known thinkers of this school of philosophy were al-Kindi [d. circ. 873], al-Farabi [d. 950], Ibn Tufail, and Ibn Rushd [d. 1198], known to the Western world of philosophy by his Latin name, Averroes.) According to Neo-Platonic Aristotelians, in every objective judgment consciousness is first active with a concept, for instance, an idea of blackness; then it recognizes the externally perceptible content by denoting it with the term "black" and thus apprehends a black thing. Accordingly, perception consists not in cognition, but in recognition—recognition of an idea in the contents of the external world. This logical priority of the idea and its role in the act of observation makes knowledge a vicious circle and subjects every existing being to the medium of an idea in its being known. This theory of knowledge is consistent with Aristotelian rationalism, because it is a necessary corollary of the proposition that idea is the essence which participates in the being of a thing. Suhurwardi, on the contrary, expounds the theory of illumination: Consciousness directly gains acquaintance with the object; the illumination or intuitive apprehension, not seeking the medium of an idea, reaches the object. Therefore, idealization follows illumination; it does not precede it.

Knowledge by illumination means that the Neo-Platonic Aristotelian formula of definition is rendered meaningless. Suhurwardi holds that definition by genus and differentia does not lead to clarity. If the percipient is acquainted with the object, definition is redundant; and if any of the terms is unknown, the definition serves no purpose. An attempt to know by (Aristotelian) definition proves a failure because the differentiating term remains unknown or known only through the object under definition, indicating that the Aristotelian process of definition does not lend to any preperceptual epistemic clarity about the object of inquiry. Since Aristotelian rationalism, including all forms of idealism, remains forever in the airy castle of ideas, it is divorced from reality. The new philosophy should be the philosophy of observation. Suhurwardi's interest in the "world of heart" led him to spiritualism and mysticism, not to science and the physical world, although his critique of logic and exposition of the nature of knowledge could become the foundation of empirical sciences. Iqbal was profoundly influenced by this criticism, and it was one of the prime sources of his strong plea for observation as the fundamental requirement for knowing the psychic world and the physical world.

Iqbal's cardinal principle of ontology eliminates the division between appearance and reality. For him "reality lives in its own appearance." Revolt against the bifurcation of the real into noumenon and phenomenon, having its own origin in Fichte, led to the rise of Hegelian idealism in the modern West; but Iqbal's revolt against dualism drew inspiration from the ontological statement of Shahab-al-Din Suhurwardi: appearance is the very nature of reality.

The Ishraqi philosophy of Suhurwardi posits the experience of ultimate reality in the symbol or idea of light. Related imagery including heavens, sun, orient, brightness, rays, radiance, weaves a comprehensive system of symbolism. This system was evolved by the mystics and gnostics of ancient Persia to indicate the experience of the Magian soul. Suhurwardi adopted the whole set of symbols but made it a part of his own philosophy of light, while he successfully eliminated the dualism of appearances and reality and the distinction between substance and function. Light by nature is diffusive; it radiates spontaneously, demonstrating its essence in activity. Since light always enlightens there can be no distinction between existential and operational aspects of its being.

By working itself out within this peculiar symbolism, the Ishraqi philosophy overcomes those philosophic problems which arise because of the structure of Greek and Persian grammar, apriorily committing one to the subject-verb-object pattern of thought. How far did Suhurwardi succeed in his attempts to overcome this linguistic predicament? This is beyond the purview of the present discussion, but it should be pointed out that in his philosophical system many of the metaphysical problems having their genesis in ordinary grammar, do not arise owing to the advantages his symbolism gives to the thinking mind. For instance, act and agent do not appear different; they become the same thing. When Iqbal tried to define "ego," he did not hesitate to employ the terminology of "actionism." However, to an untrained eye Iqbal's approach may look like crude behaviorism. But against the powerful philosophic background of Suhurwardi's thesis (recognizing being and appearance, light and brightness as identical) Iqbal's interpretation in fact spiritualizes behaviorism by eliminating the distinction between the doer and the doing, the maker and the making, the actor and the acting.

## AL-JILI: 'AMĀ, INSIGNIA OF THE INDIVIDUAL

ACTIVITY, according to Iqbal, is the fundamental of reality. Introspectively, it is ego; outwardly, it is movement. The principle of identity cannot match even for a moment this living reality. The subject-predicate form of reasoning cannot comprehend it, nor is it intelligible in the taxonomic concepts of classes. Epistemic participation in the dynamism of reality is a swing into the logic of contradictions. The thinker who pioneered this logic is not Hegel, but 'Abdūl Karīm al-Jīli (d. 1406). According to the dialectics of al-Jīli, one-ness is thesis, He-ness is antithesis, and I-ness is synthesis. A sensitive poet with an eye on human psychology, and a reputed ontologist, Al-Jīli is known to posterity for his concept of the "perfect man." Although he borrowed this concept from Ibn al-'Arabi, he made it quite his own by giving it entirely original connotations. Also, his works acquire modern significance for his analysis of religious symbolism. Of his several treatises only *Insān i-Kāmil* has survived. It is considered to be a source book of Muslim metaphysics in Persia and India.

In the words of Iqbal, al-Jīli says:

The Intellect flying through the fathomless empty space, pierces through the veil of names and attributes, traverses the vasty sphere of time, enters the domain of the non-existent and finds the essence of Pure Thought to be an existence which is non-existence—a sum of contradictions. It has two accidents, eternal life in all past times and eternal life in all future time. It has two qualities, God and Creation. It has two definitions, uncreatableness and creatableness. It has two names, God and man. It has two faces, the manifested (this world) and the unmanifested (next world). It has two effects, necessity and possibility. It has two points of view: from the first, it is non-existent for itself, but existent for what is not itself; from the second it is existent for itself, and non-existent for what is not itself.[18]

Al-Jīli thus anticipates all the necessary facets of the dialecticism of Hegel, who also conceives of ultimate reality as a totality of negations.

To al-Jīli, reality is an evolution or a journey from unfathomable obscurity to the utmost brightness of objectivity and manifestation. It is a passage through various grades of light and darkness; speeding through nature and history it comes to the full light which unifies all the contradictions (he-nesses) in the realization of absolute reality (I-ness). Iqbal's idea of self (implying that life is the life of objectivity and outward activity) is a mature and developed form of al-Jīli's idea, although it is immensely strengthened by the axioms of Hegelianism. Having thoroughly internalized the al-Jīlian concept of '*amā* (darkness as the contour of singleness for the ego), it is understandable that in his analysis of ego, Iqbal should lean more toward al-Jīli than toward Hegel, or for that matter, toward any other philosopher.

Al-Jili's concept of darkness corresponds to the modern concepts of "aesthetic or undifferentiated continuum" at the base of experience. Al-Jili treats this continuum or darkness as the universal ground of all manifest reality. No articulate consciousness is capable of referring to it; it cannot be symbolized or conceptualized; yet an awareness is there to affirm it, and therefore it is not unknowable. Al-Jili says that the all-embracing (knowable) darkness in its interior is identical with the Divine Self Himself. To the outer eye (that is, from all the standpoints of manifestation), it is beyond differentiation and thus creates the impact of blindness. It is light in itself for itself, and is darkness in itself for other selves. Therefore, it is the original symbol of the Living Ego. (Reference to 'amā is the most direct reference to the ḍhat [existential essence] that exists.)[19]

Al-Jili remarks that "darkness is the Singular *Tajallī* (light) which the Truth has chosen for itself. It is not for any otherness; consequently, the creation has no share in it."[20] Darkness is the sign of the Singular Ego. Iqbal generalized this conclusion to all the selves; not only the Divine Self, but every self has the aura of darkness as the original symbol of its own being.

There are pointers toward this generalization in al-Jili's exposition. He maintains that the concrete richness of existing self rests on a bare feeling of the existence of self, which is absolutely devoid of any content. This feeling is already sunk in the dark continuum. Every ego in its depth may feel the substrate darkness on which his self is raised. Al-Jili appeals to the reader, asking him to look into his being in order to experience the darkness, which sustains his own being. Every created ego is immersed in 'amā (the darkness). Consequently, the self-reflecting consciousness of the ego realizes its own limits, acquiring a feeling of incompleteness. Now it is at the threshold of the darkness, the border of its own being. Al-Jili states that beyond the intensive magnitude of the 'amā is the Divine Ego Himself. All individual egos have their ultimate ground in this Universal Ego. (Between them is the darkness, the 'amā, which was explained earlier.)

Iqbal absorbed this subtle analysis into his exposition not only of the nature of self but also of the relationship between the created egos and the Divine Self. For Iqbal every ego shines in itself with a private circuit of its own. This privacy is essential to its existence. (It is due to this that I cannot share your experience, and you cannot undergo mine.) The privacy which in Iqbal's thought identifies self-consciousness with self-existence makes the ego a uniquely existing individual.

"Pantheistic Sufism," remarks Iqbal, "obviously cannot favor such a view and suggests difficulties of a philosophical nature. How can the infinite and the finite egos mutually exclude each other? Can the finite ego as such retain its finitude beside the infinite ego? This difficulty is based on a misunderstanding of the true nature of the infinite. True infinity does not mean infinite extension which cannot be conceived of without embracing all available finite extensions. Its nature consists in intensity and not extensity, and the moment we fix our gaze on intensity, we begin to see that the finite ego must be distinct though not *isolated*, from the infinite."[21] Al-Jili's view that every created ego is grounded in the dark continuum, beyond which is the Ultimate Ego, is a representation of this intensive magnitude which does not admit spatial principle. Iqbal says: "Extensively regarded I am absorbed by the spatio-temporal order to which I belong. Intensively regarded I consider the same spatio-temporal order as a confronting 'other' wholly alien to me. I am distinct from and yet intimately related to that on which I depend for my life and sustenance."[22] To al-Jili, this experience of intensity is comprehended in the feeling of darkness beyond which is the unsharable divine sanctuary. Thus, there is no question of either subvergence or participation.

## WESTERN AND MUSLIM CONCEPTS OF TIME

It may have become clear by now that the problem of space and time is intimately involved in the ontology of a pluralistic universe, consisting of really existing egos. Western thought relegates this issue to the physical world, believing that time is bound up with linear motion and that space is a material principle representing the structure of corporeal events. Muslim thought, on the contrary, isolates this problem from the confines of the physical world, considering it a fundamental issue of religious and spiritual significance.

Long before Iqbal, the Mu'tazlites and the Ash'arites had discussed the problem of *jawher-i-fard* (atomlike substance), the nature of *fasl* (distance), and the implications of continuum. They had not raised these issues as intellectual exercises, but as living issues affecting the destiny of Muslim civilization. Iqbal fully appreciated the significance of their argumentation. However, for him the evolution of western thought represents spatialization of intellect, degenerating time to the problem of space, and distorting reality in the category of *absolute dispersion*. On the other hand, Muslim thought contains many incipient transspatial perceptions. The Bergsonian distinction between spatial time and real time (which for Iqbal symbolized a novelty in the historical continuity of western thought), probably comes closest to the Muslim concept. Yet Bergson cannot comprehend the notion of '*amā*, implying duration without succession, the highest space-time experience at the root of the real world, because the western mind in general is Euclidean and cannot transcend the concept of "figure." Hence geometry is one of its major accomplishments.

To the Muslim mind the problem of space is bound up with the problem of spiritual determination. Therefore it is intertwined with the problem of time. Since the dawn of Islam the story of *Mi'rāj* (the Prophet Muhammad's ascension) has been the main determinant in the crystallization of Muslim outlook. Because of the Prophet's ascension, Muslim scholars tended to entertain a pluralistic view of space and time. However, not before the advent of the pioneering works of Saccheri (d. 1819), Gauss (d. 1855), Lobachevsky (d. 1856), and Bolyai (d. 1860) did the western mind entertain a similar view. Their works unchained geometry from the law of "imaginative construction" which played a decisive role in Kant's theory of the monism of space, and made possible the mathematical conceptions of different space orders in our time. In his lectures Iqbal referred to Nāsir Tūsi (1201–1274), "who in his efforts to improve the [parallel] postulate," long before Saccheri "realized the necessity of abandoning perceptual space."[23] Once the intellect is unfettered from ordinary (three-dimensional) perception it can soar to celestial heights.

The commonwealth of egos around the Divine Ego is an ultimate fact of reality. Having a space order of its own, it is different from the space order of corporeal things. It sustains the individual egos, and has its own laws of motion. Such in essence are the implications of Iqbal's philosophy. They can be traced back to the ideas of Iraqi, who, several centuries before the modern works on the non-Euclidean or transperceptual spaces, had visualized three orders of space—the space of material bodies, the space of immaterial beings, and the space of God.[24]

(Also, he said that the space of light is different from the space of material bodies, an idea accepted as true in modern astronomy.) According to Iraqi, the element of distance is not altogether absent from these spaces. However, in divine space, God is in touch with everything. This touch is not a matter of speed, which minimizes the lapse of time in motion to zero, but involves a unique logical structure of spatiality in which time cannot be conceived of as consisting of discrete moments, one succeeding the other.

Abū Ali al-Husain ibn 'Abdūllah Ibn Sina, known to the Western world of philosophy by his Latin name, Avicenna (d. 1073), distinguished among three kinds of time: *al-zamān*, *al-dahr*, and *al-sarmadiyyān*. The first corresponds to the time of everyday perception; the second, which envelops all the *al-zamān* in its titanic embrace, is really akin to Bergson's duration. *Al-sarmadiyyān* is a time which is beyond all comprehension. Avicenna maintained that time is a projection of movement; *sarmadi* time, therefore, can be identified with divine activity. "If we look at the movement embodied in creation from the outside," remarks Iqbal, "it is a process lasting through thousands of years. . . . From another point of view the process of creation, lasting through thousands of years, is a single indivisible act, swift as the twinkling of an eye."[25] Pure time is an organic whole.

Avicenna denies the divisibility or the atomic character of movement.[26] Our point-instants are merely epistemic breakups of the spontaneous dynamism under the category of quantification, which by the logic of its own mode of *noesis* fails to grasp the nature of movement, perceiving it as discrete immobile chunks subject to infinite division. It conceives of a third point between every pair of points; in such a system movement from one point to the other is therefore either impossible or utterly unintelligible. The idea of divisibility thus tends toward the conception that movement is an illusion. (Belief in the realism of movement can be held only on the ground that infinitely divisible space and time are mere illusions.) This conclusion inspires Iqbal to formulate the concept of an open universe in which real space-time is identical with the heartbeats and dynamic flow of the ultimate reality. "The universe which seems to us to be a collection of things is not a solid stuff occupying a void. It is not a thing but an act."[27] The units of time are pure acts; they are denotable as instants. When the acts become visible they tend to appear as bodies and become measurable. This is the genesis of "space" as the form in which external reality is perceived. True reality belongs to acts, that is, to instants. Of the point-instant "the instant is the more fundamental of the two," says Iqbal, but the point is inseparable from the instant as being a necessary mode of its manifestation." This exposition of Iqbal is an elaborate and creative restatement of atomism, which was evolved and propounded by Abū al-Hassan Ash'ari (d. 935/936), Abū Bakr Baqilani (d. 1025), Imam al-Harmayn (d. 1100), Shahrastani (d. 1190), and al-Ghazzali (d. 1111).[28]

The atomic movement in the history of Muslim thought is in many ways anti-Neo-Platonic. Sometimes it is known as empiricism because of its avowed distrust of elusive speculation, and also because of its positive contribution in demonstrating the limits of theoretic reason. In establishing the superiority of faith Baqilani dismantled the categories of speculative thought. Shahrastani made his severest attacks on the doctrine of emanationism; however, it was al-Ghazzali who built a complete theology and a practical philosophy on the ruins of rationalism. He propounded the voluntaristic notion of ultimate reality: "The first principle is an omnipotent and willing agent. He does what he wills and ordains as he likes and creates . . . in whatever manner he likes."[29] His doctrine is the superstructure of Muslim atomism with all its implications.

According to the atomists, the world consists of atomic accidents, that is, monads. Their theory in its observable form is more or less akin to that of Hume and Mach, Russell and Wittgenstein. But in principle it involves the rejection of substancelike theories of space-time order, rightfully claiming a unique place in the history of global thought. The Muslim atomists maintain that space and time are a series of monads (events); there are space monads and time monads, but they are not contiguous. In fact, the atomists came close to propounding the modern theory of compact series, according to which no point is a contiguous neighbor of any other point. Consequently, there is a void between one monad and the other. A thing is not a substance but aggregate of monads. This aggregation is the genesis of spatial order—the reason why perceptible objects have magnitudes. Movement is a leap from the present to a future position. This leap constitutes the law of world order, an open growth implying a genuine increase upon the mass of events in the history of creation.

This original contribution was made, however (as already pointed out) in the background of a monistic metaphysics, giving rise to the image of a centralistic system of the objective world. Atomic accidents were interpreted as fiats of the divine will. Each of the monads, viewed externally, is an accident, whereas its inner core is an act of the will. The dynamism of the will thus generates the panorama of time. Its nolition is responsible for the death of the present, and its volition for the birth of the future. Although adhering to this theory of the root of time in the free creativity of the will, Iqbal remarks that "space and time are possibilities of the Ego, only partially realized in the shape of our mathematical space and time."[30]

Iqbal, however, makes his own contribution to the centralistic thesis of Muslim atomism in favor of a pluralistic metaphysics. He admits that the world, consisting of its atomic accidents, is a continuous creative activity of God, yet it does not entail a system of monolithic despotism. He says: "I have conceived the ultimate Reality as an ego, and I must now add that from the ultimate ego only egos proceed. The creative energy of the ultimate ego . . . functions as ego unities . . . every atom of divine existence, however low in the scale of existence, is an ego."[31] Ego acts and rebounds, responds and reacts; every monad therefore becomes in its own right a causality, which invades the environment. This conception also leads to the finite centers of energy and activity where the psychic unities are space-time matrices of their own creation. Every psychic atom in its movement spins a web of objective spatio-temporal order around its nucleus. Thus, Muslim atomism culminates in Iqbal's conception of the relativity of the space-time continuum. There are as many spacetimes as there are doers and actors, that is, egos, yet this multiplicity is ultimately grounded in the spacious presence of the Divine Ego.

## KHAWAJA MĪR DARD:
## TIME, AN ATTRIBUTE OF EXISTING REALITY

KHAWAJA MĪR DARD (d. 1784), an eighteenth-century Muslim poet-philosopher of India, maintains that time is one of the attributes of perfection of the truly existing reality.[32]

## Heritage of Islamic Thought

Khawaju Mīr Dard was born (1719) in Delhi. His father, Khawaja Nāsir was a known Sufi, who had won considerable fame for writing *Nalā-i 'Andalīb*, a treatise on metaphysics which refuted the mystic doctrine of the unity of existence. Khawaja Mīr Dard received his early education from his father and was later initiated into Sufism. During a period of spiritual retreat at age fifteen Khawaja Dard authored his first treatise on the mystery of prayers; his less known but more profound work *'Ilm al-Kitāb* deals with epistemology, ontology, gnosis, and mystic practices. In Urdu literature he occupies an abiding place as a mystic poet, and his poems are widely sung in the Sufi circles of India and Pakistan.

In establishing six gradations of temporality from *dhat* (existential essence) to accidents, Dard points out that accidents in relation to each other (coming one after another) produce *zamān-i-adaffiyāh* (relative time). Relative time is grounded in real time, which is identical with the view of an *accident* in the medium of itself. Every accident in its composition includes that temporal limit which truly constitutes its own substance. Thus Khawaja Mīr Dard eliminates the classical distinction between a thing and its time, an occurrence and its moment. He identifies its being with the time itself, indicating that the occurrence in relation to itself is *zamān-i-haqīqi* (real time). Real time is also not an ultimate fact, but a manifest aspect of *dahr-i-adaffiyāh* (relative duration), through which it springs from the *sarmadiyyati adaffiyāh* (a category of time), which may be translated as the specious presence of the *dhat* denoting its living differentiations. Visualized as attributes, such as will, consciousness, and power, these differentiations do not delimit each other as in a spatial manifold, nor do they succeed each other as in serial time, yet they are changing aspects of the existential essence indicating multiplicity in its unity, an effable experience, simultaneously involving motion and omnipresence of every distinction. This specious presence, according to Dard, is related to the *dhat* in *dahr-i-haqīqi* (real duration). The *dhat* itself is identical with itself in *sarmadiyyāt-i-haqīqi*, real presence; the latter is the highest category of time.

Against this philosophic background, Iqbal' notion of time may well be appreciated. He asserts that the spatio-temporal determination of the external world in its intensive magnitude is an organic and living whole, which in its external manifestation serializes itself into the succession of momentary "nows."

## JALĀL-UD-DIN RUMI: LOVE, THE MODE OF KNOWLEDGE

For Iqbal material experience is icy cold and deadening to the soul. Consequently, for him knowledge is insight, not just sight. In this regard he was deeply influenced by Maulana Jalāl-ud-Din Rumi (d. 1273), whom Iqbal considered his spiritual mentor. Rumi says: "The world of soul is a pure sea, whereof bodily form is the foam. Contemplate the pure sea; why have you plunged your hand into the foam? The foam never rests on the surface of the sea, because the motion of the replenishing wave does not allow it to rest."[33] True knowledge is not cognition alone, it is also affection involving the total being of the seeker. True knowledge feels the pulse of organic transformation. Ultimately the distinctions between thought and experience, will and consciousness, judgment and affection disappear. Iqbal, following his mentor Rumi, designates this mode of knowledge as love. Modern espistemologists call it *verstehen*.

Rumi is the first great thinker who explained, in his *Diwān-i-Shamsi Tabriz* and *Mathnawi*, nearly all the aspects of this mode of knowing. For him love was a principle of moral behavior. As a principle of gnosis it meant oblivion in the "great ocean" of the Beloved with the loss of consciousness. Rumi in his poetic mystical vision grasped the dialectical tensions and epistemic meanings of the love experience. Love for Rumi is not just an experience, but the specific mode of experiencing the living reality. In love the seeker's faculties develop and he absorbs the attributes of the object of experience and realizes its nature. If you ask: "What is fire? [then] become fire." "The color of iron," says Rumi, "is lost in the color of the fire; the iron has assumed the color of the fire and has become like fire. When it becomes red like gold, then its appearance boasts without words 'I am fire.' Glorified by the color and nature of fire it says, 'I am fire, I am fire, if you doubt it, then come, put your hand on me or touch my face with your face.' "[34]

Rumi contrasts love with reason, proclaiming that the latter cannot bring to open relief the real bonds which connect individuals. "How should the intellect find the way to this connection? This intellect is in bondage to separation and union." Intellect analyzes and thus divides;

it is incapable of perceiving the bonds of organic union and growth. Love, on the other hand, is a principle of unification and synthesis. "The force of attraction in every atom and one form of life losing itself in another form [assimilation] and thereby resulting in growth—all are manifestations of love."[35]

Also, for Rumi love is a metaphysical principle identical with the formidable push of life, the creative urge unfolding itself in the objective world. His epistemology is thus inseparable from his cosmology, which is evolutionary. Iqbal's evolutionism grew out of Rumi's metaphysical outlook. Life develops by evolutionary stages. From matter to the stage of *fauna*, and eventually to the more developed stage of man, life has undergone several evolutionary periods. However, even man, according to Rumi, is not the final form of evolution. He proclaims: "Dying from animality, I became a man; why should I be afraid of becoming anything less through another death? In the next step I shall die from humanity in order to develop wings like the angels. Then again I shall sacrifice my angelic self and become that which cannot enter imagination" (*Mathnavi*, III, 1–3,6).

Iqbal's concept of human destiny is essentially based on Rumi's ideas. Iqbal does not believe in the incorruptibility of human soul, and he does not follow Avicenna and al-Ghazzali in holding that the soul is immortal by nature. According to him, "Personal immortality is not ours as of right. It is to be achieved by personal effort. Man is only a candidate for it."[36] These conclusions are implicit in Rumi's concept of evolution. (However, Iqbal's contribution lies in his refutation of Nietzsche's concept of eternal recurrence and Spencer's idea of static equilibrium, both of which are different versions of inorganic mechanism and inert materialism.) With the arrival of man, the prospects of further evolution become concentrated in the creative, antonomous, and self-conscious endeavors of the ego. The cosmic force does not operate as an impersonal collective sway, using human beings as means in its irresistible impetus toward change and evolution. Such an outlook leads to the historical determinism propounded by Hegel, Schopenhauer, and Marx. Rumi's metaphysics contains an opposite orientation, which Iqbal has fully realized in his *Six Lectures*. To Iqbal, evolution has led to the arrival of man, in whom life has become self-possessed, individualized, and concentrated. On man's career as an individual, as a free, creative agent, depends the future of evolution.

## MUJADDID ALF THANI: SECRET OF THE UNION

In the notion of union in separation Iqbal found the evolution of the ultimate form of reality. Every individual in his loving embrace contains all other individuals, yet this embrace individualizes them into mutual otherness and consolidates them in their respective singularities. Iqbal says:

> Our separation is separation in union
> Separation gives to this dust [i.e., man] an insight,
> It gives the weight of a mountain to a straw.
> Separation is a token of love;
> It agrees with the nature of lovers.
> If we are alive, it is due to their affliction [of separation].
> And if we are immortal, it is due to it.
> . . .
> To live in company is real life
> Love does not acquire insight without company;
> And without company it does not become self conscious.[37]

Iqbal's vision grasped the mystery of the law of identification, in which the lover is absorbed in the existential nucleus of the Beloved, or the latter is completely absorbed in the former. According to Iqbal, identification is not at all a love experience. Love throbs on the dual reference of existential confrontation between the lover and the beloved, and its essence is separation. (Consequently, its ontological category is union-in-separation.) The discovery of this category is a major achievement of Indic Muslim thought.

Shaikh Ahmad Sarhindi (1563–1624), known to the Muslims of India and Pakistan as Mujaddid Alf Thani, articulated this category of being (union-in-separation) with a philosophic precision. In this regard Iqbal was overwhelmingly influenced by him.

Shaikh Ahmad was born in Sarhind, and received his early education from his father, Shaikh 'Abdūl Ahad. After finishing his education at an early age, Shaikh Ahmad was initiated into Sufism by his father, an eminent Sufi. He received *Khilafat* (permission to teach others) from his father in the Chishtiya and Suhurawardiya orders. At age twenty-eight he went to Delhi and joined the Naqshbandiya order; in a short time he received the *Khilafat* from Khawja Bāqī Billah.

Although Shaikh Ahmad concedes the possibility of the experience of identity with the Beloved, he looks upon it only as an immature and partial mystic experience. According to him, the *sālik* (the lover in his journey toward the beloved), at one time may find himself charged with a mono-reference experience; but he has yet to go beyond. Describing the nature of mystic endeavor, he says: "This experience is such that when he looks at the earth, he does not find it; if he turns his gaze towards the sky, he does not see it. The face of the beloved he sees everywhere, in himself, in every direction."[38] Mystic poetry is full of this theme, but Shaikh Ahmad does not rank it high. The lover, according to him, advances to a higher station from this state of unitary experience and regains his consciousness of other things. As he is not totally recovered even at the next station of love, he feels that everything, including himself, is a shadow of the beloved. This experience makes the lover lose all initiative and drive, reducing him to a mere projection. Thus, all forms of judgments are suspended in this overpowering experience. Shaikh Ahmad admits that he, too, remained for some time in this state.[39]

However, he points out that the *sālik* is bound to ascend from this shadowy stage when the vagueness and mystery that shroud the journey disappear. The *sālik* eventually realizes the separation which, even when he reaches his union, individualizes him in relation to the beloved. Man's highest achievement at the end of the mystic journey, maintains Shaikh Ahmad, is his attainment of the supreme position of *'abduhū* (His servant). Shaikh Ahmad attributed the unitary experience— identification—to the ever-varying life of the *qalb* (heart). He says, as quoted by Iqbal, "It appears to me that the recipient of it has not yet passed even one fourth of the innumerable stations of the *qalb*. The remaining three fourths must be passed through in order to finish the experience of this first station of spiritual life. Beyond this station there are other stations known as *Rūh*, *Sirra Khāfi* and *Sirr-i-Akhfā*; each of these stations which together constitute what is technically called the *'Ālam-i-Amr* has its own characteristic states and experiences."

The world of love, in mystic terminology, is the world of heart. In its expanse this world of heart touches all souls, and is therefore the world of living reality. Placing it under the concept of the *'ālam-i-amr* (the world of commandment), Shaikh Ahmad believes this world of heart has infinite stations of mystic experiences. Here the principle of existence is not just seeing, but "becoming." The doors of this world are open for a truly living individual who unfolds his creative freedom by self-direction. This, too, is the world of commandment in which purposes and values constitute the contents of reality.

Against this philosophical background, Iqbal developed his theories of religion, morality, law, and society. All these categories are forms of human activity for which man himself is responsible. According to Iqbal, man transcends every form of cosmic determinism. There is no preordination, and absolutely no immanent fatalism unfolding human history. The pages of history are adorned by man himself, because he is the prime author of his own destiny. This central theme underlies his beautiful poetry:

> Travel into yourself and see what "I" is.
> To travel into self?—It is to be born
> without father and mother,
> To catch Pliads from the edge of the roof,
> To hold eternity with a single stroke of anguish,
> To break the spell of sea and land
> The heavens are in terror of its glory
> Time and space are in its grip
> It sought refuge in the heart of man
> It is in prison and yet free! What is this
> It is the lasso, the prey and the hunter! what is this
> There is a lamp with your heart;
> Don't be negligent, you are its trustees,
> What folly that you don't look within self.[40]

Iqbal interprets the problems of man with reference to the norms of *selfhood*: man preserves himself, and for that matter his institutions, by strengthening his ego and by creating in himself the attributes of God. To Iqbal's dismay, this philosophical spiritualism remained dormant in the evolution of Muslim thought, underneath its Persian encrustation.

# 11

# Conception of Time

## S. ALAM KHUNDMIRI

IQBAL occupies a unique position in the history of Muslim thought, for he is the first great thinker of Islam who has made a serious attempt to reconstruct Islam philosophy on an existential basis, without ignoring the claims of reason to critically examine the results of intuitive experience.

What Ghazzali had failed to do, Iqbal accomplished. Abu Hamid al-Ghazzali (1058–1111) mercilessly criticized scholastic Muslim thought based on Greek logic and Neo-Platonic traditions. He refuted the claims of natural philosophy to offer an understanding of the ultimate principles, for the first time separating the realm of theology from that of natural science and making a searching analysis of the scope and limit of logical understanding. In a sense, Ghazzali anticipated Kant. But the anticipation was not of much value as their motives were fundamentally different. Kant, by prescribing limits to human understanding, wanted to make the science of nature (physics) possible and to give religion, morality, and art their proper place in the scheme of human culture. In his criticism of theology, he maintained an extremely scientific attitude and opened new possibilities of understanding religious phenomena in their own right.

Ghazzali's attitude toward science is somewhat condescending; consequently, he makes a rigorous attempt to dislodge science and philosophy from the exalted place they had formerly occupied, thus reducing them to an insignificant level. What he wanted was to make room for religion at the expense of science and philosophy. For instance, his criticism of the notion of causality is not meant to redescribe the facts of experience in a cogent manner, but to make miracles possible.

The preoccupation of Ghazzali with this orthodox viewpoint makes his whole body of thought suspect in the eyes of the philosophic-minded inquirer. His book *Ihyā' 'Ulūm al-Dīn* (Revival of the Sciences of Religion) is not so much a reconstruction of religious thought but a fervent attempt to consolidate the orthodox position and close the doors to further speculation. This closed spirit prevails in all subsequent Muslim philosophy. Moreover, with the exception of Ibn-Khaldun (1332–1406), almost all the great creative thinkers beat the same well-trodden path of trying to demonlish Graeco-Muslim philosophy, without making serious attempts to evolve new modes of thought. Most of them lacked an authentic historical consciousness, without which no serious philosophical speculation is possible. The critics of Aristotelian logic and Neo-Platonic cosmology were themselves victims of this approach, the stagnation in the field of scientific inquiry having made their thinking somewhat repetitive.

In the eighteenth century Shah Waliullah (1703–1762) of Delhi seems to have taken the crisis in Muslim thought seriously. Although he was conscious of the political challenge from the West, he appeared to be hopelessly unaware of the advances in natural science and the theory of knowledge that were developing in other parts of the world. Since the philosophy of history is originally linked with the philosophy of nature, it is not surprising that history as a category of thought is entirely absent in the writings of this otherwise great thinker.[1] Having different theoretical assumptions, Jamal-ud-Din Afghani (1839–1897) and Sir Sayyid Ahmad Khan (1817–1889) tried to fill the gap. Since their motives were practical rather than speculative, they could only initiate new movements and were not able to establish new directions for future thought.

## CONCEPTION OF LIFE AND TIME

It is from this background that Iqbal emerged as the most outstanding philosopher, being the first Muslim thinker to rechannel Islamic thought. Instead of offering an apology for what the elders had said, Iqbal introduced new categories, making a bold attempt to reconstruct Islamic philosophy on hitherto unrecognized principles. It is only with Iqbal that global consciousness mirrors itself in contemporary Muslim thought, and *Islamic thought comes of age*. He is the first philosopher, not only in Islam but the whole East, who takes life and time seriously, and, instead of explaining them away, makes them the basis of his philosophy and poetry. Perhaps no other poet and thinker, with the exception of Sri Aurobindo, has taken these fundamental facts of experience as the starting points of his art and thought.

The philosophy of the East, with very few exceptions, had been a complete negation of the principles of life, time, and change. The unreality of time was, and still remains, the dominant attitude. The social a priori of Eastern thought had been this unreality of time and the insignificance of history. Ibn-Khaldun had always been respected but could not become an essential part of Muslim culture. It is a sad commentary on the East's philosophic thinking that this celebrated Eastern thinker had to be rediscovered by the West, and thereby became a part of Eastern legacy.

Iqbal shares with Ibn-Khaldun his positive, proscientific attitude, and like him tries to approach the problem of religious consciousness from a scientific standpoint. In his speculation, Iqbal never renounces this spirit; his whole endeavor is to offer a synthetic consciousness which does not stop merely at science or at so-called religion, supposed to be an antithesis of science, but which embraces all the moments of reflective consciousness and makes the emergence of different specifications of thought possible. These specifications are not mere moments in the dialectic of thought, but are the real moments of the reality which is one, and the synthetic which manifests itself in the process of time, thus making time real. And yet, at the unitive level they transcend temporal relations without making them unreal or less real, but essential elements of total reality.

According to Iqbal, "thought is the whole in its dynamic self-expression, appearing to the temporal vision as a series of definite specifications which cannot be understood except by a reciprocal reference. Their meaning lies not in their self identity, but in the larger whole of which they are the specific parts. This larger whole is, to use the Qur'ānic metaphor, a kind of 'preserved tablet' which holds up the entire undetermined possibilities of knowledge as a present reality, revealing itself in serial time as a succession of definite concepts appearing to reach a unity which is already present in them."[2] Thus thought expressed in its dynamic movement, and reality revealing itself in the process of thought, are not fundamentally two separate realities, nor is reality a mere appearance of thought. Both of them, while retaining their separate identities at the existential level, unite as two aspects of the same process at a higher unitive level, which although eluding logical understanding, reveals itself to man at an intuitive moment, whose nature is essentially different from temporal moments. This synthetic unitive nature of reality is the fundamental concept of Iqbal; and it is by this methodology that he escapes the conclusions of subjective and absolute idealisms. Throughout its history Muslim thought had been moving between these two extremes, although without committing itself to the total implications of either.

Muslim thought represents a very interesting instance of the convergence of subjectivism and absolutism. Both tendencies agreed in the conclusion that time is an irrelevant factor and that change does not belong to the nature of reality. Time and change are either accidents or mere illusions of the perceiving mind. The Mutakallimūn (dialectical theologians) tended toward some form of subjectivism, and the Sufi scholastics toward absolutism. The ultimate source of their thought was undoubtedly the Qur'ān, but the penultimate source was the Neo-Platonic Aristotelian tradition, both of them being emphatic in their denial of time as a constituent of reality.

For the ancient Greek philosophers change represented a principle of the degradation of reality, a fall from its original purity of oneness and from a condition of rest and immobility. The concept of fall was implicit in the Platonic dialogue *Timaeus* and in the Neo-Platonic metaphysics of emanation. Plato gave a concession to time as an image of eternity, but time only belonged to the phenomenal world which was in itself unreal.

Time and the universe of sense experience go together, and as the universe of sense experience is unreal, time is also by its association with this world unreal. Time can only be called real in the sense in which an image can be called real. Since the universe of sense experience is not a proper object of knowledge, time, too, cannot be regarded a proper object of knowledge. Time comes into existence simultaneously with the world of nature, but as creation itself is not an act or event in time, time is therefore, by definition, unreal. The intelligible world, that is, the world of ideas, is eternal, and eternity, according to the interpretation of Collingwood, is "not the mere absence of time (still less, of course, . . . an infinite amount of time) but . . . a mode of being which involves no change or lapse, because it contains everything necessary to itself at every moment of its existence."[3]

The philosophy of Plato is concerned with the banishment of time and the ultimate elimination of change. Since time and change go together, they also die together. Plato sets the trend of subsequent Greek and medieval philosophy. Aristotle takes the discussion of time more seriously than Plato, but in the final analysis regards it as an almost unnecessary principle in the understanding of reality. To Aristotle time is the numbering of motion. And as motion, in his teleology, is the meaning of change, time has no ontological significance and is relegated to a position of nonentity. "Aristotle begins characteristically by relating time to motion with the most simple and sparing use of the terms, but ends by setting forth a worldview of time that in its universality and solemnity is akin to that of Plato's *Timaeus*."[4]

Plotinus, the last great philosopher of antiquity, seems to have taken time far more solemnly, since he calls it an important principle for the things of the world, but his main purpose is to show that eternity is a higher and a truer category. It was because of Plotinus, more so than Plato, that the terminology of time and eternity became current in Christian and Arab philosophy and was transmitted to the modern world. The dynamic Hebraic world view was so much influenced by the static world view of Platonism and Neo-Platonism that Christian and Muslim theology merely pushed to the background the dynamic nature of reality as revealed in the Books.

The philosophers Abū Yūsuf Ya'qūb ibn Ishāq al-Kindi (b. 9th century) and Avicenna (980–1037) found in time nothing but the relations of posterior and prior, and to make time unreal went to the extent of regarding the world itself as eternal. This concept of the eternity of the world reached its culmination in the philosophy of Averroes (1126–1198).

The Mutakallimūn, particularly of Ash'arite tradition, adopted an atomic view of time. They inferred this view, according to Maimonides (1135–1204), from Aristotle's argument in his *Physics* that space, time, and motion are correlative notions and consequently have a certain correspondence to one another.[5] The logical corollary of this atomic view of time was their occasionalistic theory of creation. Existence was regarded as an accident, a created accident that ceased to exist forthwith, but it was held that God created in the atoms another accident of the same species so long as he wished that particular species to endure.⁶ This occasionalistic explanation of the world of becoming had a far-reaching consequence in the history of Muslim thought. It quickly assumed the respectable form of true orthodoxy and became an essential element of Muslim theology. The Mutakallimūn were led by important nonphilosophic motives, a primary one being to banish human reason from a position of significance. In their enthusiasm to make God truly all-powerful, they made man a mere tool in the scheme of divine omnipotence. With time as a succession of discontinuous "news," the continuity of the human self also became a mere myth.

The absolutists were no better. They held that the world is identical with God; thus the relation between the world and God is one of identity. The affirmation of God and the negation of the world are not two different propositions. The world is imaginary, unreal, and a mere appearance. Therefore, in a mere phenomenal world, time cannot be real.

The Mutakallimūn and the Unityists had reached almost identical conclusions as far as the unreality of time is concerned. Their theological motives apart, the method of inquiry adopted by these thinkers could not lead to better results. Even Razi (865–925), the most outstanding dialectician of Islam, could not achieve a satisfactory outcome. Nevertheless, he was better than many scholastics of Islam, in that he considered time to be a fundamental fact of experience. Razi admitted that he had not been able to understand the nature of time, although he regarded it as real as an immediate datum of experience. However, it was to make motion possible that time was to be presupposed.⁷ Like Leibnitz, Razi regarded time as a basic phenomenon, but the moment he applied the logical categories, the notion became involved in logical contradictions. The experience of time is fundamental, but as logic unfortunately does not support this fact of experience, it is to be rejected. It was in such a moment of exasperation that Broad said, "so much worse for the laws of logic."

The method of the scholastic thinkers was basically logical, and the whole history of philosophy—Eastern and Western—is a testimony to the fact that the problem of time eludes all logical thinking. Truth for logic must be eternal and free from all contradictions. Time is opposed to eternity and is not free from contradictions; hence it must be false. Leibnitz considered time to be fundamental, but understood it as consisting of mere relations, because it alone could be a logical solution. Kant regarded time and space as necessary presuppositions for human experience but maintained that they involved logical contradictions when applied to reality.

Among modern philosophers, McTaggart discusses time seriously, showing how the illusion of time occurs and why one is led to believe it as a constituent of reality. He denies time, assuming that what is self-contradictory and inconceivable cannot be real. He asserts rather emphatically that "if we are to find a single cause for error, we must find it in close connection with the appearance of time, and with the reality on which that series is based."[8] What seems to be so fundamental about the experience of time, that is, the passage of the present into the past, makes time a riddle for the idealists like McTaggart and Bradley.

The denial of time is not a special privilege of the idealist. Bertrand Russell, who does not share a single belief with the idealists, is delighted to eliminate time from the scheme of human knowledge. According to him, "there is some sense in which time is an unimportant and superficial characteristic of reality. Past and future must be acknowledged to be as real as the present, and a certain emancipation from slavery of time is essential to philosophical thought."[9] This is again a good example of the convergence of the extremes of subjectivism and idealism. Certain emancipation from the slavery of time may or may not be essential to philosophic thought; but for the proper understanding of the phenomena of life and change a degree of emancipation from the slavery of logic is essential. When logic (if not wholly abandoned) is subordinated to the facts of experience, time can become a true object of knowledge. As Harris has pointed out, the mistake of the logical-minded philosopher has been to impose the limits of physical science, in the Kantian tradition, upon all human knowledge. The science of biology and psychology, dealing with nature at higher levels than physics may prove to be channels of approach to the knowledge of the ultimate reality.[10] Only when the "character of our conscious experience" is made "the point of departure in all knowledge" can the nature of time and becoming be made comprehensible.

Iqbal, like some twentieth-century philosophers, accepts time in its immediacy and certainly considers it most seriously. He had poetic vision of the highest order, making it possible for him to see reality beyond the logical categories.

## TIME AND DURATION

It was not Iqbal the philosopher who became conscious of the importance of time. On the contrary, it was the poet that forced the philosopher to look for the immediate fact of experience. As a young poet he had a vision of the devastating aspect of time.[11] The vision was later broadened, and the poet saw in time not only an agent of destruction but also a principle factor for the creation of novelty and uniqueness. Then the poet of beauty, longing for union with its eternal source, was attracted by the increasing rhythm of life. The rhythm of life is not repetitive; it is creative of new forms. Thus the poet found perpetual struggle and strife in the process of life.

In *Bāng-i-Dara* (The Call of the Highway), Iqbal's first collection of Urdu poems, one comes across symbols which are expressive of the dynamic nature of reality. He uses the traditional symbols, which instead of conveying a pessimistic meaning, communicate a feeling of hope that out of destruction new creations will emerge. It is in the "death" of the innumerable stars that he sees the emergence of a sun, and the eternal, noiseless universe appears as a vast process of change and becoming. Finally, in *Khizr-i Rah* (The Guide), the last poem of *Bāng-i-Dara*, the concept of time as a ceaseless duration emerges. Life is not measurable in serial time, it is "overflowing, eternal and evergreen."[12] The idea of the life force overcoming all the obstacles imposed by nature and the past history of mankind dominates the consciousness of the poet. The word "new" acquires the sign of "holy" for him. Man is presented as a creator of ideals, aims, and goals and the realizer of values.

Iqbal gives a new message to the traditionalists, still mourning the disappearance of old institutions and modes of life, and brings to them the sight of the new sun on the horizon. His poetic vision crystalizes the idea that human "self" is the principle of creation. The poet attaches the highest value to the self, which develops in time and accepts challenges from the world of nature and human history. This idea is fully developed in his remarkable poem *Asrār-i Khudi* (The Secrets of the Self). It was in this poem that he developed the idea of the self and its evolution in the course of time, the ever-evolving finite self being the central fact of existence. Compared to classical Sufi doctrine, the scale of value has been completely reversed. For the classical Sufi, the absolute being was the central fact, and the finite individual was completely insignificant.

In *Asrār-i Khudi*, Iqbal declares that the aspiration of the finite self is not in losing its identity but in enhancing itself and evolving within the framework of its finitude, and in seeking proximity with the infinite self of God. The relationship between God and the finite self is not that of complete identity; it is a dialectical relationship of identity-diversity. The infinite can only be understood by the analogy of the definite. The infinite self is not a static being, but a dynamic principle of creation who creates the finite self of man in his own image and places him in a world full of challenges and promises. Thus man conquers the world of nature by mastering all the faculties bestowed upon him by his creator. In this process of conquest, Iqbal believes, God becomes man's coworker and helper. The conquest takes place in time; the history of mankind is the history of the gradual mastery of nature by man.

Iqbal was greatly influenced by the "activistic," mystic poet Rumi, who looked upon evolution as a law of life. For Rumi life consisted in creative activity and in endless struggle to overcome the forces of death and annihilation. In *Asrār-i Khudi*, Iqbal aggressively attacked Plato for his conception of reality as immobile and static. Iqbal also disapproved of the Muslim Sufis who believed in the analogous doctrine of *A'yān-i Th'abita*. It was the concept of self as the ultimate principle of reality, and ceaseless activity as the nature of self, that led Iqbal to a serious consideration of the problem of time.

In *Asrār-i Khudi* Iqbal presents a monadic scheme of existence. For Iqbal self or ego is unique, a center of force whose essential nature is activity. It has a preference for solitude, although it is not a closed system. (In his later poems Iqbal uses the symbol of the royal falcon to express this love for solitude.) It is organically related to other monads, achieving completion in the course of time and experiencing time as a pure duration. (Unlike Iqbal, Leibnitz reduced time to relations, and this reduction of time to mere relations made the activistic element of his philosophy rather meaningless.)

*Asrār-i Khudi* represents Iqbal's formative period as a philosopher. In this poem the reference to time is not direct; it is implied in his philosophy of activity. In *Payām-i Mashriq* (Message of the East), which represents the fruition of Iqbal's artistic genius, his concept of time as the ultimate principle is given the best poetic expression. It is in his poem *Nawā-i Waqt* (The Melody of Time) that time is presented as the "clothing of man and the garment of God and destiny as a mere spell of time."[13] This poem describes the devastating as well as the creative aspect of time. The dominant note in many poems of this collection is the identification of the real with the living and active, and the nonreal with the motionless and changeless. As the thinker in the poet matures, the problem of time becomes central in his poetry, and gradually self and duration are identified'

In *Javid-Namah* (The Book of Eternity) Iqbal makes a clear distinction between time, space, and duration. To him it is duration which is real, time and space being derivations from this duration. *Zarvān*, the soul of space and time, tells the poet that it is by contemplation and enjoyment of duration that space and time are broken. In another verse of the same collection, space and time are regarded as the modes of life.[14] It is only when vision is deflected from the immediately present reality, that the succession of today and tomorrow is produced. In *Masjid-i Qirtabāh* (The Mosque of Cordoba), a rather well-known poem in the collection *Bāl-i Jibrīl* (Gabriel's Wing), time is linked with history, and history is presented as a continuous process of the achievements of dynamic individuals, the heroes of history, who by their constant endeavor and ceaseless activity realize values and are able to transcend the transience of successive time.[15] In this poem time appears to be a continuous series of happenings, a process of becoming, a pure duration involving no succession of day and night. In this process of becoming, only those deeds are preserved which carry the marks of a strong will, love, and inner freedom. Love is the experience of pure duration; therefore, in the life of love there is pure continuity, which is not exhausted by the mere "present." The true self resists the transience of time because it has grasped time's real essence. Only on the plane of art and love—the modes of creation—can the temporality of time be arrested and pure duration grasped. By this intuitive grasp of duration alone can history be made a creative act of the real, enduring souls. History is not a mere unfolding of the static divine will. Its course is always open with unlimited possibilities. The future is not predetermined by the past; it is an open challenge and can only be met by creative spirits.

## THE PROBLEM OF TIME

This poetic vision of the nature of time and duration is made the subject matter of philosophic speculation in Iqbal's collection of lectures, *The Reconstruction of Religious Thought in Islam*. The problem of time is its central theme. Iqbal's interest in the concept of time is not merely speculative. It has, according to him, immense practical value. In one of his lectures, he points out that the problem of time is a problem of life and death for a historically conscious and growing community.[16] The practical implications of Iqbal's belief in the reality of time are very clear. If time is an illusion, the march of history is insignificant. If the course of evolution is predetermined, then "the future" becomes a meaningless term, a mere linguistic convention. If the past, which is irrevocable, determines the entire present and future, no individual and no community can be optimistic about the future; it has already become a fact. If this proposition is false, then the whole scientific procedure becomes suspect, because, for the purposes of natural science, there must be a complete equation between the different phases of time. This equation makes scientific predictions possible. This is what has been called by Russell "a certain emancipation from slavery to time." Science is committed to a kind of determinism and it is the function of speculative philosophy to examine whether or not the applicability of this concept can be confined to a specific class of events outside of which the concept will have no relevance. The problem is not exhausted by these considerations.

Not only does logic abhor time, but systematic theology is also an enemy of time. It has not received better treatment from the mystics, as mystic experience has invariably been associated with eternity, and time is opposed to eternity. God has always been described as outside space and time, but it is obvious that space and time cannot be considered outside God in the same sense in which God is supposed to be outside space and time. The inescapable conclusion is that such terms do not correspond to anything real. Undoubtedly time is a fact of experience, but it comes into conflict with another fact of experience, that is, religious consciousness, which always tends to transcend time and time relations. It is a matter of grave importance for a religiously inclined thinker to reconcile these two divergent claims. If time is given some form of reality, it must be distinguished from the relations that time involves. To deny reality to time is relatively easy within the framework of thought, but to assert its reality is not an easy task for a philosophic thinker. It was on account of this dilemma that St. Augustine said, "If nobody asks me, I know (what time is); but if I try to explain it to one who asks me, I do not know."

Like Bergson, Whitehead, and Alexander, Iqbal is fully aware of these not easily surmountable philosophic difficulties of time. For Bergson and Alexander the problem of God and the eternity of values are not problems of serious metaphysical concern. However, for Iqbal the problem is how to reconcile eternity with change. "The ultimate spiritual basis of all life as conceived by Islam is eternal and reveals itself in variety and change. A society based on such a concept of Reality must reconcile its life with the categories of change and permanence."[17] Since the source of these eternal principles is revelation, the reconciliation is a challenging task. The problem does not end here. In the cosmology of Alexander, God is never a complete fact, for he evolves along with the world. In fact, He is the evolving world itself, always being the next stage of the evolving universe. He is not even the nisus of the creative energy. The transcendence of God never offers a serious problem to Alexander because he is committed to the imminence of the nisus. As Leighton has remarked, the emergent evolution of Alexander is a modified form of materialism.[18] There is nothing in the beginning except space and time, and it is from this primordial stuff that matter, life, and God emerge. The concept of deity is so vague that it can be easily dispensed with. It seems to be a mere relational term which relates the lower with the higher. Alexander's cosmology is Aristotelianism expressed in the language of temporal development.

Bergson does not occupy a much happier position, torn asunder because of the inherent dualism in his thought. But he could never reconcile the dualism of life and matter (as Collingwood remarked) and the dualism of intellect and intuition (as Iqbal pointed out).[19] In addition to this, God does not occupy a very enviable position in his philosophic system. In his view, God would have been happier without the insignificant place He has been asked to share with almighty life. Bergson eliminates all reference to cosmic purposes in the scheme of creative evolution. He is inclined to believe that any mention of purpose will make evolution less creative.

Of these philosophers, Whitehead is the most serious about God; his system requires a reference to eternal objects. It is a different question how devoid of eternity these eternal objects emerge in the final analysis. Whitehead has tried to prove the need for God, for him "an ultimate irrationality. For no reason can be given for the nature of God because that nature is the ground of rationality."[20] In other words, God becomes a necessary postulate to save the system from final collapse, and to provide a basis for infinite possibilities. Nature and its passage are really the ultimate principles in the philosophy of Whitehead. Similarly, the problem of the immortality of the individual self is not a very serious problem for either Bergson or Whitehead. Alexander, with his naturalistic bias, can have no love for personal immortality. He would rather ask man to face the fact of natural death with a sense of piety, leaving unfinished aspirations for future generations with a hope that the world is, after all, a continuous process of creation.

These three great philosophers of time could afford to take time seriously because the other problems of philosophy and religious life were far less important to them. Iqbal's case is entirely different; his chief motive was to reconstruct a new ideational basis for Islamic thought, and God, eternity, and personal immortality were problems which could not be treated lightly in his philosophic system. He felt obliged to demonstrate the reality of time in a particular framework. He could not say cavalierly that since time and change are real the God of personal devotion and worship is an abstraction from the real flow of life.

## INFLUENCE OF WESTERN PHILOSOPHIES

IQBAL's central problem is how to reconcile existentialism with some form of absolutism. His commitment to the metaphysical basis of the Qur'ān leads him toward the concept of absolute unity, and his preoccupation with the problem of the human situation toward a dynamic view of reality. It does not mean that his system of thought is a collection of disjointed propositions—as is the case with some of modern thinkers, notably the Marxists. He endeavors to present a coherent, systematic doctrine; his preoccupations with the problem of time itself has a religious motif. He rebels against the classical spirit of Muslim theology, imbibing the best elements of the anticlassical and romantic movements of the twentieth century and synthesizing them with the romantic traditions of Sufism.

Generally, the philosophers of time represent the fruition of the Romantic movement of the West. The reality of time, change, and becoming cannot be reconciled with a rigid, logical, and intellectualistic frame of mind. The logical view presents a picture of the world as predetermined, static, and timeless. It has no relation to time, and time has no effect on it. Time, as has been suggested by M. F. Cleugh, is logical,[21] if not illogical. Assertion about time generates an attitude of mind which, if not anti-intellectual, is suspicious of the total claims of intellect. As time cannot be grasped by intellect alone, there must be some other source of knowledge capable of giving a deeper understanding of the nature of reality, including time. For instance, Bergson's choice of intuition as the only source of "feeling" time is not an arbitrary choice. It is the result of a rigorous analysis of the scientific method, which he declares is cinematographical and best suited to a life of action, because the life of action requires only a piecemeal knowledge of reality. Bergson does not oppose the scientific method as such; he only considers it inadequate for an understanding of all the levels of reality. He concludes that there must be an alternative method which does not negate the scientific method but rises above it.

Alexander's commitment to the realistic theory of knowledge stops him at the notion of natural piety. For him philosophy becomes a descriptive scheme and not an interpretation of the facts of experience. He demands that these facts be accepted with an attitude of natural piety, observing the march of evolution with a spirit of humility not very much different from the religious attitude of abnegation. The word "emergence" has, in fact, an element of the word "holy" in Alexander's philosophy. Whitehead's mathematical genius could not lead him to the dizzying heights of anti-intellectualism, but the terminus of his philosophy is, however, the "ultimate irrationality."

Iqbal does not entirely agree with any contemporary philosopher of time, although in varying degrees he is influenced by all of them. Bergson, of course, exercised the major influence on Iqbal, but the Muslim thinker is by no means alone in his indebtedness to the French philosopher. Whitehead has, on more than one occasion, admitted that Bergson was an important influence in the development of his

## Conception of Time

philosophy of time and organism. Bergson is one of the greatest and one of the most significant factors in the making of modern philosophic thought. The post-Bergson age is qualitatively different from the pre-Bergson age. After him no philosopher could take time lightly. Although it is true that all the contemporary philosophers of time are indebted to Bergson, it is significant that none has entirely agreed with him. From Bergson to Whitehead and Iqbal, one finds a continuous enlargement of an appreciation of the problem of time.

Iqbal agrees with Bergson that the real nature of time is pure duration and that the categories of time, space, and matter are abstractions from it. Duration is a continuous flow of conscious experience never felt by the self at its intellectual plane. Bergson insists that the true essence of time and change has always eluded understanding because previous philosophers have accepted physics as the only guide for the understanding of nature. To prove this point Bergson has made a brilliant analysis of the scientific method to show how inadequate it is for the purpose of interpreting the totality of the facts of experience.

Modern science seeks laws, and its laws set forth relations between magnitudes. The magnitude to which all other magnitudes are related is time, time being an independent variable in the method of science. Bergson points out that time consists of moments, which are virtual immobilities. In its relating activity, real time, regarded as a flux, as the very mobility of being, escapes the hold of scientific knowledge. Time becomes the fourth dimension of space. It is not real time; it is spatialized time.[22] If mind and life are made the points of departure in knowledge, the whole perspective will change. In life and consciousness time makes all the difference, for life and consciousness are perpetually changing, thus making time and change identical. Time experienced by the conscious self does not resemble a line. It is the physicist's time which is conceived as a line, as a series of events lying one beside the other. Bergson admits that this conception of time has a biological utility, but at the same time it has a limited applicability. It presents a picture of the world which is predictable, determinable, and calculable.

To Bergson, it is precisely this sort of world that is needed by man in dealing with his environment. For man intellect also serves a very useful purpose. Man feels safe in this world. His actions are facilitated by a view of the world which is bifurcated into unchanging instantaneous chunks. A life of action demands that the constant flow of reality be arrested. It helps man in executing his actions successfully, but distorts his vision of reality. A full and authentic vision of reality needs an entirely different source of knowledge. This Bergson calls intuition, a direct feeling of one's own ever-glowing conscious experience of life. Inner experience of the conscious self alone reveals the true nature of reality, which is ever-flowing and constantly passing from one state into another. In this intuitive grasp the difference between the time passed and time passing is obliterated. Man lives in a pure flux of being.

Iqbal agrees with this account of time given by Bergson, and is also in general agreement with the dynamic nature of reality he presents. But Iqbal's fundamental position is different from Bergson's. He states it in one of his lectures: "Space, time and matter are interpretations which thought puts on the creative activity of God. They are not independent realities existing *per se*, but only intellectual modes of apprehending the life of God."[23] Time and again, Iqbal, in his lectures, speaks of the ultimate nature of reality as spiritual. This position is of immense value. For Bergson it is life with its creative force that is the ultimate nature of reality. It looks dynamic but creates serious metaphysical problems which become nearly insurmountable. As Collingwood has remarked, "If we cannot seriously accept Kant's theory that nature is a by-product of the thinking activity of the human mind, because we are sure that the opposite is nearer the truth, how can we accept Bergson's similar theory that the world of physics is a by-product of the self-creative activity of life? This is a new form of subjective idealism, of which we might say what Hume said of Berkley's, that the argument might admit of no answer, but it produced no conviction."[24]

As all reality cannot be reduced to the self-creative activity of life, a dualism of matter and life creeps into the philosophy of Bergson, which according to Collingwood is irreducible.[25] Matter serves a very useful purpose in Bergson's cosmology. It obstructs the creative, onward flow of life. But how can a by-product obstruct the flow of that of which it is a by-product? Unless matter is presupposed to be prior to life, it cannot perform this necessary function of obstruction. Only a unitary view of reality can satisfy metaphysical needs. It is on account of this problem that Iqbal is more in agreement with Whitehead, who adopts an "organismic" view of reality.

Whitehead and Iqbal take a position which is very close to that of

Leibnitz. Iqbal significantly substitutes the words "God" and "His creative activity" for Bergson's "life" and its creative activity. It symbolizes the parting of the ways. Iqbal agrees with Bergson that the point of departure for knowledge can only be the conscious self. Here the agreement ends. Iqbal crosses the limits of the conscious self, after finding the clue to the nature of reality, which is duration, and develops the concept of the infinite self or ego, which can experience real duration. For Bergson, life is ultimate; for Iqbal, it is a mode of the infinite being or ego. In this infinite ego, the categories of being and becoming are united. "Reality," says Iqbal, "is essentially spirit. But of course, there are degrees of spirit. I have conceived the ultimate reality as an Ego and I must now add that from the ultimate Ego only Egos can proceed. Only that is, strictly speaking, real which is directly conscious of its own reality. The degree of reality varies with the feeling of Egohood."[26] If the nature of reality is egolike, then, what is matter, which is the antithesis of ego? Iqbal says, "Matter is a colony of Egos of a low order out of which emerges the Ego of a higher order, when their association and interaction reach a certain degree of coordination."[27] There is an onward march of evolution, and the supreme infinite ego is the ultimate ground of this evolutionary movement. Iqbal tries to bridge the gap between life and nonlife, and conscious and nonconscious, by postulating a common basis and source of all becoming. If there is an intelligent super ego as the ground of all evolution, the evolution cannot be a blind process, advancing upward without any clear direction, as conceived by Bergson.

Iqbal is in fundamental disagreement with Bergson on the status of future. He partially agrees with Bergson that the time passed is different from the time passing, but he disagrees with him regarding a basic implication of his account of real time. For Bergson the past persists into and penetrates the present and the future. In the determination of the course of its movement the future has no role to play. He insists that the "portals of the future must remain wide open to reality." This view of the "open future" frees the Bergsonian scheme from any possibility of determinism. He wants to eliminate any reference to teleology, to purposes and ends, since the postulation of purpose will result in the diminution of freedom and creativity.

Iqbal rejects the conventional teleological conception of the "working out of a plan in view of a predetermined end or goal," because "it does make time unreal."[28] Iqbal believes that this view is hardly distinguishable from materialism. But he does not believe that evolution toward an end is the only explanation of the world process. Evolution is either realization of higher values or it is not evolution. As Whitehead has put it, "Possibilities do not themselves decide which of them is to be actual."[29] This would be a contradiction, since it would make the unselected possibilities impossibilities. Further, actuality cannot in advance decide upon its future stages, since futurity in its distinctive difference from pastness means a certain indecisiveness in what is future. Hence the selection of a given possibility for realization can only be creative act in the present occasion, which is itself creative.[30]

Whitehead and Iqbal agree with Broad that the future, as an event, does not exist. It is an anticipation, and anticipation does control future happenings in a certain sense. Iqbal suggests that ends and purposes form the warp and woof of man's conscious experience.[31] The notion of purpose involves a reference to the future. The past itself was the realization of once a future possibility. The present embodies the whole past and moves forward to realize some selected possibilities. "Life is only a series of acts of attention, and an act of attention is inexplicable without reference to a purpose, conscious or unconscious."[32] These purposes color not only the present state of consciousness, but also reveal its future direction.[33] Iqbal concludes that past and future both operate in the present state of consciousness and the future is not entirely undetermined, as Bergson's analysis of our conscious experience shows.

Iqbal, like Whitehead, takes both memory and imagination into account. The source of this mistake in Bergson's analysis of the future lies, according to Iqbal, "in regarding the pure time as prior to self, to which alone pure duration is predictable."[34] Further, he says, "To exist in pure duration is to be a self, and to be a self is to be able to say 'I am.' The ultimate self alone can say 'I am' in its full connotation."[35] It is the ultimate self alone for whom the non-self or the wholly "other" does not exist, as something external to it. World is the creative act of this pure self. It is a structure of events, a systematic mode of behavior, and as such organic to the ultimate self.[36] As the ultimate self is a free, creative self, nothing is predetermined in the world. "Nothing is more alien to Qur'ānic outlook than the idea that the universe is the temporal working out of a preconceived plan."[37]

## INFLUENCE OF THE QUR'ĀN

The universe, according to the Qur'ān, is likely to develop further. It is a growing universe and not an already completed product which left the hand of its maker ages ago, now lying stretched in space as a dead mass of matter to which time does nothing and consequently is nothing.[38] The universe, in brief, is finite but boundless. Iqbal agrees with the philosophers of time and particularly with Whitehead on this point. However, a serious difficulty of a theological nature arises. If the universe is not predetermined, then what is destiny? For creation and destiny go together in the Qur'ān. For this, Iqbal offers a very interesting explanation. He defines destiny as time regarded prior to the disclosure of possibilities. It is time regarded as an organic whole. "The destiny of a thing is not an unrelenting fate working from without; it is the inward reach of a thing, its realizable possibilities which lie within the depths of its nature and actualize themselves in a serial order without any feeling of external compulsion."[39] This interpretation of destiny is one of the best examples of Iqbal's philosophic genius, and is conclusively brought home in his interpretation of divine knowledge and omnipotence. If omniscience and omnipotence are given their literal meaning, then future cannot be really free. Iqbal explains that if divine knowledge is regarded as a single indivisible act of perception, which makes God immediately aware of the entire sweep of history, regarded as an order of specific events, the universe will appear as a closed universe, a fixed futurity and a predetermined, unalterable order of specific events.[40] This view will make history insignificant, and no room will be left for creation.

Iqbal suggests that divine knowledge must be conceived as a living, creative activity to which objects that appear to exist in their own right are organically related. He says that the future certainly pre-exists the past, but it does so as an end or purpose which is yet to be realized. He explains the notion of the pre-existence of the future as pre-existence in the organic whole of God's creative activity and not as a fixed order of events with definite outlines. It simply means that although God knows the future it is not the future of something external but the future possibilities of his own creative activity. This explanation gives a new meaning to the notion of omnipotence, a much-debated idea in Muslim theology. As already stated, God is absolute ego, and from this ego only egos proceed. The whole universe is a colony of egos, and some egos are endowed with the power of spontaneous action and freedom. Iqbal admits that the emergence of such free egos is a limitation on the freedom of the all-inclusive being, but he regards such a limitation as derived from his own creative freedom, allowing finite egos to be participators of His life, power, and freedom.[41] The orthodox view of omnipotence, Iqbal thinks, will make the moral evolution of man as a free spiritual being meaningless.

## THE RELATION OF GOD TO TIME

AND now, the most important question of this discussion: the relation of God to time. God is infinite, and infinity demands that He must be above time and the relations of time. He is the beginning and the end. One can think of time in God, but one cannot think of God in time. Iqbal, in one of his poems, '*La ila ill-Allah,* says: "Nā hai zamāñ nā makāñ; 'la ila ill-Allah!'" (There is neither time nor space; nothing exists absolutely except God.)[42] Here a distinction should be made between time and space as abstractions of thought and time as pure duration. Iqbal clearly says that beyond Him and apart from His creative activity there is neither time nor space to exclude him from any reference to other egos.[43] He calls space and time the possibilities of ultimate ego, only partially realized in the shape of mathematical time and space. These two statements put together do not convey a clear idea. Is man to look back to Aristotle who called matter a mere possibility? The second statement suggests this, whereas the first gives something like a Platonic solution of time and the universe of sense experience going together; and in the realm of the infinite, time having no relevance.

Whitehead, too, was not clear on this point. According to Whitehead, time outside the passage of nature is insignificant.[44] If this is the final position of Iqbal and Whitehead, then it is true that all philosophy consists of footnotes to Plato's dialogues. Iqbal is aware that this position reduces the whole philosophy of time to a farce, implying that time was taken seriously just to be abandoned when its company started to be embarrassing. This romantic engagement with time is becoming a comedy of a very low order. Iqbal endeavors to save his notion of time from utter collapse, suggesting that the infinity of the ultimate ego consists in endless inner possibilities of His creative activity, and that the universe as known is only a partial expression of them. In one word, God's infinity is intensive, not extensive. It involves an infinite series, but is not in that series.[45] The final position of Whitehead seems to be conclusive: "There is time because there are happenings, and apart from happenings and therefore, [it] will not be wrong to say that God and time are two polar concepts." Time is real because creation is a real process in time. Creation, to be true creation, must involve novelty and newness; but there must be a ground of this evergrowing and expanding universe. This will be the limit of man's knowledge.

Iqbal suggests that by intuition man may be able to grasp the idea of duration, and by analogy conceive the being of God as "a pure duration without succession." This suggests that modern philosophy has been able to overcome certain limitations imposed upon knowledge by Kant, but the reality still remains and perhaps may ever remain beyond the intellectual grasp of man. It is impossible to meditate on time and the creative passage of nature without overwhelming emotion at the limitations of human intelligence.[46] And this is what Iqbal ultimately says:

> Nā hai zamāñ na makāñ; 'la ila ill-Allah.
> 
> There is neither time nor space; Nothing exists absolutely except Allah.

# 12

# The Doctrine of Personality

## N. P. ANIKEYEV

IQBAL enjoys wide popularity not only in India and Pakistan but throughout the East, especially among Muslims. However, it should be noted that in evaluating the ideas of this outstanding thinker-poet, one notices several extreme and, in fact, mutually exclusive points of view. Reactionary forces, after stamping out everything in his works that is progressive and advanced, try to use his name and prestige to cover up and justify their own narrowly selfish and egotistical interests. Also, there are progressivists and pseudo progressivists who declare Iqbal's views reactionary and conservative on the grounds that he spoke, so they say, only to the Muslims because he derived the arguments for his theories and the awakening of the East from the Qur'ān. Finally, there are also admirers of his world view who strive with all their might to prove that Iqbal's ideas are the only true ideas, that they must become the guiding star for mankind and that they very nearly serve as its salvation in our age of general despair and hopelessness.

As far as objectively irreconcilable opinions like these are concerned, the work of Iqbal is not exceptional. It is well known that the world view of nearly all great thinkers in any area of spiritual culture has caused, in different eras, the most varied reaction in various strata of society. But in addition to this general reason for such antithetical evaluations of Iqbal, there is also another serious basis in the very nature of his views, which frequently contain inconsistencies and contradictions, and in the complexity and depth of the development of his creative and spiritual evolution, which reflected the complex and contradictory processes of India's ideological life in the first third of the twentieth century.

Iqbal's conscious activity came at the period in the development of his homeland when it had started to struggle for its liberation from colonial oppression. The basis of this struggle consisted in the requirements of India's social development, hindered by its dependence on British imperialism, which in turn perpetuated the country's feudal backwardness and institutions. But the ideological reflection of the struggle for independence and rebirth, as a rule, took the form of religious ideology in two of its basic and, in India, most widespread forms, Hinduism and Islam.

## ROLE OF RELIGION IN THE DEVELOPMENT OF AFRO-ASIAN NATIONALISMS

NEARLY all the political and spiritual leaders in India at the time, and indeed in present-day India, put forth their nationalistic, patriotic programs—even the most progressive and radical of them—under the banner of loyalty to the traditional religions of their homeland. An analagous picture was and is indeed now to be seen in the majority of the Asian and African countries fighting for their independence. Herein lies the distinctive characteristic of the development of the peoples of the East, as contrasted with the West, where the struggle against feudalism and medievalism was carried on, as a rule, under slogans of atheism, anticlericalism, and often even philosophical materialism. As is well known, this circumstance has frequently been depicted in literature as the inherent spirituality of the peoples of the East and as their age-old adherence to a traditional-religious way of life, which allegedly distinguishes the East from the materialist, utilitarian-pragmatic civilization of the West. It is precisely at this point that we have the beginning of the two concepts of Europocentrism and Orientocentrism, which at first glance seem to contrast but are in essence equally fallacious.

The question of the religiosity and traditionalism of the spiritual life of the countries in the East is a rather complicated but, more importantly, an independent subject; however, since it has a direct bearing on Iqbal's world view, at least a few words must be devoted to it. The religiosity and traditionalism of spiritual life in many of the countries of the East has been conditioned by a whole series of factors, of an objective as well as a subjective nature, among which the following may be singled out.

1. Under the conditions of the Asian and African peoples' socio-economic and cultural backwardness, caused primarily by their long sojourn in the chains of colonial slavery, and in the face of a trampling of their national cultures by foreign powers, the heritage of the past and the traditional religion stand forth almost inevitably as the symbol of national pride and distinction, and as a means of expressing patriotic emotions. Moreover, religion has been connected with and has had attributed to it all the grandeur and achievements of Indian civilization in past ages, which have proved especially dazzling against the background of the arbitrary rule and ruthlessness of the colonial systems. It is for this reason that the source of a future renaissance for the motherland was sought in religion.

2. The extensive influence of religious ideology on spiritual life in the countries of Asia and Africa is also furthered by certain features of the religions most widespread there—Islam, Buddhism, Hinduism, and others. As distinguished from the Christianity prevalent in the West, religious creeds in the East are not rigidly centralized, clearly organized religions. They lack a clergy appointed from above, standing above and opposed to laymen, and they are far more intimately intertwined with the daily life of the masses. Therefore, any social concepts in the East are most likely to find access to the popular masses, held captive by religious vestiges and prejudices, by appealing to their religious emotions and sentiments. This is why religion, more often than not, is becoming the mouthpiece of social movements, the reactionary as well as the progressive, including the national liberation movements.

3. The religiosity of the national liberation movement ideology in the countries of Asia and Africa is also determined by the character of its leadership: because of the small numbers and poor organization of the working classes in these countries, leadership is in the hands of the bourgeois and petty bourgeois classes and the nonproletarian parties. By virtue of their social nature they themselves are highly susceptible to a religious-idealistic world view and for that reason are incapable of resisting the influence of a peasant element enmeshed in religious prejudices.

4. Besides, the national liberation movement and the ideology of nationalism in the countries of the East were in the formative process during the historical period (end of the nineteenth century, beginning of the twentieth) when the capitalist system, reigning supreme in the

West, was disclosing clearly its exploitative nature, as well as its internal contradictions, and when it had begun to disregard the ideals of democracy and humanism. The colonial peoples, who had become the object of capitalism's exploitation, experienced these sides of it particularly keenly. It is completely natural that the capitalist civilization of the West not only could not be acceptable to the thinkers in the East but, on the contrary, excited the sharpest condemnation among them. Moreover, the antihumanist nature of capitalism presented itself to them as the consequence of the excessive attention paid in the West to the material side of life, which was supposed to be the result of the "worldly utilitarian" nature of Western civilization in general. It is true that the ideologies of nationalism in the East usually have not rejected the material values of life and have acknowledged them as an important and necessary element of social progress, giving the achievements of the West their due in this respect. But at the same time these ideologies have held that in order to avoid negative consequences, the material aspects of life must be subordinated to the spiritual values that allegedly find their highest expression in religion, including primarily the religions of the East.

Thus, by virtue of all these and an entire series of other reasons, religious motifs and sentiments burst forth in a mighty stream in the teachings of the overwhelming majority of the ideologists for Afro-Asian nationalisms. It is now important to stress that these reasons bear a concretely historical and socially determined character, and so there are no grounds for talk of the inherent religiosity and spirituality of the peoples of the East.

Of course, religion is far from the most adequate form of expression for the progressive substance of a national liberation movement. Nevertheless, in the majority of the countries of the East, for the reasons noted above, religion has proved to be the ideological banner of processes that in their significance for all mankind are revolutionary. Therefore the slogans "revive Hinduism" and "revive Islam" cannot always be the criteria of how reactionary one thinker or another was or one current or another was under the specific conditions in India at that time. Everything depends upon which forces backed them and what meaning they attributed to what would seem to have no relationship whatever to practical life, that is, religio-scholastic questions concerning the soul and its relationship to God and the world. When we evaluate the highly important role played by religion in India, these questions take on rather great significance even in the sphere of the political struggle. The aspect of this problem which interests us most, freed of its religious trappings, boils down ultimately to: how man should behave in society.

Some thought that since the soul had no independent existence but was an illusory manifestation of the only true and genuinely real existence, God, the absolute, etc., the ultimate meaning of life therefore consisted of merging with this absolute, of becoming one with it by renouncing, or at least having an indifferent attitude toward, the worldly vanity of vanities. Posing the question in such a way led to the preaching of asceticism, suppression of the will, and, finally, passive submission to the existing state of affairs.

Representatives of the patriotic community opposed this trend. Proceeding from the same religio-idealistic premises, they demonstrated the reality of the existence of the human personality and the human soul, the affirmation and strengthening of which are the only aim of life and purpose of man. Hence the recognition of man's high mission in this world and respect for his individuality and dignity. Such an approach provided the basis for demanding the creation of the proper conditions for developing the personality (freedom first of all), for demanding a change in the existing situation and a struggle to reform it. Such was the atmosphere in which this ideology responded to the aspirations of the progressive forces in Indian society who were interested in delivering the country from colonial dependency, weakening the bonds of feudalism, and giving full range to bourgeois attitudes. A host of representatives of the "Indian Renaissance," including S. Vivekananda, B. G. Tilak, Aurobindo Ghosh, Rabindranath Tagore, M. K. Gandhi, and others, preached these views. Among Muslims this role, to a significant degree, fell to Sir Sayyid Ahmad Khan and Muhammad Iqbal.

Iqbal is justly called the poet of philosophers and the philosopher of poets. He thought that art, including poetry, must above all shed light on life's most profound problems instead of wallowing in its trivia. It must strengthen man's creative ability and inspire him to struggle for a better life, not lure him away from this struggle, as the supporters of art for art's sake urge. "The highest art is that which awakens our dormant will-force and nerves us to face the trials of life manfully.

All that brings drowsiness and makes us shut our eyes to Reality around, on the mastery of which alone Life depends, is a message of decay and death. There should be no opium-eating in art. The dogma of art for the sake of art is a clever invention of decadence to cheat us out of life and power,"[1] Iqbal wrote in 1916. He preserved and carried this understanding of the high goals and civil calling of art through his whole life.

## THE REALITY OF PERSONALITY

THE main feature of Iqbal's works and world view is the doctrine of personality, the reality of its existence and the necessity to do everything to strengthen it. "The moral and religious ideal of man is not self-negation but self-affirmation and he attains to this ideal by becoming more and more individual, more and more unique."[2] This concept stands out in all Iqbal's works and is his determining, in fact his starting, point in his solutions to all the other cosmological problems.

Close acquaintance with the West leads the poet to the conviction that the main reason for India's backwardness (the backwardness of the entire East, for that matter) and humble position lies in its widespread and dominant systems of philosophy that preach passivity, self-denial, and indifference to the living conditions that surround man. Therefore, Iqbal directs all the enthusiasm of his works against these particular views and their chief exponents—religious Vedantism among the Hindus and the mysticism of the Sufis among the Muslims, as well as against the European varieties of idealism, to which he contrasts his theory of the soul as an active, creative source, eternally seeking and never stopping in its search. "Obviously, this view of man and the universe is opposed to that of the English neo-Hegelians as well as to all forms of pantheistic Sufism which regard absorption in a universal life or soul as the final aim and salvation of man."[3]

In order to prove the existence of the personality, Iqbal considers the entire universe and the entire material world as a composite of individual egos, isolated and separated from each other. "All life is individual; there is no such thing as universal life."[4]

Iqbal attached great importance to this point—the independence and self-determination of the ego—and considers it the basic characteristic of individuality: "The nature of the ego is such that, in spite of its capacity to respond to other egos, it is self-centered and possesses a private circuit of individuality excluding all egos other than itself."[5] In its higher manifestations—in man and in God—individuality becomes a self-contained exclusive center.[6]

The personality reveals its existence in its constant formation of desires, passions, and ideals.

> We live by forming
> We glow with the sunbeams of desire![7]

Desires and passions do not arise spontaneously, but under the influence of a yet higher emotion—love—which Iqbal has elevated to the rank of the basic, all-determining, universally known moral-philosophical category. "This word is used," Iqbal explains, "in a very wide sense and means the desire to assimilate, to absorb. Its highest form is the creation of values and ideas and the endeavor to realize them."[8]

Thus, Iqbal does not merely believe that the existence of the personality is confined only to the production of ideals and desires. They are only the initial stage of life, which in its true embodiment must manifest itself in creative activity to subordinate and reshape the external world.

In opposition to the theory that the personality as such has no objective criterion for its existence and that the fact of its so-called self-evident being is based solely on the Cartesian conviction *cogito ergo sum*, Iqbal said that the reality of the individual manifests itself not in the act of contemplation but in his purposeful, practical activity in the world, which is the only thing fashioning the personality and demonstrating its objectivity: "The final act is not an intellectual act, but a vital act which deepens the whole being of the ego, and sharpens his will with the creative assurance that the world is not something to be merely seen or known through concepts, but something to be made and re-made by continuous action."[9]

Thus, genuine individuality proves to be inseparable from activity and the active, creative life. In one of his poems Iqbal symbolizes this idea with the image of a wave, which says of itself:

> When I am rolling, I exist,
> When I rest, I am no more.[10]

Tireless functioning, activity, and the struggle against difficulties are, properly speaking, life itself, which in this manifestation is a synonym for freedom.

For Iqbal, only he who considers himself the master of life can claim the right to call himself a real man, a *momin*. He is a "true believer," because he deems himself the master of life; otherwise he is an "infidel," a *kafir*. Belonging to different religious faiths has no significance here; it is not what determines the value of the individual:

> He who feels himself lost in the world is a *kafir*.
> But he who knows, he is sovereign of the world—a *momin*.[11]

To all intents and purposes, true individuality, according to Iqbal, is characterized primarily by its activity and its active relationship to the world. On this level he deemed it possible to speak of immortality, which is not a right or quality residing in man, but which can and must be acquired in the process of constant action. Iqbal places his ideal of man so high that he proclaims him, in the highest and ultimate form of his development, an earthly god or the deputy of God on earth, a model of the harmonious combination of thought and action, instinct and reason, the model toward which it is necessary to strive and whose attainment by all people will signify the advent of the Kingdom of God on earth.

A state of lassitude and inertia indicates the absence of individuality, tantamount to its death. From this Iqbal also draws the criterion for the ethical values of good and evil: Everything that strengthens the personality is good; everything that weakens it is evil. These are the positions from which religion, ethics, and art must be evaluated. It is from these very positions that Iqbal opposed Plato: the poet perceived in the influence of Plato's teachings on Muslim ideology the main reason for the loss of its original life-affirming spirit.

> His mind's eye created a mirage.
> Since he was without any taste for action,
> His soul was enraptured by the non-existent.
> He disbelieved in the material universe
> And became the creator of invisible ideas . . .
> He dominates our thinking,
> His cup sends us to sleep and takes the
>     sensible world away from us.[12]

Asking (*swāl*) leads to the weakening, humiliation, and degradation of the personality. Under the definition of *swāl*, Iqbal says, comes everything that is achieved without personal effort, for example, the position of the rich heir or the status of a man who lives on another's thinking—in general, any blessing acquired without fighting for it. Asking makes poverty even more humiliating.

> By asking, poverty is made more abject;
> By begging, the beggar is made poorer . . .
> Seek not thy daily bread from the bounty of another . . .
> A whole ocean, if gained by begging, is but a sea of fire;
> Sweet is a little dew gathered by one's own hand.[13]

All the sobering and striking significance of these words becomes especially clear if we remember that in the India of that period sweet illusions were widespread among the intelligentsia regarding the possibility of persuading the colonial power of the necessity of giving up their domination over their country by peaceful means, through "good behavior." In the poem *Taskhīr-i Fitrat* written to the motifs of Milton's *Paradise Lost*, Iqbal says (in condemnation of these sentiments), that man can achieve his paradise not as the result of someone else's charity, mediation, or intercession, but only as the result of developing and strengthening his own personality; that is, happiness is acquired through one's own efforts and not through the remission of sins by someone else.[14]

When the question was posed this way, Iqbal could not consider the external world an illusion whose fetters bind the spirit in its drive to merge with God the Absolute. On the contrary, for Iqbal the material external world is a necessary factor of the personality's being. "Nature," he says, "is not evil, since it enables the inner powers of life to unfold themselves."[15]

## THE INDIVIDUAL IN SOCIETY

THE most intimate and direct reality, in the sphere of which all the qualities and potentialities of the individual are realized and his purpose in life effected, is society. Only here man can unfurl his creative activity, approach the ideal of man, gain freedom, and make himself

# The Doctrine of Personality

immortal. The individual personality must take a social path and devote itself to serving society. This does not at all mean the loss of its individuality; on the contrary, the social path enables personality to realize itself.

In the light of this, the futility of any comparison, even a parallel, sometimes drawn between Iqbal's ideal man and Nietzsche's *Übermensch* is obvious.[16] It is true that Iqbal spoke sympathetically of Nietzsche, but in such instances, as a rule, he had in mind the venomous attacks on certain aspects of bourgeois civilization that had attracted him to German philosophy, in particular the attacks on clericalism. Iqbal said of Nietzsche that "he plunged his sword into the heart of Europe and his hands are stained with the blood of the clergy."[17] But basically—in their concept of man and his purpose in the world—they are radically different.

In his striving for power, Nietzsche's *Übermensch* cynically tramples all the generally accepted moral and ethical values, and the people for him are a mere crowd, a herd above which he must proudly rise and reign. Iqbal, on the contrary, wants the entire people to be made up of strong, willful personalities united by the common ideals of friendship, fraternity, and mutual service. In his works Iqbal repeatedly disassociated himself outright from Nietzsche's cynical aristocratism. However, Iqbal's positive presentation of this question serves as the most convincing argument in favor of the contrast, in principle, of their views.

Only in society does man achieve self-realization, and society, in subordinating man to its social structure, makes him free.[18] Iqbal says that when man dissolves his "I" in society, he finds his true individuality in its past history, past traditions, and future achievements. The individual reflects in himself the diversity of society, and the diversity of society embodies its unity in the individual.

> For man, belonging to society is a blessing,
> Society contributes to the perfection of his qualities.
> When man identifies with society
> He is like a drop becoming the ocean within the ocean . . .
> The separate individual knows no goals or ideals
> And cannot find uses for his abilities.[19]

The personality that has entirely devoted itself to society acquires immortality, since this personality, as it were, concentrates within itself the past and future of its dominant social ideas. In other words, man's immortality must be understood not as his personal physical immortality but as the eternity and constancy of human civilization and the human intellect. In devoting himself to the service of society, man thereby makes the good of society the goal of his existence. He merges his limited and finite spiritual world with the world of society, which is immortal in its historical development and infinite in its possibilities, thus partaking of its immortality, infinitude, and omnipotence. Only the social man turns himself into the crown of creation and the master of the universe, which he must take over, subdue, and reshape: "It is the lot of man to share in the deeper aspirations of the universe around him and to shape his own destiny as well as that of the universe, now by adjusting himself to its forces, now by putting the whole of his energy to mould its forces to his own ends and purposes."[20] Once the discussion turns to this aspect of man, Iqbal truly becomes the troubador of man's creative and constructive capabilities, his unlimited possibilities for reshaping and subduing the external world: "Hard his lot and frail his being, like a rose-leaf, yet no form of reality is so powerful, so inspiring, and so beautiful as the spirit of man."[21]

In his laudation of man Iqbal places him at least on an equal plane with God the Creator, if not higher. In the anthology *Payām-i Mashriq* (Message of the East) is the famous poem *Mahawārah Ma-bayen Khudā wa Insān* (God's Talk with Man), in which man hurls a challenge at the Creator himself:

> You created the night—I lit the lamp
> You created clay—I molded the cup.
> You made the wilderness, mountains and forests
> I cultivated flower-beds, parks and gardens.
> I made a mirror from rock
> And from poison I extracted a sweet beverage![22]

You will hardly find another poet in the East in whose works the Promethian motifs are so strong.

## PERSONALITY AND THE POLITICAL SOCIETY

WHAT was Iqbal's notion of the interrelation among people in society and its social structure? The main demand on the people in what he

## The Doctrine of Personality 275

considered the ideal society was respect for one another: "The principle of the ego-sustaining deed is respect for the ego in myself as well as in others."[23] In *Javid-Namah* (The Book of Eternity) he states that "humanism means respect for man and realization of the position and place of man."

Unlike many Indian thinkers, Iqbal understood that past history offers no such ideal of society. At the same time Iqbal believed that Western civilization did not have, nor by its very nature could it have, a society in which relationships among people are based on the principle of friendship and brotherhood with one another. Iqbal's criticism of the bourgeois order is one of the most forceful and impressive sides of his work. In this respect he has been likened to a man holding a mirror before the West, not unlike Hamlet who became the eternal reproach to his mother's conscience.

During his first visit to Europe, Iqbal developed a life-long repugnance toward the atmosphere of general bickering, competition, and pursuit of wealth prevailing in the capitalist world, where everything is bought and sold for money, where spiritual values are converted to ready cash. Iqbal foresaw the precariousness of this system and while in Europe (1907) wrote these verses filled with prophetic meaning:

> O inhabitants of the West, The house of God is not a shop,
> Those things that you revere as true values are only tinsel!
> Your civilization will destroy itself
> With its own sword!
> A nest built on a rotten branch
> Cannot hold out for long![23]

Iqbal painted realistic pictures of the exploitation and the humiliating position of the common man in the competitive society of the West. In his highly artistic poem *Lenin Khudā Kay Hadhūr Mein* (Lenin before God) Iqbal presents Lenin angrily protesting to God the horrors and torments that the worker must suffer on earth under His command:

> Oh, of what mortal race art Thou the God?
> Those creatures formed of dust beneath these heavens?
> Europe's pale cheeks are Asia's pantheon,
> And Europe's pantheon her glittering metals.
> A blaze of art and science lights the West

> With darkness that no Fountain of Life dispels:
> In high-reared grace, in glory and in grandeur;
> The towering bank out-tops the cathedral roof;
> What they call commerce is a game of dice;
> For one, profit, for millions, swooping death.
> Their science, philosophy, scholarship, government,
> Preach man's equality, and drink men's blood;
> Naked debauch, and want, and unemployment—
> Are these mean triumphs of the Frankish arts!
>
> Omnipotent, righteous, Thou; but bitter the hours,
> Bitter the labourer's chained hours in Thy world!
> When shall this galley of gold's dominion founder?
> Thy world Thy day of wrath, Lord, stands and waits.[24]

During the last years of his life Iqbal demanded equality of property and liquidation of the exploitation and the clericalism that maintains the bases for this system. Thus, in the poem *Lenin before God* (already mentioned), the Creator, having heard Lenin's just protest, orders his angels to destroy injustice in the world and to destroy the palaces of all rich men and establish the rule of the people on earth.

As far as the political organization of society is concerned, Iqbal supported the secular state and was opposed to a state headed by a representative of God on earth who could screen his despotic will behind his supposed infallibility.[25] Specifically, he approved of the republican form of government, since it is, in his words, "not only thoroughly consistent with the spirit of Islam, but has also become necessary in view of new forces that are set free in the world of Islam."[26] Regarding the social bases of the ideal society, Iqbal was undoubtedly under the influence of the successful realization of the concepts of socialism in the Soviet Union. In the poem *Javid-Namah* Iqbal places in the mouth of Jamal-ud-Din Afghani a message of greeting to the Soviet people, who are putting into practice the ideals that correspond to the ideals of Islam—the annihilation of exploitation of man by man and the liquidation of the autocracy of the church and the clergy. "What is the Qur'ān? A Message of death to rich men and the weapon of the oppressed." Afghani declares to the Soviet people that "the All-High has charged you to observe justice." The experience of the Soviet people, he says, is an inspiring example for all the peoples of the East: "You have fired our hearts and we have been inspired by your experience. The West has become antiquated, but you have taken the true path and you will live eternally."[27]

## THE ROLE OF RELIGION IN THE DEVELOPMENT OF TOTAL PERSONALITY

HOWEVER, a positive attitude toward the Soviet state does not mean that Iqbal fully understood and accepted the ideas of socialism. It seemed to him that socialist ideology, and materialism in general, had as their ultimate goal only the satisfaction of people's material needs and that they were not at all concerned with the spiritual side of their existence. Thus he believed, for example, that socialism led to the impoverishment of man's spirit and fettered the inner sources of his spiritual energy. "Modern atheistic socialism, which possesses all the fervor of a new religion has a broader outlook; but having received its philosophical basis from the Hegelians of the left wing it rises in revolt against the very source which could have given it strength and purpose."[28] Socialism, like any atheistic system according, to Iqbal, is an incomplete, one-sided reflection of the needs of the individual, which are to be satisfied in their entirety and diversity only by the religious ideology of Islam, for it "requires faith in God, not in a throne. And since God is the ultimate spiritual basis for all life, faith in God is in fact elevated to man's faith in his own ideal nature."[29]

This ethical motivation greatly determines the large place religion occupies in Iqbal's specifically metaphysical and generally philosophical views. He maintains that only religious ideology gives full expression to the whole complex of problems connected with man. Therefore, philosophy and science must acknowledge religion's pre-eminence over all other intellectual tools which enable man to apprehend reality. In this cognitive process religion becomes the focus, concentrating within itself the data of science and philosophy and directing them into further research. On closer investigation one realizes that within this scheme Iqbal means by religion nothing more than a world view, a system of general methodological principles, a synthesis of specific branches of knowledge. Certain sciences, Iqbal says, are limited, since they deal only with a specific object of reality, excluding all others from their sphere of consideration. Consequently, they cannot give man a systematized picture of the totality of this reality, but only fragmentary scraps of it. In fact, for Iqbal individual sciences are like vultures that attack the dead body of nature and then fly away, each with its piece of the carrion.

Iqbal asserts that the results of all concrete sciences must be gathered at some single center and this center must naturally be religion, since it correlates the data of all diverse types of experiences with the purposeful activity of man and gives the scientist a reliable guide in his research so that his generalizations will be truly general in import. Citing Rumi's language, Iqbal compares a scientist with a hunter who first tracks the musk ox but eventually comes to the conviction that it is far more expedient to follow the smell of the ox's glands than to grope along after its tracks.[30]

Iqbal maintains that rational thought must not be considered the highest form of knowledge, but rather religious intuition, which in contrast to rational thought (which masters reality in its static state by parts and degrees), catches reality in motion as an integrated whole. However, Iqbal's intuition does not bear a mystical, irrational character; he places it above so-called rational thought only because he means by the latter ordinary superficial-empirical consciousness, based exclusively on the demands of formal logic. Its inadequacy and limitedness are what Iqbal claims intuition is called upon to compensate for; it overcomes creeping empiricism, since by nature it bears a dialectic character. Iqbal says:

> In fact, the logical understanding is incapable of seeing this multiplicity as a coherent universe. Its only method is generalization based on resemblances but its generalizations are only fictitious unities which do not affect the reality of concrete things. In its deeper movement, however, thought is capable of reaching an immanent infinite in whose self-unfolding movement the various finite concepts are merely moments. In its essential nature, then, thought is not static; it is dynamic and unfolds its internal infinitude in time like the seed which, from the very beginning, carries within itself the organic unity of the tree as a present fact.[31]

Present here is the Hegelian concept of thought as a process that in its functioning dialectically unfurls from within itself its own definitions, which prove to be, in the final analysis, ontological categories of existence.

## INTUITION AND PERSONALITY

ALTHOUGH Iqbal does not separate the highest form of consciousness, intuition, from ordinary experience and scientific thinking with an impassable wall, intuition is nevertheless qualitatively different from them in one respect: it brings man into direct contact with the eternal, intransient basis of existence, inaccessible to the senses or the rational mind because they focus their attention only on its temporary, fluctuating, changing aspects. Intuition opens to man a conception of ultimate reality whereby "diverse stimuli merge into one another and form a single unanalysable unity in which the ordinary distinction of subject and object does not exist."

Thus, for Iqbal the main determinant of ultimate reality is the unity of subject and object, of thinking and existence: "The consciousness or the idea is not something alien to, apart from the original nature of things; it is their ultimate basis and forms the very essence of their existence, entering into them at the very beginning of their existence and stimulating their progressive development toward an independent self-determined goal."[32] This unity and identity of matter and spirit, with which the development of reality logically begins and ends, Iqbal calls the supreme soul, God, the absolute ego.

Nature, or the non-I, is organically related to the supreme soul; nature is not simply a mass of pure materiality located in a void but a definite structure of events, a systematized image of their behavior. Nature is to the divine soul what the body is to the human soul—it plays the role of accumulator of its actions. In other words, Iqbal puts forth a pantheistic interpretation of the question of the interrelation between spirit and matter, between nature and God. The absolute spirit is all of reality, Iqbal says; it is immanent in nature. By knowing nature, one knows the activity of God. Consciousness of this, according to Iqbal, also imparts to the natural sciences that higher meaning in which, by themselves, they are deficient.

Iqbal understands the universe not as "a ready-made product that left the hands of the creator ages ago, but one that has just been laid out in space, like an inert mass of matter upon which time exerts no influence."[33] He believes that in the process of development the world will expand quantitatively—"This is a growing Universe," he says.

But in its development the world is not moving toward any pre-established goal, since teleology deprives the world process of its distinctiveness and creative character. "A temporal process," Iqbal wrote, "must not be regarded as a line already drawn. It is a line that is in a process of developing, the actualization of discovered possibilities. It is purposive only in the sense that it has a selective nature and develops up to its given state by means of active retention and maintenance of the past."[34]

Iqbal considered the ethical principle the chief argument against teleology: a world regarded as a process that is realizing a pre-set purpose cannot be a world of free subjects responsible for their actions. In this case it would be a kind of stage upon which puppets act, obeying strings being pulled by someone offstage. One can speak of teleology only in the sense that in the process of life's development we constantly work out new goals, tasks, and ideal values, which condition our activity.

The creative activity of the ultimate reality, the supreme soul, God, manifests itself in the formation of individual souls, egos that differ in degree of expression of the personality, the highest and most perfect form of which is achieved in man, who is called upon to become God's partner in His creative activity.

"What is matter? Colonies of egos (individualities) of a lower order from which the ego (individuality) of a higher order rises when their association and interaction achieve a certain coordination."[35] The circumstance, Iqbal says, that the higher arises from the lower does not deprive the higher of its dignity and value. The point is not origin but creative ability, meaning, and vocation. The evolution of life shows that at least in its early stages the physical subdues the spiritual, whereas subsequently the reverse is true: the spiritual subdues the physical and, in the final analysis, acquires complete independence.

## DIALECTICAL CONTRADICTIONS

THUS does Iqbal substantiate in theoretical form his doctrine of human individuality, of which an ethical characterization on a personal and social level has been given above. One cannot help but notice that the theoretical basis of Iqbal's world view suffers from a number of limitations and contradictions.

## The Doctrine of Personality 281

To begin with, the method chosen by Iqbal of seeking in the Qur'ān the substantiation and sanction for all his propositions cannot be recognized as the most successful, even for the India of that time. However, we must be immediately cautioned against exaggerating the role, significance, and relative weight of religious-Islamic ideology in Iqbal's world view. Actually, if we grasp the religious form of his teachings we will realize that what was significant to him was not so much the religion of Islam as the scientific attitude and humanitarianism of Muslim culture. He maintains, for example, that during the gloomy epoch of the Middle Ages, when the sensual world was declared to have no value, Islam began to preach the reality of the external world, laid the foundations for the modern sciences, and called on people to bring nature under their control—and that herein lies its service to world civilization.[36]

In one respect the religious-Muslim setting of Iqbal's views played a great role in the life of India; it assisted, and to some extent, especially in our times, even became the banner for the Indian Muslim elite in substantiating their right to independent territorial existence. As Iqbal Singh writes: "His [Iqbal's] fervent idealization of Islam, not merely as a religion but also as a comprehensive polity, exercised a very far-reaching restraining influence upon the Muslim intelligentsia."[37] Although in his political pronouncements Iqbal subscribed to the thought that the Muslims of India constituted a part of the population separate from the Hindus, this did not prevent him from remaining an ardent patriot of India throughout his life, grieving at her sorrows and rejoicing at her successes; he never preached religious or any other enmity between Hindus and Muslims. Therefore he is equally honored by both groups, in India as well as in Pakistan.

As for the strictly theoretical bases of Iqbal's views, they suffer from the essentially idealistic premises of his world view. For example, he does not give a convincing explanation of his conception of the ultimate reality, the absolute spirit, a failure which lies in the utter impossibility—indeed absolute—of demonstrating how the spirit, God, turns out to be the organizing principle of what spirit essentially is not, nature. His conception of God is contradictory; sometimes he speaks of him as a personality that fashions and directs the world and the behavior of the individual—a typically theological idea that rules out his own interpretation of God either as a concentrated embodiment of the highest ideal qualities of man or as synonym for the regular organization and orderliness of the world process. This initial idealistic premise to some degree determines the precariousness of the principles of the central element in his teaching—ethics.

Although Iqbal also asserts that the personality finds its individuality only in the social field, in fact he considers it a principle independent with respect to society, both in origin and existence. Thus he admits of the metaphysical opposition of personality and society, yet fails to see the complex nature of their dialectic unity and difference, when the individual receives his true existence only as the bearer of definite social functions in their economic, political, cultural, and ideological manifestations. By virtue of the specific conditions of the historical development of India, where class antagonism frequently took the form of national, religious, and caste contradictions and hid the essence of social relations, Iqbal did not perceive the class nature of the personality, thereby depriving himself of the sole basis on which this question could be solved. Therefore, his theory of the individual rests on the rather cathetic base of the abstract man torn away from the concrete base of socioeconomic relations. Iqbal does not go beyond the limits of speculative and abstract humanism; he contrasts problems of an ethical nature to social themes and sees in moral self-perfection the basic problem of educating man. In one of his speeches he said that he who intends to change conditions of existence unfavorable to him must change his internal existence.

In Iqbal's notions of the ideal organization of society one cannot help but note elements of utopianism and liberal amorphousness. Although in general outlines he also opposes exploitation and approves of socialist principles, these principles come closer to petty bourgeois, and in certain features feudal, socialism than to the socialism of Saint-Simon, Owen, and Fourier.

In general it cannot be said that Iqbal left behind a harmonious, consistent system of views; they reflect traces of the influence of many contradictory doctrines. In this connection Iqbal Singh, an Indian student of Iqbal's philosophy, points out that Iqbal's world view, like those of the majority of the outstanding people in India in the last century, from Ram Mohan Roy and Sayyid Ahmad Khan to Mohandas Gandhi, is not an integral whole but is a sort of mosaic made of different parts, although certain parts of it stand out more than others.

Of course, this characterization cannot be recognized as the chief and basic point when we begin to speak of Iqbal, but to some extent it gives an idea of his views.

## SIGNIFICANCE OF IQBAL'S MESSAGE

EVEN Iqbal himself once said that his personality consisted of a "sum of contradictions." However, all these contradictions in Iqbal's teachings do not diminish his significance as a thinker. These are the weaknesses and contradictions of a great man whose views reflect the turbulent dynamics surrounding his social activity, its revolutionary scope, its progressive trend, as well as its immaturity, weakness, and limitations. Iqbal's work bears the maximum social load: he endeavors to comprehend the most urgent problems of his own people and all of mankind, to delve into the hidden secrets of the personality's inner world and into the profound processes of the social organism with all their complexity and the diversity of their various tendencies and collisions, which are not confined to the framework of speculative, formal, and nonconflicting constructions.

Therefore it hardly makes sense to apply to Iqbal the criteria and yardsticks of professional philosophy of the sort that sees as its task the creation of a speculative system which is all-encompassing to the point of unwieldiness, detailed to the point of pedantism, technically refined to the point of abstruseness, and which pretends to originality. The history of human thought has known a great many such pretentious theories, but for all their harmony (frequently superficial) and terminological refinement they are, as a rule, isolated from the needs of real life and incapable of exerting any influence upon it.

Iqbal was hardly striving for the laurels of this type of system-creating philosopher. He is great for something else—his passionate condemnation of weak will and passiveness; his angry protest against inequality, discrimination, and oppression in all its forms—economic, social, political, national, racial, religious, etc.; his preaching of optimism, an active attitude toward life, and man's high purpose in the world; in a word, he is great for his assertion of the noble ideals and principles of humanism, democracy, peace, and friendship among peoples.

Of course, these ideals and principles are in themselves far from original; they have been defended by the progressive thinkers among all peoples at all times, for which they have even been raised to the semi-ironic title of *philosophia perennis*. Therefore it may sometimes seem that there is no particular merit in or necessity for mortifying ourselves for these principles in our enlightened century. However, despite their seeming elementariness, it is these ideals and principles that make up the moral basis of human society, and in their constant realization lies, properly speaking, the meaning of social progress. If these ideals and principles are now felt to be eternal and self-evident, it is partly because they have been preached since time immemorial by the best minds of mankind. Even in our times, defending these principles is far from quixotic. It is no accident that the ideologists of militarism, neocolonialism, chauvinism, racism, etc., view them as opposing ideas and exert no little effort in discrediting them. It is no accident that an extreme form of modern reaction and misanthropy such as fascism asserts itself only when and where these elementary norms of human morality have been trampled and crushed. They serve as an effective means of neutralizing and combating the feelings of pessimism, despair, fear, loneliness, and devastation from which certain strata of society chronically suffer and which from time to time become a kind of fashion of the day, taking on the dangerous proportions of an epidemic disease.

Furthermore, Iqbal is great because he did not pose and defend these eternal human problems abstractly, with no relationship to time and space, but defined them concretely in terms of the conditions of Indian reality, bound them with the needs of his people, and placed them in the service of their social and spiritual renaissance.

Finally, the greatness and force of Iqbal's ideals lie in the way they are presented: they do not remain only within the sphere of pure theorization and cold reasoning, which inevitably makes any thought, although most profound, the property of a comparatively narrow range of intellectuals, but are clothed in the brilliant forms of highly artistic, poetic images. This gives them the extraordinary force of emotional influence and ensures them the widest popular audience. In the depth of his views as in the force of their influence Iqbal has a complete right to a place in the ranks of such coryphaei of the human spirit as Dante, Shakespeare, Goethe, Tolstoi, and Tagore.

# IV

# ISLAMIC MYSTICISM

# 13

## Attitude toward Sufism

### ABU SAYEED NUR-UD-DIN

WHILE reconstructing religious thought in Islam, Iqbal pondered all the fundamental systems of Islamic philosophy—especially Sufism,[1] in so far as the doctrine of *Wahdat al-Wujūd* (unity of being) was concerned. He could not reconcile his interpretation of Islamic beliefs (which perhaps are closer to the spirit of Islam originally unfolded by the Prophet Muhammad) with the implications of this doctrine. He criticized the great exponents of this philosophy and rejected *Wahdat al-Wujūd*, which in his opinion contained inherent negative aspects. Although Sufism is a typical Muslim philosophy of life, it was developed gradually by eminent Sufis in the Middle East and in India and Pakistan over a period of several centuries. It attained its highest form in the doctrine of *Wahdat al-Wujūd* under the influence of pantheism, which originated in the age-old Greek thought. (This chapter concerns itself primarily with *Wahdat al-Wujūd* and Iqbal's attitude toward it.)

In a study of the history of Sufism one finds that most of the great Sufis (deeply influenced by pantheistic philosophy) tried to determine the position of God vis-à-vis man and universe. According to them, this was in a deeper sense the real Islam. Iqbal challenged this approach and then successfully established his new, positive philosophy of life under the name of *khudi* (ego or selfhood). In order to better understand the unique theory of *khudi* it is necessary to discuss pantheism and its influence on Islamic thought, which gave rise to the theory of *Wahdat al-Wujūd*.

### PANTHEISM

PANTHEISM, generally described in Sufism as *Wahdat al-Wujūd*, has certain affinities with Sufism in the sense that it has been adopted, developed, and maintained by almost all the great Sufis. Although it is not possible to draw a distinct line of demarcation between Sufism and metaphysics, it can be said that the doctrine of *Wahdat al-Wujūd* does not have as much connection with Sufism as it has with metaphysics. It is fundamentally a metaphysical problem, which owing to the passage of time and to different environments and circumstances has been mixed with Sufism and has been turned into a theoretical problem most intricate and difficult to understand.

The doctrine of *Wahdat al-Wujūd* made its way into Sufism through Neo-Platonism, which was established as an independent school of thought in the third century A.D. as the result of interpretations and commentaries of Plato's ideas. The ideas of Neo-Platonism may be summarized as follows:

1. "Existence" is actually "One" and that Existence alone is the main source of all other existence. In fact, the whole world has emerged from the Existence and finally has to go back to that "One Being." In other words, except for the One Being itself, whatever exists is merely a reflection of the One Being and does not have a permanent existence of its own. In Sufi terminology this doctrine is also called *Hama Ust* (All is He). It is also maintained by the Sufis that all things of the world have emanated from the One Being as a manifestation of Him, and that He Himself has not emanated from anything. This viewpoint is termed *Hama Az Ust* (All is from Him).

2. God is the exact universe, that is, God Himself is the universe, as if God and the universe were the same. God cannot be attributed with anything. Any interpretation of God as "Existence," "Being," "Essence," or "Life" is incomplete; God is above all these attributes. He cannot be confined within the boundary of ideas.

3. Thought cannot be made applicable to God, as it presupposes two things—the thinker and the object of thought. Thought necessitates the precondition that the thinker requires a state of mind other than that which exists within himself. (This leads to dualism, which is against the fundamental Islamic concept of *Tawhīd* [Divine unity].) God is *Wājeb al-Wujūd* and must exist complete in Himself. He is above all analysis and numerical calculation. He surrounds everything; he is unlimited. Any reference to Him is against the concept of *Tawhīd*. Any reference of knowledge and perception of Him is also wrong and against *Tawhīd*, as nothing has existence which can be known or perceived. Through

sense perception and reason one cannot reach God. For this purpose, vision, earnest desire, and eagerness is essential.[2]

When Islam gradually expanded and the Muslims left Arabia and conquered Syria, Iraq, Iran, Palestine, and Egypt, the principles of Neo-Platonism prevailed in these countries. During the period of the 'Abbasid caliphate (750–1258), Muslim scholars translated into Arabic Greek philosophy and physical sciences including medicine, astrology, geography, metaphysics, theology, psychology, logic, politics, and ethics. They also translated into Arabic the philosophy of Neo-Platonism.

Among the Muslims, al-Kindi (883) was the first who earned fame as a philosopher. Eclectic in his system, he endeavored in Neo-Platonic fashion to combine the views of Plato and Aristotle. The harmonizing of Greek philosophy with Islam begun by al-Kindi was continued by al-Farabi (d. 950) and completed by ibn-Sina (d. 1037).

Islam's basic teaching is *Tawhīd* or belief in one god. The Prophet Muhammad invited the people to accept the concept of *Tawhīd*. (In the Jahiliyah period [pagan age] the Arabs worshiped three hundred and sixty idols.) He explained to them that the numerous Gods they worshiped were all false and that the real God is One, and He alone deserves to be worshiped.

Since the pantheistic philosophy of Neo-Platonism had some resemblance to the concept of *Tawhīd*, the ascetic Sufis of the third century (A.H./ninth century A.D.) accepted it. They somehow considered this dogma as the inner aspect of *Tawhīd*, making it part and parcel of Sufism and presenting a new interpretation which did not exist in Islam. They explained it in such great detail and with such emphasis that it became a very important chapter in the history of Sufism.

Long before the advent of Islam, Neo-Platonic philosophy had completed all the stages of its development in Alexandria, and during the age of Dhu'L-Nun (d. 861) of Egypt all its principles were commonly known. Therefore, it was natural that this Egyptian Sufi should have come under the influence of Neo-Platonism. He was an enlightened philosopher, and in the words of Maulana Jami: "He was the leader and pioneer of the Sufi community."[3] Of all the strands of Neo-Platonistic philosophy, he was most influenced by the doctrine of *Wahdat al-Wujūd*. It is generally believed that this doctrine entered Islamic mysticism through his efforts. He said, for instance, that "the love of God ultimately unites man with Him. Man becomes absorbed in God. His self then does not remain his own self, but becomes a part of the self of God."4 And he said in a prayer: "O God, I never hearken to the voices of the beasts or the rustle of the trees, the splashing of waters or the song of birds, the whistling of the wind or the rumble of thunder, but I sense in them a testimony to Thy Unity (*Wahdānȳat*) and a proof of Thy incomparableness that Thou art the All-prevailing, the All-knowing, the All-wise, the All-just, the All-true, and that in Thee is neither ignorance nor folly nor injustice nor lying."5

The concepts of absorption (*istighrāq*) and annihilation (*fanā*) into God are the highlights of the doctrine of *Wahdat al-Wujūd*.

After Dhu'L-Nun, the well-known Persian mystic Abū Yazīd (Bayazid) of Bistam became the leading exponent of pantheistic philosophy. The central ideas of *Wahdat al-Wujūd* find an echo in his sayings: "Once I cried: 'O Lord, with my egoism I cannot attain to Thee and I cannot escape from my Selfhood. What am I to do?' God responded: 'O Abū Yazīd, thou must win release from thy thouness by following my Beloved, Muhammad (peace be upon him).' "6 "When I came out of myself [Bayazid] as snakes change their skins, I observed that both the lover and Beloved are one, as if two manifestations of one self. For, in the domain of *Tawhīd* (Divine Unity) only one can be seen."7

The conflict between the extreme form of Sufism and *Sharīʿa* (the canon law of Islam) initiated by the ideas of Bayazīd came to a head-on collision in the time of the well-known mystic, Hussain Ibn Mansūr al-Hallaj, whose life was sacrificed at the altar of the *Sharīʿa*.8 However, pantheistic philosophy came into vogue with the Spanish-Arab mystic Shaikh Muhy al-Din Ibn al-ʿArabi. He was born in Murcia (Mursiyah) in 1165 and flourished mainly in Seville until 1201–1202, when he made the pilgrimage to Mecca, after which he remained in the East till his death in Damascus in 1240. Ibn al-ʿArabi presented pantheistic philosophy under the name of Islamic mysticism. In his principal works (*Al-Futūhāt al-Makkiyah* [The Makkan Revelations] and *Fusūs al Hikmāh* [The Bezels of Wise Precepts]) all the principles of Neo-Platonism were amalgamated with Sufism in such a manner that no distinction could be made between them.

As a pantheistic monist, Ibn al-ʿArabi firmly believed that things pre-exist as ideas (*aʿyān thābitah*) in the knowledge of God, whence they emanate and wither they return. The world is merely the outer aspect of God, who is its inner aspect. Between the Essence and its attributes, that is, God and the universe, there is no real difference. (Here Muslim mysticism passes into pantheism.) It is useless for Sufis, in the judgment of Ibn al-'Arabi, to search for God beyond this universe. The true mystic in fact has but one guide—the inner light.

Ibn al-'Arabi insisted with utmost assurance that pantheistic monism was the only reality of Islam. He sought support of his assertion in the Qur'ān and in the Traditions of the Prophet Muhammad. For instance, the Qur'ān says: "And we are nearer to Him than the great artery." Ibn al-'Arabi believed that this verse of the Qur'ān implied that "God Himself is the limbs and parts of the body of the servant." Interpreting the Tradition (He created Adam in the image of Himself), he said that man possessed all the attributes of God.

This pantheistic theory (*Wahdat al-Wujūd*) popularized by Ibn al-'Arabi had a deep impact on contemporary Sufis and also on those who came after him. Gradually the principles of this doctrine became so common among Muslims that almost all learned people with an inclination toward Sufism came under its spell. The Arabic, Persian, and Urdu poets who pretended to be Sufis interjected these ideas into their verses. In this way Muslim mysticism was Hellenized, and the real spirit (*Tawhīd*) of Islam gradually vanished. These alien Platonic and Neo-Platonic ideas became familiar among Muslims because of Ibn al-'Arabi, and in a true sense he alone was responsible for their popularity.

For Iqbal it was an inescapable law of nature that nations rise and fall because of their *khudi* (egohood, that is, self-realization). Only that nation—with all its power and dignity—which realizes the value of its self and makes it strong can survive in this world. Muslims in India and Pakistan or elsewhere, in the eyes of Iqbal, were no exception to this rule. His elegant verses repeatedly pointed out that as long as the Muslims focused their attention upon realizing their *khudi* they were crowned with glory and power; their decline started with loss of *khudi*. Iqbal believed that the root cause of the negation of *khudi* for individuals and nations was the unhealthy impact of pantheism, the doctrine of *Wahdat al-Wujūd*, which had entered Islamic mysticism through Neo-Platonism. Iqbal's philosophy is therefore an indictment of Plato and his Sufi followers.

## CRITICISM OF PLATO

BEFORE Plato, his master Socrates (d. 399 B.C.) believed that true knowledge could be attained by *ideas* alone. Thus he recognized the supremacy of ideas over material things. But Plato went one step further, asserting that in reality only *ideas* or *forms of knowledge* existed, and that the material world, along with all its contents, had no independent existence and was ever-changing. Whatever meets the eye is nothing but an illusion; the conscience deceives man, for it is not possible to know reality. In fact reality exists nowhere in this material world, as reality can be applied only to a thing which is free from transformation. Since the universe is ever-changing, the sense of reality cannot be applied to it.

Iqbal rejected Plato's ideas in the allegorical story *Tiger and Sheep* narrated in his philosophical Persian poem *Asrār-i Khudī* (The Secrets of the Self). In this allegory the sheep very tactfully teaches the tiger the lesson of self-negation:

> O plotters of evil, bethink yourselves of good!
> Who so is violent and strong is miserable:
> Life's solidity depends on self-denial.
> The spirit of the righteous is fed by fodder:
> The vegetarian is pleasing unto God.
> The sharpness of your teeth brings disgrace upon you
> And makes the eye of your perception blind.
> Paradise is for the weak alone,
> Strength is but a means of perdition.
> It is wicked to seek greatness and glory,
> Penury is sweeter than princedom.

The moral of the tale is that negation of the self is a doctrine invented by subject peoples in order that by this means they may sap and weaken the character of their rulers. Iqbal believed that Plato followed the sheep's doctrine by presenting the theory of ideas. He cautioned his audience to be on their guard against the impact of Plato's life-negating theories:

> Plato, the prime ascetic and sage,
> Was one of that ancient flock of sheep.

> His Pegasus went astray in the darkness of idealism
> And dropped its shoe amidst the rocks of actuality.
> He was so fascinated by the invisible
> That he made hand, eye, and ear of no account.
> "To die," said he, "is the secret of life:
> The candle is glorified by being put out."
> He dominates our thinking,
> His cup sends us to sleep and takes
>                 the sensible world away from us.
> He is a sheep in man's clothing,
> The soul of the Sufi bows to his authority.[9]

In Iqbal's eyes Plato was the godfather of those Sufis who believed in the doctrine of *Wahdat al-Wujūd*. After Ibn al-'Arabi, the most influential exponents of this doctrine were Iraqi (d. 1287) and Khāwja Hāfiz, the celebrated Persian poet. Hāfiz, thoroughly influenced by Neo-Platonism, expressed through his charming verses a sleepy and intoxicating philosophy of life. The uncertainty of the existence of the world, negation of the self, abandoning of action, and drinking of wine are the main themes of his captivating poetry. According to the doctrine of *Wahdat al-Wujūd* (as already stated) the world and its contents have no existence; whatever is perceived is only an illusion; existence is only "one" and that is God. Everything else is naught. Illustrating the unreality of the world, Hāfiz says:

> Companion and singer and cup-bearer, all is He,
> Thought of water and clay [material things] in life is false.
> Our existence is such a riddle O Hāfiz
> That investigation of it is an enchantment and a fiction.
> The result of the workshop of the world, all these do not exist,
> Bring forth wine, as the causes of the world,
>                 all these do not exist.
> The world and the business of the world
>                 are all nothing and worthless,
> Thousands of times I have pondered on this point.

If the world and its business is nothing and worthless, then man is also naught. All else but God is naught; nothing else exists. Therefore, for Hāfiz, the idea of human self is irrelevant:

> Thought of self and vision of self in the world of fraud is "Naught,"
> It is infidelity in this creed to have self-decoration and self-conceit.
> As long as thou look'st after the wisdom and reason,
>                        thou wilt be deprived of revelation;
> One thing I tell thee, don't see toward thee, thou wilt be free.

If the human self is nothing, then it is useless to face the problems of life with manly spirit and participate in the struggle for survival. If something is available without effort, that is well and good:

> The result of the workshop of the world, all these do not exist,
> Bring forth wine, as the causes of the world, all these do not exist,
> Wine of two years old, and beloved of fourteen years of age;
> This is sufficient for me, association of youngs and olds.[10]

Along with Plato, Iqbal criticized Ḥāfiẓ in a bitter tone and warned the people in very impassioned language to avoid his philosophy. Iqbal says:

> Beware of Ḥāfiẓ the drinker,
> His cup is full of the poison of death.
> His garment of abstinence is mortgaged to the cup-bearer.
> Wine is the remedy for the horror of the resurrection.
> There is nothing in his market except wine—
> With two cups his turban has been spoiled,
> He is a Muslim but his belief wears the thread
>                        of an unbeliever.
> The beloved's eyelashes make holes in his faith.
> His proposition is nothing but chit-chat.
> His hand is short as the date on the date trees.
> He is a sheep and he has learnt how to sing.
> He has learnt coquetry and whims and elegance.
> His fascination is poison and that's all,
> He gives weakness the name of strength,
> His musical instrument leads the nation astray.
> His congregation is not worthy for the pious ones,
> His cup is not suitable for the ingenious ones.
> Go independent of the congregation of Ḥāfiẓ,
> Beware of sheep and beware.[11]

When the first edition of *Asrār-i Khudi* came out in 1914 attacking Khāwja Ḥāfiẓ, it raised a storm of controversy among mystically inclined Muslims, including the conservative Urdu poet Akbar Allahabadi, Khwaja Hasan Nizāmi of Delhi, Pīrzada Muzaffar-ud-Din Ahmad, and Maulana Feruz-ud-Din Ahmad Tughrayee. The latter two wrote in reply to *Asrār-i Khudi* and in defense of Hāfiz two complete *mathnavis*, *Ramūz-i-Bekhudi* (The Mysteries of Selflessness) and *Lisān-ul-Ghā'ib* (Tongue of the Unseen). They went so far as to pass some discourteous remarks about Iqbal. But as Iqbal by nature was a peace-loving man, he did not like to enter into such uncalled-for controversies, and thus omitted the offending verses from his *mathnavi* in its second edition. The omitted verses on Hāfiz have, however, lately been included by Feruz-ud-Din Ahmad Tughrayee, S. A. Vahid, and Anwar Hārith in their collections *Lisan-ul-Ghā'ib*, *Baqiyāt-i-Iqbal*, and *Rakht-i-Safar*, respectively.

Iqbal was right in critizing Hāfiz. Then why did he eliminate his indictment of Hāfiz in the second edition of his *mathnavi*? Khalīfah 'Abdūl Hakīm, one of the authorities on Iqbal and a close associate of the poet, explains the reason: "Iqbal dropped the name of Hāfiz from *Asrār-i Khudi* in its second edition. Once I inquired about this from him. He replied: 'My views are the same. I have omitted the name of Hāfiz expediently; otherwise, I was afraid that due to this controversy, people might oppose the aim of the philosophy of *Khudi* presented by me. If they do not consider Hāfiz to be such a poet as I depicted, then let them do so. But they must think over my contention so far as literature is concerned.' "[12]

In Iqbal's view, Khāwja Hāfiz was not a Sufi. One cannot be a Sufi merely by using the terms and language of Sufism, as one cannot be a clergyman merely by wearing a cowl. Sufis give instructions for action; this is missing in Khāwja Hāfiz.

In accordance with the doctrine of the unity of being, the Sufis, in general, advocated that for the sake of knowledge of God man should annihilate his self in God. But Iqbal, on the contrary, taught that, following the famous Sufi proverb Whoever has known his self, verily he had known his God, man should properly realize his self and know it fully, as it deserves. Then he should attain knowledge of God. For Iqbal, knowledge of God was dependent on knowledge of *khudi* (self), as if, without proper knowledge of self, it were not possible to have knowledge of God.

Whereas for Shaikh Muhy al-Din Ibn al-'Arabi the basis of all knowledge was the doctrine of the unity of being, and therefore it was essential for man, for the sake of knowledge of God, to annihilate his self in God and become absorbed in Him, the foundation of the thought of Iqbal is *khudi*. Thus, contrary to Ibn al-'Arabī, gnosis of God is dependent on the realization of self, the maintenance of self, and the firmness of the idea of self. As such *khudi* and God become reciprocal. Iqbal sings:

> Far, Far from every other go,
> With the one Friend upon the road;
> Seek thou of God thyself to know,
> And seek in selfhood for thy God.
> In the selfhood is hidden Godhead,
>   Search O ye careless,
> This is for thee now only the way of
> Taking advice for the goal.[13]

Thus Iqbal expounded the dynamic theory of self in contrast to the passive and static doctrine of the unity of being (*Wahdat al-Wujūd*) and opened a new chapter in the history of Islamic mysticism.

## DEFINITION OF KHUDI

In Persian and Urdu literature the term *khudi* has been used to mean vanity, pomp, and arrogance. For example, Maulana Rumi says:

> *Pas khudi rā sir bā-bur ba zulfiqār*
> *Bekhudi shau fani wa dervish wār.*
> Cut the head of *khudi* with the sword
> You are without self, be absorbed and dervishlike.

Iraqi uses this term in a similar manner:

> *Awwal aȳn ast wa ākharesh dāni chīyst*
> *Khud rā z-khudi-i khud ba-perdaftan ast.*
> The beginning is this, do you know what's its end?
> To relinquish the self from one's own self.

The famous Urdu poet Sauda expresses these sentiments:

> *Hāy' puhanchā nah gayā qayd-i Khudi say ūs tak
> Apany hee dām say chutana mujhay dushwar hūwā.*
> Alas, I could not reach Him from the prison of self,
> It has been difficult to be released from my own trap.

And Akbar Allahabadi says:

> *Mitā dow rang wahdat mein Khudi kā rang ay Akbar
> Agar sābat kiya chaho tum apana mu'taber honā.*
> Efface the color of *Khudi* from the color of unity O Akbar,
> If thou wishest to prove thyself to be reliable.[14]

Thus critics alleged that Iqbal propagated boorish ideas of personal arrogance. This misunderstanding was rooted in the traditional meaning of *khudi*. Iqbal explained that by the term *khudi* he never meant vanity or arrogance, but self-realization and self-assertion, which refines human personality and helps man to achieve God-gifted greatness. He writes in the preface of *Asrār-i Khudi*: "Yes, as regards the term *Khudi* it is necessary to clarify that this term has not been used in the meaning of 'Vanity,' as it is commonly used in Urdu literature. Its meaning is only self-realization and self-assertion."

*Khudi*, in Iqbal's own words, "is an emotional unity or a bright thing of the conscience by which all human ideas and inspirations are enlightened. This is an eternal reality, which is a binding force for the scattered and unlimited mental states. It is a silent force which is anxious to come into action."[15] He expresses these ideas in his verses:

> A silent force but anxious to come into action,
> By action (again) bound to the causes of action.
> Its place is within the heart of man, as Iqbal says:
> The abode of *Khudi* is within your heart.
> As the sky is within the pupil of the eyes.

According to Iqbal, "All life is individual; there is no such thing as universal life. God Himself is an individual. However, He is the most unique individual. The universe, as Doctor McTaggart says, is an association of individuals; but we must add that the orderliness and adjustment which we find in this association is not eternally achieved and complete in itself. It is the result of instinctive or conscious efforts.

We are gradually traveling from Chaos to Cosmos and are helping in this achievement." Iqbal adds:

> This universe is yet perhaps incomplete, as every
> moment comes the sound: "Be and it was."[16]

Iqbal also believes that the universe is not a complete act: it is still in the course of formation. There can be no complete truth about the universe, for the universe has not yet become "whole." "The process of creation is still going on, and man too takes his share in it, inasmuch as he helps to bring order into at least a portion of the chaos." There is also an indication regarding this fact in the Qur'ān: "*Fa Tabaraka Allahu Ahsan-Al-Khaleqīn*" (Blessed is God, the best of those who create). This passage indicates that, besides God, there is the possibility of other creators, although they might be of lower status and dependent on God, the best of those who create. Iqbal explains this delicate point in his work *Payām-i-Mashriq* (Message of the East), enumerating the rare qualities of *khudi*:

> You made the night, and I the lamp,
> And You the clay and I the cup;
> You—desert, mountain-peak, and vale;
> I—flower-bed, park, and orchard; I
> Who grind a mirror out of stone,
> Who brew from poison honey-drink.[17]

Therefore, the moral and religious ideal of man is certainly not self-negation, but self-affirmation. His capacity for self-realization is not like that of the drop of water which passes away into the sea and loses its individual existence; it is more like that of a drop of water which becomes a pearl in the sea. Following the famous Tradition "Takhallaqū bi-Akhāq Allah" (Create in yourselves the attributes of God), man should attain more and more nearness to a unique God. Thus man becomes unique by becoming more and more like the most unique individual.

However, unlike the Sufis, Iqbal does not seek union with God, since complete union between the Creator and the creature is not possible. He once remarked: "How can I meet Him. I am the servant and He is God. My relation to Him is only that of a servant. If I am told that God is coming to meet me, I shall run far away. Because if the ocean unites with a drop of water, the drop will certainly lose its existence.

... I want to maintain myself as a drop of water; I do not want to perish myself, but wish to create in me the qualities of the ocean." Thus Iqbal seeks *firāq* (separation) instead of *wiṣāl* (union) with God:

> In the state of burning and passion separation is better than union,
> In union, the death of desire; in separation
>                                 the enjoyment of seeking.
> O! thou, nearer the soul, but hidden from the sight;
> Thy separation is happier to me than the union of others.
> If union be the end of love, beware!
> More blest than this are sighs and fruitless plaints.

In developing the idea of man's servanthood, Iqbal was considerably influenced by Shaikh Ahmad Sarhindi (commonly known to the Muslims in India and Pakistan as the Mujjadid Alf Thani). Shaikh Ahmad believed that the last station of the *sālik* (devotee) is not *Wahdat al-Wujūd* (unity of being), but rather *abdeyat* (servanthood). The *maqām-i abdeyat* (station of servanthood) is a stage in mysticism in which a devotee can realize that he is merely a servant of God and nothing more. The station of union with and absorption in God claimed by the devotee under the influence of *Wahdat al-Wujūd* is but a transitory phase. Servanthood is perpetual since God is God and man is His creature. Iqbal believes that servanthood is the highest achievement of man, freeing him from all bondage:

> When the station of servanthood is fortified,
> The beggar's bowl becomes the magic cup that (Emperor) Jamshid bore.

For Iqbal God's servant is elevated by *khudi* and strengthened by His love. According to the poet, the accomplishment of Islam is also dependent upon love. In *Masjid-i Qirtabāh* (The Mosque of Cordoba), a charming poem in *Bāl-i Jibrīl* (Gabriel's Wings), Iqbal wrote several captivating verses highlighting the dimensions of dynamic love of God.

> Love is Gabriel's wing, Love is Muhammad's strong heart,
> Love is the envoy of God, Love the utterance of God.
> Even our mortal clay, touched by Love's esctasy, glows;
> Love is new pressed wine, Love is the goblet of kings,
> Love the priest of the shrine, Love the commander of hosts,
> Love the son of the road, counting a thousand homes.
> Love is the plectrum that draws music from life's taut strings,
> Love is the warmth of life, Love is the radiance of life.[18]

Now one comes to the basic question about the mystic faith of Iqbal: if he was opposed to the doctrine of *Wahdat al-Wujūd* (unity of being), what did he really believe in? In one word, the answer is *Tawhīd* (unity of God). This does not mean, however, that he negated the *kasrat* (plurality of life). In Iqbal's mind the antithesis of *Tawhīd* was not *kasrat* but *shirk*, the attempt to associate an animate or inanimate object with the unity of God. And this is exactly what the Qur'ān says: "Verily I [Muhammad] am also a human being like thee; it is revealed to me that verily thy God is one God. Then those who gave desire to meet his God should do good deeds; and in the service of God none else should be associated."[19]

In explaining the doctrine of *Wahdat al-Wujūd*, Sufis generally use the terms *bahr* (ocean) for God and *qatra* (drop) for man. Iqbal also used the term "ocean" for God, but for man he coined a fresh term—"shining pearl." He did not agree with the Sufi view that man is a trivial drop of water, longing to lose its existence in the ocean. Instead Iqbal's drop has the capacity within itself to be a shining pearl. He prayed to God:

> If I am a shell, then the dignity of my pearl is in your hand,
> But if I am an earthen vessel, then make me a royal gem.

Indicating his need of God, Iqbal said:

> My thought is so high—only due to his favor.
> A stream not caring for the coast—is only due to his favor.

Regarding *Tawhīd*, Iqbal also believed in the Sufi proposition of *Hama Az Ust* (All is from Him). After creation man had become independent, attaining this status because of the mercy of God. If there had been no God, Iqbal believed, man's existence also would not have been possible:

> *Khudi* achieved manifestation due to God's manifestation,
> *Khudi* obtained existence due to God's existence.
>
> I don't know where this shining pearl would have been,
> If there had not been the ocean.

Unlike the Sufis, Iqbal did not teach renunciation of the world; on the contrary, he endeavored to make both the religious life and the material world harmonious in the light of the teaching of Islam.

# 14

# The Demise of Fatalism

## M. T. STEPANYANTS

THE acceptance of religion as the most perfect form of social consciousness constitutes Iqbal's philosophical world outlook. "Philosophy," he wrote, "must recognize the central position of religion and has no other alternative but to admit it as something focal in the process of reflective synthesis."[1] Iqbal did not deny the importance of science and philosophy in the process of cognition, but he held that ultimately only religion can save unfortunate mankind from all its calamities. Of all the religions he gave preference to Islam as the most perfect.

Recognizing that "conservatism is as bad in religion as in any other department of human activity," Iqbal admitted the need to "reconstruct" the religious teaching of Islam.[2] Although he took into full account the "philosophical traditions of Islam," he tried very hard to reform Islam in the light of more "recent developments in the various domains of human knowledge."[3] Of the philosophical heritage of Muslim thinkers Iqbal was most of all attracted by the philosophy of the medieval mystics—the Sufis.

The influence of Sufism was greatest on Iqbal's theory of knowledge and concept of personality. To a large extent Iqbal assimilated the Sufist interpretation of intuition and its role in the process of cognition. His understanding of the relationship between man and God and his concept of the "perfect man" and the ways of achieving this perfection were largely derived from the ideas of al-Ghazzali, Rumi, Ibn al-'Arabi, and al-Jili.

However, it is noteworthy that Iqbal never accepted the Sufi world outlook as a whole. His attitude toward Muslim mysticism was critical, and as the years passed his criticism became increasingly sharper. Iqbal, for example, did not subscribe to the view of al-Ghazzali, who treated intuition in isolation from reason. For Iqbal intuition and thinking were two interconnected and necessary processes of cognition.[4]

## STRUGGLE: THE ESSENCE OF MAN

IQBAL vehemently criticized Sufism for its advocacy of shunning everything that links man with the mundane world and thereby achieving, through the release of the particle of the divine essence contained in man, his merger with the substance with God. Iqbal perceived in Sufism the danger of reducing all human activity to passive mystical contemplation. Criticizing Sufism, he wrote: "The ultimate aim of the ego is not to *see* something, but to *be* something.... The end of the ego's quest is not emancipation from the limitations of individuality; it is, on the other hand, a more precise definition of it. The final act is not an intellectual act, but a vital act which deepens the whole being of the ego, and sharpens his will."[5]

Muhammad Iqbal, expressing the spirit of the new times, championed creative activity and struggle as the true expression of man's essence, being convinced that the "world is not something to be merely seen or known through concepts, but something to be made and re-made by continuous action."[6] He maintained that mysticism "destroy[ed] the ego's creative freedom" and therefore "medieval mystic technique" could no longer serve as a method for cognizing truth.

In order to work out a new method Iqbal turned to the experience of the West. "With the reawakening of Islam," he wrote, "it is necessary to examine, in an independent spirit, what Europe has thought and how far the conclusions reached can help us in the revision and, if necessary reconstruction, of theological thought in Islam."[7] Iqbal therefore borrowed from the West the intellectual tools most appropriate for his philosophical concepts.

His main aim was to construct a philosophic system that would be based on a "modernized" religious philosophy of Islam. He sought to demonstrate that Islam had not become obsolete and that its precepts only had to be expressed in terms and concepts of the new age. Hence Iqbal strove to find points of contact between Muslim philosophy and contemporary Western philosophy. For example, he was especially drawn by the epistemological concepts of Kant and Bergson because they could be enlisted as proof of the "correctness" and "modernity" of the philosophy of Islamic Sufism. The Sufis claimed that the possibilities of reason were limited and that "ultimate problems" could be cognized only with the help of the intuition of mystic experience.

Nor is it accidental that Iqbal turned to Fichte's philosophy. In the latter's interpretation of the concept of ego he found definite points of contact with the philosophy of Muslim medieval mystics who claimed the inseverable connection of the human "I" with divine substance. Moreover, in the pluralism of Leibnitz Iqbal saw a similarity with the pluralistic concept of the philosophy of *kalām* (scholastic theology).

In short, Iqbal accepted from Western philosophy ideas which could be reconciled or in some way "combined" with the Muslim philosophical traditions. However, Iqbal's attitude toward the philosophy of Nietzsche has become controversial. Some students of Iqbal claim that his entire philosophy is a kind of repetition of Nietzschean philosophy. For example, E. G. Browne defines Iqbal's philosophy as mainly an adaptation of Nietzschean philosophy.[8] A diametrically opposed view is held by some who fully deny the influence of Nietzsche on Iqbal, asserting that there is nothing in common between their philosophies.[9]

Both extreme views seem to miss the point. Iqbal undoubtedly felt the influence of Nietzscheanism but, far from becoming its follower, he sharply criticized it. To a certain extent the attraction of Nietzscheanism was determined by another, no less important, premise (mentioned earlier) from which Iqbal proceeded in working out his philosophical system. That was primarily the pragmatic one of the need to create *a philosophy of action* in the period of an incipient national liberation movement in India. That is why Iqbal was drawn by the ideal of the Nietzschean superman, a personality of strong will capable of "heroic existence."

Nietzsche's criticism of Christian asceticism which dooms man to slavish passivity appealed to Iqbal because he himself was bitterly opposed to the asceticism preached by Muslim mystics. Iqbal borrowed from Nietzsche some images, including those of diamond and coal, as symbols of firmness and lack of will.

Although attracted by Nietzsche's philosophical writings and literary talent, Iqbal never did accept the very essence of Nietzscheanism. He admitted that Nietzsche had the ability of "divine seeing," and in this sense the ability to become a prophet. But Nietzsche, maintained Iqbal, could not become one, because he relied solely on his own faculties and did not have in his spiritual life "guidance from without." Moreover, the principles of his philosophy could be carried out only by the elite, by strong personalities, as opposed to the "herd."[10] Nietzsche's atheism and cynical aristocratism made Nietzschean doctrines unacceptable to Iqbal, who based his entire world outlook on faith and believed in the inseverable connection of man with God and society.

After examining the main spiritual sources of Iqbal's philosophical views an analysis of some aspects of his world outlook is in order. In constructing his ontological conception, Iqbal tries critically to revise the philosophical doctrine of *kalām* (scholastic theology) "to turn the Ash'arite scheme of atomism into a spiritual pluralism."[11]

He regarded quite positively the *mutakallimūn* (dialectical theologians') idea of being as a whole, especially stressing its dialectical nature. Iqbal regarded as "dialectical" the postulate of *kalām* about the unlimited number of atoms constantly created by God and also the proposition about accidents, the attributes of substances created each time anew by God. Iqbal saw in all these assertions an expression of the idea that everything in the world is in constant flux and subject to change.

What Iqbal objected to most was the *mutakallimūn* proposition that all atoms and all substances are similar, while reason or the soul is nothing but one of the accidents of substance. His criticism of this proposition was evidently determined by two causes. In the first place, he acted here from consistent positions of monistic idealism. Second, he criticized the *mutakallimūn* because, by recognizing the soul (reason) only as one of the attributes of substance, they assumed the position of "pure materialism" and thereby "oppose[d] the real trend of their own theory."[12]

Indeed, the *mutakallimūn* interpretation makes it possible to draw a conclusion regarding the existence of two substances: one possessing the apperception of reason (that is, the spiritual) and the other devoid of it (that is, the material). Iqbal opposed this dualism. "Reality is essentially spirit," he asserted. "The whole world is an expression of the Ultimate Reality—of God."[13]

God is the Ego (with a capital letter) which engenders a plurality of egos, each of which is his self-expression. "The world in all its details, from the mechanical movement of what we call the atom of matter to the free movement of thought in the human ego, is the self-revelation of the 'Great I am.'" Egohood is most perfectly expressed in man. "That is why," Iqbal concluded, "the Qur'ān declares the Ultimate Ego to be nearer to man than his own neck-vein."[14]

Assertion of various levels of substance enabled Iqbal to revise one more proposition of the *kalām* philosophy. According to the Ash'arite interpretation, all bodies are composed of identical atoms and differ from each other only by accident. Thus man consists of the same substance as a worm. Man, as everything else in the world, possesses no internal potential and does only what is preordained by God. For Iqbal such an interpretation of man's place and role in the universe was unacceptable. He believed (as noted before) in the creative activity of the human ego and in man's definite freedom of choice and action. That is why Iqbal claimed that the ego's substances differ, depending on the degree to which they express the Divine Ego.

"Man," Iqbal stated, "in whom egohood has reached its relative perfection, occupies a genuine place in the heart of Divine creative energy and thus possesses a much higher degree of reality than things around him. Of all the creations of God he alone is capable of consciously participating in the creative life of his Maker."[15] (Iqbal admitted that in his criticism of Ash'arite philosophy he was guided by the traditions of Muslim thought.) This statement undoubtedly contains a measure of truth, and apparently the pantheistic school of Sufism exerted here a great influence on Iqbal. But, in the opinion of this author Iqbal's main reasons for revising the *kalām* theory of being were the new sociopolitical conditions demanding fresh approaches to many philosophical problems, including the position of man and his role in society.

The form in which Iqbal's concept of being was expressed resembled in many respects Leibnitz's monadology. This similarity is very clearly visible in Iqbal's followers, who include contemporary Pakistani philosophers, especially Khalifah 'Abdūl Hakīm, M. M. Sharīf, and others. Iqbal's interpretation of the essence of being was the basis on which he and his followers developed their epistemological and ethical concepts.

In the philosophy of Muslim mystics (especially in the thought of al-Ghazzali) Iqbal found the most suitable approach to the problem of knowledge. What attracted Iqbal to al-Ghazzali was that his philosophic aim in the eleventh-century world of Islam was similar to Iqbal's own, namely, "securing for religion the right to exist independently of science and metaphysics."

In his lectures *The Reconstruction of Religious Thought in Islam*, Iqbal compared al-Ghazzali with Kant, saying that the mission of both was "apostolic" in the sense that both proceeded from positions of scepticism in the period of the greatest advance of rationalism and eventually succeeded in restoring religion to its rightful position. From Iqbal's viewpoint there was, however, an important difference between al-Ghazzali and Kant. "Kant, consistently with his principles, could not affirm the possibility of a knowledge of God," whereas al-Ghazzali, "finding no hope in analytic thought, moved to mystic experience, and there found an independent content for religion."[16]

Although Iqbal had a high regard for al-Ghazzali's philosophy, he nevertheless pointed to an essential shortcoming in his philosophical world outlook—his failure to understand that "thought and intuition are organically related." Iqbal believed that thought and intuition were noncontradictory: "They spring up from the same root and complement each other. The one grasps Reality piecemeal, the other grasps it in its wholeness. The one fixes its gaze on the eternal, the other on the temporal aspect of Reality."[17]

In contrast to most religious philosophers, Iqbal considered it necessary to subject the "data" of mystic experience to an intellectual and pragmatic test. He asserted that "critical interpretation" or "intellectual test" by philosophers "leads us ultimately to a reality of the same character as is revealed by religious experience." As for the "pragmatic test," it is a function of prophets. Iqbal was a religious ideologist and he always remained on religious grounds; simultaneously, however, he was an ideologist of the rising bourgeois class and of the national liberation movement. Therefore, his philosophy reflected the progressive tendency to renounce the blind following of religious dogmas and to develop the creative activity of man's reason. This progressive tendency was further developed in Iqbal's ethical concepts.

## MAN, THE PARTNER OF GOD

IN view of India's national bourgeoisie's determination to overthrow foreign domination and take vigorous action against colonialism, Iqbal the poet and philosopher rejected the fatalism preached by Islamic mysticism and advocated recognition of man's freedom of will. He regarded man as a creator, as a partner of God the Maker. In his poem *Mahawārah Ma-bayen Khudā wa Insān* (God's Conversation with Man), man speaks to his maker as an equal:

> God
> I made this world, from one same earth and water
> You made Tartaria, Nubia, and Iran.
> I forged from dust the iron's unsullied ore,
> You fashioned sword and arrowhead and gun;
> You shaped the axe to hew the garden tree,
> You wove the cage to hold the singing-bird.
>
> Man
> You made the night, and I the lamp,
> And You the clay and I the cup;
> You—desert, mountain-peak, and vale;
> I—flower-bed, park, and orchard; I
> Who grind a mirror out of stone,
> Who brew from poison honey-drink.[18]

The recognition that man is a creator who transforms the world left to God only the role of the prime impulse which created the world and then gave man full freedom of action. Seeking to resolve this contradiction, Iqbal asserted that God in this way consciously limited his omnipotent will. "It (this limitation) is born out of His own creative freedom whereby He has chosen finite egos to be participators in His life, power, and freedom."[19] For Iqbal recognition of the freedom of the will was a prerequisite for the awakening in people of faith in their powers and potentialities. Describing man as a coworker of God the Maker, Iqbal sought to convince his compatriots of the need for action and energetic intervention in the reconstruction of social life.

Iqbal accepted in his own way the Sufist interpretation of the relationship between good and evil. In contrast to the Qur'ān, which states that whatever good falls to the lot of man comes from Allah and whatever evil befalls man comes from himself (Sura, IV, 81), medieval Sufis asserted that both good and evil in the world came from God. Muslim mystics held that evil was objective and necessary as a requisite for the realization of good. Just as a bird can fly only by overcoming the resistance of the air, so man can become pious only by overcoming evil. That is why man has no right to complain about the existence of evil, but must accept it as necessary.

Borrowing this concept of evil from the Sufis, Iqbal transformed it into a contingency for realizing good. But as an ideologist of the rising national bourgeoisie, the spirit of pessimism and passivity underlying the writings of the medieval mystics was abhorrent to him. Also, in order to solve the problems of relationship between good and evil, Iqbal was attracted by the romantic and dynamic European bourgeois philosophy of the seventeenth and eighteenth centuries.

As a poet Iqbal perceived Western philosophical ideas chiefly through literature. That is why, for example, he, in a way borrowed the dialectical concept of good and evil from the poetry of Goethe and Milton. The problem of the relationship between good and evil is solved by reinterpreting the Biblical legend (Sura, VII, 10–24) about the Fall of Man and his eviction from paradise. In contrast to the traditional religious interpretation of the legend, Iqbal welcomed the Fall of Man as the manifestation of the first act of his free will. "Man's first act of disobedience," he wrote, "was also his first act of free choice."[20] Since good is a product of free choice, it may be said that evil creates good. Iqbal's Iblīs-Satan, like Goethe's Mephisto is a part of "the eternal force always striving for evil which created only good." Without it life would be devoid of dynamism, and dead passivity would prevail in this world. As in Milton's *Paradise Lost*, Satan in Iqbal's *Javid-Namah* (The Book of Eternity) is more attractive than God because he symbolizes a more dynamic and creative spirit. Addressing God, Iblīs says:

> You created the stars, but they owe their movement to me.
> The world's hidden life comes from me, not from you.
> You breathed life into man's body, but it owes its dynamism to me.
> You followed the road of passivity, while I urged all to act.
> This Adam wrought of clay, devoid of vision and of narrow horizon
> Was begotten by you, but he will mature under my guidance.

The revolutionary spirit of Iqbal's concepts of good and evil corresponded to the sentiments of the Muslim bourgeoisie during the period of its development and emergence in the political arena. Recognition of the objective existence of evil was then in its interests. This made it possible to explain all social difficulties and hardships not by subjective means, but by the existing evil personified by colonialism and feudalism. By advocating the close connection of good and evil and their transmutation the bourgeoisie thereby sought to substantiate and justify its action against the social and political order of the day. Disobedience, active protest, and even violence, regarded by the prevailing morality as evil, were pictured by bourgeois ideologists as forces creating good.

# 15

# Mystic Impact of Hallaj

## ANNEMARIE SCHIMMEL

IQBAL appreciated the ideas of Hussain Ibn Mansūr (known to history as Hallaj, i.e., the wool carder), the ninth-century mystic, only in the later period of his life. Earlier he had written a sharp condemnation of Hallaj's mystic doctrines in his *Development of Metaphysics in Iran* (1908). This change in attitude is evident in Iqbal's *Javid-Namah* (The Book of Eternity), which he composed toward the end of his creative years.

In the last sections of *Javid-Namah* appear the three *zindīqs* Hallaj, Ghālib, and Tahira.[1] In the Heaven of Jupiter, generally considered to be the dwelling place of religious leaders, the three mystic-poets wander about. The pure spirit of these great lovers leads Iqbal to probe the deepest mysteries of being and not-being, of predestination, and of the role of the Prophets and Satan. Here in the firmament of Jupiter Hallaj is the main speaker, whereas Tahira and Ghālib sing only two brief songs.

The late discovery of Hallaj by Iqbal helped crystallize the poet's ideas of love and its significance for Muslim India. To understand the influence of Hallaj and his work on Iqbal, it is necessary to examine his life and his mystic ideas.

Hussain Ibn Mansūr al-Hallaj was born in Bayda, a little town in Iran in 859. From his native province, Fars, he went to Baghdad, the center of mystic life during the ninth and tenth centuries. In Baghdad the classical *Tasawwuf* (mysticism) had developed, beginning with the austere, ascetic preacher Hasan al-Basri (d. 728) and the ardent lover Rabi'a (d. 801), and leading to the sober, self-controlled al-Harith b. Asad al-Muhasībi (d. 837), to Sari al-Saqati, and finally to al-Junayd (d. 910).[2] Besides these great teachers there lived a great number of Sufis, trying to experience the gnosis, the love of God, the *Tawhīd* (belief in one God), and striving for the *fanā fillāh* (the passing away from self) and the *baqā billāh* (remaining in God).

Hallaj joined other mystics, but was not on very good terms with his master, al-Junayd (who is said to have cursed him). He then journeyed to Mecca. After about a year's stay, Hallaj went to India, perhaps with a view to acquiring some knowledge of Yoga practices. Upon his return to Baghdad in 913, the government, in concert with most of the *Fuqha* (jurists) and even many Sufis, accused him of impiety and conspiring with the Karmatians.[3] Hallaj was imprisoned, and on March 26, 922 he was cruelly put to death.[4] Most of the contemporary Sufis contended that Hallaj's execution was a punishment, willed by God, because the mystic had openly announced the mystery of divine love. He had exclaimed, "Āna' l-Haqq" (I am the creative truth), a statement utterly unacceptable to orthodox Muslims and moderate mystics. Therefore, most of the Sufis of the time (with the exception of Shaikh Ibn al-Khafif and 'Ali Rudhbāri)[5] neither agreed with Hallaj's mystic theories of the *huwa huwa* (man is the personal and living witness of God) nor understood the meaning of his famous statement "Āna' l-Haqq." This is not at all the cry of an intoxicated lover who has lost self-control, but the quintessence of his mystic doctrines, which should not be interpreted in a pantheistic sense.

## LEGEND OF LOVE

SOMETIME after his death the personality of Hallaj was transformed by legend, and perhaps by deeper understanding. He now stands out "pre-eminently as a man of sorrows striving with all his heart to fulfil the Divine Command no matter at what cost of suffering to himself."[6] He has become the prototype of the great lover, who sheds his blood in endless love and becomes *Mansūr* (victorious) at his death on the gibbet. Maulana Jalāl-ud-Din Rumi (d. 1273), the greatest mystical poet of Persia, once compared the red rose on its bough to Mansūr al-Hallaj. His famous *Mathnawi* and his *Diwān* are filled with allusions to the martyr of love. The impact of Hallaj's mystic personality and ideas is most clearly felt, however, in the poetry and prose of Farīd-ud-Din 'Attār (d. 1220). He considered Hallaj his spiritual guide and once again made his name famous in the Persian-speaking world.

From its beginnings, Turkish poetry sings the story of Hallaj's love and the dangerous ways of love and affliction. A number of details from Hallaj's life are quoted by the poet Nesimi (d. 1417), who was killed for heterodoxy, and thus, like his master, "performed the ablution for prayer with his own blood."[7] In the sixteenth century, Pīr Sultān Abdāl was imprisoned and suffered wounds "not by the stones thrown at him but only by the rose thrown by his friends," just as Hallaj had suffered when his disciple Shiblī threw a rose at him. Without mentioning Hallaj's works, Oriental poets have borrowed the symbols of true love; the story of the moth throwing itself into the flame is a centuries-old symbol of the *fanā fillāh* (the passing away from self). In his famous work, *Kitāb al-Tawasin*, Hallaj describes in short harmonious sentences the lot of the lover who, after reaching the point of union, will never return to his earthly companions.

During the Middle Ages Hallaj had become not only the poetical hero of painful love, but also, in the view of later Sufism, a representative of the concept of *Wahdat al-Wujūd* (pantheistic monism). This doctrine had been fully developed in the mystical philosophy of Ibn al-'Arabi in the thirteenth century. Later Muslim mystics became deeply submerged in the idea of *Wahdat al-Wujūd*, and the works of classical Sufis, including al-Junayd and Hallaj, were interpreted in the light of Ibn al-'Arabi's monistic philosophy. The development of Indo-Muslim poetry (especially the songs of the Punjabi and Sindhi mystics), is the most charming expression of these thoughts.[8]

After Ibn al-'Arabi's time, the ideas of classical *Tasawwuf*—stressing the transcendency of God, and the relation of man to Him as that of a creature to his creator or a lover to his beloved—were completely transformed and interpreted according to the system of great Spanish theosophists. It was this distorted picture of Hallaj, as seen in the mystical poetry of India and Persia, which Iqbal knew from his early childhood.

## IQBAL'S ATTITUDE TOWARD HALLAJ: 1908

IN the poems of the Punjabi folk poet, Bullhe Shah, Iqbal could see Hallaj praised as the first man openly to announce the essential unity of God and the soul, and the first martyr of love killed by the fanatical theologians, who were far from understanding the mystery of divine love. From Persian and Urdu poetry Iqbal must have known the confrontation of the pulpit (the seat of the dry-as-dust theologians), and the gibbet (the place where the ascension of the great mystic Hallaj occurred).

Iqbal did not appreciate these mystic ideas, however, when he saw the dangerous consequences of a monistic system of thought, realizing that such an interpretation was not compatible with the prophetic spirit of Islam. Discussing different aspects of Sufi metaphysics, Iqbal wrote in his doctoral dissertation (1908) that the Sufi "school became wildly pantheistic in Hussain Mansūr al-Hallaj who, in the true spirit of the Indian Vedantist, cried out—I am God—'Aham Brahma Asmi.' "[9] He echoed similar sentiments about Hallaj in the verse of the *Zabūr-i 'Ajam*, first published in June 1927:

> Do not speak of Shankara and Mansur!
> Search for God always in the way of the Ego!
> Be lost in thyself in order to realize the Ego!
> Say "Āna' l-Haqq," and become the Siddīq of the Ego!

Here, Iqbal brackets Hallaj with the most erudite commentator of the *Upanishads*, Shankara, who is perhaps the greatest representative of pure "mysticism of infinity" and the most important philosopher of Vedanta.[10]

Between writing his doctoral dissertation and composing the *Zabūr-i 'Ajam*, Iqbal became familiar with French Orientalist Louis Massignon's studies on the mystic doctrines of Hallaj. Massignon introduced the scholarly world to the Persian mystics in 1914 when he edited and published Hallaj's *Kitāb al-Tawasin*.[11] Eight years later he published his monumental treatise on Hallaj, *La Passion d'al-Hosayn ibn Mansour al-Hallaj* (1922). Iqbal probably read the *Kitāb al-Tawasin* in 1918 or 1919. He referred to it in a letter (May 17, 1919) to Maulana Aslam Jairajpūri, admitting that the fundamental ideas of Hallaj had now become clear to him. Nevertheless, as yet, he showed no sympathy for the famous martyr of love.

Massignon, however, had succeeded in proving that in the theology of Hallaj the pure transcendency of God is maintained at the same time as is His presence by his grace in the heart of the believer—when it has been purified by the observance of spiritual discipline and rites. Man is created in order that the love of God may be apparent in the world. He is an image of God Himself, and God has chosen him from eternity to eternity by looking at him in love. Thus man becomes endowed with the divine attributes, *huwa huwa* (He He). Adam is said to have been created from the not-being (not emanated from God), and from that his spirit is also created. Hallaj holds that "the Divine Unity does not result in destroying the personality of the mystic, but it makes him more perfect, more sacred, more divine, and makes him its free and living organ." According to Hallaj, the mystery of creation can only be understood if one realizes that the fundamental nature of the divine essence is love, creative love, "essential desire," as Massignon pointed out.[12]

Hallaj, in order to describe divine love, uses the term *'ishq*, a word that means dynamic love, but its connotation was in Hallaj's days suspect even among the Sufis. For the relationship between man and God not even the term *mahabbat*, a more static conception of love, had been accepted by the pious Muslims of the ninth and early tenth centuries. This *'ishq*, which Hallaj describes as the divine essence, is an active and creative force; it tries to draw man nearer to God. The goal of divine grace is to make man partake of this essential love.

Love involves numerous afflictions—separation from people, from family and friends, as well as tears, grief, and sighs. Iqbal has rightly given the following words to Hallaj in *Javid-Namah*:

> No life
> It is to live without a Secret Smart
> Do learn to hold a fire beneath thy feet.[13]

This type of love means longing for death; the real lover hopes to be slain as an offering, thus fulfilling religious duty. That is why Hallaj's beautiful prayers repeat the cry: "Kill me, my intimate, for in being killed is my life." These passionate words are the beginning of Hallaj's well-known *qasīda* (Diwan No. 10), which was studied by later mystics, including Suhrawardi Halabi, Ibn al-'Arabi, and especially Maulana Jalāl-ud-Din Rumi. The Maulana has alluded to this *qasīda* several times in *Mathnawi* (V, 2675; VI, 4062), making it familiar to later generations of mystical poets.[14]

However, it is doubtful that Hallaj uttered his controversial statement "Āna' l-Haqq" in the presence of his master, Junayd. It is preserved in the sixth chapter of *Kitāb al-Tawasin*. The meaning of *haqq* in this context is the creative essence of God, the creative truth. It is the cry of someone who feels that the *ruh natiqāh* (the uncreated divine spirit) has transformed him and that he is the living witness of God, the uncreated spirit of God being united by divine grace with the created spirit of man.

Following generations of Sufis have tried to explain this dangerous statement of the martyr-mystic in different ways, its theological foundation being forgotten by most of them. According to some of the Sufis, Hallaj in ecstasy completely lost his personality, and God spoke through his mouth. In the view of Abū-Hamid al-Ghazzali (d. 1111), the great scholastic theologian who always took the orthodox attitude, Hallaj's exclamation was a delusion, and—if announced in public—a dangerous delusion, an exaggerated utterance of the heart when it was intoxicated with love so deep that it could not feel the difference between itself and the Beloved. But it may also be the illumination brought by the divine name *al-Haqq* into the heart of the believer meditating on it. Only in the *Mishkāt al-Anwār* does al-Ghazzali agree that a vision of divine beauty could have led Hallaj to that cry. Nevertheless, when quoting Hallaj's sayings and prayers, al-Ghazzali seldom mentions his name.

The most charming explanation of *Āna' l-Haqq* is given by 'Abdūl Qādir Gilāni (d. 1166). Some of the metaphors used by this great Iraqi mystic are very close to those used by Iqbal:

One day the reason of one gnostic flew away from the tree of his outward form and came into Heaven, where it broke through the ranks of the angels. It was one of the falcons of the world whose eyes were covered by the hood called "Man has been created weak" (Qur'ān, IV, 32). He did not find in Heaven anything he could hunt, and when he saw the prey "I have seen my Lord" he was bewildered that this goal said to him, "Where so ever turn there is the Face of God" (Qur'ān, II, 122). He descended again, in order to gain a thing which is more precious than fire at the bottom of the sea; and he turned the eyes of his reason and did not see but his traces, and he returned and did not find in this world another goal than his Beloved. And he became glad and said, with the intoxication of his heart, Ana' l-Haqq, singing tunes which are not allowed to mankind, and whistling in the garden of Existence in a way that is not given to the Sons of Adam, and he modulated his voice in such a manner that it brought him to death.

In the commentary of Gilāni the motif of the bird is clear. Iqbal has, in the Jupiter-Sphere, painted Hallaj as an always-flying, birdlike spirit, an allusion to the lyrical words of Hallaj's commentator, Ruzbihān Baqli, who called his spiritual master "the King of the birds of love." And the idea that angels and even God are the "prey of the longing heart," occurs often in Iqbal's poetry.

Gilani's ideas are viewed from the standpoint of the *Wahdat al-Shahūd*: the vision of God is the real prey of the seeker. He has, on the other hand, touched the problem of the *ifsha as-sirr*. Since it is forbidden to tell people the great mysteries of divine love and union, Hallaj, who did not refrain from revealing these secrets, had to be punished.

Contrary to the ideas of Gilāni, the explanation of *Ānaʾ l-Haqq* offered by the Spanish mystic Ibn al-ʿArabi (1115–1240) is in the light of his monistic philosophy. He alters the expression *al-Haqq* to *Haqq* and says: "I am truth, I am the mystery of God's truth in visible things." Like Maulana Rumi, Iqbal's spiritual guide, he compares the situation of the one who cries "Ānaʾl-Haqq" to that of iron cast into the fire (Math. II, 1347): the color of iron lies in the color of fire; iron calls: "I am the fire, you may touch me and understand that I am really fire. . . ." That means that the union is not substantial (for iron remains materially and substantially iron), but is a union of attributes: iron takes the heat and the color of fire. In order to express the union of the human and the divine, the iron-and-fire symbol has been used by mystics of all religions, from orthodox Greek, Catholic, and Protestant writers to the Hindu sage Lal Das, a friend of Prince Dara Shikoh. Dwelling upon the theme of *Ānaʾl-Haqq*, Jalāl-ud-Din Rumi offers a fascinating explanation in his verses:

> To say "I" in due time is Divine Grace,
> To say "I" in undue time is a curse,
> The "I" of Mansur became grace,
> That of Pharaoh became a curse.
> (Math. II, 2522)

## IQBAL'S ATTITUDE TOWARD HALLAJ: 1928

IN Hallaj's concept of *Āna'l-Haqq* may be found an interesting parallel to Iqbal's problem of the ego. Discussing Hallaj's mystic ideas in one of his lectures delivered in Madras in 1928, Iqbal revealed his changed attitude toward the martyr, acknowledging especially the divine side of Hallaj's "I":

Devotional Sufism alone tried to understand the meaning of the unity of inner experience which the Qur'ān declares to be one of the three sources of knowledge, the other two being History and Nature. The development of this experience in the religious life of Islam reached its culmination in the well-known words of Hallaj: "I am the creative Truth." The contemporaries of Hallaj, as well as his successors, interpreted these words pantheistically; but the fragments of Hallaj, collected and published by the French Orientalist M. Massignon, leave no doubt that the martyr saint could not have meant to deny the transcendence of God. The true interpretation of his experience, therefore, is not the drop slipping into the sea, but the realization and bold affirmation in an undying phrase of the reality and permanence of the human ego in a profounder personality. The phrase of Hallaj seems almost a challenge flung against the *Mutakallinūn*.[15] The difficulty of modern students of religion, however, is that this type of experience, though perhaps perfectly normal in its beginning, points, in its maturity, to unknown levels of consciousness. . . .[16]

Furthermore, Iqbal compared Hallaj to his respected teacher, Professor John McTaggart of Cambridge University, saying that "Hallaj's phrase—I am the Creative Truth—was thrown as a challenge to the whole Muslim world at a time when Muslim scholastic thought was moving in a direction which tended to obscure the reality and destiny of the human ego. He never ceased to utter what he had personally seen to be the truth until the *mullas* of Islam prevailed upon the state to imprison him and finally to crucify him." However, McTaggart's emphasis on personal immortality, as Iqbal pointed out, "even at the expense of the transcendent God of Christian theology at a time when this important belief was decaying in Europe,"[17] forms the *tertium comparationis* between the modern British philosopher and the medieval Muslim mystic.

Defining the nature of *imān* (belief) as "a living assurance begotten of a rare experience," Iqbal also discussed Hallaj's divine "I" in relation to other luminaries of Islam:

> In the history of religious experience in Islam which, according to the Prophet, consists in the creation of divine attributes in man, this experience has found expression in such phrases as "I am the creative truth" (Hallaj), "I am Time" (Muhammad), "I am the speaking Qur'ān" ('Ali), "Glory to me" (Bayazid). In the higher Sufism of Islam, unitive experience is not the finite ego effacing its own identity by some sort of absorption into the infinite ego; it is rather the infinite passing into the loving embrace of the finite.[18]

However, it is more than doubtful whether a comparison of the above-mentioned theopathic utterances is justified, since the genuineness of two of them is highly questionable. Nevertheless, it is interesting to note how Iqbal managed to use these estatic words to prove his theories. Further, he saw the application of *Āna'l-Haqq* not only to the individual (who may preserve his personal self in union with God), but also to the community of the faithful. In a group of quatrains in his posthumous work *Armaghān-i-Hijaz* (p. 97 ff.), Iqbal maintained that an ideal nation was that which realized *Āna'l-Haqq* in its striving and proved to be the creative truth, a living and active reality which witnessed God's reality by its own national or supranational life. He said:

> If the individual says *Āna' l-Haqq*, punishment is justified,
> If a nation says it, it is not improper.

Having overcome his first, critical interpretation of Hallaj's ideas, Iqbal saw in the mystic a sublime example of living faith. It is therefore not astonishing that in the *Javid-Namah* the famous Sufi is presented as representative of a truly dynamic individual, perhaps a forerunner of the poet himself. Iqbal even put into Hallaj's mouth a *ghazal* (lyric) (which had appeared earlier in *Payām-i Mashriq*), and called him the ardent preacher of desire and free will. More than that, these two topics in the chapter "Heaven of Jupiter" are especially interesting, although their discussion in conjunction with Hallaj may at first sight seem strange to those readers who are not acquainted with his philosophy. Nevertheless, one must admire Iqbal's erudition and art because he chose, in addition to the notorious and perhaps dangerous doctrine of

*Āna'l-Ḥaqq*, other important ideas of Hallaj, including the prophetology and the concept of Satan as the only true worshiper. (These concepts are discussed by Hallaj in his *Kitāb al-Ṭawāsīn*.)

The beautiful lines in *Jāvīd-Nāmah* explaining the meaning of *'abduhū* (His servant), in which Hallaj praises the Prophet in sweet and ardent verses, were no doubt composed by Iqbal under the influence of the *Kitāb al-Ṭawāsīn*. The chapters "Ṭasīn al-Fahm" and "Ṭasīn an-Nuqṭā" of the *Kitāb al-Ṭawāsīn* praise the high qualities of the Prophet Muhammad, alluding to his *Mi'rāj* (ascension) and to the mysterious words of the *Sūrat an-Najm*. In the first chapter, "Ṭasīn as-Sirāj," Hallaj sings in very exuberant language the attributes of the Prophet, "whose light was created before all things, whose being preceded the not-being, whose name existed before the Divine Pen, and who came before all mankind, who is the Lord of mankind, whose name is Ahmad. . . ." According to an old mystic tradition, *'abduhū* is the most honored rank that man can reach; in the *Sūrat al-Isrā* the deepest mystery of the ascension is alluded to with the words "Praised be He Who travelled at night with His Servant".

It is, therefore, impossible to imagine a rank higher than that of *'abduhū*. Its importance was again underlined by the famous Indian reformer of the seventeenth century, Shaikh Ahmad Sarhindi, and his followers in the Naqshbandiya order. He even contrasted the rank of *'abduhū*, the modest status of the Prophet, to the arrogance of Hallaj, who claimed to be "the creative truth," without properly recognizing the role of the Prophet in Hallaj's system of thought.

Although Iqbal was not very faithful to Hallaj, especially in his treatment of the mystic's doctrine of *fanā* (annihilation), he was able to summarize the ideas of early Islamic mysticism on Paradise in the alleged words of Hallaj:

> The ascetic is a stranger in this world,
> The lover is a stranger in this world.

For the real lover does not wish anything but God himself, a subject often treated in Sufism, beginning with Rabi'a and her fellow-mystics and continued by Iqbal. Paradise is only a veil which separates the lover from his Beloved. Those who adore God in the hope of paradise are like hirelings, expecting from their Lord a good reward. Even the ascetic who has given up this world longs for paradisean rewards and hopes to find in paradise all the pleasures he refrains from enjoying on earth. As for the real lover, he flies from paradise toward the vision of the Beloved and is never satisfied with the created pleasures of a future life.

Just as Iqbal developed the thoughts of Hallaj in the *'abduhū* verses of *Javid-Namah*, he similarly stressed his idea of Iblīs (Satan). In the chapter "Heaven of Jupiter" Satan appears at the end. Hallaj, answering a question of the poet, says before vanishing:

> We are but ignorant; he [Satan] knows reality
> And nothingness. His old revolt has taught
> To us this secret: that the fallen know
> Delight of rising and that from the pain
> Of less flows forth the joy of more.[19]

What kind of secret is this, and what is the nature of this mystery? The clue to understanding it is provided by Ruzbihān Baqli, who explains Hallaj's ideas in his commentary on the Qur'ān. Discussing the meaning of Sura II, verse 32, Baqli writes:

Hallaj says: "When *Iblīs* was ordained to prostrate before Adam he said to the Almighty: 'Has somebody else taken away the honor of the prostration from my heart so that I should prostrate before Adam? If Thou hast ordained that, Thou hadst forbidden it first.' God said: 'I will punish Thee with everlasting punishment!' Satan asked: 'While punishing me, wilt Thou look at me?' God answered: 'Yes!' And Satan said: 'Thy looking at me is enough to let me bear Thy punishment. Do whatever Thou wilt!' He said: 'I will make Thee rajīm!' He said: 'Do what Thou willest!' "

According to Hallaj, Iblīs was glad to be honored by the "garment of curses." Later Sufism expressed the view that Iblīs, the true lover, would gladly accept punishment from the hand of his Beloved if the Beloved continued to look at him while chastising him. In this form 'Attār and some other Sufis, including Shah 'Abdūl Latīf, the great mystical poet of Sindh, accepted Iblīs as the lover, who would never adore anyone other than God. Although outwardly disobeying His order, Iblīs obeyed the hidden will of God, who never allowed anyone to be worshiped besides Himself. Thus, in this strange manner Iblīs becomes the only true worshiper in the two worlds.

But that is only a small part of the great problem of Iblīs and his act of disobedience as shown in Hallaj's work. In the "Tasīn al-Azal wa-l-iltibās" (Tasīn VI), this problem is discussed with greater clarity. Here Hallaj points out that there are no real *muwāhhids* (confessors of God's unity) in the world, except Iblīs and Muhammad. Since the latter is the treasurer of divine grace, Iblīs must be called the recipient of divine wrath, who remained in himself, whereas the Prophet went away from himself. Iblīs, in Hallaj's words, goes so far as to declare that an individual's denying is the declaration of God's holiness, but he makes the mistake of seeing Adam only in his outward form, as a figure of clay and water, not perceiving the divine spark in him. According to Hallaj, Iblīs boasts of his service to God before the creation of man, and because of his pride he prefers everlasting separation to one loving prostration. In this chapter of the *Kitāb al-Tawasin*, Iblīs also meets Moses and tells him that he not only remembers his Beloved, but is always mentioned along with Him, both at the beginning of the recitation of the Holy Book (when the *"a'ūdh Bi-Allah min al-shaytān al-rajīm"*[20] is recited before the *"bi-smi Allah al-Rahmān al-Rahīm"*)[21] and in other verses of the Qur'ān (i.e., *"wa-inna 'alayk la'ntī ilā yawm al-dīn"*).[22] True to his logic, Iblīs accuses Moses of polytheism because he bowed his head before the Burning Bush and looked at the mountain, and thus saw created things beside God.

Finally, Hallaj compares his situation to that of Iblīs and Pharaoh—each of them pretended to something, be it the negation ("I do not prostrate") of Iblīs, or the pride ("I am God") of Pharaoh, or Hallaj's "I am the creative truth." All of them are ready to die or to be punished, but not to give up their pretentions. Reading "Tasīn al-Azal wa-l-iltibās," one understands better the verses from Rumi's *Mathnawi*, in which "I" of Hallaj and that of Pharaoh are held to be two completely different things.

The ideas of Hallaj formulated in the *Kitāb al-Tawasin* help in appreciating the significance of the great scenes "Appearance of Satan" and "Satan's Complaint" in the Jupiter-Sphere of *Javid-Namah*. Many famous Sufis have inherited these seemingly strange ideas of Hallaj and interpreted them in their own light. Al-Ghazzali goes so far as to say in his account of the story of Iblīs and Moses: "He who does not learn the *tawhīd* (acknowledgment of God's Unity) from Iblīs is a heretic (*zindīq*)." Iqbal expresses these positive qualities of Iblīs in wonderful words when he has Hallaj say:²³

> To burn in his fire is to love; without his flame
> No burning be. He is antecedent in
>     service and love, therefore, unschooled.
> Man in his mysteries remains. Tear off
> The cloak of orthodoxy that constrains;
> And from him learn the unity of God.²⁴

That is the last advice given by Hallaj to the poet before he continues his flight in eternal desire and never-resting love.

The name of the martyr-mystic occurs once more in the *Javid-Namah*. It is in connection with a spirit that flies in never-ending circles between the heavenly spheres and paradise—the spirit of Nietzsche, whom Iqbal calls "a Hallaj without a gibbet":

> "Who is this frenzied man?"
> I asked. And Rumi said, "The German seer
> Is he, who lives betwixt two worlds. His flute
> Contains an ancient melody. Nor chains
> Nor cross did come his way; yet he too gave
> The antique message that once Hallaj brought.
> His speech is bold, his thought sublime, his words
> Have like a sword cut up the West in twain
> His coevals his emotions could not track;
> And thought him mad whom ecstasy possessed."
>
> A Hallaj, lonely in his town,
> Whose life, the Mullahs spared, physicians claimed.
> "None was there in the West who concord knew
> And so his music broke his harp. None showed
> The wanderer his way; so chaos grew in his experience."
>
> All life explains the signs
> Of self, whose stages are the "no" and "but."
> He lingered at the point of "no" and failed
> To gain the stage of "but"; nor realised
> The rank and reach too of "His worshipper."
> A light illumined him, yet unaware
> He was of it, as of the roots remains
> The fruit.²⁵

## Mystic Impact of Hallaj

Iqbal became acquainted with Nietzsche's work quite early. Although the ideas of the German philosopher deeply influenced his philosophy of activity, they could not be more than a milestone on his spiritual journey. He saw quite clearly that the imperfections of Nietzsche's one-sided doctrine prevented man from achieving the noble rank of 'abduhū. The Iqbalian superman becomes perfect as he draws closer to his creator. The Nietzschean superman, on the contrary, enters a world where God is dead. Yet, a certain admiration for the tragic figure of Nietzsche is always visible in Iqbal's poetry and prose.

Hallaj and Nietzsche were both conceived by Iqbal as fighters against fossilized and petrified religious systems, and this similarity led them toward the same fate. And this is what Iqbal felt about himself. Already in 1917, Iqbal warned some friends not to explain his concept of the ego (which had appeared in the *Asrār-i Khudi* [The Secrets of the Self]). He couched this warning in a Persian verse, pointing to the fate of Hallaj:

> On the gibbet thou canst say it,
> But on the pulpit thou canst not say it.

And two decades later he summed up:

> The mystery is unfolded in two words:
> The place of love is not the pulpit but the gibbet.

Iqbal openly compared himself to Hallaj. He put into the mouth of the martyr-mystic (in the great scene in Jupiter-Heaven in *Javid-Namah*) verses of unforgettable beauty. Hallaj, in his memorable monologue, tells the poet that the sound of the trumpet of resurrection had been in his breast, but his people had preferred to go toward the cemetery, and he complains that the theologians of his time do not know that the Spirit, the *ruh Allah*, is from the *amr Allah*, as stated in the Qur'ānic revelation (Sura, XVII, 8f). The same sentiments were expressed by Hallaj in the beautiful lines of his *Diwān*:

> By God, the breath of the (uncreated) Spirit breathes
> into my body like Israfil's blowing into the trumpet!

Love was, for him, the real resurrection. Hallaj sang the great threnody for all those who were spiritually dead and had never felt the enrapturing force of love which bears the greatest afflictions without complaint, nay, with utmost joy.

Iqbal admired the qualities of brave love, activity, and loving desire in the great mystic. He felt that he, too, was called to blow the trumpet of resurrection in his country, to help to shape a living world and to stimulate mankind by the message of eternal desire. In this vein spoke Hallaj, as he was made to address Iqbal in the *Javid-Namah*:

> The voice of resurrection shot its call
> Forth in my breast; I saw a people who
> Were hastening to their graves; the faithful lived
> Much as the infidels; "No God save God,"
> They said, but the reality of self
> They did reject.
>
> Each hearth doth secretly
> Communion have with it, within this grey
> Old church. Whoever from its fire did fail
> To take his share died unaware of self.
> Its light both India and Iran have
> Beheld, but who also sees its flame
> Is rarely met. Of both its light and fire
> I gave the tidings. Seest thou not my sin,
> My friend, my confidant, fear for thyself.
> Thou too repeatest what I did, thou too
> Wouldst lief attempt to resurrect the dead.[26]

# V

# POETRY

# 16

## Conception of Poetry and the Poet

### HADI HUSSAIN

NO poet, not even Milton, ever took his art more seriously than Iqbal did; none, not even Shelley or Dante, claimed for it a higher place among human activities or employed it in the service of a more far-reaching purpose. In the midst of his multifarious pursuits—philosophy, religion, mysticism, even politics—poetry was Iqbal's real vocation all his life. In fact, his excursions in these and other realms were all in the nature of explorations for ore to be refined into poetic gold. His approach to everything was that of a poet, for poetry was the core of his being. His whole *Weltanschauung*, his vision of God, man, and the universe, is a poet's vision illumined by a fiery heart at its center. His God is the archetypal poet, the supreme creative artist, incessantly creating out of a grand passion of self-expression.

Iqbal's ideal man is God's apprentice and helpmate in this creative activity, always adding to the Master's work and daring even to improve upon it, because he has a personality of his own to express. His universe is that perfect poem yet to be written, which God and man are writing in collaboration, as some of the great epics of ancient times are written, but which will never be completed; for it will continue to grow in the very process of being composed. This is the essence of poetry, no matter by what name it is called.

Iqbal's conception of poetry is of a piece with his cosmology. In a poetic universe poetry is life and life poetry, and both are endless creation. The creative impulse, originating in God's self, which is the primal source of all being, flows through innumerable human selves into the sea of becoming which is life.

> Life is a boundless sea,
> Whose every drop's heart is a restless wave,
> It knows no tranquil state,
> Because it must continually create.[1]

The most restless drop in life's sea is the poet's heart. For one thing, the poet has more than the ordinary human need of self-expression, which is the fountain of all creative activity; for it is what generates, sustains, and multiplies life. For another, it is not merely an individual human heart beating in the poet's breast, but the universal heart; also, his is the voice of the whole humanity. He forges links of sympathy between man and the things that surround him, reveals to him the mysteries that lie behind the obvious and the familiar, and gives him an insight into the secrets of his own self. He creates things by naming them, for by doing so he invests essence with attributes and brings them within man's ken. He imparts to man a vision of the unity that underlies the diversity of phenomena and an awareness of the coherence behind the apparent incoherence of things.

The poet thus reduces man's chaotic world to order and makes life meaningful for him. He extends the frontiers of man's consciousness beyond the world he knows, thus enabling him to transcend the limits of his temporal experience and see his finite existence as part of infinity. By virtue of these activities the poet wields a great deal of influence over man's moral and spiritual development in both the individual and the social domains. As an individual he helps man to realize the full potentialities of his natural endowments, to face up to the hostile forces arrayed against him with courage and determination, and to reshape the world around him in accordance with his aspirations and ideals. He spurs man to greater effort in order to realize his immense possibilities.

> You are a sword; come forth out of your sheath;
> Fulfill your task. Remove the mask from
> The face of all your possibilities.
> Seize sun and moon and stars. Illuminate
> Your night with the strong light of certainty.
> Bring out the Shining Hand from underneath
> Your cloak. If one looks right into one's heart,
> One sows a spark, but reaps a star.[2]

He reminds man that it is his divinely appointed destiny to rise from one state of being to another.

> To reach no end, to travel on
> Without a stop is everlasting life.
> Our range is from the ceiling of the skies

> To the sea's floor, and Time and Space are both
> Dust lying on our path.³

The process of evolution does not stop even after death.

> There are a thousand worlds along our way.
> How can journey's course come to a point and stay?
> Be steadfast, traveler, in both life and death;
> Take in your stride all worlds along your path.⁴

In man's social life, too, the poet is his philosopher, friend, and guide. He creates in the individual members of society a concern for its progress as a whole and unites them in bonds of solidarity. Thus the society develops into an organic whole, a living individual with a heart, a mind, and a soul of his own. The poet stirs up new impulses in the society, places high ideals before it, and inspires it with the will to strive for their achievement. When the social organism loses its zest for life, he pours his own life's blood into its veins. When its outlook becomes warped, its values fade, its energies flag, and no hope of its progress through peaceful evolution remains, he breathes the wind of revolution in it. He gives it a new ethos, a new set of values, a new philosophy of life.

Thus the poet helps in shaping the human personality and human destiny, both within the span of the individual life and in the perspective of history—and in both cases against the background of eternity. Speaking for the poet in his own person, Iqbal claims:

> The destinies of worlds are shaped behind
> The awnings of my mind,
> And revolutions are brought up
> In my heart's lap.
> I spent a moment in my inner solitude,
> And there emerged a world which knows no finitude.
>     . . .
> I witness life and death engaged in transitory strife,
> But have my eyes fixed firmly on eternal life.⁵

## POETIC PASSION

IN short, the poet is a leader, a teacher, a reformer, a sage—all these together. The unifying principle that activates this composite personality is poetic passion, the passion to create ever new, ever more beautiful and perfect forms embodying man's ever-growing aspirations. Another name for this poetic passion is love. It is a heightened state of the soul, which raises man above his ordinary self, increases his powers of perception, refines his feelings, broadens his sympathies, animates his imagination, and, above all, makes a sense of power well up from within him. This sense of power is a dynamic, outgoing urge to take hold of things and remodel them so as to make them better than they are. Iqbal maintains that love beautifies, sublimates, and idealizes:

> It is a touchstone for the gold of beauty.
> It both uncovers beauty and preserves
> Its sanctity. Its aspirations soar
> Beyond the summit of the skies, beyond
> This world of quantity, cause and effect.
> Since what it sees can never be described
> In words, it throws the veil off its own soul.
> Love sublimates all passions and invests
> With worth much that is worthless. Without love
> Life is a funeral, a joyless thing,
> A celebration of decay and death.
> Love meliorates man's mental faculties
> And burnishes a stone into a mirror.
> It gives to men with living hearts the light
> Of Mount Sinai and to the artist's hand
> It gives the miracle-performing power
> Of Moses' Shining Hand. All that exists,
> All that is possible, yields to its might;
> And in this bitter, gloomy world it is
> A gushing fountain of sweetness and light.
> The ardor of our thought comes from its fire.
> Its work is to create and to breathe life
> Into what it creates.[6]

Such being their origin, poetic creations are not mere slavish imitations of nature, lifeless reproductions of things in the external world, but living images of things as they exist in the poet's perfection-seeking soul and as they ought to be in nature. Whether poet or painter, the artist who merely imitates nature is untrue to his vocation:

## Conception of Poetry and the Poet

>He goes to Nature with a begging bowl
>For beauty's alms: a robber in disguise,
>He steals from Nature, itself destitute.
>To seek for beauty outside of yourself
>Is wrong: what ought to be is not before
>Your eyes, all ready-made for you to see.
>A painter who surrenders himself to
>The forms of Nature loses the form of his Self
>In imitating mere external forms.
>He does not smash the crystal images
>Of our false gods with granite strokes
>From his creative brush. His canvases
>Show Nature captive, lame and helpless in
>Its multicolored garment as if it
>Were a straightjacket made to hold it down.
>The moths he paints burn at an alien flame
>And have no living flame within themselves.
>His picture of today reflect no vision of
>Tomorrow and his eye can never penetrate
>The curtain of the sky; for in his breast
>There beats no fearless, enterprising heart.[7]

On the other hand:

>The artist, when he adds to Nature, brings
>To light the secret of his inner Self.
>Although a sea that needs no increment
>He yet receives full tribute from the streams
>Of other minds. He makes good life's defects,
>And shows it ways of being beautiful.
>The houris he creates are lovelier
>Than those of Heaven: the images he shapes
>Are more authentic than Lat and Manat.[8]
>Denying them is like denying God.
>He brings into existence a new world
>And gives a new life to the heart of man.
>He is a sea which hurls its wave upon
>Itself and which casts its pearls at our feet.
>Out of the fullness of his soul he fills
>All voids. His pure heart is the touchstone
>Of the beautiful and the ugly, and
>His art a mirror which reflects them both.[9]

The truth of the poetic creations is a higher form of truth than mere literal faithfulness to appearances; it is an unveiling of reality, residing neither in the world of sense perception nor in its abstraction, the world of the intellect, but in the world of the soul, the world of essence. The power to perceive this essential reality is not given to ordinary mortals, not even to the philosopher or the scientist, who are concerned only with rationally analyzable or empirically verifiable data. The only persons besides the poet who are vouchsafed knowledge of the truth that lies beyond proof or verification are the prophet and the saint—like the poet, men of passion, whose souls are aflame with love. The prophet embodies his vision of reality in the poetry of action, and the poet in the poetry of words; the saint absorbs it in himself, thus becoming a living poem. The poet is closer to the prophet than to the saint in that, like the former and unlike the latter, he transforms subjective into objective reality—his own inner states of being into concrete facts and situations, adding new dimensions to life. Although the media of the prophet and the poet are different, their product is the same—man's moral and spiritual regeneration or, in concrete terms, a morally and spiritually regenerated society—and this product is clearly envisaged and consciously willed by both of them. Their activities are, therefore, fully purposive, notwithstanding the fact that they are the outcome of inspiration, divine in the case of the prophet and intuitive in that of the poet.

## THE PERFECT MAN

THE charismatic character of poetic activity and the messianic role assigned to the poet entail a high degree of moral responsibility. In entrusting him with a gift of such vital importance to humanity, God has chosen the poet as an instrument for the fulfillment of His high purpose, which, on the temporal plane, is the advancement of humanity and, on a supratemporal plane, the creation of the perfect man, who is the *beau idéal* of all created things and is destined to be God's comate in eternity. The poet should, therefore, so exercise his art as to help man forward on his journey to perfection. His life's work should itself form a stage of that journey. In other words, he should himself be the forerunner and prototype of the perfect man—rebel, iconoclast, revolutionary, hero of mortal strife, champion of high ideals, and prophet of human progress.

It bears eloquent testimony to Iqbal's belief in this sublimated role of the poet that he sees himself in it, in much the same way as, for example, Homer, according to Longinus, often sees himself to live the great lives of his heroes or as Milton enjoins that one who hopes to write "of laudable things ought himself to be a true Poem." Iqbal's frequent claims of divine frenzy, inspired wisdom, intuitive foresight, and heroic courage are not mere braggadocio or attitudinization in the rather naïve tradition of Persian poetry. On the contrary, they sound like genuine appeals to the reader to take him for a serious poet, one who has something more to offer than mere entertainment. Conscious of the presence of these qualities in himself, he is anxious to make sure that the reader takes them into account so that he approaches him in a receptive frame of mind. His hieratic role not only entitles him, but makes it necessary for him, to speak in an oracular manner. His claims are not the pretensions of a pseudoprophet or a mystagogue, but the manifesto of a man with a mission who cannot afford to let false modesty prevent him from stating his qualifications.

Here is a typical passage in this vein out of a varied assortment:

> . . . A tiny mote,
> I hold the shining sun in fee,
> And I have countless mornings up
> My sleeve. My dust is brighter far
> Than Jamshid's world-reflecting cup;
> For it reflects things that still are
> The future's shadow-shapes.
> . . .
>
> My mind is a rare instrument,
> Which gives birth to new strains
> Strange to the hearer's ears.
> I am a newborn sun,
> Unused to the ways of the firmament;
> The stars are not yet on the run
> Before my light's advance.
> My rays have yet to dance
> On the sea's waves. The mountain bears
> No mark of my red henna-dye.
> The universe's eye
> Is not yet used to me.

I tremble with the fear
Of having to appear;
For night has ceased to be,
And dawns at last my day.

    . . .

I am that music which does not require
To be plucked out of strings.
I am tomorrow's poet's voice,
Which in today's void sings.
Alas! my age is ignorant
Of being's mysteries.

    . . .

I have no hope in my contemporaries;
And if my Mount Sinai
Is lit up, that is for
A Moses who has yet to come.
This age's sea is quiet to the core
Like dew, whereas my very dew
Is like a sea in storm.
My song is from another world,
A call to the road, a bell tolled
For caravans not yet in view.
O many poets were reborn
After their death: they shut their own
Eyes, but they opened ours.
They pulled their precious substance out of dust
And grew upon their graves like flowers.
The desert they passed silently
Like the steps of a dromedary.
But, lover that I am, to wail
Is my vocation; and a boom
Of lamentation like the crack of doom
Heralds my progress on the trail
I blaze. My voice outsings
My instrument's capacity;
But I am not afraid to snap its strings.

    . . .

I have been given access to the springs
Of everlasting life, and I evoke
The living soul of things.

> Mere particles of dust are quickened by
> My song and, growing wings of light, they fly
> Like glowworms. There has been
> No one before me who has sung
> Of truths that lie concealed,
> No one whose thought has strung
> Pure pearls of wisdom such as mine.[10]

## PURPOSIVE POETRY

SIMILARLY, when Iqbal denounces poets and poetry, he is thinking of poets and poetry not deserving of their name because they are decadent, life-negating, and subversive of human progress. Not to speak of poetry which addresses itself to the baser side of human nature, he condemns even poetry which is technically excellent but yields nothing more than mere aesthetic pleasure; for such poetry weakens the will to action and is therefore immoral. For instance, although he was a great admirer of Hāfiz as a master craftsman of Persian poetry, who, he acknowledged, could pack into single words meanings which others could not express in whole *ghazals* (lyrics), he inveighed against him for his quietism, his epicureanism, his libertinism, his indifference to the great historical events that were taking place around him and the soporific effect of his mystical eroticism. It is this kind of poetry which Iqbal intends to disavow; but he disavows it in words which convey the impression that he has no use for poetry of any kind. Here, for example, is a specially violent outburst:

> No good will ever come from any churlish boor
> Who lays the charge of versifying at my door.
> I do not know the alley where the poet's sweetheart dwells;
> I have no lovelorn heart which someone's coldness ails.
> Mere humble dust, I yet do not lie on the street
> To be a carpet under beauty's feet.
> Nor is there in my dust
> A heart made clamorous by lust.[11]

The disclaimer is aimed at the *fin-de-siècle* erotic poetry which was fashionable in Urdu when Iqbal started his poetic career; but Iqbal seems to be repudiating all poetry, although actually intending only to repudiate this one kind. In the passage quoted below, however, he is more specific: the target is unmistakably decadent poetry, the poetry of people on the downgrade, as were the Indian Muslims of that period, whom he particularly had in mind:

> Woe to the nation which regales itself
> On death, whose poet has no zest for life.
> He holds the mirror up to ugliness,
> Presenting it as beautiful. His song
> Is like a poisoned lancet in the heart.
> His kiss drains roses of their youthful bloom.
> He robs the nightingale's heart of the joy
> Of soaring while it sings. His opium dulls
> Your mind. His entertainment costs you dear:
> The price you pay for it is life itself.
> He warps the cypress's tall stateliness.
> He turns proud eagles into timid quails.
> His Muse is a seductive nymph; beware
> Its fatal siren song, which will allure
> You into the depths of the sea to drown.
> His music so bewitches hearts that they
> Court death, mistaking it for very life.
> He takes away all gusto from your soul:
> He steals the ruby from your inner mine.
> He dresses loss in the guise of gain,
> And he transforms all virtue into vice.
> He casts you into contemplation's sea,
> And makes you unfit for an active life.
> He makes what is poor in you poorer still
> His wine damps the spirits of the company.
> In his cloud there is no electric charge.
> His garden is a mere hallucination,
> A mere mirage of color and of smell.
> His beauty is a stranger to all truth.
> In his sea there are only blemished pearls.
> He teaches you that sleep is preferable
> To wakefulness. His breath puts out your fire.
> His nightingale pours pure gall into hearts,
> And underneath his rosebush lurks a snake.
> Beware his vat, his goblet, and his cup;
> Beware his poisonous, although sparkling, wine.[12]

An illustrative list of the favorite themes of decadent art (it is painting in this instance, but could well be poetry) is given in the following passage:

> A monk caught in the snare of carnal lust;
> A beauty with a bird imprisoned in
> A cage; a king with bended knees before
> A hermit wrapped up in a patchwork cloak;
> A man from the hills with a firewood load;
> A lovelorn maiden going to a temple;
> A yogi sitting in a wilderness;
> An old man tortured by the pains of age,
> Whose candle is about to flicker out;
> A minstrel with an alien instrument,
> So deeply lost in its strange melodies
> That if a nightingale—an alien bird,
> Again—were to break into song, the shock
> Would surely make his instrument's strings snap;
> A young man wounded by a glance's shaft;
> A child astride his aged father's neck.[13]

It would be wrong to conclude from the foregoing quotations that Iqbal has an ambivalent attitude toward poetry and that he is rent by a conflict between the poet and the moralist in him. The conflict is there, but it is only on the surface. At bottom it has been resolved by a belief in the inherent moral value of true poetry. Poetry and ethics, in their higher reaches, are for Iqbal both motivated by a quest for human perfection. In this quest these traditional opposites find their synthesis by a Hegelian dialectic, acquiring the name of great poetry, and the distinguishing mark of the great poet, the poet dedicated to this quest, is the aura of the perfect man which encircles him.

One last item that completes this description of the poetic origin and character of Iqbal's conception of poetry is the fact that he has for the most part used the medium of verse to expound it. His prose writings on the subject are few and far between, consisting of a handful of introductions to his own or other people's works and occasional articles. These contain some observations on the nature and function of poetry, too casual and too meager to constitute anything like a systematic treatment, not to speak of a theory. (That is why this writer has refrained from using the word "theory" in the title of this chapter and has confined himself to quotations from Iqbal's poetical works.)

In dealing with a poet like Iqbal who melted everything in the furnace of his poetic imagination before he put it into his verses, it is hardly worthwhile to try to trace the sources of his ideas in other people's writings. However, for the sake of assigning his conception of poetry its proper place in the vast literature that exists on the subject, an attempt is made here to discuss briefly the obvious affinities it seems to have with other well-known conceptions. These are the conceptions of Plato, the *Sturm und Drang* school of German literature, Nietzsche, Carlyle, and Shelley.

## CRITIQUE OF THE PLATONIC CONCEPTION OF POETRY

IQBAL's relationship with Plato is an interesting subject for study, a violent clash of philosophical theory along with a shared moral enthusiasm. Here is what Iqbal thinks of Plato and his philosophy:

> That hermit, Plato the philosopher,
> Was of the herd of goats of ancient times.
> His steed, lost in the dusk of intellect,
> Lagged in its race up the ascent of life.
> Charmed by the suprasensible, he lost
> Faith in his hands and feet, his eyes and ears.
> He taught that the essence of life is in death;
> The candle only shines to be put out.
> He holds sway over all our thought.
> What he serves us is a narcotic drug.
> He is a goat disguised in human clothes,
> And his writ runs over the mystic's soul.
> He let his intellect soar in the clouds
> And thought the world of sense to be a myth.
> His is to analyze the elements
> Of Life: to lop the branches of its tree.
> He presents loss to us as gain and says
> That what we think exists does not exist.
> His spirit went to sleep and dreamed a dream;
> His intellect created a mirage.

> Living in a phantasmagoric world,
> He had no gusto for activity,
> Denying this world of phenomena,
> He fabricated an ideal world—
> A world which cannot be perceived or known.
> This world of actualities, where things
> Occur, is good enough for living men;
> Let the dead have the whole ideal world.[14]

This is a poet's rejection of a life-denying philosophy. Alive as he is in every pore of his being to the beauty and wonder of the daylight world of reality, the world of living men and concrete objects, the poet cannot reconcile himself to a shadowy region of prenatal memory haunted by ghosts of "ideas." He has nothing to do with a metaphysical figment of this kind. His business, on the contrary, is to seize the world of concrete reality and beautify it.

> The poet's breast is beauty's fountain head,
> A Mount Sinai, a source of heavenly light.
> His eyes makes what is beautiful more so;
> His magic adds to Nature's native charm.
> The nightingale sings with his fiery breath;
> The color in the rose's cheek is lent
> By him. It is his flame that brightly burns
> In the moth's heart. Love's tales are colorful
> Because in telling them he makes them so.
> In his dust are contained all earth and sea;
> New worlds are in the making in his mind;
> His thought consorts with moon and stars.
> No ugliness exists for him, because
> No matter what he touches he adorns.
> His tears, which issue from a spring he has
> In the depths of his soul, like Khizar's spring
> Of immortality, revives the world.
> Eternally.[15]

But in rejecting Plato's world of ideal archetypes Iqbal is speaking not merely as a metaphysician but also as a moralist. A lost paradise of perfection which can never be regained and which cannot, in fact, even be known, can only breed spiritual nostalgia and moral passivity. Plato's philosophy led him to denounce poetry for its epistemological failure to mirror reality in terms of the utopia visualized by that philosophy and for its consequential moral failure to be truthful. By a strange piece of poetic justice, a philosophical poet two-and-a-half centuries later condemned that philosophy as being both epistemologically and morally worthless, and claimed for poetry a higher level of achievement in both these spheres than philosophy—whether Plato's or anybody else's—can dream of. If Plato criticized the creations of poetry as images of images, shadows of illusions, Iqbal calls into question the very reality which, according to Plato, poetry fails to represent.

Indeed, the representing of Plato's picture of reality—if it could be represented—would be for Iqbal in itself an immoral act; for it would amount to repeating lies and bodying forth illusions at the expense of the living truths of common human experience. The reality that Iqbal wants poetry to represent is not some perfect world irretrievably lost in the mists of man's ethereal past, but a world of the future. This world of the future is perfect in a different manner from Plato's world of ideas: it is a world which man's desires and aspirations are progressively shaping for him in his imagination and which is promised to him on this earth—and afterward in heaven too—as the reward of physical and spiritual endeavor.

Plato's poet, having an impossible moral task to perform, namely, to represent the unknowable, is condemned to failure from the very first. Plato does, it is true, concede the possibility of poetry being written which would approximate philosophy in stating universal truths and which would, therefore, be morally commendable; but he cites no instance of such poetry. In making this concession he probably had in mind his own philosophical works, which are written in poetic language without being in verse. So far, however, as poetry actually in existence at that time was concerned, he condemned it wholesale and recommended the expulsion of all poets, including even Homer and the great Greek tragedians and comedians, from his ideal republic as men whose works were likely to have a baneful influence on the upbringing of its citizens.

For this indiscriminate condemnation of poets—and unjust condemnation of the great ones—moral retribution has been visited upon Plato rather severely at Iqbal's hands. Iqbal has expelled him from the Valhalla of great philosophers and preceptors of civilization. Iqbal himself is more just in his moral judgment of poets. For one thing, his criterion is general enough to be applicable universally: a good poet, in the simplest terms, is one who helps the construction of a healthy and progressive society in the broad perspective of history. For another thing, his criterion is realistic and capable of being satisfied; it does not require the poet to do the impossible. There are many poets who have actually satisfied it, and Iqbal is generous in paying tribute to them.

Although Iqbal and Plato disagree about the moral criterion to be applied to poetry, they are at one in regarding the poet as a person with a special gift of nature, which they describe by similar names, such as divine frenzy, inspired mania, and suprarational intuition. There is, however, a subtle difference. According to Plato, the poet is not morally responsible for his utterances, since in the act of composition he is under the influence of unknown external powers; in fact, it is as a morally irresponsible person that he is disqualified for the citizenship of Plato's ideal republic. For Iqbal, on the other hand, the inspiration of the poet, the true poet that is, contains within it a deep-seated sense of moral responsibility: he is conscious that he owes a duty to God to use His Gift in the best interests of the world of men, which is God's main concern. It is this consciousness which saves him from the excesses to which the unbridled exercise of his power would render him liable.

Plato's poet is a moral failure because, in the first place, he cannot live up to Plato's philosophy, and, in the second place, he has no moral sense—he is altogether a pretty poor specimen of humanity. However, the philosophy that Iqbal's poet has to live up to in his creations is a natural product of the human mind, heart, and soul in their moments of exaltation. It is a philosophy of hope and aspiration, and the poet reflects it more or less spontaneously through a process of empathy because in the act of composition he is in a similar state of exaltation. Since the philosophy is inherently moral, the poet, in making his creations reflect it, is *ipso facto* acting as a moral being. All that is required of him is that he espouse it sincerely and reflect it faithfully. The more he does so the greater is his rank as a poet.

## HEDONISM OF THE *STURM UND DRANG* SCHOOL

The aesthetic theory of the *Sturm und Drang* school was a kind of transcendental hedonism. For members of this school, poetry along with the other fine arts was the generator of a feeling of intense pleasure, a tumultuous rapture, an access of obscure, ineffable impressions that flooded the soul. In this state, which was akin to mystical ecstasy, there occurred an inner expansion of the whole being so that, transcending all barriers of sense and intellect, it was immersed in the absolute. What the poet presented was not, therefore, an imitation or even an embellishment of nature or, in other words, a reproduction or refinement of sense impressions or primary feelings, but transcendental reality, the ideal hidden behind the veil of the actual, the infinite presented in finite form. Poetry was thus a manifestation of the divine principle of creative energy which pervades the universe and which keeps the human soul in a constant ferment of self-expression. It was a higher mode of revelation of reality than philosophy as well as a revelation of its conceptual elements, whereas philsophy only dealt with concepts shorn of all concreteness. By virtue of his enriching the world of existence the poet was God's deputy on earth, his colleague in creation, and as such a kind of demigod or superman.

Iqbal is at one with this school of thought except for its hedonistic aspect. Whereas the *Stürmer und Dränger*, getting bogged down in a kind of pseudomysticism, regarded the spiritual rapture produced by poetry as an experience desirable for its own sake, Iqbal requires it to transform itself into something of moral value in terms of action. In fact, the only kind of pleasure he accepts as a legitimate product of poetry is that which either accompanies the impulse to action or ensues the satisfaction of that impulse. Iqbal calls it by different names, all suggesting a dynamic content, such as ardor, fervor, enthusiasm, gusto for action, zest for life. There is no room in his philosophy of poetry for the static pleasure of pure contemplation, much less for the spurious pleasure of feeling like a demigod or superman without acting like one.

## THE FRENZY OF NIETZSCHE AND THE HERO OF CARLYLE

IQBAL's conception of poetry, like his philosophy, shares some important features with Nietzsche's, but in both cases there is a fundamental difference—the presence of Iqbal's work of a religious and moral content which was missing in Nietzsche's. For example, with Iqbal as with Nietzsche, the self is the motive and formative force behind life; but whereas Nietzsche's self operates in a moral vacuum where there are no other selves, not even God's, to be dealt with, Iqbal's self has other selves to contend against in evil and to co-operate with in good so that humanity as a whole may grow through moral endeavor in accordance with God's purposes.

Again, both Nietzsche and Iqbal dream of a man who has become perfect through overcoming human frailties; but whereas Nietzsche's superman is an amoral individual beyond good and evil enjoying complete mastery over everything and everybody else, Iqbal's perfect man is a representative member of a perfect society. As regards their concepts of art, including poetry, both Nietzsche and Iqbal believe in what they call emotion, passion, frenzy and by other names having similar connotations as the motive force behind artistic creation, in contradistinction to reason, intellect, logic, etc. They also share a vitalistic point of view. Thus, Iqbal's attack on Plato's idealism has in it echoes of Nietzsche's attack on the rationalism of Greek philosophy and on the Apollonianism of what he regarded as the decadent period of Greek art and poetry.

The resemblance ends here. With Nietzsche the creative passion behind art and poetry is a blind force—Dionysian power, symbol of the eternal will—destroying the Apollonian illusion of enlightenment, beauty, order, and reason simply for the sake of asserting the permanence of change and the supremacy of the irrational and immoral will to live. There is no purpose impelling it other than creation for creation's sake. With Iqbal, on the other hand, the will to live has a moral impulse behind it—an impulse divinely provided by the embodiment of the will to live in many individual selves. At its highest this moral impulse assumes the form of love, in which one self identifies itself with others and feels an urge to re-create them in accordance with some ideal of perfection conceived by it. Such, according to Iqbal, is poetic passion in its purest form.

Parallel to Nietzsche's two categories of art, the Apollonian and the Dionysian, Iqbal makes a distinction between two categories into which poetic creations can be divided. He calls these *jamāl* and *jalāl*, the nearest English equivalents of which are "beauty" and "sublimity," respectively. The chief components of beauty are charm, grace, elegance, proportion, tenderness, and other pleasing features; those of sublimity are power, grandeur, vastness, exaltedness, overwhelmingness, and other awe-inspiring characteristics. Beauty and sublimity are the two broad categories into which the Qur'ānic attributes of God, and derivatively the attributes of nature and man, are divided. Whereas Nietzsche is partial to Dionysus as against Apollo, Iqbal holds the scales even between beauty and sublimity, and commends a balanced combination of them in poetic creations as well as in human personality. Referring to their chief ingredients, charm and power, Iqbal says:

> Divorced from power, charm is sorcery;
> Combined with power, it is prophethood.[16]

His ideal poetry is not, therefore, mere sound and fury, nor is his ideal man, the perfect man, merely a personification of naked power. Nor, as a logical corollary, is his poet in the role of the perfect man a demoniac hero, but rather has the lineaments of Carlyle's hero as poet. Like Carlyle's poet-hero he is a *vates*, combining in himself the personalities of prophet and poet, who, to quote Carlyle, "have penetrated both of them into the sacred mystery of the universe, what Goethe calls 'the open secret.' . . . That divine mystery, which lies everywhere in all beings, 'the Divine Idea of the World, that which lies at the bottom of Appearance,' as Fichte styles it; of which all Appearance, from the starry sky to the grass of the field, but especially the Appearance of Man and his work, is but the *vesture*, the embodiment that renders it visible. . . . The *Vates*, whether Prophet or Poet, has penetrated into it; is a man sent hither to make it more impressively known to us." The resemblance does not end here. Iqbal's perfect man as poet, like Carlyle's poet-hero (*vates*-prophet and *vates*-poet combined) is both a revealer and creator of beauty and a builder of man's moral nature. "These two provinces," says Carlyle, "run into one another and cannot be disjoined."[17]

Iqbal's conception of poetry had so close an affinity with Shelley's that the following passages, quoted by way of illustration from Shelley's *A Defence of Poetry*, the most affirmative glorification of poetry and the poet in all Western literature, could very well have been written by Iqbal:

Poets, according to the circumstances of the age and nation in which they appeared, were called in the earlier epochs of the world, legislators, or prophets: a poet essentially comprises and unites both these characters.

For he not only beholds intensely the present as it is, and discovers those laws according to which present things ought to be ordered, but he beholds the future in the present, and his thoughts are the germs of the flower and the fruit of latest time.

A poet participates in the eternal, the infinite, and the one; as far as relates to his compositions, time and place and number are not.

Poetry is indeed something divine. It is at once the centre and circumference of knowledge. . . . It is at the same time the root and blossom of all other systems of thought.

A poet, as he is the author to others of the highest wisdom, pleasure, virtue and glory, so he ought personally to be the happiest, the best, the wisest, and the most illustrious of men.

The most unfailing herald, companion, and follower of the awakening of a great people to work a beneficial change in opinion or institution, is poetry. Poets are the hierophants of an unapprehended inspiration, the mirror of the gigantic shadows which futurity casts upon the present. . . . Poets are the unacknowledged legislators of the world.[18]

But, although these claims imply that poetry has a high moral value as one of the potent forces that shape human progress and civilization, Shelley denies that great poetry has a conscious moral aim. Poetry, according to him, is conducive to moral improvement only in the sense that it stimulates, broadens, and educates the imagination, which, he maintains, is the chief instrument of moral action. In fact, he dismisses poetry written with a conscious moral purpose as second-rate. Not so Iqbal. For him great poetry is consciously—and passionately—moral in that it proceeds from love, which is essentially an ameliorative emotion; it is a product of moral fervor.

Iqbal's advocacy of didactic poetry, poetry which addresses itself to the improvement of society, is saved from degenerating into a variant of the Marxist theory of art by his deep-seated belief in the freedom of the human ego, on the one hand, and by his emphasis upon spiritual as against moral values, on the other. Just as the mystique of dialectical materialism with its view of history as a class struggle for economic power was diametrically opposed to Iqbal's view of history as a continuous progress of the human soul toward perfection, similarly the Marxist subservience of art to party politics and to "socialist realism" ran counter to Iqbal's conception of poetry as a free expression of the human personality, as an outcome of the creative impulse.

In Urdu literature Iqbal found the ground prepared for his purposive view of poetry by Hali, author of a long poem (*Muṣṣadas*) bewailing the cultural, political, and economic decline of Indian Muslims and of a treatise on poetry (*Muqqadmā Shʻr wa Shāʻri*) criticizing the highly artificial traditions of Urdu poetry and its concentration upon undignified and immoral erotic themes. Iqbal carried the movement initiated by Hali out of the ivory tower of pure aestheticism in which Urdu poets had been living for generations, as if in a fool's paradise, while vast political and social changes had been taking place around them.

But the main source of Iqbal's inspiration, both in his poetry and in his conception of poetry, was the Persian mystical poet, Rumī, author of the great *Mathnawi*, which has been hailed as "a Qurʼān in Pahlawi." Rumi was Iqbal's ideal poet, his hero among poets, the embodiment of his idea of the perfect man as poet; and it is frequently by assuming Rumi's mantle that he derivatively invests himself with the attributes of the poet playing the role of the perfect man.

# 17

## Iqbal and Western Poets

### S. A. VAHID

IQBAL knew several languages and had read poetry of different countries in original or in translation. Early in his career he taught English poetry in a college in Lahore. It was inevitable that a poet of his broad and versatile sensibility should respond to these contacts with poets of other languages in an effective manner. Early in his career, he translated or adapted into Urdu some English poems, especially those of Cowper, Tennyson, and Emerson. When reading passages from English poets with his students he would sometimes remark that those lines were beautiful but he would have expressed his ideas in a slightly different form, and there and then he would compose some lines. Thus it will be interesting to trace the affinity that he displays with other Western poets, as it will also enable us to appreciate his versatile, poetic genius.

The main characteristic of Iqbal's art was a synthesis of romanticism and classicism. He started writing poetry in the classical style but was soon attracted by the romanticism of the English poets, especially Wordsworth. During his stay in Lahore (toward the end of the last century and in the beginning of the present one), romanticism appealed to him greatly. His admiration for the English romanticists, especially Wordsworth and Shelley, continued throughout his life. As his philosophical studies deepened, Iqbal was attracted by the problem of good and evil and the role of Satan in human evolution. This naturally drew him to Milton. He was also interested in Goethe. Writing about the great Urdu and Persian poet Ghālib (1796–1869) in 1903, he said:

> Ah! you are resting in the ruined Delhi
> Your fellow bard is sleeping in the garden of Weimar.
> (*Bāng-i-Dara*, p. 10)

After Iqbal's return from Europe, a theme which fascinated him considerably was the Ascension of the Prophet. He then wrote several short poems on the significance of this theme for mankind. He thought of writing a long poem on the subject, but meanwhile there appeared the work *Islam and the Divine Comedy*, which showed the indebtedness of Dante to the tradition of Mi'rāj (the Ascension of the Prophet) and to the Muslim writers for the design of his great poem. Probably this quickened Iqbal's interest in a subject which had always appealed to him, and he studied the works of various Muslim writers on apocalyptic subjects. This led Iqbal to write his *magnum opus*, *Javid-Namah* (The Book of Eternity), whose comparison with Dante's *Comedy* provides some interesting material for students of *Weltliteratur*.

## IQBAL AND WORDSWORTH

AMONG the English romantic poets the ideas of Wordsworth and Browning impressed Iqbal greatly. Very few languages of the world have produced poetry of nature to match that of the English language, and it is admitted that Wordsworth (1770–1850) is the greatest poet of nature in that language. The conception that nature is alive was present in other poets only as a germ, but it reached its full growth in Wordsworth's poetry. The outer universe lay open before the poet's eyes and ears, and he felt that it spoke through his senses to his soul.

According to Wordsworth, the universe is animated by soul, an active principle, and to this he gave a personality and called it nature. Each object acquired from nature not only its own distinct soul and character, but also its distinct work. For Wordsworth there was one personal spiritual life which had infinitely subdivided itself through all the forms of outer life, which could realize an undivided life at any moment, but which also lived a distinct life in every part. It became possible for the poet to communicate with any one manifestation of the life in a tree, or a flower, or a cloud, and also to communicate with the whole. When the poet communes with the living soul of nature, he is in contact not just with nature, the poetic creation of the imagination, but with the spirit of God, who abides as life in all.[1]

In the early stages of his career Iqbal agreed with Wordsworth completely, but later he developed his philosophy of ego, which held that throughout the universe there was a rising note of "egohood." Every object in the universe has an individuality which becomes personality in man. According to both Iqbal and Wordsworth, intercommunication between man and different objects in the universe is possible.

For Wordsworth there are some special characteristics of the life of nature. The first characteristic is that it is a life of enjoyment; the second characteristic is the spirit of quietude which pervades nature, and the third is the constant intercommunion between man and nature. Iqbal agreed with Wordsworth so far as these characteristics are concerned. He believed that the life of nature was the life of enjoyment and that, in spite of struggle, there was happiness in nature. Thus he wrote:

> Hail the Season! Hail the Spring!
> Stars of the Pleiades have issued from the meadows.
> How sweet the melody! How charming the sound!
> That emanates from the solitude of shrubbery!
> In the body life, in the life wish is generated
> By the melody of a starling and the song of a nightingale.
> One feels like saying that the Almighty
> Has put Paradise amongst the mountains.
> (*Payām-i Mashriq*, p. 133)

Every line of this poem reflects the happiness which the poet sees in nature. Iqbal associated everything in nature with quietude; one of the reasons why he loved to be with nature was because he longed for this quietude. In his poem *Ayk Arzū* (A Wish), he says:

> I run away from noise and my heart longs for
> Quiet which even speech will envy.
> I long for quietude and I have but one wish
> To own a hut amongst the hills.
> (*Bāng-i-Dara*, p. 35)

The following lines of Wordsworth's *The Prelude* depict the intercommunication between man and nature:

> Wisdom and Spirit of the universe!
> Thou Soul that art the eternity of thought
> That givest to forms and images a breath
> And everlasting motion, not in vain

> By day or starlight thus from my first dawn
> Of childhood didst thou intertwine for me
> The passions that build up our human soul.
> Not with the mean and vulgar works of man,
> But with high objects, with enduring things
> With life and nature, purifying thus
> The elements of feeling and of thought,
> And sanctifying by such discipline
> Both pain and fear, until we recognize
> A grandeur in the beatings of the heart.
>
> (Book I, 401–414)

Iqbal says:

> The self-sown tulip's temper I know well,
> Within the stem the rose's scent I smell,
> The meadow songster loves me as a friend,
> The tone wherein he carols I can tell.
>
> (*Payām-i Mashriq*, p. 68)

Wordsworth's conception of nature, in the last stage of his development, corresponds to a remarkable degree with Iqbal's conception in his first stage of development. The difference in the two poets' conception was that while Wordsworth was only a partial pantheist and regarded God as immanent in nature but transcendent for man, for Iqbal God was immanent in nature and man. In his boyhood, nature was Wordsworth's playground, in his adolescence the poet came to love nature for her own sake, and later in his life he discovered in nature the divine. Curiously enough, the process was reversed in Iqbal. Early in his poetic career, Iqbal saw the divine in Nature; later on he came to love nature for her own sake and regarded her as having an ego.

There is a striking resemblance in the ideas of Wordsworth and Iqbal in other minor matters also. During communion with nature Wordsworth used to go into ecstasy. Iqbal, too, used to go into a trance:

> The mountains, the sea, and the setting of the sun,
> There I saw God without any veils!
>
> (*Javid-Namah*, p. 188)

A partial resemblance in their sense endowment lay in the fact that Wordsworth excelled in two senses—seeing and hearing; other senses meant nothing to him. Iqbal excelled in seeing and hearing, but also had a fine sense of smell. Thus, whereas Iqbal speaks about the fragrance of flowers, for Wordsworth fragrance meant nothing.

Singing of the beauties of nature, both Wordsworth and Iqbal impress upon man the significance of his mission and the supreme importance of his work. Their poetry takes man to heights of spiritual and moral elevation, touched even in the greatest poets only in the moments of their highest exultation. Above all, they both proclaimed the true function of the poet in society and exalted the poet's office.

Although both Wordsworth and Iqbal have left great poetry of nature, there is a significant difference between them. Wordsworth is a poet of nature, and as Walter Raleigh has said: "Nature, as he tells in the *Prelude*, held for long an exclusive place in his affections. When the feeling for humanity was aroused in him by suffering, Man was still subordinate to Nature in this sense that he was always conceived in a larger setting, exhibited in close relations with a greater whole, and played around by the emotions that it begets."[2] On the other hand, Iqbal, in spite of his superb poetry of nature, is a poet of man. Even when painting beautiful scenes of nature in vivid detail, he never forgets for a moment the position of man in the universe or his mission. He even goes so far as to maintain that in spite of all the charm and beauty of nature, man's works of art are more exquisite than all that nature has to offer. He seems to agree with Sir Thomas Browne when the latter says: "Art is the perfection of Nature."[3]

Summing up, it can be said that Wordsworth and Iqbal are not merely poets of nature, they are prophets of nature. Although they are masters at depicting natural scenes, they are not content merely with depicting scenes; through Nature they both want to illuminate problems facing man, each according to his own light. They both found in nature a solution to the riddle of human life and to the conflict of good and evil, but the intuition of this solution came to them through different channels. Intuition came to Wordsworth through nature and to Iqbal through religion. Whereas "Wordsworth makes Nature the author and finisher of his faith,"[4] Iqbal does not. For Iqbal, the author of his faith is man and his "self." And yet, both Wordsworth and Iqbal were inspired by a burning zeal to come to man's succor in his struggle against the forces of materialism and all that is ugly in human life. No wonder Iqbal wrote about Wordsworth that he "saved me from atheism in my student days."[5]

## IQBAL AND MILTON

WHILE his love of nature and romanticism were attracting Iqbal toward Wordsworth, his interest in the problem of good and evil in human life drew him to another great English poet, John Milton (1608–1674). Milton's choice diction, the stateliness of his rhyme, and the sublimity of themes touched in his poems impressed Iqbal greatly, so much so that very early in his career he wrote to a friend that he wanted to write a poem on the model of Milton's *Paradise Lost*. At another time he told a friend that he wanted to write, on the model of *Paradise Regained*, a poem dealing with the tragedy of Kerbala, in which the Prophet's grandson and his companions were massacred mercilessly. Admiration for the genius of Milton could not have been expressed in a more fitting way. A critical study of the life, art, and thought of Milton and Iqbal reveals a remarkable parallelism between these two great poets. Almost from boyhood both Milton and Iqbal took poetry seriously and labored by study and self-discipline "to write something that the world would not willingly let die,"[6] and at thirty Milton was "perhaps the most accomplished young man in England."[7] The same can be said about Iqbal; after his return from England in 1908, he was one of the most accomplished young men on the Indian subcontinent. Not only was he regarded as a leading poet of the subcontinent, but his books and his lectures in Lahore and Aligarh had marked him out as the leading intellectual of Muslim India.

In their subsequent careers, there was a remarkable resemblance in many respects. They both took an active part in politics. In connection with his political activities, Milton issued pamphlets; Iqbal issued press statements and delivered political speeches. In poetry, both Iqbal and Milton wrote in two languages: Milton, in Latin and English, Iqbal, in Persian and Urdu. Although, according to the accepted opinion, Milton's best poetry is written in his mother tongue, it is a moot point whether Iqbal has left greater poetry in Urdu or Persian. Both were erudite scholars. Whereas Milton's language shows Latin solidity, Iqbal's language always shows an exuberance of Arabic words and phrases. A charge frequently leveled against Milton is that he corrupted the English language; similar charges were leveled against Iqbal. Both poets adopted a musical and resounding style, which displays extraordinary beauty, variety, and rhythm.

Adam is the central figure of Milton's epic poem, and in the literary sense is his hero, and it can be said that Iqbal is a poet of man. He says:

> For many my eyes shed tears
> Till I succeeded in unveiling the secrets of life.

Early in his life Milton's dominating idea was to write a great poem —great in theme, in style, and in attainment. It was the same with Iqbal.

Although the versatile genius of both Milton and Iqbal is admitted by everyone, the importance of Milton as a thinker was not fully realized until recently.[8] One cannot notice any close affinity between the ideas of Milton and Iqbal, but certain resemblances are striking. Both Milton and Iqbal attach the highest importance to liberty in the development of human personality. Milton's opinion of the importance of liberty is beautifully expressed in *Paradise Lost*:

> But man over man
> He made not Lord; such title to himself
> Reserving, human left from human free.

Iqbal says:

> Under subjugation the heart dies in the body
> Under subjugation the soul is a burden to the body.
> Under subjugation the infirmity of old age comes in youth
> Under subjugation the lion of the forest becomes imbecile.
> (*Zabūr-i 'Ajam*, p. 248)

But it is in dealing with the problem of evil in the life of man that the greatest similarity between these two great poets has been seen. How can evil find a place in a world under divine ordering? Milton undertakes to expound upon this in his great epic, and his answer to the question is the traditional Christian reply, that Satan or the Devil is responsible for all the evil in the world. Iqbal is faced with the same question. "How is it, then, possible to reconcile the goodness and omnipotence of God with the immense volume of evil in His creation?"[9] In tackling the problem of evil in this world, Iqbal also refers to Satan. (A study of the character of Satan as depicted by Milton and Iqbal is of absorbing interest.)

Whereas Milton believes in the story of the Fall of Man as given in the Book of Genesis, Iqbal relies on the story as related in the Qur'ān. According to Milton, Satan is an archangel, if not the first archangel, and he is inclined to give Satan pre-eminence over all angelic beings. There is a rebellion in heaven, and the immediate cause is the proclamation that all should worship the Messiah as their head. Satan resents the command and in his defiance draws away a third of the angels from their allegiance to God. Milton in his *Paradise Lost* represents the archangel more as the foe of God than of Christ.

These narrations differ in important details. Iqbal points out the salient features of the story as related in the Qur'ān:

Thus we see that the Qur'ānic legend of the Fall has nothing to do with the first appearance of man on this planet. Its purpose is rather to indicate man's rise from a primitive state of instinctive appetite to the conscious possession of a free self, capable of doubt and disobedience. The Fall does not mean any moral depravity; it is man's transition from simple consciousness to the first flash of self-consciousness, a kind of waking from the dream of nature with a throb of personal casuality in one's own being. Nor does Qur'ān regard the earth as a torture-hall, where an elementary wicked humanity is imprisoned for an original act of sin. Man's first act of disobedience was also his first act of free choice; and that is why, according to the Qur'ānic narration, Adam's first transgression was forgiven.[10]

While the legends on which Milton's and Iqbal's poems are based vary in details, the conflict between God and Satan, between good and evil, retains its enthralling interest in both. Against God who stands for harmony, order, and love Milton and Iqbal set Satan who stands for disorder in the hope of inflicting pain upon God; Iqbal's Satan wants to create disharmony to prove that God's trust in man was misplaced. In Milton, Satan, when incensed with envy and injured vanity at the elevation of Christ to share the glory of the Deity, decides to revolt. In Iqbal's version, Satan in his pride refuses to render obeisance to man and prefers to create disorder to demonstrate that he was right in his refusal.

But there is a difference between Milton and Iqbal when they are depicting Satan's character. Although Milton ascribes to Satan great grandeur and splendor, he also attributes to him a gradual, but definite, fall in character after the Fall. Once Satan believes that no conciliation with God is possible, he becomes desperate and decides to destroy everything. There is no such decay in the character of Iqbal's Satan. In Iqbal, as in Milton, Satan displays a very complex character, but the absence of gradual decay in Iqbal's work makes the portrayal of his character less difficult from the artistic point of view.

Although Satan's character in Milton's and Iqbal's works shows many points of resemblance, it must be pointed out that from the artistic point of view Iqbal shows a more rationalistic realization of the part evil plays in human life. According to Iqbal, Satan is neither a rebel against God nor an enemy of man. He is fulfilling his allotted role in the scheme of things, and that role is not only important but essential if the moral and spiritual evolution of man is to be maintained.

Milton has described Satan and the problem of evil mainly in his masterpiece *Paradise Lost*. Iqbal has dealt with the subject in several poems; other more pressing works did not allow him to deal with this subject in one long poem. The important poems in which Iqbal deals with the subject are *Taskhīr-i Fitrat* in *Payām-i Mashriq* (Message of the East), *Iblīs awr Gabriel* in *Darb-i Kalīm* (The Rod of Moses), *Iblīs Ki Majlis* in *Armaghān-i Hijaz*, and some others.

At times the two poets painted the same scenes, and it is interesting to note the similarity of language and ideas employed by them on such occasions; for example, when the angel Michael bids good-by to Adam and Eve, Milton describes the scene in the following lines:

> To whom thus also th' Angel last repli'd;
> This having learnt, thou hast attained the sum
> Of wisdom; hope no higher, though all the Stars
> Thou knew'st by name, and all th' ethereal Powers,
> All secrets of the deep, all Nature's works
> Or works of God in Heaven, Air, Earth or Sea,
> And all the riches of the World enjoy'dst,
> And all the rule, one Empire; only add
> Deeds to thy knowledge answerable, add Faith,
> Add Virtue, Patience, Temperance, add Love,
> By name to come call'd Charity, the soul
> Of all the rest; then wilt thou not be loath
> To leave this Paradise, but shalt possess
> A paradise within thee, happier far.
> . . .
> That ye may live, which will be many days,
> Both in one Faith unanimous though sad,

> With cause for evils past, yet much more cheered
> With meditation on the happy end.
> (*Paradise Lost*, XII, 574–587; 602–605)

In Iqbal's poem angels bid farewell to Adam:

> Thou hast been given the restlessness of Day and Night,
> We know not whether thou art made of clay or mercury,
> We hear thou art created from clay,
> But in thy nature is the glitter of Stars and Moon.
> Thy melody unravels the secret of life
> For it is Nature that has attuned thy organ.
> (*Bāl-i Jibrīl*, p. 177)

Iqbal deals with this subject again in another poem in which the spirit of earth greets Adam:

> Open thine eyes; behold the earth, the stars, the atmosphere!
> Behold awhile the sun rising from the east,
> Behold this unveil'd vision hid in the veils of light!
> Behold the anguish and torment of the days of separation!
> But be not overwrought, behold the contest of Hope and Fear.
> These clouds and thunders are for thee to control,
> The high vault of the Heavens and the silence of space,
> These mountains, these deserts, these oceans and the winds.
> Till yesterday the angel's charm fascinated thee,
> Today in Time's mirror behold thy own charm.
> (*Bāl-i Jibrīl*, p. 178)

In Milton, Adam admits that even his Fall is to be valued as the occasion for the eventual triumph of goodness:

> O goodness infinite, goodness immense!
> That all this good of evil shall produce,
> And evil turn to good.
> (*Paradise Lost*, XII, 469–71)

In Iqbal, when man appears before God on the Day of Judgment, he expresses similar sentiments:

> O Thou whose sun gives light to the star of life,
> With my heart thou hast lighted the candle in this world.
> I went under the earth, I went over the sky,
> Under my domain are the atom as well the glittering Sun.

Although his guile has led me astray from the path of rectitude,
Forgive my wrongs and accept my excuse for the sin.
Intelligence ensnares the one endowed with cunning and guile;
Satan, born of fire, performs obeisance to man of clay!
*(Payām-i Mashriq*, p. 100)

Thus it will be seen that Milton and Iqbal, in spite of religious and cultural differences, display some affinity in their thought and a remarkable kinship of poetic genius. Those resemblances only serve to emphasize the universality of their art. They both infuse courage and faith in man by pointing out that partial evil in life only contributes to universal good. According to both, man can triumph over evil by doing his duty in the face of all obstacles. Thus both bring to man, when he is overwhelmed by frustration and disappointment, a message of cheer and hope.

## IQBAL AND GOETHE

As remarked above, Iqbal was very widely read and was equally at home in Eastern and Western cultures, but it can be safely said that apart from his Islamic background he was largely a product of German culture. The study of German thought and German literature had greatly influenced his views on life. He had studied deeply all the important German thinkers; we have only to mention Kant, Hegel, Fichte, and Nietzsche. In literature he had studied the works of Goethe, Schiller, Heine, and other poets. Even when he was a student in Europe his admiration for Goethe's *Faust* was unbounded. Later in his career he showed his admiration for Goethe's transcendent genius in different ways. Hence it will be interesting to trace the points of similarity in the works of these two literary giants. Goethe was born on August 28, 1749 and died on March 22, 1832. Iqbal was born on November 9, 1877 and died on April 21, 1938. Thus the ages of these two geniuses are separated by a gulf of nearly a century. In spite of this wide gulf and cultural differences, very rarely in the literary history of the world have two great poets displayed such affinity in their poetic sensibility.

Iqbal freely expresses his admiration for the supreme literary genius of Goethe in his poems. In the introduction to his *Payām-i Mashriq* he wrote:

> The Western sage, the German poet
> A votary of Persian manners,
> He was born and nurtured in a garden
> I spring but from arid soil.
> (*Payām-i Mashriq*, p. 2)

But perhaps the greatest tribute Iqbal paid to Goethe is contained in the poem *Jelāl wa Goethe*:

> The sage from Germany in Paradise
> Chanced to meet the sage from 'Ajam,
> Rumi said: 'O poet of transcendent genius
> You chase angels and capture the Almighty.
> (*Payām-i Mashriq*, p. 246)

In the footnote to the above poem Iqbal says about Goethe's masterpiece, *Faust*: "In this drama the poet has, while dealing with the legend of the pact between Dr. Faust and Mephistopheles, described the various stages in the development of man with such beauty and charm that it is impossible to think of greater artistic perfection."[11]

Another link between Goethe and Iqbal is the fact that Iqbal translated some of Goethe's poems. It is not very often that one master translates the poetical compositions of another. Although there are translations of several great poets in prose as well as verse, the supreme art of the original is not always reflected in the translation. Iqbal added the following note to his translation of Goethe's *Mahomets Gesang*: "This is a free translation of Goethe's poem known as *Mahomets Gesang*. In the poem, which was written by Goethe long before the *Divan*, the poet has beautifully described the Islamic ideal of life. Actually this poem was supposed to be a fragment from an Islamic drama which the poet could not finish. The present translation is intended to illustrate Goethe's point of view."[12]

The original poem as well as the translation is superb, as the following extract will show:

> See the rock-born stream!
> Like the gleam
> Of a star so bright!
> Kindly spirits,
> High above the clouds,
> Nourished him while youthful.

In the copse between the cliffs.
Young and fresh,
From the clouds he danceth
Down upon the marble rocks;
Then tow'rd heaven
Leaps exulting.[13]
     (*Mahomets Gesang*)

Look how beautifully the stream runs,
Like gleaming stars in meadowland,
She was sleeping in the cradle of clouds,
Suddenly opened the yearning eye in the lap of crags,
Her gliding among pebbles produces music,
Her face is without blemish like a mirror.
Towards the ocean how lustily she goes,
Unique in herself, stranger to others she rolls.
     (*Payām-i Mashriq*, p. 15)

Iqbal wrote poems on subjects on which Goethe had also written. Out of these, *The Houri and the Poet* is the most remarkable. A poet in his wandering finds his way into heaven. He is so absorbed in his own thoughts that the charms of that place fail to attract him. In despair a houri addresses him thus: "You are a strange fellow. You do not seem to have any craving for the refreshing drinks available here—nor any use of my looks. All that you seem to be interested in is the creation of an imaginary world of your own." The poet replies indifferently: "I do not find any fascination in this place; its tranquility is boring. And I can never rest, my restless nature is always yearning for the more beautiful."

Both Goethe and Iqbal have in their poems displayed artistic presentation, grace of style, and the power of originality. The two poets, owing to close affinity in their sensibility, express their sentiments in language which bears marks of close resemblance. For instance, in Goethe's *Faust* (p, 19), his main character says:

> Here stand I, ach, Philosophy
> Behind me and Law and Medicine too
> And, to my cost, Theology—
> All these I have sweated through and through
> And now you see me a poor fool
> As wise as when I entered school!

Iqbal expresses the same sentiments in the following lines:

> Friends are happy that a wanderer has reached the destination,
> And I am still confused, after having acquired all knowledge and learning.
> (*Zabūr-i 'Ajam*, p. 69)

Welcoming man, the spirit of earth says in Iqbal:

> Image of Clay! Behold the reward of ceaseless toil.
> (*Bāl-i Jibrīl*, p. 179)

Goethe voices a similar exhortation to man in the following words:

> Should a man strive with all his heart
> Heaven can foil the devil.
> (*Faust*, p. 298)

In Goethe the spirit tells Faust:

> At the whirring loom of Time I weave
> The living clothes of the Deity.
> (*Faust*, p. 23)

In Iqbal time says:

> I provide robes for Man and living clothes for Deity.
> (*Payām-i Mashriq*, p. 103)

In order to elucidate the affinity of sensibility between Goethe and Iqbal, reference must be made to a great phenomenon in the literary history of the world, Goethe's *West-Östlicher Divan*. In Germany a literary movement known as *Weltliteratur* tried to produce translations not only from European languages but also from Eastern languages. This interest in Eastern culture was further stimulated by the translation of Hāfiz by the Viennese Orientalist Hammer-Purgstall. After reading this translation in the summer of 1814, Goethe discovered in the poetry of Hāfiz something which not only attracted him but also had great affinity with trends in his own creative genius. The result was that Hāfiz provided a great stimulus to an immense creative effort which resulted in Goethe's *Divan*.

In his opinion about the *Divan*, Heine says: "The charm of the book is inexplicable; it is a native nosegay sent from the West to the East, composed of the most precious and curious plants: red roses, hortensias, like the heart of a spotless maiden, purple digitales, like the long finger of a man, fantastically formed rancuculi, and in the midst of all sittest and tastefully concealed, a tuft of German violets. This nosegay signifies that the West is tired of their icy cold spirituality, and seeks warmth in the strong and healthy bosom of the East."[14]

The *Divan* is divided into several books. In *Hāfiz Namah* and *Suleika Namah*, the names under which Goethe immortalized his love for Marianne von Willemer, are books of personal confessions in which lyric fervor is dominant. *Schekensbuch* is a glorification of the power of Dionysus in which the intoxication produced by wine is compared to divine ecstasy. The remaining books are didactic; critics and students alike contend that they contain some of the ripest fruits of Goethe's philosophy of life.

A work of such sublime beauty by a great master challenged Iqbal and evoked a response in him which gave the world a masterpiece in the Persian language. It was apparent from the *Divan* that according to the German sage the West was seeking spiritual sustenance from the East, and Iqbal, most generously, offered it. In *Payām-i Mashriq* his creative genius offered spiritual warmth as well as strength.

On the cover of the *Payām* are written the words: "In response to the *Divan* of the German Poet." This is the highest compliment that one great poet could pay to another. In the *Divan* Goethe wrote:

> God is of the East possessed
> God is ruler of the West
> North and South alike, each land
> Rests within the gentle hand.[15]

And on the cover of the *Payām* Iqbal, most appropriately, quoted the following verses of the Qur'ān:

> To God belong East and West.

As regards the book itself, Iqbal said: "I need hardly say anything about the *Payām-i Mashriq*, which has been written a hundred years after the *Western Divan*. The reader will himself see that its main object is to bring out those social, moral and religious truths which have a bearing on the spiritual development of individuals and communities."[16] By reason of its breadth of emotional and intellectual appeal, its great wealth of art and variety of poetic form, *Payām-i Mashriq* deserves to be ranked among the classics of the world and is without question a masterpiece of Persian language. There is no doubt that the appeal of *Payām-i Mashriq* is wider than that of the *Divan*.

But, in addition to the tributes Iqbal paid to Goethe and his poetic genius in various forms, the remarkable kinship of creative power that these two masters display goes much deeper. The most significant affinity between the two great poets is apparent in the synthesis of romanticism and classicism they attained in their art. Although they worked at different times and had fundamental differences in their cultural backgrounds, this synthesis was achieved by each.

Romanticism has assumed two different manifestations; first, there is the romantic attitude of mind, a feature of thinking which can be found in all ages, in most thinkers and in literary men, but which is naturally more preponderant in some than in others. Second, there is the European Romantic movement, primarily a literary movement, which originated in a revolt against the formalities and conventions of classicism. It was characterized in the nineteenth century by concentration on the subjective aspects of life and nature and by free use of imagination. The movement swept across the whole of Europe toward the close of the eighteenth and the beginning of the nineteenth centuries, but it had distinctive features in each country.

As is well known, eighteenth-century Europe was characterized by rationalism in philosophy as a reaction to religious bigotry. As a result, religious dogmas were questioned, and reason became the sole standard of judgment. However, philosophers like Kant and Rousseau brought down the whole edifice of rationalism. Rousseau pleaded strongly that emotions, passions, instincts, and intuitions be given a place along with reason in man's life. In Germany Herder led this revolt against rationalism and reason. Herder, like his master Rousseau, stressed the claims of feeling as against intellect, of the individual against the society. He thought that the essence of poetry lay in "energy," that energy was the gift of nature, the mother tongue of human race. During his stay in Strassburg (1770–1771) Goethe came in contact with Herder and was greatly influenced by him. In fact, he became the leader of the movement and gave it its fullest expression in his early writings. It was under these circumstances that German Romanticism was born. Originally the movement aimed at liberating human personality from the fetters of social convention and social morality, but it was soon realized that this enthusiasm for liberation had to be kept within limits.

The leaders of the Romantic movement in Germany, Goethe and Schiller, although at first extremely individualistic, eventually toned down with a new classical objectivity. Therefore, Goethe "was at once the embodiment of classicism and the fountainhead of the Romantic School, and symbolized the reconciliation of both in the marriage of Helen and Faust."[17]

Like Goethe, Iqbal achieved a fusion of romanticism and classicism gradually. Classicism in Iqbal was adherence to the traditions of the old Urdu and Persian poets. When Iqbal started writing poetry in Sialkot he followed the classical Urdu masters in diction, imagery, and form. He continued to do this in Lahore. His early poems bear the full impress of classicism in this sense. He gave a good deal of time and labor to the mastery of classical traditions and his attachment to Dāgh (1831–1905), a classical Urdu poet of great repute, completed his apprenticeship in the old traditions. But during his stay in Lahore, Iqbal came in contact with the Urdu poets of the romantic school. His studies of English poetry, especially Wordsworth, also attracted him to romanticism. Thus Iqbal also attained the fusion of classicism and romanticism which characterized his poetry for the rest of his life. With him the period of pure classicism did not last long.

Although Iqbal and Goethe display great similarity in their art, their classicism connotes adherence to different traditions. After the attainment of the synthesis of romanticism and classicism, however, literary art achieves transcendental heights in the hands of both. It was this synthesis which enabled them to keep control over their imaginations and to produce poetry of great perfection; moreover, it gave their art a universal humanism. But the different ways in which the two masters attained it left a mark on their works. In Goethe, the synthesis resulted in many paradoxes. A comparison of his early works with his later ones reveals marked contrasts in theme and style: *Wilhelm Meister* seems the direct opposite of *Werther*, and *Iphigenie* the opposite of *Prometheus*. Against this, Iqbal attained a synthesis very early in his career and retained it throughout. There is no doubt that Iqbal's ideas underwent important changes at different periods of his life, but it can be safely said that the synthesis of romanticism and classicism continued to characterize his art. The result is that the balance of thought and emotion, the mellowed maturity that are found only in the later works of Goethe, distinguished all the works of Iqbal.

Apart from the basic similarity of their poetic art (as exhibited in the synthesis of classicism and romanticism), there is also general agreement in the thought of Goethe and Iqbal on most of the fundamental problems with which man is faced. Through the ages thinkers have given a good deal of thought to the problem of evil in the world, and yet the problem whether a benevolent and beneficent God ever created evil remains unsolved. As Iqbal says: "How is it possible to reconcile the goodness and omnipotence of God with the immense volume of evil in His creation? The painful problem is really the crux of theism."[18]

According to Goethe, evil is the obverse of good, and both together form a higher unity. The fact that in *Faust* Mephistopheles is among the Lord's retinue implies that evil is part of God's system. Although Goethe realizes that error, imperfection, and conflict are bound to occur in human life and effort, he still believes that human life is innately good. Goethe's view of evil was Pelagian: "What we call evil is only the reverse of good which belongs as necessarily to its existence and to the whole as the torrid zone must burn Lapland freeze in order that there may be a temperate region." In Goethe's view, there are two forces in life—good and evil—which work in opposite directions but ultimately cooperate in carrying out the divine purpose. Goethe does not believe in the dualism of Mani or early Christian thinkers, yet he does not shut his eyes to the evil in the world. It is the action and reaction of good and evil that brings out the best in man.

> In the floods of life, in the storm of work,
> In ebb and flow,
> In warp and weft,
> Cradle and grave,
> An eternal sea,
> A changing patchwork,
> A glowing life,
> At the whirring loom of Time I weave
> The living clothes of the Deity.[19]
>
> (*Faust*)

Iqbal agrees with Goethe in this view of evil; according to him, "Good and evil, therefore, though opposites, must fall within the same whole. There is no such thing as an isolated fact; for facts are systematic wholes the elements of which must be understood by mutual reference.

Logical judgment separates the elements of a fact only to reveal their interdependence."[20] Iqbal has expressed the same view again and again in his poems; for instance, in *Payām-i Mashriq* he says:

> How should I describe good and evil,
> The problem is complex and the tongue falters to speak!
> Outside the bough you see flower and thorn
> Inside it there is neither flower nor thorn.
> (*Payām-i Mashriq*, p. 54)

While the existence of evil is explained by both Goethe and Iqbal, the nature of evil can best be illustrated only by reference to the Devil. Goethe and Iqbal did this by making the Devil the chief agent of evil: Mephistopheles in Goethe, Iblīs in Iqbal.

In the history of human thought there are two contradictory views about the Devil: according to one view, adopted in most of the Scriptures, he is represented as the hideous creature who was punished for disobedience and who is now always trying to tempt man away from the path of rectitude, his aim being to show to the Almighty that His trust in man was misplaced. But slowly this view underwent a change. Satan, or Iblīs as Iqbal calls him, is no longer regarded as evil incarnate. He no doubt represents an egotist who believes in a philosophy of negation, but at the same time he possesses many admirable qualities. His self-confidence, determination, and dynamic energy are remarkable. The role of Iblīs is to excite and create. He can make nothing but is effective in other ways. Goethe describes Mephistopheles in the following words:

> A part of that Power
> Which always wills evil, always procures good.
> (*Faust*, p. 47)

In Iqbal, Iblīs advises Gabriel to question the Almighty:

> Whose blood has imparted color to man's story?
> (*Bāl-i Jibrīl*, p. 194)

Thus, the role of Satan in the life of man is the same according to Iqbal and Goethe. In this apparent evil lies the secret of all good. No life is worth living where there is no evil and no struggle against it. In the

*Prologue*, it is made clear that the universe is a constantly growing, living process through struggle. Raphael declares:

> The chanting sun, as ever, rivals
> The chanting of his brother spheres
> And marches round his destined circuit—
> A march that thunders in our ears.
> His aspect cheers the Hosts of Heaven
> Though what his essence none can say,
> These inconceivable creations
> Keep the high state of their first day.

To this Gabriel answers:

> And swift, with inconceivable swiftness
> The earth's full splendour rolls around,
> Celestial radiance alternating
> With a dread night too deep to sound.

And Michael responds:

> And storms in rivalry are raging
> From sea to land, from land to sea,
> In frenzy forge the world a girdle
> From which no inmost part is free.
> (*Faust*, p. 13)

In contrast to the harmony of the universe, the earth, with its inconceivable speed, typifies imperfection, disharmony, and strife. Change, incompleteness, light and darkness, and violence and strife are characteristics of life on earth. But it is this very disharmony and strife which makes moral activity possible. Unlike those writers who have depicted Satan as inhabiting hell and planning his nefarious activities from there, Goethe describes Mephistopheles in the *Prologue* as one of the elite of God in heaven. Iqbal places him in the planet of Jupiter—in company with the great Muslim mystic Mansūr al-Hallaj (859–922) and the renowned poet Ghālib (1796–1869), who refused to accept residence in paradise and preferred to be constantly traveling about the universe.

It is the ideal of ceaseless activity and dynamic life that Goethe's Mephistopheles and Iqbal's Iblīs place before man. Pointing to this role of Satan, the Lord says in *Faust* (p. 16):

> Man finds relaxation too attractive—
> Too fond too soon of unconditional rest;
> Which is why I am pleased to give him a companion
> Who lures and thrusts and must, as devil, be active.

In *Bāl-i Jibrīl* (Gabriel's Wing), Iblīs himself says:

> My boldness has imparted the handful of clay
>     yearning for growth,
> My temptations form the warp and woof of
>     reason and intellect.
> You see the strife of good and evil from the shore.
> Who is facing the storm? You or I?
>             (*Bāl-i Jibrīl*, p. 193)

Satan is not only a devil but is also a servant of God. While working evil on men he is full of contempt for them in view of the ease with which he can beguile them.

> Your suns and worlds mean nothing much to me;
> How men torment themselves, that's all I see.
> The little god of the world, one can't reshape, reshade him,
> He is as strange today as that first day you made him.
>             (*Faust*, p. 14)

Speaking in a similar strain, Iblīs, in Iqbal, complains to the Almighty about the ease with which he can overcome man:

> O Lord of good and evil!
> Man's company has debased me.
> What is this man? A handful of straw!
> For straw a spark from my fire is sufficient.
>             (*Javid-Namah*, p. 160)

When striving, man no doubt commits mistakes, but these occasional lapses do not condemn him to eternal punishment. So long as man persists in his creative activity, the Lord is there to help him. Mephistopheles uses all his devices and even employs the spirit of earth to tempt Faust into accepting conditions not conducive to the fulfillment of the divine plan, but in the end Faust is delivered and God's confidence in Faust is justified, and Mephistopheles fails to win the bet he offered in heaven. The Lord accordingly intervenes; Mephistopheles' influence ceasing, as he had been told, at Faust's death. Iqbal says: "Freedom is thus a condition of goodness. But to permit the emergence of a finite ego who has the power to choose, after considering the relative values of several courses of action open to him, is really to take a great risk, for the freedom to choose good involves the freedom to choose what is the opposite of good. That God has taken this risk shows His immense faith in man; it is for man now to justify this faith. Perhaps such a risk alone makes it possible to test and develop the potentialities of a being who was created of the goodliest fabric and then brought down to the lowest of the low."[21] Faust has justified this faith placed by the Lord in him. According to Iqbal, "This is the point where faith in the eventual triumph of goodness emerges as a religious doctrine."[22] Thus it will be seen that Goethe and Iqbal explain beautifully the existence of evil in the world, and they both elucidate the role which the Devil plays in the moral and spiritual evolution of man.

Another point of resemblance between Goethe and Iqbal is the important role they assign to love in the life of man. Goethe emphasizes the importance of love in the following lines:

> The changing Essence which ever works and lives
> Wall you around with love, serene, secure.
> *(Faust, p. 201)*

Iqbal says:

> 'Tis Love that paints the tulip petal's hue
> 'Tis Love that stirs the spirit's bitter rue
> If thou couldst cleave this carrion of clay,
> Thou shalt behold within, Love's bloodshed too.
> *(Payām-i Mashriq, p. 13)*

In spite of all the importance that Goethe attaches to love, he uses the term in a very restricted sense. Although he recognizes the redeeming and purifying influence of love, he does not recognize the omnipotent and invigorating effect of love on man as Iqbal does. For Iqbal love is a cosmic force which controls the whole universe and a factor which controls the human destiny. It is through love that man can conquer time and space and can acquire mastery over the forces of nature. The conception of love in the wide sense in which Iqbal uses it is not found in Goethe.

Neither Goethe nor Iqbal believe in the doctrine of original sin; and both reject the doctrine of vicarious atonement. Both believe that all that man wants to attain he must attain by his own efforts. Faust acknowledges, at the close of his career, that the individual life has no real meaning except as an integral part of the whole pattern of humanity. In this connection Iqbal says:

> You seek peace of mind, peace of mind means naught;
> To shed tears for the weal of fellow beings is something.

Although Goethe and Iqbal display such affinity in their art and thought, there are certain differences between them. As a literary artist Goethe demonstrates much greater versatility. Iqbal was supreme as a poet, but he did not write drama in verse or prose; Goethe, on the other hand, wrote novels, long and short; essays, reviews, and all kinds of poetry. Thematically, Goethe dealt with the development of man as an individual; Iqbal dealt with man's development as an integral part of society. In the occupational sphere, Goethe was, in addition to being a literary artist, an administrator; Iqbal was a poet, politician, philosopher, religious reformer, and lawyer. (Goethe had been trained as a lawyer but had given up practice after a brief trial; Iqbal practiced law all his life.) And yet, in spite of all differences, the two great masters displayed unusual kinship of genius. Showing the way to overcome the Devil in man, they have shown the way to synthesize conflicting forces in an individual, and it is in the synthetic genius of their work that they have proved great benefactors of mankind.

## IQBAL AND DANTE

IQBAL also displays a significant affinity of poetic sensibility with the great Italian poet Dante, despite the gulf of six centuries that separates them. As regards their religion, their cultural background, their traditions and language, no two poets could have been more different, yet there is kinship among them, mainly through the apocalyptic works *Divine Comedy* and *Javid-Namah* (The Book of Eternity).

Dante was born in Florence, and his family was supposed to have descended from the "noble seed of the Roman founders of the city." The city's population was, at the time of Dante's birth, divided into two groups, Ghibellines and Guelphs; the Ghibelline part consisted of feudal aristocracy, and the Guelph of lesser nobility and artisans, corresponding to the middle class in modern society. While still young, Dante learned by himself the art of "discoursing in rhyme" (*La vita nuova*, III, 9). The grace and beauty of a Florentine lady, Rice, daughter of Folco Portinari and later the wife of Simone de' Bardi, created a great impression upon Dante, who called her Beatrice. Dante collected all the poems he had written to celebrate Beatrice in a volume called *La vita nuova*.

Meanwhile, great class struggles had started in Florence, and the main conflicting factions were the offshoots of the Guelph party called the Blacks and the Whites. The Blacks were ready to compromise with the church to gain power, but the Whites wanted independence from both the state and the church. In 1301 the Commune decided to send an embassy to the Pope to counteract the intrigues of the Blacks. Dante was one of the three chosen to represent the Commune. After a time the Pontiff sent the other two to Florence for negotiations and kept Dante back. While Dante was at the Pontiff's court, the Blacks overpowered the Whites in Florence. His house was plundered, and he was fined 5,000 florins, banished for two years, and perpetually banned from public office.

Exile widened Dante's horizon and made of the Florentine a citizen of Italy. A few years later he wrote that "the world was his fatherland as the sea is the common country of the fishes."[23] Dante did everything to free himself of the charge of Ghibellinism. Furthermore, he tried to establish his reputation by the composition of great works. Thus appeared the two treatises *De vulgare eloquentia* and the *Convivio*, which were composed between 1304 and 1307. For him the world was without justice; only greed, envy, and violence were everywhere triumphant. Pondering the cause of so much evil, Dante undertook a work which would portray the ravages of such widespread depradation and which would persuade the people to return to the right path. Work on the *Convivio* and *De vulgare eloquentia* was interrupted and the work was undertaken to which Dante dedicated the remaining years of his life. He called it the *Comedy*, but future generations called it the *Divine Comedy*.

Here a brief description of Iqbal's reasons for composing *Javid-Namah* is in order. During his stay in Europe for higher studies (1905–1908) Iqbal became seriously concerned about the colonial domination of the Indian subcontinent. He came to believe that the cause of

Muslims' decadence was their belief in doctrines which inculcated otherworldliness. As a reaction to this situation Iqbal developed his doctrine of the *khudi* (ego). Pondering the causes of evil and depravation in the world, he came to the conclusion that their effects could better be shown in an allegory. This world would not only receive warnings from the other world, but also moral instructions from well-known historical personalities. Thus was conceived Iqbal's *Javid-Namah*, named after the poet's son Javid.

Iqbal lived to write some great poems after *Javid-Namah*, but for the purposes of a comparative study of Dante and Iqbal it is appropriate to focus our critical appreciation on the two classics—the *Divine Comedy* and *Javid-Namah*. Both poets have attempted to depict the destiny of the soul through the allegory of a sublime vision. Although there is a remarkable resemblance in the art of the two masters and also in their ideas on some fundamental problems which face mankind, it must be made clear that Iqbal did not take Dante's masterpiece as his model. Dante is not himself the first in the long series of apocalyptic writers. According to Fisher, "The *Divine Comedy* owes much to the Dream of Scipio and to the Sixth Book of the Aeneid, but a theme of a visit to the other world was neither original with Virgil nor was it principally confined to the writers of pagan antiquity."[24]

Recent researches have established that Dante was indebted mainly to Muslim sources for the original conception of his great poem. Although this question had aroused the curiosity of many scholars—even in the last century—it obtained rich documentation and precise information through *La escatalogía Muslimana en la Divina Comedia* of a Spanish Orientalist, Miguel Asín Palacios. The thesis of Asín's book was that an analogy existed between the representation of "beyond" in Dante's *Comedia* and that of the Muslim writings regarding the fate of souls after death and the last judgment, the most prominent being *Durratul Fakhira* of al-Ghazzali and the *Mi'rāj Namah*. Miguel Asín wrote: "It not only confirmed that in Muslim sources there were to be found prototypes of features in the *Divine Comedy* hitherto regarded as original because nothing similar to them had been discovered in the Christian legends, its predecessors; it further revealed the no less Muslim origin of many of those medieval legends themselves. It let in a flood of light upon the whole problem."[25] The researches of Nounerat de Villard and Cerulli have also established beyond all doubt that Western versions of Mi'rāj (the Prophet Muhammad's Ascension) were available to Dante. Also, in Ibn al-'Arabi's *Futūhat-i-Makkiā* and Muarri's *Al-Ghufrān* description of the *Mi'rāj* is in almost identical terms.

In tracing the influence of Dante on Iqbal it should be kept in mind that Iqbal was intimately acquainted with the Muslim conception of life after death through the traditions of *Mi'rāj*, immortalized in various *Mi'rāj Namahs*, and also through the writings of various Muslim scholars recording their mystic experiences of visions.

The subject of the Ascension of the Prophet had always interested Iqbal. He had studied Ibn al-'Arabi and Muarri, and was aware of *Futūhat-i-Makkia* and *Al-Ghufrān*. He had read the vast literature on the *Mi'rāj*. Evidence indicates that at one time Iqbal planned to write a poem on the Ascension of the Prophet. However, the researches of Miguel Asín on the influence of the Muslim sources on Dante attracted Iqbal's attention and stimulated his creative genius to compose *Javid-Namah*. Thus, although Dante cannot be regarded as a source of inspiration for Iqbal, perhaps he can be correctly described as a stimulant. There is nothing uncharitable in this, as Miguel Asín says: "It is now admitted that the essential trait of genius does not lie in the absolute novelty or originality of the work of art; neither can it consist in the power, the prerogative of God alone, of creating both Form and Matter out of nothing."[26]

Dante's poem the *Divine Comedy* is divided into three parts, *Inferno*, *Purgatorio*, and *Paradiso*. In *Paradiso* Dante visits the Seven Spheres, the Heaven of Fixed Stars, the Primum Mobile, and the Empyrean. In *Javid-Namah* Iqbal does not visit Inferno and Purgatorio, and instead of seven planets he visits only six. Moreover, he does not visit the Heaven of Fixed Stars and the Primum Mobile, but visits the Empyrean. It took Dante ten years to write the *Divine Comedy*, which contains fourteen thousand lines, whereas it took Iqbal three years to write *Javid-Namah*, which contains nearly four thousand lines. A line of the *Divine Comedy* has ten or eleven syllables, but a line of *Javid-Namah* has twenty-two syllables. Thus the number of words used in the *Javid-Namah* is about half of those used in the *Divine Comedy*. Obviously, Iqbal worked on a smaller canvas than Dante did.

Iqbal portrays nothing corresponding to Dante's *Inferno*, but he meets traitors in the Sphere of Saturn, which is equivalent to the Ninth Circle (Ring Antenora) in the *Inferno*, where Dante has put the traitors.

The *Qulzam-i-Khūni* (Ocean of Blood) corresponds to the Seventh Circle of Dante's *Inferno*.

As regards the journey in the other world, Dante is accompanied by Virgil, Matelda, Beatrice, and St. Bernard. Out of these four, Matelda and St. Bernard play only minor roles, but Virgil accompanies Dante throughout the *Inferno* and *Purgatorio*, and Beatrice accompanies him in *Paradiso*, except in Canto XXXI where she leaves him to take her seat in the Third Circle beside Rochels. When Dante first sees Virgil he addresses him thus:

> O glory and light of all the poet's throng!
> May the ardent study and great love serve me now
> Which made me to peruse thy book so long!
> Thou art my Master and my Author thou.[27]
> (*Inferno*, I, 82–85)

In another place Dante addresses Virgil as "Thou that honored'st all learning and art." Virgil fills the first two books of the poem. In making him so central and so admirable, and then completely excluding him from the story, Dante took a great risk which only the very greatest of artists could venture to take. The theme of the *Comedy* is that Virgil is fundamental and indispensable; yet the way he is suddenly left out is perplexing. The whole structure of the poem quivers under the shock, and stability is restored only by the intense and concentrated brilliance of the scene that follows between Dante and Beatrice. Various scholars and commentators have tried to explain the omission of Virgil from *Paradiso*, but it would be correct to say that Dante, in taking this great artistic risk, allowed his faith to override his judgment and artistic sense.

Unlike Dante, Iqbal is accompanied throughout the journey by Rumi; moreover, his behavior in the presence of the guide contains no paradoxes and needs no long explanations from the commentators. Appearing from behind a mountain just as Virgil does, Rumi is Iqbal's constant guide. And throughout the poem Iqbal displays feelings of respect toward and confidence in him. This attitude saves Iqbal from the many paradoxes which Dante creates by his treatment of Virgil.

An important characteristic of both poems, the *Divine Comedy* and *Javid-Namah*, is their imagery: both symbolic and pictorial. In symbolic imagery Iqbal and Dante do not use personified abstractions. Instead they use historical personages, who are symbolic images of the qualities they represent. One advantage of this method is that since the images in the poems are actual human beings, their interests and conversations need not be confined to the qualities they represent symbolically. The symbols employed in both poems are natural as against conventional. Occasionally, Dante uses personified abstractions, but Iqbal never uses them. The allegorical imagery of Dante and Iqbal, being based on natural symbolism and purporting to display an universal pattern in each case, is susceptible of being interpreted in many ways and at many different levels. This gives a universal appeal to the poems.

The pictorial imagery in the *Divine Comedy* and *Javid-Namah* is so superb that they can be regarded as wonderful picture books. Both Dante and Iqbal are masters of description, and, by means of delicate descriptive touches, they build up vast landscapes as beautiful in grand outlines as they are correct in minute details. Depicting the flowery dell known as the Valley of Kings, Dante says:

> Gold and fine silver, crimson, pearly white,
> Indigo, smooth wood lustrous in the grain,
> Fresh flake of emerald but that moment split,
> Could none of them in color near attain,
> The flowers and the grass in that retreat,
> As less with greater rivalleth in vain.
> (*Purgatorio*, VII, 73–78)

Describing the abode of kings, Iqbal says:

> Its blossom-laden boughs, its hyacinths,
> Its roses and its cypresses appeared
> As paintings of blithe spring—so delicate
> Were they. The flower petals and the leaves
> Of trees acquired continual colours new
> From an urge to self expression; magic was
> There in the breeze, which yellow turned to red
> Before the eye could wink; on every side
> The fountains sprayed their pearls
> While heavenly birds sang anthems constantly.
> (*Javid-Namah*, p. 202)

There is such an affinity of sensibility in Dante and Iqbal that very often the language used by one closely resembles the language used by the other. In the *Inferno*, for example, when Dante is assailed by doubts, Virgil tells him to cast them away in the following words:

> And like a man of quiet discernment, "Here
> Lay down all thy distrust," said he; "reject
> Dead from within thee every coward fear."
> (*Inferno*, III, 13–15)

In *Javid-Namah*, Iqbal describes a similar situation in these words:

> Rumi said: "Get rid of doubts,
> Get used to the ways and customs of heavens."
> (*Javid-Namah*, p. 30)

In the same work Iqbal says:

> He drew my hands towards him gently,
> Walked fast and reached the brink of an abyss.
> (*Javid-Namah*, p. 32)

Similar instances abound throughout the two poems. The most striking feature in both Dante and Iqbal is the importance they attach to love in human life. As remarked by George Santayana, "The background and the starting point of everything in Dante is the *intelletto di amore*, the genius of love." In Canto XXIV of *Purgatorio* Dante declares:

> I am one who hearkens when
> Love prompteth, and I put thought into word
> After the mode which he dictates within.
> (*Purgatorio*, XXIV, 52–54)

And Iqbal asserts in *Javid-Namah*:

> Love is Power and a clear argument;
> Love holds supremacy over the worlds.

Both Dante and Iqbal mention the different roles love and knowledge play in human development, but Dante is not as emphatic as Iqbal on the lesser role assigned to knowledge. According to Dante, both love and knowledge are complementary and not rivals. According to Iqbal, knowledge is desirable and even essential for man, but the important role in human affairs is reserved for love. Another point on which Dante and Iqbal display a remarkable resemblance of thought is their conception of hell and heaven. What is the exact nature of hell and heaven? Dante gives the answer in *Paradiso*:

> Nor has this heaven any other where
> Than in the mind of God.
> *(Paradiso,* XXVII, 109-110)

As regards the divine mind, he says:

> Here where is centred every when and where.
> *(Paradiso,* XXIX, 12)

In Dante's view, hell is heaven in reverse; it is "reality seen farther than it can ever be in this world." Thus hell is where one makes it. For Iqbal, heaven is not a holiday and hell is not a pit of everlasting torture inflicted by a revengeful God; they are merely corrective experiences. In Iqbal's words: "Heaven and Hell are states, not localities. Their descriptions in the Qur'ān are visual representations of an inner fact, i.e., character. Hell in the words of the Qur'ān is God's kindled fire which mounts above the hearts, the painful realization of one's failure as a man. Heaven is the joy of triumph over the forces of disintegration. There is no such thing as eternal damnation in Islam."[28] Dante does not agree with Iqbal; according to him, damnation is eternal in most cases.

Thus, whereas Dante and Iqbal agree on several problems facing mankind, they differ on some important points. Both have described Satan in their poems, but their conceptions of Satan differ fundamentally. Satan in the *Divine Comedy* is a static figure, ice-bound, who does no more harm than mangling three treacherous persons. According to Iqbal, Satan is a dynamic character who, although always trying to tempt men from the path of rectitude, is a necessary part of God's plan. He is, in his own way, only fulfilling God's will.

The symbolism adopted by Dante and Iqbal is natural, yet that used by Dante is at times very confusing. Certain symbolic figures in his work, like the Furies, the old man of Crete, Geryon, Cato, and the Serpents provide great difficulty for the subtlety of commentators. This is not the case with Iqbal. There is, however, one fundamental difference between Dante and Iqbal to which reference must be made here. Fisher says that in the *Divine Comedy* "there is violence, obscenity, and grotesqueness."[29] These factors are totally absent in the *Javid-Namah*. There are many lines in the *Divine Comedy* which cannot but offend non-Christian readers. They smack of vulgarity and represent a serious blemish in a great artist.

## IQBAL AND BROWNING

IQBAL displayed a great affinity of thought with another English poet, Robert Browning. His appreciation of Browning was based on their mutual admiration for vitalism. Both preached a message of faith and cheerfulness and brought to distracted humanity moral succor. Although both poets were romantic in temper, they did not follow the Romantic tradition of the English poets in concentrating entirely on nature or on the private emotional life of the individual. Rather, they dealt with the numerous problems that arise out of the contact of man with his fellow human beings. In *Pauline*, Browning expresses the purpose of his poetry in the following words:

> 'T was in my plan to look on real life,
> The life all new to me; my theories
> Were firm, so them left I, to look and learn
> Mankind, its cares, hopes, fears, its woes and joys;
> And, as I pondered on their ways, I sought
> How best life's end might be attained—an end
> Comprising every joy. I deeply mused.

In his *Asrār-i Khudi* (The Secrets of the Self), Iqbal writes:

> No one hath told the secret which I will tell
> Or threaded a pearl of thought like mine,
> Come, if thou wouldst know the secret of everlasting life,
> Come, if thou wouldst win both earth and heaven!
> (*Asrār-i Khudi*, p. 6)

In *The Statue and the Bust* Browning explains that ceaseless activity is better than a life of hesitation and sloth. He goes so far as to say:

> Oh a crime will do
> As well, I reply, to serve for a test.

And Iqbal says in *Gulshan-i Rāz-i Jadīd* (A Rose Garden of a New Secret):

> Life exists in not reaching the end—
> Immortal life lies in being always on the journey.
> Lie constantly in ambush against yourself,
> Fly from doubt to certitude.

In this ceaseless activity man is sure to encounter obstacles and will at times face failures; but these obstacles and failures only add to the fruitfulness of his efforts. Browning advises in *Rabbi Ben Ezra*:

> Then, welcome each rebuff
> That turns earth's smoothness rough,
> Each sting that bids nor sit nor stand but go!
> Be our joys three parts pain!
> Strive, and hold cheap the strain;
> Learn, nor account the pang; dare, never grudge the throe!

Iqbal says:

> The Truth is: thine enemy is thy friend (in disguise)
> His existence crowns thee with glory
> To the seed of man the enemy is a rain-cloud:
> He awakens its potentialities
> The sword of resolution is whetted by the stones in the way.
> And put to proof by traversing stage after stage.
>
> (*Asār-i Khudi*, p. 59)

But according to both Browning and Iqbal, all this activity can be fruitful only if it is in alliance with the spiritual background of life. Browning illustrates this beautifully in his poem *Abt Vogler*.

One of the reasons why Iqbal criticizes Western culture is that he believes it has allowed forces of materialism to displace its spiritual basis. Regarding the spiritual orientation of society, he says: "It is the invisible mental background of the act which ultimately determines its character. An act is temporal or profane if it is done in a spirit of detachment from the infinite complexity of life behind it; it is spiritual if it is inspired by that complexity."

The two poets share a buoyant faith in life here and hereafter, which provides unlimited scope for human development. To them life does not mean only life here and now, but extends beyond to eternity. And death is merely a passing phase. Browning once remarked, "Never say of me that I am dead," and Iqbal says:

> I tell you the sign of a Perfect Man:
> When death comes he greets it with a smile.

Both poets preach strenuous activity, but it must be noted that their ideal of unceasing effort is not extraneous; it lies in the self of the individual, who continues to strive, sometimes succeeding and sometimes failing, but never abandons his endeavors. In their poetry there is the same activity of intellect, the same rush of thought through the impassioned mind. But there is one difference between them; the harshness and grotesqueness so noticeable in Browning are not found in Iqbal.[30]

Apart from the poets mentioned above, Iqbal has shown his appreciation of some other Western poets also. He has written poems or verses on the Hungarian Patufi, the English poet Byron, and the German poet Heine.

Thus it can be seen that Iqbal displays kinship of artistic genius and affinity of thought with some great Western poets, especially Dante, Milton, Goethe, Wordsworth, and Browning. That he displays affinity with great craftsmen and thinkers so diverse in their geniuses is an index of the universality of his art and the breadth of his sensibility.

# APPENDIX

# Letters of Iqbal to Jinnah

DURING 1936–1937 Iqbal wrote eight letters to Jinnah. He wrote these letters as the president of the Punjab Provincial Muslim League, seeking Jinnah's advice about the politics of the Punjab. Two of them (included here) vividly express Iqbal's convictions regarding the future of Muslims in India. The eight letters were published by Jinnah before 1947, along with a foreword. The foreword is Jinnah's testimonial to Iqbal's role in the organization of the Muslim League in the Punjab and his concern for the development of a Muslim state, which, less than ten years after his death, was officially proclaimed the Islamic Republic of Pakistan. Jinnah's foreword and Iqbal's two most crucial letters are reproduced below.

## JINNAH'S FOREWORD

THE letters which form the subject of this booklet were written to me by the sage, philosopher and national poet of Islam, the late Dr. Sir Muhammad Iqbal, during the period May 1936 to November 1937, a few months before his death. This period synchronises with a very eventful period in the history of Muslim India—between the establishment of the All-India Muslim League Central Parliamentary Board in June 1936 and the great historic sessions at Lucknow in October 1937.

If the Central Parliamentary Board with its Provincial Branches marked the first great attempt on the part of the Muslim League to rally round the Muslim opinion to contest the approaching elections, under the Government of India Act of 1935, for Provincial Legislatures on the League ticket, the Lucknow Session indicated the first stage in the reorganisation of the Muslim League on a popular basis and as the only authoritative and representative organisation of Muslim India. Both these high objects were attained in great part owing to the invaluable support that I obtained through the sincere efforts and patriotic and selfless activities of many friends like Sir Muhammad Iqbal, amongst others. The League gained from strength to strength in this short period. In each of the Provinces where the League Parliamentary Board was established and the League parties were constituted we carried away about 60 to 70 percent of the seats that were contested by the League candidates. Hundreds of District and Primary Leagues were established in almost every Province from the farthest corner of Madras to the North-West Frontier Province.

The league gave a staggering blow to the so-called Muslim Mass Contact Movement which was started by the Congress to disrupt Muslim ranks and to overawe the League into submission. The League emerged triumphant in most of the by-elections and shattered the intrigues and machinations of those who hoped to create the impression that the Muslim League Organisation had no support of the Muslim people.

Within eighteen months before the Lucknow Sessions [October, 1937], the League had succeeded in organising Muslims as one party with an advanced and progressive programme and had brought under its influence even those Provinces which for lack of time or preparation had not been sufficiently benefited by the activities of League Parliamentary Boards. The Lucknow Sessions furnished an unmistakable evidence of the popularity that League commanded among Muslims of all groups and ranks.

It was a great achievement for the Muslim League that its lead came to be acknowledged by both the majority and minority provinces. Sir Muhammad Iqbal played a very conspicious part, though at the time not revealed to the public, in bringing about this consummation. He had his own doubts about Sikandar-Jinnah Pact being carried out and he was anxious to see it translated into some tangible results without delay so as to dispel popular misapprehension about it, but unfortunately he has not lived to see that the Punjab has all round made a remarkable progress and now it is beyond doubt that the Muslims stand solidly behind the Muslim League Organisation.

With this brief historical background in mind, the letters can be read with great interest. It is, however, much to be regretted that my own replies to Iqbal are not available. During the period under reference I worked alone unassisted by the benefit of a personal staff and so did not retain duplicate copies of the numerous letters that I had to dispose of. I made enquiries from the Trustees of Iqbal's estate at Lahore and was informed that my letters are not traceable. Hence I had no alternative but to publish the letters without my replies as I think these letters are of very great historical importance, particularly those which explain his views in clear and unambiguous terms on the political future of Muslim India. His views were substantially in consonance with my own and had finally led me to the same conclusions as a result of careful examination and study of the constitutional problems facing India, and found expression in due course in the united will of Muslim

India as adumbrated in the Lahore resolution of the All-India Muslim League, popularly known as the "Pakistan Resolution," passed on 23rd March, 1940.

I

*Confidential*                                                       Lahore
28th May, 1937

My dear Mr. Jinnah,

Thank you so much for your letter which reached me in due course. I am glad to hear that you will bear in mind what I wrote to you about the changes in the constitution and programme of the League. I have no doubt that you fully realise the gravity of the situation as far as Muslim India is concerned. The League will have to finally decide whether it will remain a body representing the upper classes of Indian Muslims or Muslim masses who have so far, with good reason, taken no interest in it. Personally, I believe that a political organisation which gives no promise of improving the lot of the average Muslim cannot attract our masses.

Under the new constitution* the higher posts go to the sons of upper classes; the smaller ones go to the friends or relatives of the ministers. In other matters too our political institutions have never thought of improving the lot of Muslims generally. The problem of bread is becoming more and more acute. The Muslim has begun to feel that he has been going down and down during the last 200 years. Ordinarily, he believes that his poverty is due to Hindu money-lending or capitalism. The perception that it is equally due to foreign rule has not yet fully come to him.

The atheistic socialism of Jawaharlal is not likely to receive much response from the Muslims. The question therefore is: how is it possible to solve the problem of Muslim poverty? And the whole future of the League depends on the League's activity to solve this question. If the League can give no such promises I am sure the Muslim masses will remain indifferent to it as before.

Happily there is a solution in the enforcement of the Law of Islam and its further development in the light of modern ideas. After a long and careful study of Islamic Law I have come to the conclusion that if this system of Law is properly understood and applied, at last the right to subsistence is secured to everybody. But the enforcement and development of the Shariat of Islam is impossible in this country without a free Muslim

---

*This refers to the Government of India Act, 1935.

state or states. This has been my honest conviction for many years and I still believe this to be the only way to solve the problem of bread for Muslims as well as to secure a peaceful India. If such a thing is impossible in India the only other alternative is a civil war which as a matter of fact has been going on for some time in the shape of Hindu-Muslim riots. I fear that in certain parts of the country, e.g. N.W. India, Palestine may be repeated.

Also, the insertion of Jawaharlal's socialism into the body-politic of Hinduism is likely to cause much bloodshed among the Hindus themselves. The issue between social democracy and Brahmanism is not dissimilar to the one between Brahmanism and Buddhism. Whether the fate of socialism will be the same as the fate of Buddhism in India I cannot say. But it is clear to my mind that if Hinduism accepts social democracy it must necessarily cease to be Hinduism. For Islam the acceptance of social democracy in some suitable form and consistent with the legal principles of Islam is not a revolution but a return to the original purity of Islam. The modern problems therefore are far more easy to solve for the Muslims than for the Hindus.

But as I have said above in order to make it possible for Muslim India to solve the problems it is necessary to redistribute the country and to provide one or more Muslim states with absolute majorities. Don't you think that the time for such a demand has already arrived? Perhaps this is the best reply you can give to the atheistic socialism of Jawaharlal Nehru.

Anyhow I have given you my own thoughts in the hope that you will give them serious consideration either in your address or in the discussions of the coming session of the League. Muslim India hopes that at this serious juncture your genius will discover some way out of our present difficulties.

Yours sincerely,<br>(Sd.) Muhammad Iqbal

P.S. On the subject-matter of this letter I intended to write to you a long and open letter in the press. But on further consideration I felt that the present moment was not suitable for such a step.

## II

*Private and Confidential*       Lahore
June 21st, 1937

My dear Mr. Jinnah,

Thank you so much for your letter which I received yesterday. I know you are a busy man; but I do hope you won't mind my writing to you so often, as you are the only Muslim in India today to whom the community has a right to look up for safe guidance through the storm which is coming to North-West India, and perhaps to the whole of India.

I tell you that we are actually living in a state of civil war which, but for the police and military, would become universal in no time. During the last few months there has been a series of Hindu-Muslim riots in India. In North-West India alone there have been at least three riots during the last three months and at least four cases of vilification of the Prophet by [the] Hindus and [the] Sikhs. In each of these four cases, the vilifier has been murdered. There have also been cases of burning of the Koran in Sind.

I have carefully studied the whole situation and believe that the real cause of these events is neither religious nor economic. It is purely political, i.e. the desire of the Sikhs and [the] Hindus to intimidate Muslims even in the Muslim majority provinces. And the new constitution is such that even in the Muslim majority provinces, the Muslims are made entirely dependent on non-Muslims. The result is that the Muslim Ministry can take no proper action and are even driven to do injustice to Muslims partly to please those on whom they depend, and partly to show that they are absolutely impartial.

Thus it is clear that we have our specific reasons to reject this constitution.[1] It seems to me that the new constitution is devised only to placate the Hindus. In the Hindu majority provinces, the Hindus have of course absolute majorities, and can ignore Muslims, altogether. In Muslim majority provinces, the Muslims are made entirely dependent on Hindus. I have no doubt in my mind that this constitution is calculated to do infinite harm to the Indian Muslims. Apart from this it is no solution of the economic problem which is so acute among Muslims.

The only thing that the communal award grants to Muslims is the recognition of their political existence in India. But such a recognition granted to a people whom this constitution does not and cannot help in solving their problem of poverty can be of no value to them.

The Congress President has denied the political existence of Muslims in no unmistakable terms. The other Hindu political body, i.e. the Mahasabha, whom I regard as the real representative of the masses of the Hindus, has declared more than once that a united Hindu-Muslim nation is impossible in India. In these circumstances it is obvious that the only way to a peaceful India is a redistribution of the country on the lines of racial, religious and linguistic affinities. Many British statesmen also realise this, and the Hindu-Muslim riots which are rapidly coming in the wake of this constitution

---

*This refers to the Government of India Act, 1935.

are sure further to open their eyes to the real situation in the country. I remember Lord Lothian* told me before I left England† that my scheme‡ was the only possible solution of the troubles of India, but that it would take 25 years to come.

Some Muslims in the Punjab are already suggesting the holding of a North-West Indian Muslim Conference, and the idea is rapidly spreading. I agree with you, however, that our community is not yet sufficiently organised and disciplined and perhaps the time for holding such a conference is not yet ripe. But I feel that it would be highly advisable for you to indicate in your address at least the line of action that the Muslims of North-West India would be finally driven to take.

To my mind the new constitution with its idea of a single Indian federation is completely hopeless. A separate federation of Muslim provinces, reformed on the lines I have suggested above, is the only course by which we can secure a peaceful India and save Muslims from the domination of non-Muslims. Why should not the Muslims of North-West India and Bengal be considered as nations entitled to self-determination just as other nations in India and outside India are?

Personally, I think that the Muslims of North-West India and Bengal ought at present to ignore Muslim minority provinces. This is the best course to adopt in the interest of both Muslim majority and minority provinces. It will therefore be better to hold the coming session of the League in the Punjab, and not in a Muslim minority province. The month of August is bad in Lahore. I think you should seriously consider the advisability of holding the coming session at Lahore in the middle of October when the weather is quite good in Lahore. The interest in the All-India Muslim League is rapidly growing in the Punjab, and the holding of the coming session in Lahore is likely to give a fresh political awakening to the Punjab Muslims.

Yours sincerely,<br>
(Sd.) Muhammad Iqbal<br>
Bar-at-Law

*He was the author of the so-called Lothian Report, which determined the electoral provisions of the Government of India Act, 1935.

†Iqbal had been in England for the Third Round Table Conference in 1932.

‡This refers to Iqbal's plan for India's regional distribution, which he had described in 1930 in his Presidential Address at Allahabad.

# NOTES & BIBLIOGRAPHY

# Notes

## CHAPTER 1

1. There is considerable confusion about the exact date of birth of Iqbal; 1873 and 1876 have also been mentioned as Iqbal's year of birth. After thoroughly examining this problem, S. A. Vahid, an outstanding Pakistani scholar of Iqbal, has deduced 1877 as the most probable year of Iqbal's birth. This author has accepted his version. See S. A. Vahid, "Date of Iqbal's Birth," *Iqbal Review* (Karachi), 1966, p. 27.
2. Josef Korbel, *Danger in Kashmir* (Princeton, University Press, 1954), p. 13.
3. Sālik, *Dhikr-i Iqbal*, pp. 7–10; see also Farūqi, *Sīrat-i Iqbal*, p. 48.
4. *Ibid.*, p. 12.
5. *Ibid.*, pp. 13–14.
6. Hakīm, *Fiker-i Iqbal* (1961), p. 15.
7. See Ghulam Rasūl Mehr, *Matālab Asrar wa Ramūz* (Lahore, Ghulam Ali, 1960), p. 238; see also Nadwi, *Iqbal-i Kāmil*, pp. 4–5.
8. Iqbal, *Ramūz-i-Bekhudi* (1959), pp. 151–53; Arberry, *The Mysteries of Selflessness* [Iqbal's *Ramūz-i-Bekhudi*], pp. 46–47.
9. Shaikh Muhammad Ismaʿīl, ed., *Maktūbāt-i Sir Sayyid* (Lahore, Majlis Traqqi-i Adab, 1959), pp. 293–308; see especially Sir Sayyid's letters to Sayyid Mīr Hasan numbered II, V, and VIII. Hasan was one of the close confidants of Sir Sayyid in the Punjab. After the founding of the Muslim Educational Conference, Sayyid Mīr Hasan regularly attended its annual sessions.
10. For a detailed literary review of Dāgh's poetry see ʿAbdūl Islam, *Shiʿr al-Hind* (Azamgarh, 1949), I, 315–39.
11. Sir ʿAbdūl Qādir, "Daybachah," in Iqbal, *Bāng-i-Dara* (1946), p. z.
12. ʿAtiya Begum Faizee, *Iqbal* (1956), pp. 110–12.
13. See Mehr and Dilawari, eds., *Sarūd-i Raftah*, pp. 80–82; see also Iqbal, "Ruʿbian," *Kashmir Gazette* (Lahore), September 15, 1901.
14. *College Magazine* (Aligarh), February 1898, p. 71; Sayyid Sulaiman Nadwi, *Hayat-i Shibli* (Azamgarh, 1943), p. 2 ff.
15. *Ibid.*, p. 139.
16. Sālik, *Dhikr-i Iqbal*, p. 65.
17. *Kashmir Gazette* (Lahore) October 1901; *Paysā Akhbār* (Lahore), September 1901; Muhammad ʿAbdullah Qurashi, "Maulavi Mahbūb ʿAlam Awr Iqbal," *Iqbal Review* (January 1963), pp. 4–5.

18. Shaikh Nizām-ud-Din Awliya (generally known as Mahbūb-i Ilahi . . . the beloved of God), is one of the most popular mystics among the Muslims of India and Pakistan. Migrating in the thirteenth century from Bukhara (now in the USSR), the saint's ancestors went to Lahore, and from there moved to Badaūñ, settling ultimately in Delhi. Shaikh Nizām-ud-Din Awliya was born in 1236 and died in 1324. He was not only an accomplished Sufi, but was also an acknowledged scholar. Under his influence and that of his disciples, including Shaikh Nasīr-ud-Din (Charāgh-i Delhi), Shaikh Akhi Sirāj-ud-Din (Bengal), Khawja Burhān-ud-Din Gharīb (Deccan), and Shaikh Sharaf-ud-Din Bū Ali Qalander (Panipat), Islam spread peacefully into different parts of India. Also, a Chinese disciple of the saint established the Nizamiyya Sufi order in China. The present mausoleum over the grave of Shaikh Nizam-ud-Din Awliya was constructed by Sultan Muhammad bin Tughlaq (1325–1351). Cf. Sayyid Sbah-ud-Din 'Abdūr Rahmān, *Bazm-i Sufiyya* (Azamgarh, 1949), pp. 180–81, 223, 234; Khalīq Ahmad Nizāmi, *Tarīkh Mashaikh-i Chisht* (Delhi, 1953), pp. 171–75.

19. Iqbal, "Iltajā-i Masafer: Ba Dargah Hadrat Mahbūb Ilahi Delhi," *Makhzan* (Lahore), October 1905; see particularly Mir Ghulam Bhīk Nayrang's introductory note. Bhīk says that "after visiting the saint's mausoleum Iqbal went to the grave of Mirza Ghālib and kissed it tenderly." See also Ghulam Rasūl Mehr, *Matālab Bāng-i-Dara* (Lahore, Kitab Manzil, n.d.), pp. 96–97.

20. A scion of Mughal nobility in the Punjab, Mirza Ghulam Ahmad of Qadian (1835–1908) was the founder of the Ahmadi movement. Initially, the movement won the acclaim and admiration of the Muslims for its defense against the attacks of the Arya Samaj on Islam. In this respect the *Barahīn-i Ahmadiyya* of the founder was hailed as a monumental study in modern *'ilm al-kalām* (dialectical theology). Subsequently, however, Ahmad claimed to be a prophet and the promised Messiah, demanding the allegiance of all Muslims and non-Muslims. Although professing to revitalize Islam and the *Shari'a* of the Prophet Muhammad, he split the Muslims by enjoining his followers in 1898–1900 to pray separately and not to intermarry with other Muslims. For a lucid statement of the Ahmadis' beliefs and the history of the movement, see Mirza Bashīr Ahmad, *Silsala-i Ahmadiyya* (Qadian, 1939), pp. 84–85 ff.; Mirza Bashir-ud-Din Mahmūd Ahmad, *Ahmadiyyat Ya'ni Haqīqi Islam* (Qadian, 1935), pp. 17–19 ff.

21. 'Abdūl Majīd Sālik, *Sar Guzasht* (Lahore, Qawmi Kutab Khan, 1955), pp. 16–17.

22. *Roadād Anjuman-i-Himāyat-i-Islam*, Lahore, February 23, 24, 25, 1900, pp. 30, 31.

23. Ibid., p. 36. This refers to the masters of the *marthiya* (elegy) form in Urdu poetry, that is, Mir Babar Ali Anīs (1802–1874) and his rival Salamat Ali Debīr (1803–1875).

24. Kiernan, *Poems from Iqbal* (1955), p. 8.

25. Khansar, which lies about a hundred miles northwest of Isfahan, was the birthplace of several Persian poets.

26. Nicholson, *The Secrets of the Self* [Iqbal's *Asrār-i Khudi*] (1960), pp. 14–15; see also Muhammad Iqbal to Tamkīyn Kazmīy, August 16, 1928, *Anwār-i Iqbal*, ed. Bashīr Ahmad Dar, (Karachi, Iqbal Academy, 1967), p. 156.

27. Sadiq, *A History of Urdu Literature*, p. 358.

28. Nabaneeta Sen, "An Aspect of Tagore; Criticism in the West: The Cloud of Mysticism," *Mahfil* (Chicago), III, I, (1966) 20, "He lives today in Bengal as he did fifty years ago . . . for most non-Indians, he is no longer living. He is an isolated figure. For us, he is not part of a living tradition." Edward E. Dimock, "Rabindranath Tagore, 'The Greatest Baul of Bengal'," *The Journal of Asian Studies*, XIX, 1 (November 1959), 34.

29. Persian was the official language of the Delhi Sultanate (1206–1517) and the Mughal Empire in India (1526–1857), and the medium of instruction in the Muslim schools. In the earlier period, that is, the Ghazanvide period, (1014–1160), the literary and poetical works of the Indic Muslims were not different in style and diction from the works of Iranis, Tadjiks, or Afghans.

During the past three hundred years the cultural and educational contacts between the Afghan, Tadjik, Irani, and Indic Muslims (the latter being mostly the descendants of the former three) have virtually disappeared. Consequently, Persian in these lands has developed in isolation, creating a certain strangeness in idioms and expressions, just as American English today sounds strange to a supercilious Briton. Iqbal was not educated in Iran, and despite his admiration for Iran, never visited it. Consequently, Iqbal has often been criticized for using words and expressions no longer in Iran's poetic use. See Aqa Mujtaba Maynavi, *Allama Iqbal*, trans. by Sufi Ghulam Mustafa Tabasam (Lahore, Bazm-i Iqbal, 1955), pp. 4–5.

30. Nicholson, *The Secrets of the Self* (1960), p. vii. Nicholson, however, translated the second edition of *Asrār-i Khudi*, in which Iqbal had made certain changes.

31. Wahīd-ud Din, *Ruzgār-i Faqīr*, I, 35.

32. For Iqbal's attitude toward Sufism see two excellent studies: Jagan Nath Azad, *Iqbal Awr Us Kā Ahad* (Allahabad, Adarah-i Anīs-i Urdu, 1960), pp. 50–85; Nur-ud-Din, *Islami Tasawwuf Awr Iqbal*.

33. (Faizee), *Iqbal*, p. 4.

34. *Ibid.*, pp. 86–98.

35. *Ibid.*, pp. 80–81.

36. *Ibid.*, pp. 23, 88.

37. Hakīm, *Fiker-i Iqbal*, pp. 66–67.

38. Iqbal to Miss Faizee, March 30, 1910, in (Faizee), *Iqbal*, p. 129.

39. *Ibid.*, pp. 73–74.

40. *Ibid.*, pp. 110–11.

41. Sālik, *Dhikr-i-Iqbal*, p. 69.

42. (Faizee), *Iqbal*, pp. 124–25.

43. Iqbal to Niyāzi, March 27, 1935, in Sayyid Nazīr Niyāzi, *Maktūbāt-i Iqbal* (Karachi, Iqbal Academy, 1957), p. 266.

44. Wahīd-ud-Din, *Ruzgār-i Faqīr*, II, 169–70.

45. *Ibid.*, I, 222.

46. Iqbal to Niyāzi, May 2, 1935, in Niyāzi, *Maktūbāt-i Iqbal*, pp. 269–70. Faqīr Sayyid Wahīd-ud-Din has compiled the figures of Iqbal's books sold since their first editions. (These figures do not include the pirated editions which Indian publishers have put out since 1947.)

| TITLES | YEARS | EDITIONS | NUMBERS |
|---|---|---|---|
| Asrār-i Khudī (Persian) | 1915–1959 | VI | 13,000 |
| Payām-i Mashriq (Persian) | 1923–1958 | IX | 18,000 |
| Bāng-i-Dara (Urdu) | 1924–1962 | XXII | 114,000 |
| Zabūr-i 'Ajam (Persian) | 1927–1959 | VII | 164,000 |
| Jāvid-Nāmah (Persian) | 1932–1959 | IV | 6,000 |
| Bāl-i Jibrīl (Urdu) | 1935–1962 | XII | 62,000 |
| Pas Chā Bayad Kard Ay Aqwām-i Sharq (Persian) | 1926–1959 | IV | 11,000 |
| Darb-i Kalīm (Urdu) | 1936–1959 | X | 43,000 |
| Armaghān-i Hijaz (Persian, posthumously published) | 1938–1959 | VII | 22,000 |
| | | | 453,000 |

See Wahīd-ud-Dīn, *Ruzgār-i Faqīr*, I, 215–16.

47. Muhammad Din Fauq, "Doctor Shaikh Sir Muhammad Iqbal: Mukhtaser Sawaneh Hayat," *Nayrang-i Khayāl* (Lahore), September–October 1932, p. 38; Beg, *The Poet of the East*, p. 31; Beg's translation has been slightly modified by the authors.
48. *Civil and Military Gazette* (Lahore), November 30, December 8, 1926.
49. Iqbal, *The Reconstruction of Religious Thought in Islam* (1958), pp. v–vi.
50. Wahīd-ud-Dīn, *Ruzgar-i Faqīr*, I, 184.
51. Kiernan, *Poems from Iqbal*, pp. 55–56.
52. Wahīd-ud-Dīn, *Ruzgār-i Faqīr*, p. 135.
53. Ibid., p. 136; Sālik, *Dhikr-i Iqbal*, p. 180.
54. Kiernan, *poems from Iqbal*, pp. 37–38.
55. Iqbal, *Mathnavi Pas Chā Bayad Kard Ma' Masafer* (Lahore, Ghulam Ali, 1936), pp. 24–28 of *Masafer*.
56. Shamloo [Latīf Ahmad Sherwānī], *Speeches and Statements of Iqbal* (Lahore, Al-Manar Academy, 1948), pp. 205–7.
57. Niyāzi, *Maktūbat-i Iqbal*, pp. 135, 266, 277.

# CHAPTER 2

1. 'Atta Allah, *Iqbal Nama* (Lahore, 1951), II, 67.
2. Hafeez Jalandhari, "Maulana Girāmi," *Mah-i Nav* (Karachi), IX, 5 (August 1956), pp. 16 ff.
3. Sālik, *Dhikr-i Iqbal*. pp. 271–89.
4. 'Atta Allah, *(Iqbal Nama)*, II, 111.
5. Mahmūd Nizāmi, ed., *Malfūzat-i-Iqbal* (Lahore, 1949), pp. 75–76.
6. Ibid., p. 318.
7. Ibid., pp. 55–56.
8. Ibid., pp. 249–50.

Notes: Chapter 4        395

9. *Ibid.*, pp. 112–335. For other narratives of Iqbal's profoundly emotional reaction to the mention of the Prophet Muhammad, see also Pervaiz, *Iqbal awr Qur'ān* (1955), p. 158.

10. Sālik, *Dhikr-i Iqbal*, pp. 232–33.

11. 'Abd al-Haqq, *Chand Ham 'Asr*, pp. 142–43; Sālik, *Dhikr-i Iqbal*, p. 234; *Ganjha-i Girañmayā*, p. 150.

12. Nizāmi, *Malfūzat-i-Iqbal*, pp. 130–33, 134–39, 229–31.

13. *Ibid.*, p. 230.

14. *Ibid.*, p. 310.

15. *Ibid.*, 171; Sālik, *Dhikr-i Iqbal*, p. 267.

16. The canned sacred water from the well of Zamzam is generally included among the souvenirs from the holy cities of Mecca and Medina.

17. Nizāmi, *Malfūzat-i-Iqbal*, pp. 293–95.

18. *Ibid.*, pp. 43–47, 64.

19. *Ibid.*, 162; cf. Iqbal, *Zabūr-i 'Ajam* (1948), pp. 253–58. This section of the book is entitled Question VIII in the section "Gulshan-i Rāz-i Jadīd."

20. Nizāmi, *Malfūzat-i-Iqbal*, p. 58.

21. The movement of the people of *Hadith* represents that phase in the recent development of Islam in which the corrective for the accretions of later centuries is found in the cultivation of *Hadith* studies, which provide intimate touch with the spirit of the Prophet Muhammad.

22. *Ijtihād* is the term used for exertion in interpreting applied theology and jurisprudence in Islam.

23. Nizāmi, *Malfūzat-i-Iqbal*, pp. 66–67.

24. *Ibid.*, pp. 314–17.

25. *Ibid.*, pp. 130–31.

26. *Ibid.*, p. 168.

27. *Ibid.*, pp. 185–86.

## CHAPTER 4

1. Harold Laswell, *World Politics and Personal Insecurity* (New York, Free Press, 1950), p. 3.

2. Harold Laswell and Abraham Kaplan, *Power and Society* (New Haven, Yale University Press, 1950), p. 240.

3. *Encyclopedia of Islam* (London, 1960), II, 361–62.

4. See Saiyad Athar 'Abbas Rizvi, *Muslim Revivalist Movements in Northern India in the Sixteenth and Seventeenth Centuries* (Agra, University Press, 1965), pp. 31–39.

5. Mīr 'Abdūl Wāhid Bilgrami, "Haqāiq-i Hind" (Ahsan Collection, Aligarh University, Aligarh, India), f. 10b; Rizvi, *Muslim Revivalist Movements*, p. 61.

6. For the Mujaddid's efforts to uproot the *Din-i Ilahi*, and for his contribution to the development of the *Wahdat al-Shahūd* doctrine of Sufism, see his *Maktūbat-i Imam-i Rabbāni*, 3 vols. (Lucknow, Nole Kishore Press, n.d.); Muhammad Manzūr

Nu'mānī, *Tadhikra Imam-i Rabbāni Mujaddid Alf Thani* (Lucknow, Kutb Khana Al-Furqān, 1960); Muhammad Farmān, *Hayat-i Mujaddid* (Lahore, Bazm-i Iqbal, 1959); Burhan Ahmad Faruqi, *Mujaddid's Conception of Tawhīd* (Lahore, Ashraf, 1940).

7. Iqbal, *The Development of Metaphysics in Persia*, (1959), p. x.
8. "Daybachah-i Asrār-i Khudi," in Wahīd-ud-Din, *Ruzgār-i Faqīr*, II, 49.
9. *Ibid.*, p. 51.
10. For ecology, see R. D. Mckenzie, "The Ecological Approach to the Study of the Human Community," *The American Journal of Sociology* (November 1924), pp. 287–301 (hereafter abbreviated as *AJS*); James A. Quinn, "Topical Summary of Current Literature on Human Ecology," *AJS*, No. 46 (1940), pp. 191–226; Robert Ezra Park, "Human Ecology," *AJS* (July 1936), pp. 1–15.
11. Iqbal, "Qawmi Zindgi," *Makhzan* (Lahore), October 1904; March 1905; Sayyid 'Abdūl Wāhid Mu'inī, ed., *Maqalāt-i Iqbal* (Lahore, Ashraf, 1963), pp. 39–62.
12. Commenting on Shivaji's struggle against the Mughal Emperor Aurangzeb 'Alamgīr, Nehru said: "Shivaji was the symbol of resurgent Hindu nationalism, drawing inspiration from the old classics, courageous, and possessing high qualities of leadership. He built the Marathas as a strong unified fighting group, gave them a nationalistic background, and made them a formidable power which broke up the Mughal Empire." Jawaharlal Nehru, *The Discovery of India* (Calcutta, Signet Press, 1946), p. 319.
13. Javid Iqbal, ed., *Stray Reflections* (Lahore, Ghulam Ali, 1961), pp. 44–46.
14. Abraham is said to have overthrown the idols standing in the Holy House at Mecca. See Qur'ān, XXII, 27; cf. Arberry, *The Mysteries of Selflessness*, p. 17.
15. See Punjab, *Jullunder Settlement Report* (1881), pp. 70–72; Punjab, *Amritsar Settlement Report* (1892), p. 73; see also Sir Malcom Darling, *The Punjab Peasant* (London, Oxford University Press, 1947), pp. 172–73.
16. *Ibid.*, pp. 14–15, 21.
17. For instance the first graduate from the Government College in Lahore received his degree in 1870, and the Punjab University did not come into being until 1882. See Azim Husain, *Fazl-i Husain* (Bombay, Longmans, Green, 1946), p. 76.
18. The highest title was that of *Sir*. Other titles, in order of their importance were *Khan Bahādur* and *Khan Sahib* for the Muslims, and *Ray Bahādur* and *Ray Sahib* for the Hindus. They were very much reminiscent of the Mughal titles.
19. *Ibid.*, pp. 150–53.
20. Chaudhry Khaliq-uz Zaman, *Pathway to Pakistan* (Lahore, 1961), p. 37; Batalvi, *Iqbal Kāy Akhari Dow Sāl*, pp. 70–75.
21. See Ishtiaq Husain Qureshi, *The Struggle for Pakistan* (Karachi, University Press, 1965), pp. 46–47; Zaman, *Pathway to Pakistan*, p. 37.
22. See *Vox Populi Series*, 1932, Vol. IV.
23. Lajpat Rai, *Autobiographical Writings* (New Delhi, 1965), pp. 88–95.
24. This imperial interpretation was refined and elaborated by English administrators and scholars. The most notable examples were W. H. Moreland, *India at the Death of Akbar* (London, 1920) and Sir Percival Griffiths, *The British Impact on India* (London, 1965). The theory of the crown's ownership of land was probably due to misunderstanding of the pre-British systems. During the Classical Age (c. 300–700 A.D.)

of India land was divided into three categories: ". . . fallow or waste land owned by the state, which was generally donated by way of salary; cultivated land owned by the state and treated as crown land which could be donated but probably seldom was, because it was already under plough and providing an income; and finally, privately owned land." Romila Thapar, *A History of India* (Baltimore, 1966), I, 146. With, slight modification the successive Muslim dynasties including the Mughal maintained the same system.

25. Iqbal's speech on the budget, 1927–1928, delivered in the Punjab Legislative Council, March 5, 1927; quoted in Shamloo, *Speeches and Statements of Iqbal*, p. 63.

26. *Ibid.*, p. 75.

27. *Ibid.*, p. 80.

28. *Ibid.*, p. 85.

29. Iqbal, *Bāl-i Jibrīl*, p. 161; Kiernan, *Poems from Iqbal* (1955), p. 45.

30. Iqbal's cut motion on the government's demand for a grant under "Education," March 10, 1927, in Vahid, ed., *Thoughts and Reflections of Iqbal*, p. 313.

31. Husain, *Fazl-i Husain*, p. 134.

32. Punjab, *Report on the Progress of Education: 1921–1922* (Lahore, n.d.), Chapter XI.

33. Vahid, *Thoughts and Reflections of Iqbal*, pp. 334, 341; Shamloo, *Speeches and Statements of Iqbal*, pp. 83, 89.

34. Azim Husain, one of the sons of the Unionist party's founder, Mian Fazl-i Husain (and currently one of the secretaries of the Ministry of External Affairs, Government of India) says: "Mahasabha representatives like Monohar Lal and Dr. Gokal Chand Narang were kept in office against the wishes of the Unionist Party. . ." He claims that the British governor used the officially nominated members to give majority to the unpopular minister of education Monohar Lal. See Husain, *Fazl-i Husain*, p. 165. Iqbal, however, suspected a covert alliance between the Unionists and the governor of the province regarding the education minister's appointment.

35. Vahid, *Thoughts and Reflections of Iqbal*, p. 323.

36. Shamloo, *Speeches and Statements of Iqbal*, p. 70.

37. Vahid, *Thoughts and Reflections of Iqbal*, p. 321.

38. See M. H. Saiyid, *Muhammad Ali Jinnah* (Lahore, Ashraf, 1953), pp. 238–39.

39. Rajendra Prasad, *India Divided* (Bombay, 1947), p. 127.

40. Waheed-uz-Zaman, *Towards Pakistan* (Lahore, Publishers United, 1964), pp. 34–35.

41. The Nehru Committee, author of the Report, consisted of the following: (1) Pandat Motilal Nehru (chairman); (2) Ali Imam (Muslim); (3) Shuaib Qureshi (Muslim); (4) M. S. Aney (Hindu Mahasabha); (5) M. R. Jayakar (Hindu Mahasabha); (6) G. R. Pradhan (Non-Brahman Hindu); (7) Sardar Mangal Singh (Sikh League); (8) Sir Tej Bahadur Sapru (Liberal, Hindu); (9) N. M. Joshi (Labor).

42. These four amendments were: (1) That Muslim representation in the Central Legislature should not be less than one-third; (2) That in the event that adult suffrage, as proposed in the Nehru Report, is not granted, the Punjab and Bengal should have seats only on a population basis, subject to re-examination after ten years; (3) That the residuary powers should be vested in the provinces and not in the center; (4) That

separation of Sindh from Bombay and the elevation of the North-West Frontier Province as a governor's province should not be made contingent on the establishment of the Nehru constitution. See Rafi Ahmad Kidwai, *Proceedings of the All-Parties National Convention, Calcutta, 1928*, All-Parties National Convention, Allahabad, 1929, p. 78.

43. *Paysā Akhbār*, December 10, 1927; *Inqalāb*, November 11, 1927.
44. Shamloo, *Speeches and Statements of Iqbal*, pp. 163–64.
45. Sir Reginald Coupland, *India: A Restatement* (London, Oxford University Press, 1945), p. 130.
46. Aga Khan, *The Memoirs of Aga Khan* (London, Cassell, 1954), p. 210.
47. Coupland, *India: A Restatement*, p. 330.
48. Khan, *The Memoirs of Aga Khan*, p. 228.
49. *Ibid.*, p. 229.
50. Iqbal, "Presidential Address: Delivered at the Annual Session of the All-India Muslim Conference at Lahore on March 21, 1932," in Vahid, *Thoughts and Reflections of Iqbal*, p. 198; see also Sir Percival Griffiths, *The British Impact on India* (London, Frank Cass, 1965), p. 330.
51. *Ibid.*, p. 201.
52. In the Punjab, where Muslims constituted 57 per cent, Hindus 27 per cent, and Sikhs 13 per cent of the population, Muslims received 49 per cent, Hindus 27 per cent, and Sikhs 18 per cent of the total seats in the legislature. Similarly, in Bengal where Muslims formed 55 per cent and Hindus 43 per cent of the total population, Muslims received about 48 per cent and Hindus 43 per cent of the total provincial seats. Qureshi, *The Struggle for Pakistan*, p. 64.
53. *Inqalāb*, January 3, 1932.
54. Iqbal's Presidential Address to the All-India Muslim Conference, March 21, 1932; quoted in Vahid, *Thoughts and Reflections of Iqbal*, pp. 215–19.
55. In 1938, Iqbal invited Maulana Abul 'ala-Maudūdi, the founder of the Jama't-Islami, to establish in the Punjab an Islamic Research Institute. After the establishment of Pakistan the Central Institute of Islamic Research was created in Karachi, and the Adareh Thaqafat-i Islamia was founded in Lahore. During the first Constituent Assembly of Pakistan, a proposal for the creation of the '*ulamā*' board was adopted. These organizations, at least in idea, owe their existence to Iqbal's suggestions of 1932.
56. *Civil and Military Gazette* (Lahore) June 7, 1936; see also Husain, *Fazl-i Husain*, p. 308.
57. *Civil and Military Gazette*, May 9, 1936; also in Batalvi, *Iqbal Kāy Akhari Dow Sāl*, pp. 312–13.
58. *Ibid.*, pp. 343–34.
59. *Ibid.*, p. 352. (1) They were Malik Barkat Ali; (2) Raja Ghazanfar Ali Khan; (3) Khalifah Shuja'-ud Din; (4) Malik Zamān Mahdi Khan; (5) Sardar Karīm Bakhsh; (6) Mushtaq Ali Khan; (7) Mian 'Abdūl Majīd; (8) Muzaffar Ali Khan Qizilbash. *Ibid.*, p. 360.
60. Coupland, *India: A Restatement*, pp. 153–54.
61. *Ibid.*, p. 182.

62. Some Pakistani scholars have maintained that Nehru adopted the Muslim mass-contact campaign with the advice and consent of Abul Kalam Azad (see Batalvi, *Iqbal Kāy Akhari Dow Sāl*, p. 391). That he was opposed to a special membership campaign among the Muslims was categorically stated in 1937 by Azad. In a letter to Ghulam Rasūl Mehr, Azad (asserted): "It cannot be said that whatever provincial office-holders of the Congress do is always in harmony with the principles and the central administration of the Congress. In the course of several movements my attention was drawn to one or two incidents when special arrangements were made to hire Muslim volunteers and special funds were set aside for this purpose. Forcefully, I forbade that, and for one case I appointed an investigating committee. It is entirely possible that in some places small funds might have been spent to gain the support of some Muslims, but what can be gained by this? The big question is this: Does the central organization of the Congress regard such expenditures permissible, and ever set aside funds for this purpose? My answer is no; *al-hamd al-Allah* (praise to God) spinning of lies is not my habit." Abul Kalam Azad to Ghulam Rasūl Mehr, June 17, 1937; in Ghulam Rasūl Mehr, *Naqsh-i Azad*, (Lahore, Kitāb Manzil, 1959), p. 136.

This letter inclines the author to think that the Muslim mass-contact campaign was probably undertaken by Nehru in disregard of Azad's views.

63. *Civil and Military Gazette*, April 28, 1937.
64. Iqbal to Jinnah, August 11, 1937, in *Letters of Iqbal to Jinnah* (1956), p. 25.
65. *Ibid.*, p. 26.
66. Batalvi, *Iqbal Kāy Akhari Dow Sāl*, p. 483; also Iqbal to Jinnah, October 7, 1937, in *Letters of Iqbal to Jinnah*, p. 28.
67. *Ibid.*, pp. 486, 544.
68. *Ibid.*, pp. 487–88; Coupland, *India: A Restatement*, p. 183. The author is indebted to B. A. Dar for giving him the draft of the "Pact" from his files.
69. On the instruction of Iqbal, the secretary of the Provincial League Ghulam Rasūl Khan, sent on October 22, 1937 ninety membership blanks to the Unionists, but Sir Sikander advised them not to sign them. Batalvi, *Iqbal Kāy Akhari Dow Sāl*, pp. 515–16.
70. Iqbal to Jinnah, November 1, 1937. in *Letters of Iqbal to Jinnah*, p. 30.
71. Literally translated, the name means the Punjab Landowners' League.
72. Iqbal to Jinnah, November 10, 1937, in *Letters of Iqbal to Jinnah*, pp. 31–32.
73. *Civil and Military Gazette*, December 5, 1937.
74. See also his famous poem *Punjab Kāy Pīr Zaduñ Say* (To the Punjab Pīrs) in *Bāl-i Jibrīl* (p. 211), composed in the mid-1930s:

> Closed is the long roll of Saints; this land
> Of the Five Rivers [Punjab] stinks in good men's nostrils.
> God's people have no portion in that country
> Where lordly tassel sprouts from monkish cap;
> That cap bred passionate faith, this tassel breeds
> Passion for playing pander to Government.

Kiernan, *Poems from Iqbal*, p. 58.

75. Shamloo, *Speeches and Statements of Iqbal*, pp. 219–20.

76. Batalvi, *Iqbal Kāy Akhari Dow Sāl*, p. 613.
77. *Ibid.*, p. 629.
78. *Ibid.*, p. 640.
79. *Ibid.*, pp. 641-44.
80. In the general elections of 1946 the League won 75 out of 86 Muslim seats. The Unionist party was reduced to an insignificant group of 20. Four Unionists later defected to the League (raising the League's strength to 79), and six joined the Independent and other blocs, further reducing the Unionist group to ten. However, the Congress entered into an alliance with the Akali Sikhs and the Unionists to form a coalition ministry, which remained in power until 1947. See Qureshi, *The Struggle for Pakistan*, pp. 244-45; Abul Kalam Azad, *India Wins Freedom* (New York, Longmans, Green, 1960), p. 152. Azad has claimed that the creation of this coalition was hailed as an extraordinary feat of his statesmanship.

# CHAPTER 5

1. Hafeez Malik, *Moslem Nationalism in India and Pakistan* (Washington, D.C., Public Affairs Press, 1963), p. 217.
2. "Some Materials for a History of the Freedom Movement in India; collected from Bombay Government Records" (Bombay, 1958), II, 71.
3. Iqbal, "Sha'ir," in *Bang-i Dara*, p. 53.
4. *Ibid.*, p. 88.
5. A. H. al-Biruni [S. M. Ikram], *Makers of Pakistan and Modern Muslim India*, p. 176.
6. *Ibid.*, p. 174.
7. Iqbal, "Sha'ir," p. 119.
8. Muhammad Ali, *My Life: A Fragment* (Lahore, Ashraf, 1946), p. 167.
9. *Ibid.*, p. 166.
10. Iqbal, *Payām-i Mashriq* (1958), p. 258.
11. Iqbal, *Darb-i Kalīm* (1959), p. 139.
12. Iqbal, *Payām-i Mashriq*, pp. 230-31.
13. *Ibid.*, For a detailed examination of this poem, see N. I. Prigarinaya's article, "Humanism in Iqbal's Philosophical Lyric Poetry of the 1920s," *The Peoples of Asia and Africa* (Moscow), No. 5 (May 1965), pp. 95-107.
14. Iqbal, *The Reconstruction of Religious Thought in Islam* (1954), p. 163 (hereafter noted as *The Reconstruction*).
15. *Ibid.*
16. *Ibid.*, p. 2.
17. See Bausani, "Iqbal's Philosophy of Religion and the West," in *Crescent and Green*, p. 139.
18. Iqbal, *The Reconstruction*, pp. 68, 70.
19. Bausani, "Iqbal's Philosophy of Religion and the West," p. 140.
20. Iqbal, *The Reconstruction*, p. 78.
21. *Ibid.*, p. 22.

22. *Ibid.*, pp. 171–72.
23. Daud Rahbar, "Shah Waliullah and Ijtihād: 'iqd al-Jīd Fī Ahkām al-ijtihād wa-l Taqlīd," *The Muslim World*, XLV, 4, (October 1955), 352–57.
24. Iqbal, *The Reconstruction*, p. 97.
25. *Ibid.*
26. *Ibid.*, pp. 97–98.
27. Nicholson, *The Secrets of the Self* (1944), pp. 89–90.
28. *Ibid.*, p. 105.
29. *Ibid.*, p. 106.
30. Iqbal, *The Reconstruction*, p. 198.
31. *Ibid.* p. 14.
32. *Ibid.*, p. 154; see also Malik, *Moslem Nationalism in India and Pakistan*, p. 242.
33. Iqbal, *Bāng-i Dara*, p. 280.
34. Iqbal, *The Reconstruction*, pp. 154, 162.
35. Iqbal, "Reply to Questions Raised by Pandit Jawahar Lal Nehru," in Vahid, *Thoughts and Reflections of Iqbal*, pp. 256–90.

## CHAPTER 6

1. Iqbal, "Presidential Address: Delivered at the Annual Session of the All-India Muslim Conference at Lahore on March 21, 1932," in Vahid, *Thoughts and Reflections of Iqbal*, p. 197.
2. H. L. Chopra, "Iqbal and India," *Indo-Iranica* (Calcutta), XV (June 1961), 33.
3. Iqbal, *Bāng-i-Dara* (1946), pp. 88–89.
4. *Ibid.*, pp. 62–73.
5. *Ibid.*, pp. 32, 66.
6. Iqbal, "Extract from a letter to Sir Younghusband in the *Civil and Military Gazette*, July 30, 1931," in Shamloo, *Speeches and Statements of Iqbal*, p. 169.
7. Iqbal, *Bāng-i-Dara*, pp. 19, 82, 87, 88; referred to in Ramsay MacDonald's *Awakening of India* and also in Syed Ross Masood, "Some Aspects of Urdu Poetry," *The Atheneum* (London), 1920, p. 60.
8. Singh, *The Ardent Pilgrim*, pp. 24–25.
9. Iqbal, *Bāng-i-Dara*, p. 66.
10. Iqbal, "Self in the Light of Relativity," in Vahid, *Thoughts and Reflections of Iqbal*, p. 115.
11. Iqbal, *The Reconstruction*, preface.
12. Mehr and Dilawari, *Sarūd-i Raftah*, p. 41; Iqbal, *Bāng-i-Dara*, p. 42.
13. E. M. Forster, "The Poetry of Iqbal," *The Atheneum*, December 5, 10, 1920, p. 804.
14. W. Cantwell-Smith, *Modern Islam in India* (London, Victor Gollancz, 1946), p. 113.
15. Qur'ān, II, 28–31; Iqbal, *The Reconstruction*, p. 13.
16. Iqbal, *Bāng-i-Dara*, pp. 118, 138.

17. Iqbal, "Islam as a Moral and Political Ideal," in Vahid, *Thoughts and Reflections of Iqbal*, p. 51; Iqbal, *Bāng-i-Dara*, p. 144.
18. Iqbal, *Bāng-i-Dara*, p. 138.
19. Forster, "The Poetry of Iqbal." p. 803.
20. Shamloo, *Speeches and Statements of Iqbal*, p. 73.
21. Vahid, *Thoughts and Reflections of Iqbal*, p. 173.
22. *Ibid.*, p. 51.
23. J. Iqbal, *Stray Reflections*, p. 95.
24. Vahid, *Thoughts and Reflections of Iqbal*, pp. 287–88.
25. J. Iqbal, *Stray Reflections*, pp. 26–27.
26. Shamloo, *Speeches and Statements of Iqbal*, p. 224.
27. *Ibid.*, p. 237.
28. Vahid, *Thoughts and Reflections of Iqbal*, p. 376.
29. *Ibid.*, p. 60.
30. J. Iqbal, *Stray Reflections*, p. xxi.
31. Shamloo, *Speeches and Statements of Iqbal*, pp. 72–73.
32. Iqbal, *Ramūz-i-Bekhudi*, 1st ed. (1918), preface; quoted in Vahid, *Iqbal, His Art and Thought* (1959), p. 237.
33. Dickinson, Review of *The Secrets of the Self* by Muhammad Iqbal, *The Nation* (London), December 24, 1920, p. 458.
34. Vahid, *Thoughts and Reflections of Iqbal*, pp. 98–99.
35. Arberry, *Persian Psalms* [Iqbal's *Zabūr-i 'Ajam*] (1961), p. 75.
36. Vahid, *Thoughts and Reflections of Iqbal*, p. 163.
37. *Ibid.*, p. 167.
38. *Ibid.*, p. 162.
39. *Ibid.*, pp. 379, 381.
40. Shamloo, *Speeches and Statements of Iqbal*, p. 210.
41. *Letters of Iqbal to Jinnah* (1963), p. 14.
42. *Ibid.*, p. 18.
43. Vahid, *Thoughts and Reflections of Iqbal*, pp. 167, 170, 171.
44. Shamloo, *Speeches and Statements of Iqbal*, p. 222.
45. Khalifah 'Abdūl Hakīm, *Islam and Communism* (Lahore, Institute of Islamic Culture, 1953), pp. 136, 150.
46. *The Encyclopedia of the Social Sciences*, 15 vols, in 8 (London, Macmillan, 1957), XIII, 189.
47. Kiernan, *Poems from Iqbal*, (1955) pp. 42–43.
48. *Ibid.*, p. 72.
49. Shamloo, *Speeches and Statements of Iqbal*, p. 167.
50. M. D. Taseer, Introduction to Kiernan, *Poems from Iqbal* (1947), pp. 14–15; Shamloo, *Speeches and Statements of Iqbal*, p. 167.
51. *Letters of Iqbal to Jinnah*, p. 19.
52. *The Concise Encyclopedia of Western Philosophy and Philosophers* (London, Hutchinson, 1960), p. 117.
53. Cantwell-Smith, *Modern Islam in India*, p. 113.
54. *Ibid.*

55. *The Encyclopedia of the Social Sciences*, XIII, 188.
56. Iqbal, *Khizr-i-Rah*, trans. by Latīf, in *The Influence of English Literature on Urdu Literature*, p. 132.
57. Shamloo, *Speeches and Statements of Iqbal*, p. 168.
58. *Ibid.*, p. 169; J. Iqbal, *Stray Reflections*, p. 120.
59. J. J. Houben, "The Individual in Democracy and Iqbal's Conception of *Khudi*," in *Cresent and Green*, pp. 152, 159.
60. Kashyap, "Sir Mohammad Iqbal and Friedrich Nietzsche," *Islamic Quarterly*, II, 1 (1955), 185.
61. Vahid, *Thoughts and Reflections of Iqbal*, pp. 83–84.
62. *Ibid.*, pp. 51, 53.
63. Arberry, *The Mysteries of Selflessness*, pp. 5–8.
64. Vahid, *Thoughts and Reflections of Iqbal*, p. 51.
65. Houben, "The Individual in Democracy and Iqbal's Conception of *Khudi*," p. 157.

## CHAPTER 7

1. With fewer than two thousand verses, *Ḍarb-i Kalīm* is divided into six parts according to theme. The title of the first part is "Islam and Muslims," and that of the second is "Knowledge and Education." The remaining parts are: "The Woman," "Literature and the Arts," "Politics of East and West," and a concluding cycle of twenty poems, "Ideas of Mihrāb Gūl Afghan."
2. In this article Professor Marek has chosen certain themes to highlight Iqbal's views on the international politics of the 1930s, his concepts of democracy and nationalism, his opinions on the nature of the influence of Western intellectuals on Indian artists, and his appreciative views of socialism. The translations of the cited verses are Professor Marek's, unless otherwise indicated.
3. Iqbal, *Pas Chā Bayad Kard Aqwām-i Sharq?* (1958), pp. 58–59.
4. *Ibid.*, p. 38.
5. Iqbal, *Ḍarb-i Kalīm* (1958), p. 147.
6. *Ibid.*, p. 158.
7. *Ibid.*, p. 22.
8. *Ibid.*, p. 23.
9. The theme of the discourse between the pirate and Alexander is probably derived from an old French ballad of Villon, which Iqbal might have read:

> There lived a man named Diomed when Alexander emperor was
> A robber on the seas was he and bowed to none but pirate's laws
> Until at last one day, in chains, he stood before the angry king
> Who pondered should this captive live enchained or from his masthead swing.
> "Why, Diomed," the sovereign asked, "should you in piracy engage?"
> "But why, my Lord," his captive said, "should piracy a king enrage?"
> "My craft is light, my arms are few and hamper me as plunderer.
> "With armaments as you, my Lord, I should, as you, be emperor!"

10. Iqbal, *Darb-i Kalīm*, pp. 157, 168.
11. *Ibid.*, p. 161.
12. The Turkish Sultan Selim I (1512–1520) captured Syria and Palestine in 1516 and Egypt and Arabia in 1517. As protector of Mecca and Medina he received the title of caliph, which he carried forward as Turkish sultan. The captured countries remained under the rule of the Turks until 1920. Spain was captured in 711 by the Muslim commander Mūsā ibn Nuṣair in 756; the Caliphate of Cordova was then established. It collapsed in 1031. For details, see Philip K. Hitti, *History of the Arabs* (London, Macmillan, 1956), 493 pp.
13. Iqbal, *Darb-i Kalīm*, p. 159.
14. Kiernan, *Poems from Iqbal* (1955), p. 74.
15. Because of World War II the federal provisions of the 1935 Constitutional Reforms simply did not go into effect.
16. Iqbal, *Darb-i Kalīm*, pp. 146–47.
17. Kiernan, *Poems from Iqbal*, p. 78.
18. Iqbal, *Darb-i Kalīm*, pp. 78–79.
19. Kiernan, *Poems from Iqbal*, p. 76.
20. Yusūf Salīm Chishti, *Sharh-i Darb-i Kalīm* (Lahore, n.d.), p. 470.
21. Iqbal, *Darb-i Kalīm*, pp. 169–70.
22. Mustafa Kemal Pasha Ghazi Ata Turk was born in 1880. He was elected president of the Turkish Republic on October 28, 1923 and began energetically to institute social reforms in order to modernize backward Turkey and come closer to Europe culturally. Rezashāh Pahlāvī, originally an officer in a Cossack brigade, became prime minister of Iran in 1921 and in 1925 was declared hereditary king of Iran. He imitated Kemal Pasha and began to build a modern industry, transportation, and schools.
23. Kiernan, *Poems from Iqbal*, p. 72.
24. Iqbal, *Darb-i Kalīm*, p. 150.
25. See Iqbal, "Our Prophet's Criticism of Contemporary Arabian Poetry," *New Era* (1916), p. 251. See also Hafeez Malik, "The Marxist Literary Movement in India and Pakistan," *Journal of Asian Studies*, XXVI, 4 (August 1967).
26. Ja'ffrī, *Taraqqī pasand Adab* (Aligarh, 1951), p. 114.
27. Iqbal, *Darb-i Kalīm*, p. 121.
28. *Ibid.*, p. 130.
29. Iqbal, *Darb-i Kalīm*, p. 135.
30. Kiernan, *Poems from Iqbal*, p. 70.
31. Iqbal, *Darb-i Kalīm*, p. 138.
32. *Ibid.*, p. 143.
33. Cantwell-Smith, *Modern Islam in Iudia*, p. 132.
34. Iqbal, *Darb-i Kalīm*, p. 139.
35. *Ibid.*, p. 69.

# CHAPTER 8

1. Iqbal, *Bāl-i Jibrīl*, trans. by A. Q. Niaz. Another translation of this poem appears in Kiernan, *Poems from Iqbal*.

2. Quoted by K. G. Saiyidain in *Iqbal as a Thinker* (Lahore, Ashraf, 1952), p. 100.
3. Iqbal, *Payām-i Mashriq*, quoted in Siddiqi, *The Image of the West in Iqbal*, p. 32.
4. Iqbal, *The Reconstruction*, (1951), p. 151.
5. Unfortunately, the author cannot pinpoint this particularly neat phrasing of a commonly voiced attitude. For other examples, see Lawrence C. Little, ed., *Toward Better Education in Moral and Spiritual Values* (Pittsburgh, University of Pittsburgh, 1953).

## CHAPTER 9

1. B. A. Dar, *Iqbal's "Gulshan-i Rāz-i Jadīd" and "Bandagi Namah"* (Lahore, Institute of Islamic Culture, 1964), pp. 17-19, 24, 25, 31-32.
2. *Ibid.*, pp. 26, 71-72; Iqbal, *Bāl-i Jibrīl*, p. 88.
3. Iqbal, *The Reconstruction*, (1951), pp. 15-16.
4. R. Adamson, *Fichte* (New York, Philosophical Classics, 1903), p. 128.
5. Iqbal, *The Reconstruction*, p. 31.
6. *Ibid.*, p. 31.
7. Nicholson, *The Secrets of the Self* (1961), p. 16.
8. Dar, *Iqbal's "Gulshan-i Rāz-i Jadīd,"* pp. 17-18.
9. *Ibid.*, pp. 18-19.
10. Iqbal, "Self in the Light of Relativity," in B. A. Dar, *A Study in Iqbal's Philosophy*, p. 401.
11. Arthur Schopenhauer, *The World as Will and Idea*, trans. by Holdene and Kemp (London, 1883), III, 300.
12. William Wallace, *Life of Schopenhauer* (London, n.d.), p. 59.
13. Schopenhauer, *The World as Will and Idea*, I, 191-92; III, 112.
14. Satischandra Chatterjee and Dhirendramohan Datta, *An Introduction to Indian Philosophy* (Calcutta, 1960), p. 347.
15. Surendranath Dasgupta, *A History of Indian Philosophy* (Cambridge, University Press, 1957), I, 75.
16. *Ibid.*, p. 76.
17. Schopenhauer, *The World as Will and Idea*, I, xiii.
18. *Ibid.*, p. xii.
19. *Ibid.*, pp. 300, 531.
20. Iqbal, *The Reconstruction*, p. 88.
21. Nicholson, *The Secrets of the Self*, pp. 17-18.
22. *Ibid.*
23. Iqbal, *Payām-i Mashriq*, pp. 234-35.
24. Iqbal, *Bāl-i Jibrīl*, p. 171.
25. Nicholson, *The Secrets of the Self*, p. 26.
26. Dar, *Iqbal's "Gulshan-i Rāz-i Jadīd,"* p. 23.
27. *Ibid.*, pp. 24, 26.
28. Iqbal, *The Reconstruction*, p. 50.

29. Iqbal, *Asrār-i Khudi*, pp. 82, 83.
30. Iqbal, *The Reconstruction*, pp. 52–53.
31. Nicholson, *The Secrets of the Self*, pp. 23, 24.
32. *Ibid.*, pp. 25, 26.
33. Iqbal, *The Reconstruction*, pp. 60–61.
34. Nicholson, *The Secrets of the Self*, see pp. xvii–xix.
35. Iqbal, *The Reconstruction*, p. 184.
36. Friedrich Nietzsche, *Thus Spake Zarathustra* (New York, MacMillan, 1911), p. 263.
37. *Ibid.*, pp. 5, 8, 11, 79–80, 108, 419.
38. George Allen Morgan, *What Nietzsche Means* (New York, 1941), p. 53.
39. Iqbal, *Javid-Namah*, p. 177.
40. Morgan, *What Nietzsche Means*, p. 11.
41. Nietzsche, *Thus Spake Zarathustra*, p. 66.
42. Morgan, *What Nietzsche Means*, p. 179.
43. Iqbal, *Bāng-i Dara*, p. 140.
44. Iqbal, *Pas Chā Bayad Kard*, pp. 26–27; *Ḍarb-i Kalīm*, p. 47; Badr and Hunain were the two famous battles fought by the early Muslims under the guidance of the Prophet Muhammad. Hussain, son of Ali, was the grandson of the Prophet, who is the martyr of Islam.
45. Iqbal, *Pas Chā Bayad Kard*, pp. 20–21.
46. Iqbal, *Ḍarb-i Kalīm*, pp. 60–61.
47. Iqbal, *Javid-Namah*, pp. 146–50.

# CHAPTER 10

1. Iqbal to Sirāj-ud-Din Paul, July 10, 1916, in Allah, *Iqbal Nama*, I, 34.
2. *Ibid.*, p. 35.
3. Quoted in Vahid, *Thoughts and Reflections of Iqbal*, pp. 101–2.
4. Iqbal to Akbar Allahabadi, June 11, 1918; and to Sulaiman Nadwi, February 1, 1924, in Allah, *Iqbal Nama*, I, 50, 128.
5. For a classical representation of this image, see *Lam'āt-i Iraqi* in Fakhr-ud-Din Iraqi's *Kulliyāt*, ed. by Sa'īd Nafīsī (Tehran, Kutab Khana Sanai, 1338 Fasli), pp. 388–409.
6. K. Bader, "The Development of Religious Thought in India," *Iqbal* (Lahore), July 1964, p. 42.
7. For metaphysical details, see Shaikh Ibrahīm Gazur-i-Ilahi, *The Secret of Anāl Haqq*, trans. into English by Khajan Khan (Lahore, Ashraf, 1965), pp. 34–48.
8. Asadūllah Khan Ghālib, *Kulliyāt-i Ghālib* (Lucknow, Nol Kishore Press, 1925), pp. 103–5.
9. Cf. Khalifah A. Hakīm, "Religion and Symbolism" (Unpublished Ms., Iqbal Academy, Karachi, Pakistan), p. 15.
10. Azīz Ahmad, *Studies in Islamic Culture in the Indian Environment* (Oxford, 1964), p. 231.

11. 'Abdūl Qādir Ali of Cairo ed., *Rasā'il al-Junayd* (London, Luzac, 1962), p. 100 ff.
12. Ahmad, *The Pilgrimage of Eternity* [trans. of Iqbal's *Jāvid-Nāmah*] pp. 118–20.
13. Quoted in A. J. Arberry, *Sufism* (London, George Allan & Unwin, 1950), p. 59.
14. Shahab-al-Din Suhurwardi, *Hikmat al-Ishrāq*, trans. into Urdu by Mirza Hadi Ruswā (Hyderabad-Deccan, Osmania University Translation Bureau, 1925), pp. 14–36.
15. *Ibid.*, p. 143 ff.
16. *Ibid.*, pp. 20–36.
17. *Ibid.*, pp. 244–49.
18. Iqbal, *The Development of Metaphysics in Persia* (1964), p. 117 ff.
19. 'Abdūl Karīm al-Jili, *Insān-i Kāmil*, trans. into Urdu by Fazl Miran (Gujrat, West Pakistan, 1908), p. 90.
20. *Ibid.*, p. 92.
21. Iqbal, *The Reconstruction*, (1951), p. 164.
22. *Ibid.*, pp. 164–65.
23. *Ibid.*, p. 184.
24. *Ibid.*, p. 185.
25. *Ibid.*, p. 48.
26. Sohail A. Afnan, *Avicenna, His Life and Works* (London, George Allen & Unwin, 1958), pp. 212–13.
27. Iqbal, *The Reconstruction*, p. 51.
28. M. M. Sharif, *Muslim Thought: Its Origin and Achievement* (Lahore, Ashraf, 1951), p. 75.
29. Abū Hamid al-Ghazzali, *Tehafat al-Falasifa*, trans. into English by S. A. Kamali (Lahore, Pakistan Philosophical Congress, 1963), p. 88.
30. Iqbal, *The Reconstruction*, p. 64.
31. *Ibid.*, p. 71.
32. Khawaja Mīr Dard, *'Ilm al-Kitāb* (Delhi, Matba -i Ansari, 1883), pp. 301–5.
33. Jalāl-ud-Din Rumi, *Diwān Shamsi-i-Tabriz*, trans. by R. A. Nicholson (Cambridge, University Press, 1952).
34. Khalifa A. Hakīm, *Metaphysics of Rumi* (Lahore, Institute of Islamic Culture, 1959), pp. 36–37.
35. *Ibid.*, pp. 37–38.
36. Iqbal, *The Reconstruction*, p. 119.
37. Dar, *Iqbal's "Gulshan-i Rāz-i Jadīd,"* pp. 30–31.
38. Shaikh Ahmad Sarhindi, *Maktūbāt* (Amritsar, 1911), Letter No. 253.
39. *Ibid.*, Letter Nos. 38, 39, 66, 77, and 253.
40. Dar, *Iqbal's "Gulshan-i Rāz-i Jadīd,"* pp. 36–37.

# CHAPTER 11

1. This judgment on Shah Waliullah's inability to appreciate history as a category of thought is not shared by other scholars; however, (it must be admitted), not enough investigative work has been done on this aspect of Shah Waliullah's thought.

Cf. A. J. Halepote, *Philosophy of Shah Waliullah* (Lahore, University of the Punjab Press, 1956; for limited use only); Sbih Ahmad Kamali, "The Concept of Human Nature in *Hujjatullah Balighah*" (Ph.D. dissertation, Institute of Islamic Studies, McGill University, 1959); Sbih Ahmad Kamali, "Hikmat-i Waliullahi Meiñ Tarīkh Kā Martabah," *Islamia 'Ulūm Majalhā* (Aligarh), June and December 1963; also, Hafeez Malik, *Shah Waliullah and the Muslim Renaissance in India* (a forthcoming study).

2. Iqbal, *The Reconstruction* (1958), p. 6.
3. R. G. Collingwood, *The Idea of Nature* (Oxford, University Press, 1957), p. 74.
4. John F. Callahan, *Four Views of Time in Ancient Philosophy* (Cambridge, Mass., Harvard University Press, 1948), p. 87.
5. Majid Fakhri, *Islamic Occasionalism* (London, George Allen & Unwin, 1958), p. 27.
6. *Ibid.*, pp. 27–28.
7. Abu Bakr Muhammad ibn-Zakariyā al-Razi, *Kitāb al-Mabahith al-Mashrīqyā* (Hyderabad-Deccan, Majlis Da'rat al-Ma'rif al-Nizamīya, 1943), Vol. I, Part II, p. 648.
8. M. F. Cleugh, *Time and Its Importance in Modern Thought* (London, Methuen, 1937), p. 160 ff.
9. Bertrand Russell, *Our Knowledge of the External World* (London, George Allen & Unwin, 1952), p. 171.
10. Errol E. Harris, *Nature, Mind and Modern Science* (London, George Allen & Unwin, 1954), p. 390.
11. Iqbal, "Haqīqat-i Hussan," in *Bāng-i Dara*.
12. *Ibid.*
13. Iqbal, *Payām-i Mashriq* (1958), pp. 102–3.
14. Iqbal, *Javid-Namah* (1959), pp. 21–22.
15. Iqbal, *Bāl-i Jibrīl* (1964), pp. 126–36.
16. Iqbal, *The Reconstruction*. See the sixth lecture, "The Principle of Movement in the Structure of Islam," pp. 146–80.
17. Iqbal, *The Reconstruction*, p. 147.
18. Joseph Alexander Leighton, *Man and Cosmos* (New York, Appleton, Century, 1922), pp. 236–37.
19. Collingwood, *The Idea of Nature*, p. 140; Iqbal, *The Reconstruction*, p. 53.
20. F. S. C. Northrop and Mason W. Gross, eds., *The Adventure of Ideas* (New York, 1953), p. 249.
21. Cleugh, *Time and Its Importance in Modern Thought*, p. 28.
22. Henri Bergson, *Creative Evolution*, trans. by Arthur Mitchell (New York, Modern Library, 1944), Chap. 4, pp. 357–75.
23. Iqbal, *The Reconstruction*, p. 66.
24. Collingwood, *The Idea of Nature*, p. 140.
25. *Ibid.*, p. 141.
26. Iqbal, *The Reconstruction*, p. 73.
27. *Ibid.*, p. 106.
28. *Ibid.*, p. 55.

29. Alfred North Whitehead, *The Concept of Nature* (New York, 1920), p. 148.
30. *Ibid.*, p. 149.
31. Iqbal, *The Reconstruction*, p. 54.
32. *Ibid.*, p. 56.
33. *Ibid.*, p. 55.
34. *Ibid.*, p. 57.
35. *Ibid.*, p. 57.
36. *Ibid.*, p. 46.
37. *Ibid.*, p. 56.
38. *Ibid.*, pp. 56–57.
39. *Ibid.*, pp. 50–51.
40. *Ibid.*, p. 79.
41. *Ibid.*, p. 80.
42. Iqbal, *Ḍarb-i Kalīm* (1959), p. 7.
43. Iqbal, *The Reconstruction*, p. 65.
44. Whitehead, *The Concept of Nature*, p. 200.
45. Iqbal, *The Reconstruction*, p. 65.
46. Whitehead, *The Concept of Nature*, p. 244.

## CHAPTER 12

1. Nicholson, *The Secrets of the Self*, (1955), p. xxii.
2. *Ibid.*, pp. xviii–xix.
3. *Ibid.*, p. xviii.
4. *Ibid.*, p. xvii.
5. Iqbal, *The Reconstruction of Religious Thought in Islam* (1954), p. 72.
6. Nicholson, *The Secrets of the Self*, p. xix.
7. *Ibid.*, p. 27.
8. *Ibid.*, p. xxv.
9. Iqbal, *The Reconstruction*, p. 198.
10. Iqbal, *Payām-i Mashriq* (1954), p. 150.
11. Iqbal, *Ḍarb-i Kalīm* (1954), p. 39.
12. Nicholson, *The Secrets of the Self*, pp. xxiii, 57–58.
13. *Ibid.*, pp. 39, 40, 41–42.
14. Iqbal, *Payām-i Mashriq*, pp. 97–101.
15. Nicholson, *The Secrets of the Self*, p. xx.
16. See, for example, P. T. Raju, *Idealistic Thought of India* (London, 1953), p. 393.
17. Iqbal, *Payām-i Mashriq*, p. 241.
18. Iqbal, *Asrār-o-Ramūz* (Lahore, 1948), p. 99.
19. *Ibid.*, pp. 97, 98, 99.
20. Iqbal, *The Reconstruction*, pp. 12, 112.
21. *Ibid.*
22. Iqbal, *Payām-i Mashriq*, p. 132.

23. Iqbal, *Bāng-i-Dara* (1953), p. 150.
24. Kiernan, *Poems from Iqbal* (1955), pp. 42–43.
25. Iqbal, *The Reconstruction*, p. 155.
26. *Ibid.*, p. 157.
27. Iqbal, *Javid-Namah*, pp. 88, 120–122.
28. Iqbal, *The Reconstruction*, p. 188.
29. *Ibid.*, p. 147.
30. *Ibid.*, p. 91.
31. *Ibid.*, p. 6.
32. *Ibid.*, pp. 18–19, 31.
33. *Ibid.*, pp. 55, 106–7.
34. *Ibid.*, p. 55.
35. *Ibid.*, p. 106.
36. *Ibid.*, pp. 14–15.
37. Singh, *The Ardent Pilgrim*, p. 156.
38. *Ibid.*, p. 233.

# CHAPTER 13

1. In his *mathnawi Asrār-i Khudi*, Iqbal indicted Hāfiz and other Sufis for creating a spiritual malaise in the Muslim world. Iqbal attributed the lack of zest for life in the East to the spread of Sufism (mysticism) among the Muslims. In order to appreciate Iqbal's reasons for criticizing Sufism, it is necessary to know its history, its schools of interpretation, and the manner in which it spread (particularly the W*ahdat al-Wujūd* variety) to India. The first part of this chapter deals primarily with the genesis of Sufism, and the second part highlights Iqbal's attitude toward it.
2. Quasem Ghani, *Tarikh-i-Tasawwaf Der Islam* (Tehran, 1322 A.H.), pp. 105–7.
3. 'Abdūr Rahmān Jami, *Nahfat al-Uns* (Lucknow, 1915), p. 33.
4. Mustafa Halīm Pasha, *Tarikh-i-Tasawwaf-i Islam*, trans. by Ra'īs Ahmad J'affri (Lahore, 1950), p. 122.
5. Arberry, *Sufism*, pp. 52–53.
6. *Ibid.*, p. 55.
7. Farīd-ud-Din 'Attār, *Tadhkirah al-Awliyā* (Bombay, n.d.), p. 101.
8. For the ideas of al-Hallaj and his impact on Iqbal, see Professor Annemarie Schimmel's chapter, pp. 310–324.
9. Nicholson, *The Secrets of the Self* (1960), pp. 51–52, 56–57.
10. Khāwja Hāfiz, *Diwān-i Hāfiz*, compiled by Muhammad Qazvini and Quasem Ghani (Tehran, 1941), pp. 52, 174, 297.
11. Iqbal, *Rakht-i-Safar*, compiled by Muhammad Anwar Harith, pp. 117–119.
12. Khalifah 'Abdūl Hakīm, *Urdu* (New Delhi), Iqbal number, October 1938, p. 824.
13. Arberry, *Persian Psalms* (1951), p. 69.
14. Jalāl-ud-Din Rumi, *Mathnawi* (Tehran, 1897–1901), Vol. VI, p. 375, line 2;

Irawu, *Kulliyat* (Kannpur, 1909), p. 197; Sayyid Safi Haider, *Tasawwaf Awr Urdu Sha'iri* (Lahore, 1948), pp. 126, 139.

15. Iqbal, "Daybachah: *Asrār-i Khudi*," in Tasadaq Husain Tāj, ed., *Muḍamīn-i-Iqbal* (Hyderabad-Deccan, 1943), pp. 48, 53.
16. Iqbal, *Bāl-i Jibrīl*, p. 44; the poet alludes to the Qur'ānic phrase "Kunfā Yakūn," "[God said] Be and it was."
17. Kiernan, *Poems from Iqbal* (1955), p. 94.
18. *Ibid.*, p. 38.
19. Qur'ān, xviii, 110.

## CHAPTER 14

1. Iqbal, *The Reconstruction*, p. 2.
2. *Ibid.*, p. 183.
3. *Ibid.*, p. vi.
4. *Ibid.*, p. 196; Vahid, *Iqbal, His Art and Thought* (1959), p. 76.
5. Iqbal, *The Reconstruction*, p. 198.
6. *Ibid.*
7. *Ibid.*, p. 8.
8. E. G. Browne, *A Literary History of Persia* (Cambridge, 1924), IV, 41; Radhakrishnan, *History of Philosophy: Eastern and Western*, I, 512; Raju, *Idealistic Thought of India*, p. 393.
9. Vahid, *Iqbal, His Art and Thought*, p. 97.
10. Iqbal, *The Reconstruction*, p. 195.
11. *Ibid.*, p. 72.
12. *Ibid.*, p. 70.
13. *Ibid.*, p. 71.
14. *Ibid.*, p. 72.
15. *Ibid.*
16. *Ibid.*, p. 5.
17. *Ibid.*, pp. 2–3.
18. Kiernan, *Poems from Iqbal*, pp. 93–94.
19. Iqbal, *The Reconstruction*, p. 84.
20. *Ibid.*, p. 85.

## CHAPTER 15

1. *Zindīq* is a convenient portmanteau term of abuse used by the Muslim zealots to cover a multitude of suspected heresies. Asadūllah Khan Ghālib (d. 1869) was a famous Urdu-Persian lyrical poet of India. Qurat-ul-'Ain Tahira belonged to the Babi sect and was killed by the Persian orthodoxy in 1822. She is one of the best poetesses of Iran.
2. For the life and ideas of these Sufis, see Arberry, *Sufism*, pp. 31–63.
3. "This name was given to the rebel federation of Arabs and Nabataean peasants,

which were organized in Lower Mesopotamia after the . . . war of the Zandj (877). These federations were based on a system of Communism in which initiation was necessary. This political movement was eventually captured by an ambitious family, the Isma'ili dynasty, which founded the Fatimid Anti-Caliphate in 910. Finally the Karmatian movement succumbed with the Isma'ili dynasty before the counter-stroke of the crusades." For further details, see "Karmatians," in M. Th. Houtsma et al., eds., *The Encyclopedia of Islam* (London, Luzac, 1927), II, 767. See also Hitti, *History of the Arabs*, pp. 444-45.

4. At Hallaj's trial, the prosecution insisted that he should be tried for including the pilgrimage to Mecca among the class of religious obligations that are not binding. This doctrine, together with the charge that he was in secret correspondence with the Karmatians, may have cost him his life. The fact that he declared himself to be essentially united with God was only one of the four heads under which he was arraigned. By itself, it might not have secured his condemnation, although his ideas were generally abominable to Muslim orthodoxy. An account of the trial, condemnation, and execution of Hallaj is given by Miskawaihi, ed., *Amedioz and Margoliouth*, I, 76-82. See also Reynold A. Nicholson, *The Idea of Personality in Sufism* (Cambridge, University Press, 1923), pp. 27-28.

5. Annemarie Schimmel, ed. and trans., *The Sirah of Ibn al-Khafif* (Ankara, 1955).

6. R. A. Nicholson, *Commentary of the Mathnawi*, Gibb Memorial Series, New Series, Vol. VII (London, 1925).

7. 'Attār, *Tadhkirah al-Awliyā*, ed. and trans. by R. A. Nicholson (London, 1904), II, 143.

8. The writer has tried to show elsewhere how Hallaj has become the hero of Sindh mystical folk poetry (*Numen*, IX, 1932).

9. Iqbal, *The Development of Metaphysics in Persia* (1959), p. 89.

10. Hindu sacred literature includes different types, namely the *Samhita* or collection of verses (*Sam*, together, *hita*, put; they are *Rig-Vida*, *Sama-Veda*, *Yajur-Veda*, and *Atharva-Veda*), *Brahmanas*, *Aranyakas*, and the *Upanishads*. According to Hindu belief, the Vedas "were revealed as commandments and prohibitions to show the true path of happiness. The *Upanishads* only revealed the ultimate truth and reality, a knowledge of which at once emancipates a man." The *Upanishads* are also known by another name, *Vedanta*, as they are believed to be the last portions of the *Vedas* (*Veda* + *anta*, end). More than 200 *Upanishads* are said to have been composed, although the earliest (no more than 13) were composed by 500 B.C. They continued to be written during Muslim rule in India. In 1917, 112 *Upanishads* were published by the Nirnaya-Sagara Press in Bombay.

Shankara, the celebrated exponent of Vedanta philosophy, was born between 700 and 800 A.D. in the Malabar country in the Deccan, India. His main works are his *Bhasya* (Commentaries) on the ten *Upanishads* (i.e., *Isa*, *Kena*, *Katha*, *Prasna*, *Mundaka*, *Mandukya*, *Aitareya*, *Taittiriya*, *Brhadaranyaka*, and *Chandogya*), and on the Brahma-Sutra. In the words of Dasgupta, the main idea of the *advaita* (non dualistic) Vedanta philosophy as taught by the Shankara school is that "the ultimate and absolute truth is the Self, which is one, though appearing as many in different individuals. The World, also apart from us the individuals, has no reality and has no other truth to show than this Self—*Vedanta* sought to reach beneath the surface of appearances, and inquired after the final and ultimate truth underlying the microcosm and the macrocosm, the subject and the object." For a detailed discussion of Vedanta philosophy, see Dasgupta, *A History of Indian Philosophy*, pp. 13, 28-30, 439 ff; see also Arthur A. MacDonell, *A History of Sanskrit Literature* (London, William Heinemann, 1905), pp. 385-407.

11. *Tawāsin* is the plural of *Tasin*, the mysterious letters at the beginning of Suras XXVI, XXVII, and XXVIII.

12. See Hosayn ibn Mansour al-Hallaj, *Kitāb al-Tawāsin*, ed. and trans. by Louis Massignon, (Paris, 1914), pp. 129 ff.

13. Ahmad, *The Pilgrimage of Eternity* [Iqbal's *Javid-Namah*], p. 113. See also the more philological translation by A. J. Arberry, *Javidnama* (London, 1966).

14. The most touching story explaining the identity of love and suffering is described by Farīd-ud-Din 'Attār: "They asked Hallaj: 'What is love?' He answered: 'You will see it today and tomorrow and the day after tomorrow.' That day they cut off his hands and feet, the next day they killed him, and the third day they gave his dust unto the wind . . . ." 'Attār, *Tadhkirah al-Awliya*, II, 142.

15. Muslims believe that the Qur'ān and Islamic theology are the summation of religious law and experience. Their original contribution, therefore, was made in the borderland between philosophy and religion on one hand and philosophy and medicine on the other. In the course of time Muslim authors came to apply the word *falasifah* or *hukamā* (philosophers or sages) to those philosophers among them whose speculations were not limited by religion, reserving the term *Mutakallimūn* or *ahl al-Kalām* (speechmakers, dialecticians) for those whose system was conditioned by subordination to revealed religion. *Kalām* slowly came to mean theology and *Mutakallim* became a synonym for theologian. For Muslim philosophy, see Y. J. De Boer, *The History of Philosophy in Islam*, trans. by Edward R. Jones (London, Luzac, 1961), and 'Abdus Salām Nadvi, *Hukamā-i Islam*, 2 vols. (Azamgarh, 1953-1956).

16. Iqbal, *The Reconstruction of Religious Thought in Islam* (1958), p. 96.

17. Shamloo, *Speeches and Statements of Iqbal*, p. 152.

18. Iqbal, *The Reconstruction*, p. 110.

19. Ahmad, *Pilgrimage of Eternity*, p. 125.

20. "I take refuge in Allah from the accursed devil."

21. "In the name of Allah, the merciful, the compassionate."

22. "My curse shall be upon you until the Day of Judgment" (Sura, XXXVIII, 78).

23. In these verses Iqbal is faithful to the spirit of the *Kitāb al-Tawāsin*.

24. *Ibid.*

25. Ahmad, *Pilgrimage of Eternity*, pp. 139-40.

26. *Ibid.*, pp. 115-16.

## CHAPTER 16

1. Iqbal, "Gulshan-i Rāz-i Jadīd," in *Zabūr-i 'Ajam* (1958), p. 224. All quotations in this chapter have been translated by the author.

2. *Ibid.*, p. 243.
3. *Ibid.*, pp. 231–32.
4. *Ibid.*, p. 222.
5. *Ibid.*, p. 205.
6. Iqbal, "Bandagi Namah," in *Zabūr-i 'Ajam*, pp. 263–64.
7. *Ibid.*, p. 255.
8. Two idols in the Ka'bah at Mecca, which were worshipped by the Arabs before the advent of Islam. For detailed information about their origin, see Hitti, *History of the Arabs*, pp. 98–99.
9. Iqbal, "Bandagi Namah," p. 256.
10. Iqbal, *Asrār-i Khudi* (1959), pp. 4–6.
11. Iqbal, "Gulshan-i Rāz-i Jadīd," p. 204.
12. Iqbal, *Asrāri- Khudi*, pp. 39–40.
13. Iqbal, "Bandagi Namah," p. 254.
14. Iqbal, *Asrār-i Khudi*, pp. 34–35.
15. *Ibid.*, pp. 37–38.
16. Iqbal, "Bandagi Namah," p. 264.
17. Thomas Carlyle, *The Hero as Poet* (London, Oxford University Press, 1940), pp. 254–99.
18. Percy Bysshe Shelley, *A Defence of Poetry* (New York, 1965), pp. 31, 32, 70, 75, 80.

# CHAPTER 17

1. Stopford A. Brooke, *Theology in the English Poets* (London, J. M. Dent, 1926), p. 83.
2. Walter Raleigh, *Wordsworth* (London, E. Arnold, 1937), p. 185.
3. Sir Thomas Browne, *Religio Medici*, Letter XVI.
4. Norman Lacey, *Wordsworth's View of Nature* (Cambridge, University Press, 1948), p. 50 ff.
5. J. Iqbal, *Stray Reflections*, p. 54.
6. Francis Durham Grierson and J. C. Smith, *A Critical History of English Poetry* (London, Chatto & Windus, 1945), p. 160.
7. *Ibid.*, p. 158.
8. B. Rajan, *"Paradise Lost" and the Twentieth-Century Reader* (London, Chatto & Windus, 1950), p. 13.
9. Iqbal, *The Reconstruction of Religious Thought in Islam* (1958), p. 76.
10. *Ibid.*, p. 80.
11. Iqbal, *Payām-i Mashriq*, p. 150.
12. *Ibid.*, p. 152.
13. E. A. Bowering, *The Poems of Goethe Translated in the Original Metre* (London, George Bell, 1881), p. 167.
14. *Ibid.*, p. 383.
15. *Ibid.*, p. 386.

## Notes: Chapter 17

16. Iqbal, *Payām-i Mashriq*, p. k.
17. L. Willoughby, *The Romantic Movement in Germany* (London, Oxford University Press, 1930), p. 1.
18. Iqbal, *The Reconstruction*, p. 7.
19. This translation, as well as translations of other extracts from Goethe's *Faust*, are by Louis MacNiece (London, Faber & Faber, 1949).
20. Iqbal, *The Reconstruction*, p. 81.
21. Iqbal, *The Reconstruction*, p. 8.
22. *Ibid.*, p. 84.
23. Michele Barbi, *Life of Dante*, trans. and ed. by P. G. Ruggiers (Berkeley, University of California Press, 1954), pp. 17-19.
24. H. A. L. Fisher, *A History of Europe* (London, E. Arnold, 1935), p. 285.
25. Miguel Asín, *Islam and the Divine Comedy*, trans. and abr. by Harold Sunderland (London, John Murray, 1932), p. xiv.
26. *Ibid.*, p. xv.
27. Translations of all extracts from Dante's *Divine Comedy* are by Laurence Binyon in *The Portable Dante* (New York, Viking, 1947).
28. Iqbal, *The Reconstruction*, p. 116.
29. Fisher, *A History of Europe*, p. 285.
30. Grierson and Smith, *A Critical History of English Poetry*, p. 220.

# Selected Bibliography

## HAFEEZ MALIK

THE bibliography consists of two parts: the first part (Works by Iqbal) contains Iqbal's prose and poetry arranged chronologically and indicated by roman numerals, under each of which are listed commentaries, translations, and critical studies by other scholars in various languages; a subsection within this part lists all the articles Iqbal has published in both Urdu and English.

The second part contains general and specialized works on Iqbal in all those languages in which significant studies on his philosophy and poetry have appeared. For each item an attempt has been made to supply an adequate bibliographical reference—the name of the author, the title of the study, the name and place of the publisher, and the year of publication. However, this was not possible in all cases, because the publishers in certain countries are not careful about these essentials. If the study offers meaningful insights it has been included even though a full citation could not be given.

In preparing this bibliography I consulted three bibliographies and included several items from each. *Iqbaliyāt Kā Tanqīdi Ja'izā*, by Qaḍi Ahmad Miañ Akhtar (Karachi, 1955), the most comprehensive and critical bibliographical study yet to appear in Urdu, is the bane of the meticulous scholar and librarian. It often fails to mention the full name of the authors, the title of the studies, and other relevant information necessary for reference and cataloguing. However, the two other annotated bibliographies in English supply much of the information missing from Akhtar's bibliography: *Bibliography of Iqbal*, by 'Abdul Ghani and Khawja Nūr Ilahi (Lahore: Bazm-i Iqbal, 1955), and *Gabriel's Wing*, by Annemarie Schimmel (Leiden: E. J. Brill, 1963), pp. 388-414.

## WORKS BY IQBAL AND THEIR COMMENTARIES

### BOOKS

I. *The Development of Metaphysics in Iran*. Cambridge: University Press, 1908. Originally a Ph.D. dissertation submitted to Munich University.

Iqbal, Muhammad. *The Development of Metaphysics in Persia*. Lahore: Bazm-i Iqbal, 1959, 1964.

II. *Asrār-i Khudi* (Persian Mathnavi). Lahore: Ghulam Ali, 1915, 1959.

Ahmad, Pīrzade Muzaffar. *Rāz-i Bekhudi*. Delhi, 1918. Critical of Iqbal. For a rebuttal of Ahmad's arguments against Iqbal, see Maulana Aslam Jairajpuri's article in the monthly *Al-Nāzir* (Lucknow), February, 1919, reprinted in *The Jauhar*, Iqbal number (Delhi: Jamia Milia).

Ahsan, Syed Ali. Bengali verse translation. Dacca, n.d.

Arberry, A. J. *Notes on Iqbal's "Asrār-i Khudi."* Lahore, 1955.

Azzam, 'Abdūl Wahhab. Arabic verse translation. Karachi: Iqbal Academy, n.d.

Chishti, Yusūf Salīm. *Sharh-i Asrār-i Khudi*. Lahore, n.d.

Enver, Ishrat H. *Mathnawi Surūd-i Bekhudi*. Aligarh, 1954. A reply to Iqbal's philosophy of *khudi*.

Fazil, 'Abdūr Rashīd and Sayyid Muhammad. *Tarjumān-i Khudi* (Urdu translation in verse). Karachi, 1956.

Khan, Samandār. Baluchi translation. Karachi, n.d.

Mannan, Sayyid 'Abdūl. Bengali prose translation. Dacca, n.d.

Na'im ur-Rahmān, M. "*Asrār-i Khudi*, or *The Secrets of the Self*," *Indian Review* (Madras), XXII (1921).

Nicholson, R. A. "*The Secrets of the Self*: A Muslim Poet's Interpretation of Vitalism," *The Quest*, July 1920.

Nicholson, Reynold A. *The Secrets of the Self*. Lahore: Muhammad Ashraf, 1944, 1955, 1960, 1961.

Qurashi, Muhammad 'Abdūllah. *Ma'raka-i Asrār-i Khudi* [The Struggle about the *Asrār-i Khudi*]. Lahore: Bazm-i Iqbal, n.d.

Rahman, S. 'Abdūr. *Tarjumān-i Asrār* (Urdu translation in verse). Lahore, 1952.

Tarlan, Ali Nihat. *Esrar ve Rumuz* (Turkish translation). Istanbul, 1958.

Venkata Rao, P. K. "The Secrets of the Self: A Study of Iqbal's Poem *Asrār-i Khudi*," *Triveni* (Bangalore), XIV (1942).

Wasif, Muhammad Bakhsh. Sindhi verse translation. Karachi, n.d.

III. *Ramūz-i-Bekhudi* (Persian Mathwani). Lahore, 1918, 1959.

Ahmad, Admuddin. Bengali translation. Shantiniketan, n.d.

Arberry, A. J. *The Mysteries of Selflessness* (English verse translation). London: John Murray, 1953.

Bajnuri, 'Abdūr Rahmān. "The *Asrār* and *Rumūz*," *East and West*, August 1931. Urdu translation of both appears in *Nayrang-i Khayāl* (Lahore), Iqbal number (September–October, 1932).

"Freedom of Man," *Thought* (Delhi), February 1950.

Kakawi, Arshad. "From Self to Selflessness," *Iqbal* (Lahore), October 1960.

Khan, Samandār. Baluchi translation. Karachi, n.d.

Osman, Professor Mohammad. *Asrar O Rumūz par Nazar*. Karachi: Iqbal Academy, 1961.

Tarlan, Ali Nihat. Turkish prose translation. Istanbul, 1958.
Wasif, Muhammad Bakhsh. Sindhi translation. Karachi, n.d.

IV, *Payām-i Mashriq* (Persian). Lahore, 1923. 1954, 1958.

Arberry, A. J. *The Tulip of Sinai*. London: The Royal India Society, 1947.
Azzam, 'Abdūl Wahhab. Arabic verse translation. Karachi: Majlis-i Iqbal, n.d.
Bara, Kalam-ud-Din. *Payām-i Aftab*. Amritsar, 1923. Critical of Iqbal.
Mainosh, Sher Muhammad. Pashto translation. Karachi: Iqbal Academy, 1962.
Marek, Jan *Poselsti z vychodu*. Prague, 1960. Czech translation of selected poems with illustrations.
Meyerovitch, E., and Mohammad Achena. *Message de l'Orient* (French prose translation). Paris, 1956.
Nicholson, R. A. "The Message of the East," *Islamica*, I (1925). Urdu translation of this article in *Nayrang-i Khayāl* (Lahore), Iqbal number (1925).
Sarkosh, Sher Ali Khan. *Jam-i Mashriq Mulakhas Payām-i Mashriq* (Urdu translation in verse of "Dedication"). Lahore, 1923.
Schimmel, Annemarie. *Botschaft des Ostens* (German verse translation). Wiesbaden, 1963.
Tāriq, 'Abdūr Rahmān. *Ruh-i Mashriq* (Urdu verse translation). Lahore, 1952.
Tarlan, Ali Nihat. *Sarktan Haber* (Turkish prose translation). Ankara, 1956.

V. *Bāng-i-Dara* (Urdu). Lahore, 1924, 1946, 1953.

Arberry, A. J. *Complaint and Answer* (English verse translation). Lahore, 1955.
Bannerth, E. "Islam in Modern Urdu Poetry," *Anthropos*, XXXVII–XL (1942–1945). A translation of Iqbal's *Shikwah* and *Jawab-i Shikwah*.
Husain, Altaf, *The Complaint and the Answer*. Lahore, 1943.
Muhammad, Sultan. *The Complaint and Answer* (Bengali translation). Rangpur, 1959.
Niaz, A. Q. *Khizr-i-Rah*. Lahore, 1951. Translation of selected poems.
Mustafa, Kavi Ghulam. Bengali translation. Dacca, 1961.
Zakheli, Rahat. Pashto translation. Karachi: Iqbal Academy, n.d. The only complete translation of the book.

VI. *Zabūr-i 'Ajam* (Persian). Lahore, 1927, 1948, 1958.

Arberry, A. J. *Persian Psalms*, Parts I and II (English verse translation). Lahore, 1948, 1951, 1961.
Bausani, A. "Il Gulsan-i Rāz-i Gadidid Muhammad Iqbal," *Ann. dell' Istituto Univ. Orienti di Napoli*, New Series VIII (1959).
Dar, B. A. "Gulshan-i Rāz-i Jadīd," *Iqbal* (Lahore), IV (1957).
Kakakhel, Sayyid Taqwimul Haq. Pashto translation. Karachi: Iqbal Academy, 1961.
Mundai, Sayyid 'Azīmuddin. Gujrati translation. Karachi: Iqbal Academy, 1960.

VII. *Six Lectures on the Reconstruction of Religious Thought in Islam.* Lahore, 1930.

Haq, 'Abdūl. Bengali translation published serially in the *Massik Muhammadi. Iqbal Review* (Dacca), April, 1960.

Iqbal, Muhammad. *The Reconstruction of Religious Thought in Islam* (with an added seventh chapter "Is Religion Possible?"). London, 1934. Lahore: Muhammad Ashraf, 1951, 1954, 1958.

Mas'ūd, Akhtar. "Islami tamaddun ki Ruh" (Urdu translation of the fifth lecture). *Chatān* (Lahore), II (April 25, 1949), 15.

Meyerovitch, E. *Reconstruire la pensée religieuse de l'Islam.* Paris, 1955.

"Mutala-'a-i Qanūn-i Islami." (Urdu translation of the sixth lecture). *Chiragh-i Rah* (Karachi), XII (September–October 1958), 7.

Niāzi, S. Nazīr. *Tashkīl-i Jadīd-i ilahiyāt-i Islamiyā* (Urdu translation). Lahore, 1958.

VIII. *Javid-Namah* (Persian). Lahore, 1932, 1959.

Ahmad, Shaikh Mahmud. "Invocation," *Islamic Culture* (Hyderabad-Deccan), 1948. English translation of the first twenty-five pages of *Javid-Namah.*

———. *The Pilgrimage of Eternity* (English verse translation). Lahore, 1961. Foreword by S. A. Rahman.

Badawi, Lutfullah. Sindhi translation. Karachi: Iqbal Academy, 1962.

Bausani, A. *Il Poema celeste.* Rome: Istituto per il medio ed Estremo Oriente, 1952.

Hamza, Amīr. Pashto translation, Karachi: Iqbal Academy, 1962.

Meyerovitch, E., and Mohammad Mokri. *Le Livre de l'éternité* (French prose translation). Paris, 1962.

Schimmel, Annemarie. *Buch der Ewigkeit* (German verse translation). Munich, 1957.

———. *Gavidname* (Turkish prose translation with extensive commentary). Ankara, 1958.

———. "Einige Benerkungen zu Muhammad Iqbal's *Gavidname,*" *Die Welt des Orients,* 1959.

———. "Muhammad Iqbal: The Ascension of the Poet," *Die Welt des Islam* (Leiden), New Series III (1954).

———. "The *Javidname* in the Light of Comparative History of Religions," *Pakistan Quarterly* (Karachi), VI (n.d.), 4.

Vallino, M. "Recente Eco Indo-Persiana della *Divina Commedia:* Mohammad Iqbal," *Oriente Moderno,* XII (1932), 210–23. Translation of an article in the *Muslim Revival* (Lahore), I (June 1932), 183–200.

IX. *Pas Chā Bayad Kard Ay Aqwām-i Sharq* (Persian). Lahore, 1936, 1958.

Siddiq, Zafar Ahmad. *Hikmat-i Kalīmi* (Urdu verse translation). Delhi, 1955. Compared in *Islamic Culture* (Hyderabad-Deccan) 1955, p. 235.

X. *Masafer* (Persian). Lahore, 1936, 1964.

XI. *Bāl-i Jibrīl* (Urdu). Lahore, 1936.

    Asīr, 'Abdūllah Jān. *Palwashe* (Pashto translation). Karachi, 1959.
    Kiernan, V. G. "The Mosque of Cordova," *Pakistan Quarterly* (Karachi), II (1952), 3.

XII. *Darb-i Kalīm* (Urdu). Lahore, 1936, 1954, 1958, 1959.

XIII. *Armaghān-i Hijaz* (Persian and Urdu). Lahore, 1938.

    Badawi, Lutfullah. Sindhi translation. Karachi: Iqbal Academy, 1959.
    Tāriq, 'Abdur Rahmān, *Rumuz-i Fitrat* (Urdu verse translation). Lahore, 1950.

*Collections of Iqbal's Unpublished or Dispersed Poems*

    Bausani, A. "Sette poesie inedite di Muhammad Iqbal," *Il Punto nelle lettere e nelle Arti* (Roma), II (1953), 3.
    Harith, Muhammad Anwar. *Rakht-i Safar*. Karachi, 1952. Reviewed by Azīz Ahmad in *Mah-i Nav* (Karachi), April 1952.
    Hyderabadi, 'Abdur Razzāq. *Kulliyāt-i Iqbal*. 1923. A Collection of Urdu poems published without the poet's permission.
    Iqbal, Muhammad. *Baqiyāt-i Iqbal*. Lahore: Nawa-i Waqt (Lahore), 1954.
    Mehr, Ghulamn Rasūl, and Sādiz Ali Dilawari, eds. *Sarūd-i Raftah*. Karachi, n.d. Lahore, Ghulam Ali, 1959.
    Vahid, S. A. *Baqiyāt-i Iqbal*. Lahore, 1954.

*Translations of Selected Poems*

    Ashraf, Muhammad. *The Devil's Conference*. Gujrat, 1951.
    Bausani, A. *Poesie di Muhammad Iqbal*, Parma, 1956.
    Faridi, Mugīth-ud-din. "Ma'arif-i Iqbal" (Lahore), Urdu verse translation of some of Iqbal's poems. *'Alamgīr*, Silver Jubilee number 1950.
    Kiernan, V. G. *Poems from Iqbal*. Bombay: Kutub, 1947. Translated from Urdu. Introduction by M. D. Taseer. Also: London: John Murray, 1955.
    Metzemakers, L. A. V. M. and Voten, Bert. *De Roep van de Karavan, Moehammad Iqbal, Dichter van Pakistan*. The Hague, 1956.
    Mustafa, Kavi Ghulam. *Kalām-i Iqbal*. Karachi: Iqbal Academy, n.d. A Bengali translation of some of Iqbal's poems.
    Nūraddin, Amīra. *Gems of Iqbal*. Baghdad, n.d.
    Rahmān, Mizānur. Bengali translations of *Shikwah*, poems from *Bāl-i Jibrīl*, and *Darb-i Kalīm*. Puthir, n.d.
    Rampuri, Shafāq. "Khitab ba Aqwam-i Sharq" (Urdu verse translation of Iqbal's poems), *Tazyana* (Lahore), February 25, 1929.
    Sorley, H. T. *Musa Pervagans*. Aberdeen, 1953.
    Taseer, M. D. "Musawat-i Islamiya," *Nayrang-i Khayāl, Salnamah* (Lahore), 1930. Urdu verse translation of Iqbal's *Hikayat-i Sultan Murād wa Miañ Mīr*.

## ARTICLES

"A Plea for Deeper Study of the Muslim Scientists," *Islamic Culture* (Hyderabad-Deccan), III (1929), 201–9.

"Doctrine of Absolute Unity As Explained by 'Abdūl Karīm al-Jilani," *Indian Antiquary* (Bombay), XXIX (1900). Reprinted in *Islamic Review*, May 1959.

*Iblīs Kī Majlis-i-Shūra*. Gujrat: Urdu House, 1951.

*'Ilm al-Iqtisād* [Economics]. Karachi: Iqbal Academy, 1901, 1961.

"Inner Synthesis of Life," *Indian Review*, (Madras), XXVII (1926).

*Iqbal Nama: Majmūa'-i-Makatīb-i-Iqbal* [Iqbal's letters], ed. by Shaikh 'Atta Allah. Lahore, 1951.

*Islam and Ahmadism*. Lahore: Iqbal Academy, 1945. Also published in *Islam* January 22, 1936.

"Islam and Khilafat," *Sociological Review* (London), 1980. Urdu trans. Ch. Muhammad Husain. Lahore, 1923. Reprinted in *Iqbal* (Lahore), IV (1956), 2.

"Islam as a Moral and Political Ideal," *Observer* (Lahore), April 14, 1909. Also in *Hindustan Review*, XX, 1909. Reissued with critical remarks by Hafiz Sarwar. Lahore, 1910.

"Is Religion Possible?" in *Proceedings of the Aristotelian Society*. London, 1932–1933. Reprinted as the last chapter of *The Reconstruction of Religious Thought since 1934*.

"Khushhal Khan Khatak: The Afghan Warrior Poet," *Islamic Culture* (Hyderabad-Deccan), 1928.

Iqbal to Dr. Nicholson, January 24, 1927. Reproduced in *Dawn*, April 21, 1949.

*Letters of Iqbal to Jinnah*. Lahore: Muhammad Ashraf, 1943, 1956, 1963.

"McTaggart's Philosophy," *Indian Art and Letters* (London), VI, 1932. Reproduced in *Truth* (Lahore), July 1937.

"Notes on Muslim Democracy," *The New Era* (Allahabad), 1916.

"On Corporeal Resurrection after Death," *Muslim Revival* (Lahore), September 1932. Reproduced in the *Civil and Military Gazette, Supplement* (Lahore), April 20, 1952.

"Our Prophet's Criticism of Contemporary Arabic Poetry," *The New Era* (Allahabad), 1915.

"Political Thought in Islam," *Hindustan Review*, December 1910, January 1911.

"Self in the Light of Relativity," *The Crescent* (Lahore), 1925. Reprinted in B. A. Dar, *A Study in Iqbal's Philosophy*. Lahore: Muhammad Ashraf, 1944.

"Urdu Zabān Panjab mein," *Makhzan* (Lahore), October 1902. Reprinted in *Maḍamīn-i Iqbal*, n.d.

## GENERAL AND SPECIALIZED WORKS ON IQBAL

Abdullah, Sayyid. "Iqbal Awr Siyasiyat," *Ma'arif* (Azamgarh), March–April 1946.

Abdullah, S. M. "Nachruf auf Iqbal," *Moslemische Revue* (Berlin), XIV (1938).

Ahmad, Azīz. *Iqbal and the Recent Exposition of Islamic Political Thought*. Lahore: Muhammad Ashraf, 1950.

———. "Iqbal et la théorie du Pakistan," *Orient*, V (1961), 1.
———. "Iqbal's Political Theory," *Thinker* (Lahore), 1944.
———. "Sources of Iqbal's Perfect Man," *Iqbal* (Lahore), July 1958.
Ahmad, Farosh. "Iqbal's Concept of Self and the Belief in the Hereafter," *Iqbal Review* (Karachi), January 1962.
Ahmad, Khurshid. "Iqbal and the Islamic Aims of Education," *Iqbal Review*, October 1961.
———. "Iqbal and the Reconstruction of Islamic Law," *Iqbal Review*, April 1960.
Ahmad, Mian Bashir. "Iqbal's Political Ideas," *Islamic Culture* (Hyderabad-Deccan), 1944.
———. "Rumi and Iqbal," *Islamic Review*, XL (1952).
Ahmad, M. M. "Iqbal's Appreciative Self," *Iqbal Review* (Karachi), October 1961.
Ahmad, Zia-ud-Din. "The Poet as a Political Thinker," *Dawn, Special Supplement*, April 21, 1950, pp. 10, 11.
Ahsan, 'Abdūl Shakoor. "Intuition and Intellect in Iqbal's Poetry," *Pakistan Times, Supplement*, April 21, 1951, p. 8.
———. "Iqbal and Nature," *Pakistan Times, Supplement*, April 21, 1953, pp. 5, 6, 7.
———. "Western Imperialism As He (Iqbal) Saw It," *Pakistan Times, Supplement*, April 21, 1952, p. 8.
Ahsan, Ali. "Poetry and Philosophy in Iqbal," *Iqbal Review*, October 1960.
Akbar Ali, Shaikh. *Iqbal: His Poetry and Message*. Lahore: Mir Muhammad Nawab Din, 1932.
Ali, S. Amjad. "Iqbal in Foreign Lands," *Pakistan Quarterly* (Karachi), III (1953), 1.
Anand, Mulk Raj. *Golden-breath Studies in Five Poets of the New India*. London: Dutton, 1933.
———. "Poetry of Sir Muhammad Iqbal," *Indian Art and Letters* (London), 1931, p. 5.
Anikeyev, N. P. "Obscestvenno-politiceskie vzgljydy M. Iqbala" [The Politico-social Ideas of Muhammad Iqbal], *Sovetskoe Vostokovedenia*, March 1958.
"An Interview with Munīra Banu, Allama Iqbal's Only Daughter Relates What Daddy Looked Like," *Times of Karachi, Special Supplement*, April 21, 1954.
Ansari, Zafar Ishaq. "Iqbal and Nationalism," *Iqbal Review*, April 1961.
Arberry, A. J. "Iqbal Commemoration, 1950," *Dawn*, Magazine Section May 7, 1950, p. 13.
Arnold, Thomas W. *The Faith of Islam*. London, 1928.
Asad, Muhammad. "Iqbal's Role in Muslim Thought," *al-Islam*, IV (n.d.), 146.
*Aspects of Iqbal: A Collection of Selected Papers*. Lahore: Intercollegiate Muslim Brotherhood, 1938.
Azhar, A. D. "Iqbal as a Seer," *Iqbal Review*, October 1961.
Badawi, Lutfullah. *Hayāt-i Iqbal* (Sindhi). Karachi: Iqbal Academy, 1958.
Bakht, Muhtaram Md. Sha'bān. "Sha'ir-i Mashriq Allama Iqbal," *Vaien Zindaei*, April 1960.
Bashir, Ahmad Mian. "Rumi and Iqbal: A Medieval and a Modern Philosopher Poet, *Islamic Review*, XL (1952), 4, pp. 31–37.

Batalvi, 'Ashaq Husain, *Iqbal Kāy Akhari Dow Sāl*, Karachi, 1961.

Battersby, Abdulla. "Iqbal: Poet, Politician and Philosopher," *Civil and Military Gazette* (Lahore), April 20, 1952.

Bausani, Alessandro. "Classical Muslim Philosophy in the Work of a Muslim Modernist: Muhammad Iqbal (1877-1938)," *Arch. Gesch. d. Philosophie* (Berlin), XLII (1960), 3.

———. "The Concept of Time in the Religious Philosophy of Muhammad Iqbal," *Die Welt des Islam* (Leiden), New Series III (1954).

———. "Dante and Iqbal," *East and West*, II (1951). Reprinted in *Pakistan Miscellany* (Karachi), 1952 and *Crescent and Green*. London: Cassell, 1955.

———. "Iqbal's Philosophy of Religion and the West," *Pakistan Quarterly* (Karachi), II (1953), 3. Reprinted in *Crescent and Green*. London: Cassell, 1955.

———. "Muhammad Iqbal's Message," *East and West*, I (1950).

———. "Satana nell'opera filosofico-poetica di Muhammad Iqbal," *Riv. degli Studi Orientali*, XXX (1957).

———. *Storia delle Letterature del Pakistan*. Milano, 1958.

Beg, Abdulla Anwar. *The Poet of the East. The Life and Work of Dr, Shaikh Sir Muhammad Iqbal, the Poet-Philosopher*. Lahore: Muhammad Ashraf, 1939. Lahore: Qawmi Kutab Khana, 1940. Lahore, 1961.

———. "Iqbal, the Poet-philosopher," *Pakistan Review*, II, 2 (1954), pp. 31-33, 36.

———. "Iqbal and the New World," *Times of Karachi, Special Supplement*, April 21, 1954.

Bilgrami, H. H. *Glimpses of Iqbal's Mind*. Lahore, 1954.

———. "Iqbal's Concept of Democracy Based on Islamic Principles," *Islamic Literature*, April 1954.

———. "Iqbal: His Approach to the Spirit of Islamic Culture," *Art and Letters* (India and Pakistan), XXIII, 1 (1949), 16, 23.

———. *Iqbal's Mind and Thought*. Lahore, 1954. Six articles on different aspects of Iqbal.

———. "Iqbal's Theory of Knowledge and Its Significance in His Poetry," *Islamic Literature*, III, 5 (1951), 244-54.

Biruni, A. H. al- [S. M. Ikram]. *Makers of Pakistan and Modern Muslim India*. Lahore: Muhammad Ashraf, 1950.

Boxanyi, A. "Iqbal's Philosophy," *Pacific Revue des Asiatiques* (Paris), 1953-54.

Brailvi, 'Ibādet. *Jadīd Shaʿirī*. Lahore, 1962.

Brohi, A. K. "Iqbal as a Philosopher Poet," *Iqbal Review*, April 1961.

Chagla, A. G. "Some Aspects of Iqbal's Thought," *Triveni* (Bangalore), XVIII, 2 (June 1946), 93-102.

Chakravarty, Amiya. "Iqbal, India's Muslim Poet," *Asia* (New York), (1938), 559-62. Also in the *Statesman*, Magazine Section, 1939.

———. "Sir Muhammad Iqbal," *Voice of Islam* (Singapore), January and February 1939, pp. 19-23.

Chishti, Yusūf Salīm. "God and the Concept of Self," *Iqbal Review* (Karachi), January 1962.

Cragg, K. *The Call of the Minaret*. New York, 1956.

Dadashi, Yakub. "What Turkey Thinks of Allama Iqbal," *Dawn*, April 21, 1954, p. 5.
Daʻi ul-Islam, Muhammad Ali. *Iqbal wa shiʻr-i farisi*. Hyderabad-Deccan, n.d.
Dar, B. A. *Iqbal and Post-Kantian Voluntarism*. Lahore, n.d.
———. *A Study in Iqbal's Philosophy*. Lahore, 1944.
Dev, G. C. *Idealism and Progress*. Calcutta, 1952.
Din, Faqīr Sayyid Wahīd ud-. *Ruzgār-i Faqīr*. 2 vols. Karachi: Line Art Press, 1966.
Dinsawi, M. Bashir ul-Haq. *Tabarrukāt-i Iqbal*. Delhi, 1959.
———. *Islahāt-i Iqbal*. Patna, n.d.
"Dr. Muhammad Iqbal and the Ahmaddiyya Movement," *Review of Religions*, XXXV (1936).
Edib, Halide. *Inside India*. London, 1937.
Enver, Ishrat Hasan. "Ethics of Iqbal," *Islamic Literature*, September 1956.
———. "Metaphysics of Iqbal." Ph.D. dissertation, Aligarh, Muslim University, 1944.
Faizee, ʻAtiya Begum. *Iqbal*. Bombay: Academy of Islam, 1947. Translated into Urdu by Ziauddin Ahmad Burney. Karachi: Iqbal Academy, 1956, 1960.
———. "Iqbal As I Knew Him," *Pakistan Times, Special Supplement*, April 21, 1950.
Farūqi, Abū Tahir. *Sīrat-i Iqbal*. Lahore: Qawmi Kutab Khana, 1938. Lahore, 1939.
Fernandez, A. "Man's Divine Quest, Appreciation of the Philosophy of the Ego According to Sir Muhammad Iqbal," *Annali Lateranensis* (Rome), XX (1956).
Figar, Abdur Rahman. "Iqbal's Philosophy of Revolution," *Pakistan Quarterly* (Karachi), IX (1959), 4.
Fuck, J. "Der Sunnitische Islam," in B. Spuler, *Handbuch der Orientalistik*. Leiden: Abschnitt, 1961, Vol. I, p. 8.
Ghaffar, Abdul. "The Divine Comedy of Modern India: An Evaluation of Iqbal," *Contemporary India*, II (1936), 255–60.
Gibb, H. A. R. "Iqbal, Sir Muhammad (1876–1938)," in the *Dictionary of National Biography*, 1931–1940. London: Oxford University Press, 1949. Pp. 266–73.
———. *Modern Trends in Islam*. Chicago, 1947.
Hakīm, Khalifah ʻAbdūl. "Allama Muhammad Iqbal," *Pakistan Quarterly* (Karachi), VIII (1959), 2.
———. "The Concept of Love in Rumi and Iqbal," *Islamic Culture* (Hyderabad-Deccan), 1950.
———. *Fiker-i Iqbal*. Lahore, 1957. Lahore, Bazm-i Iqbal, 1961.
———. *Hayāt-i Iqbal*. Lahore, n.d.
———. "Rumi, Nietzsche and Iqbal," *Thinker* (Lahore), 1944.
———. "Time and Space in Iqbal's Philosophy," *Pakistan Calling*, April 1951. Also in *Pakistan Times, Supplement*, XXI (1952), 4.
Hameed, Abdul. "Iqbal's Conception of History against Marxist and Hegelian Background," *Civil and Military Gazette, Supplement* (Lahore), April 20, 1952, p. iv.
Hamid, Khwaja Abdul. "Development of Iqbal's Poetic Thought," introductory essay in V. G. Kiernan, trans., *Poems from Iqbal*, Bombay: Kutub, 1947. Pp. 125–33
———. "Iqbal's Philosophy of Human Ego," *Vishvabharati Quarterly*, September 1943.

Harre, R. "Iqbal, A Reformer of Islamic Philosophy," *The Hibbert Journal* (London), July 1958.

Hasan, Nazir. "Iqbal's Conception of Art," *Eastern World* (London), 7 (February 1953), 27.

Hasan, Reyazul. "Il Poeta Musulmano Indiano Mohammad Iqbal," *Oriente Moderno* (Rome), XX (1940).

Hayit, B. *Mohammad Iqbal und die Welt des Islam.* Cologne, 1956.

Houben, J. J. "The Individual in Democracy and Iqbal's Conception of *Khudi*," *Pakistan Quarterly*, IV (1954), 1. Reprinted in *Crescent and Green.* London: Cassell, 1955.

Husain, Iqbal. "Study of Iqbal's Poetry," *Hindustan Review*, 75 (October and November 1942), 207–9.

Hussain, Massood. "Muhammad Iqbal, philosophe-poète." Ph.D. dissertation, University of Paris, 1953.

Hyder, S. *Progress of Pakistan.* Lahore: Lion Press, 1947.

Iqbal, Shaikh Javid. "Development of Muslim Political Philosophy in the Indo-Pakistan Sub-continent." Ph.D. dissertation, Cambridge University 1960.

Islam, Zirul. *Glimpses of Modern Urdu Literature.* Allahabad: Kitabistan, 1945.

———. "Growth of Muslim Politics in India, Influence of Iqbal and Jinnah," *Civil and Military Gazette, Supplement,* September 13, 1953, pp. ii, iv.

Jafri, F. S. "Iqbal's Revaluation of Islamic Policy," *Times of Karachi, Special Supplement,* April 21, 1954.

———. "Muhammad Iqbal (1873–1938): The Man Who Conceived Pakistan," *Islamic Review*, XXXVII, 4 (1949), 8–13.

———. *Spirit of Pakistan.* Karachi: Ansari Publications, 1951.

Jalāli, al-Sayyid Hāmid al-. *Allamah Iqbal Awr Un Kī Pahli Biywi.* Karachi, 1967.

Jinnah, M. A. "Message on the Occasion of Celebration of Iqbal Day at Lahore, 9th December, 1944," in J. D. Ahmad, ed., *Some Recent Speeches and Writings of Mr. Jinnah.* 2 vols. Lahore: Muhammad Ashraf, 1947. Vol. II, pp. 231–32.

Kamali, A. H. "The Nature of Experience in the Philosophy of Self," *Iqbal Review*, October 1960.

———. "The Philosophy of Self and Historicism," *Iqbal Review*, July 1961.

Kashyap, Shubhash. "Sir Mohammad Iqbal and Friedrich Nietzsche," *Islamic Quarterly* (London), II, 1 (April 1955), 185.

Khalid, Abdul Aziz. "Iqbal—An Assessment," *Outlook* (Karachi), II, 1 (March 1953), 7–13, 31.

Khan, Mohammad Ahmad. *Iqbal Kā Siyāsi Karnāmā.* Karachi, 1952.

Khan, Saʻadat Ali. "A Note on Iqbal," *Indian Art and Letters* (London), New Series XVII, 1 (1943), 71–73.

Khan, Yusūf Husain. *Rūh-i Iqbal.* Hyderabad-Deccan, 1942.

Khan, Zulfiqar Ali. *A Voice from the East.* Lahore, 1922.

Khatoon, Jamilah. *The Place of God, Man and Universe in the Philosophical System of Iqbal.* Karachi: Iqbal Academy, 1962.

Kilani, Nagib al-. *Iqbal, ash-shaʻir ath-thaʻir.* Cairo, 1962.

Kitagawa, J. M. *Modern Trends in World Religions.* Lasalle, Illinois, 1959.

Kurucu, A. V. *Bujuk Islam Sairi Dr. Muhammad Iqbal, yazan Ebu'l-Hasan El-Nedevi, tercume ve tahsiye eden Ali Ulvu Kurucu.* Ankara, 1957.

Latīf, Syed 'Abdūl. "Iqbal and World Order," *Osmania Magazine* (Hyderabad-Deccan), XI (1938), 5.

——. *Influence of English Literature on Urdu Literature.* London: Forster Groom, 1924.

——. *Islamic Cultural Studies.* Lahore, 1952.

Lichtenstadter, I. *Islam and the Modern Age.* London, n.d.

McCarthy, E. "Iqbal as a Poet and Philosopher," *Iqbal Review*, October 1961.

Maitre, Luce-Claude. "Un Grand Humaniste Oriental, Mohammad Iqbal," *Orient*, XIII (1960). Translated as "Iqbal, A Great Humanist," *Iqbal Review*, April 1961.

——. *Introduction à la pensée d'Iqbal.* Paris, 1955. Translated into English by M. A. M. Dar. *Introduction to the Thought of Iqbal.* Karachi: Iqbal Academy, 1961.

Malik, Hafeez. "Iqbal's Conception of Ego," *The Muslim World* (Hartford), April LX (1970) 2.

——. "An Appreciation of Guru Nanak in Iqbal's Poetry," *Studies in Islam* (Delhi), July 1968.

——. "The Impact of Ecology on Iqbal's Thought," *Iqbal Review* (Karachi), October 1968.

Marek, Jan. *Life and Work of Muhammad Iqbal* (Czech). Ph.D. dissertation, Caroline University, Prague, 1958.

——. "The Date of Muhammad Iqbal's Birth," *Archiv Orientalani* (Prague), 26 (1958).

——. "Islamic Studies in Czechoslovakia," *Journal of the Pakistan Historical Society*, X, 4 (1962).

Masdoodi, Abdullah al-. "Iqbal on Taxation and Fiscal Policy," *Iqbal Review*, January 1961.

Menon, K. P. S. "Message of Iqbal," *Indian Review*, 2c (1925), 506–9.

Merad, A. "Muhammad Iqbal," *IBLA* (Tunis), XVIII (1956).

Meyerovitch, E. "Iqbal, poète et philosophe," *Église Vivante*, VI (n.d.), 218.

Minowi, M. *Iqbal-i Lahori sha'ir-i farsigūyi Pakistan.* Teheran, 1327 sh. Supplement to the journal *Yaghma.*

Mohammad, Anwar Ali. "Iqbal's religiose Ideen." Ph.D. dissertation, University of Marburg, 1954.

Mohan, Singh Diwana. *Handbook of Urdu Literature.* Lahore: Carrers, 1942.

Moin, Mohammad. "Iqbal wa Iran-i bastan," *Iqbalnama* (Teheran), 1330 sh.

——. "Mi'rāj-i Iqbal," *Iqbalnama* (Teheran), 1330 sh.

Moosvi, Z. H. "Iqbal and the Arab World," *Illustrated Weekly Pakistan*, 4 (April 20, 1952), 32, 34.

Muslih, Abū Muhammad. *Iqbal awr Qur'ān.* Hyderabad-Deccan, n.d.

Nadwi, 'Abdūl Islam. *Iqbal-i Kāmil.* Azamgarh: Matba'a-i Ma'rif, 1964.

Nadwi, Sayyid Sulaiman, *Sayr-i Afghanistan.* Hyderabad-Deccan, 1945. Describes Iqbal's visit to Afghanistan.

Nadwi, Sayyid Wahid Qaisar. "Iqbal awr Bengali Adab," *Mah-i Nav* (Karachi), April 1952.

Namus, Shujaʻ. *A Discussion on Iqbal's Philosophy of Life*. Lahore, 1948.
Niāzi, Sayyid Nazīr. *Iqbal Ka Mutulaʻa*. Lahore, 1941.
Noman, Muhammad. *Our Struggle, 1857-1947. A Pictorial Record*. Karachi: Pakistan Publications, 1954.
Northrop, F. S. C. "Iqbal through U.S. Eyes," *Dawn*, Magazine Section, May 11, 1952, p. 12. Also a chapter in his book *World and U.S. Foreign Policy*. New York: Macmillan.
Nur-ud-Din, Abū Sayeed. *Islami Tasawwuf Awr Iqbal*. Karachi: IqbalAcademy, 1959.
O'Malley, L. S. S., ed. *Modern India and the West; A Study of the Interaction of Their Civilizations*. London: Oxford University Press, 1941.
Parvaiz, Ghulam Ahmad. *Iqbal awr Qur'ān*. Karachi, 1955. Karachi: Idare-i tulu al-Islam, 1957.
"Persian Movement in German Literature," *Pakistan Quarterly* (Karachi), VI (n.d.), 4.
A Punjabi. *Confederacy of India*. Lahore: Shah Nawaz Khan, 1939.
Qādir, Sir ʻAbdūl. "Modern Urdu Literature," *Hindustan Review*, 71 (December 1938), 285-94.
———. "The Seer and the Mystic," *Pakistan Times*, Special Supplement, April 21, 1950, pp. 5, 7, 8.
———. "Sir Muhammad Iqbal. The Great Poet of Islam, 1873-1938," in L. F. Rushbrook Williams, ed., *Great Men of India*. Bombay: Home Library Club, 1939.
Radhakrishnan, S., et al., eds., *History of Philosophy: Eastern and Western*. 2 vols. London: Allen and Unwin, 1952. "Iqbal," Vol. I, pp. 541-45.
Rafīq, Sayyid Ahmad. *Iqbal Kā Nazariye-i Akhlāq*, Lahore, 1960.
Rafiuddin, Mohammad. "Iqbal's Concept of Evolution," *Iqbal Review*, April 1960.
———. "Iqbal's Idea of the Self," *Iqbal* (Lahore), I (1953), 3.
———. "The Philosophy of Iqbal," *Iqbal Review*, October 1961.
Rahman, Muhammad Khalilur. "Iqbal and Nationalism," *Pakistan Review*, II, 4 (1954), 27-30.
Raja, Rao, and Iqbal Singh, eds. *Changing India*. London: Allen and Unwin, 1939.
Raju, P. T. "The Idealism of Sir Mohammad Iqbal," *Vishvabharati Quarterly*, VI (August-October 1940), 2.
Roop, Krishna. *Iqbal*. Lahore: New India Publications, 1945.
———. "Iqbal, Poet and Preacher," in V. P. Varma, ed., *Modern Trends: A Collection of Poems, Short Stories, Plays, and Articles by Some Eminent Writers in the Punjab*. Lahore: New India Publications, 1944. Pp. 34-44.
Ross, E. Denison. "Sir Muhammad Iqbal," *Urdu* (Hyderabad-Decca), 18 (1938), 737. Obituary note.
Roy, N. B. "The Background of Iqbal's Poetry," *Vishvabharati*, September 1920.
Sabzawari, Shaukat. Falsafa-i Iqbal Kā Markazi Khayāl," *Maʻarif* (Azamgarh), February 1946.
Sadiq, Muhammad. *A History of Urdu Literature*. London: Oxford University Press, 1964.
Saiyidayn, K. G. *Iqbal's Educational Philosophy*. Lahore: Muhammad Ashraf, 1945. Translated into Bengali by S. A. Mannan. Karachi: Iqbal Academy, 1960.

———. *Iqbal the Man and His Message*. London, 1949.
Saksena, Ram Babu. *History of Urdu Literature*. Allahabad, 1940.
Sālik, 'Abdul Majīd. *Dhikr-i Iqbal*. Lahore: Bazm-i Iqbal, 1955.
———. *Muslim Thaqafat Hindustan meñ*. Lahore, 1961.
Schimmel, Annemarie. *Aspetti spirituali dell'Islam*. Venice, 1960.
———. "The Idea of Prayer in the Thought of Iqbal," *The Muslim World* (Hartford), XLVIII (July 1958).
———. "Mohammad Iqbal and German Thought," *Mohammad Iqbal, PGF*, (Karachi), 1960.
———. "Time and Eternity in Muhammad Iqbal's Work," in *Proceedings of the 10th International Congress for the History of Religion*. Marburg, 1962.
———. "The Western Influence on Sir Muhammad Iqbal's Thought," in *Proceedings of the 9th International Congress for the History of Religions*. Tokyo, 1960.
———. *Gabriel's Wing*, Leiden: E. J. Brill, 1963.
———. "Zur Anthropologie des Islam," *Anthropologie Religieuse* Suppl. Number II (1955).
Sen, S. "Moslem Political Thought since 1858," *Indian Journal of Political Science*, VI, 2 (1944), 97–108.
Shafi, Ahmad. "A Poet of Islam," *Modern Review*, December 1933, pp. 619–24.
Shafi, Mian Muhammad. "Iqbal's Conception of Social Democracy," *Pakistan Times, Special Supplement*, April 21, 1954.
———. "Last Days of the Poet of Islam," *Civil and Military Gazette, Supplement* (Lahore), April 20, 1952, pp. i, iv.
Shahidullah, Muhammad. *Life of Iqbal* (Bengali). Dacca, n.d.
———. *Shikwah* and *Jawab-i Shikwah* (Bengali translation). Dacca, 1954.
Shaikh, Hasiena. *The Conception of the Perfect Man in Iqbal*. Karachi: Iqbal Academy, n.d.
Sharif, M. M. "Genesis of Iqbal's Aesthetic," *Iqbal* (Lahore), I, 1 (1952), 19–40.
———. "Iqbal's Theory of Art," *Iqbal* (Lahore), II, 3 (January, 1954), 1–18.
———. "Iqbal's Conception of God," *Islamic Culture* (Hyderabad-Deccan), 1942. Reprinted in *Thinker* (Lahore), 1944.
Shaukat Ali, K. "Where Did Iqbal Live? From Sialkot to the Mazar near Badshahi Mosque," *Times of Karachi, Special Supplement*, April 21, 1954.
———. "Letters of Allama," *Pakistan Times, Supplement*, April 21, 1951, p. 5.
Siddiqi, 'Abdul Laith. "Iqbal awr Bedil," *Intikhāb-i Mah-i Nav* (Karachi), 1958.
Siddiqi, H. "Iqbal's Legal Philosophy and the Reconstruction of Islamic Law," *Progressive Islam* (Amsterdam), 1955, pp. 3–4. Also in *Islamic Literature* (Lahore), 1956.
Siddiqi, M. Razi-ud-Din. *Iqbal's Conception of Time and Space*, Hyderabad-Deccan: Hyderabad Academy, Serial Number 6 (1944), Article Number 7.
Siddiqi, Mazharuddin. *The Image of the West in Iqbal*. Lahore: Bazm-i Iqbal, 1956.
Singh, Iqbal. *The Ardent Pilgrim*. London: Longmans, Green, 1951.
Sinha, Sacchidanand. *Iqbal, His Poetry and Message*. Allahabad, 1947.
A Student of Literature [pseud]. "Iqbal the Poet-Philosopher of Islam," *Hindustan Review*, 71 (September and October 1938), 147–64.
Symonds, Richard. *Making of Pakistan*. London: Faber and Faber, 1951.

Taj-ud-Din, Pīr. "Iqbal's Political Career," *Pakistan Times, Supplement*, April 21, 1951.

Taseer, Muhammad Din, "Iqbal and Modern Problems," *Pakistan Times, Supplement*, April 21, 1952, pp. 5, 6.

———. "Iqbal's Conception of Perfect Man," *Pakistan Calling*, IV, 8 (April 1951), 7–8.

———. "Iqbal the Universal Poet," *Pakistan Quarterly* (Karachi), V (1955) 3.

———. "Iqbal's Theory of Art and Literature," *Pakistan Quarterly* (Karachi), (1952), 15, 71.

Vahid, S. A. *Introduction to Iqbal*. Karachi, 1954.

———. *Iqbal, His Art and Thought*. Hyderabad-Deccan, 1944. London, 1959.

———. "Iqbal: An Estimate of His Work," *Islamic Review*, XXXIX, 3–4 (1951), 21–23.

———. "Iqbal and His Poetry," *Islamic Review*, XLII, 4 (1954) 30–34.

———. *Thoughts and Reflections of Iqbal*. Lahore: Muhammad Ashraf, 1964.

———. "Iqbal's *Payām-i-Mashriq*." *Dawn*, Magazine Section, September 2, 1951, p. 12.

Vaswani, K. N. "Iqbal—An Appreciation," *Triveni* (Bangalore), New Series XI, 11 (May 1939), 18–23.

Vecchiotti, J. *Pensatori dell'India contemporanea*. Rome, 1959.

Venkata Rao, P. K. "The Secrets of the Self: A Study of Iqbal's Poem *Asrār-i-Khudi*," *Triveni* (Bangalore), XIV, 4 (1942), 246–49.

Von Glasenapp, H. *Die indische Welt*. 1948.

Von Veltheim-Ostrau, H. H. *Tagebucher aus Asien*. Hamburg, 1956.

Waheed, K. A. "Pakistan, the Realization of Iqbal's Dream," *Pakistan Calling*, VI, 8 (1952), 9–10.

Wali, Mustazid al-Rahman. "Iqbal's Doctrine of Destiny," *Islamic Culture* (Hyderabad-Deccan), 1939.

Whittemore, R. "Iqbal's Pantheism," *Review of Metaphysics*, September, 1956.

Williams, L. F. Rushbrook, ed. *Great Men of India*. Bombay: Times of India, 1941.

Yusuf Ali, Abdullah. "Doctrine of Human Personality in Iqbal's Poetry," *Essays by Diverse Hands, The Transactions of the Royal Society of Literature of the United Kingdom*, ed. by St. John Ervine, New Series 18 (1941), pp. 89–105.

Zarīf, Qadi Muhammad. *Iqbal Qur'ān Ki Raushani meiñ*. Lahore, n.d.

Zia-ud-Din, M. "Iqbal the Poet-philosopher of Islam," *Vishvabharati Quarterly*, New Series IV (May–July 1958), 1.

Zor, Sayyid Muhyiaddin Qādiri. *Shād-i Iqbal*. Hyderabad-Deccan, 1942.

# Contributors

LYNDA P. MALIK is Assistant Professor of Sociology at Villanova University. In 1967 she received an award from Alpha Chapter of Phi Delta Gamma (Graduate Women's Honor Society) in recognition of her outstanding work in her doctoral program.

MUHAMMAD DAUD RAHBAR is Associate Professor of Religion at Boston University. From 1957 to 1959 he taught Urdu literature and Pakistan studies at the University of Ankara, Turkey.

JAVID IQBAL, a son of the poet-philosopher, is a practicing attorney in Lahore, Pakistan. He holds a Ph.D. degree from Cambridge University and is the author of *The Ideology of Pakistan and Its Implementation* (Lahore, 1963).

L. R. GORDON-POLONSKAYA, a prominent Soviet Indologist, is on the staff of the Institute of the Peoples of Asia, USSR Academy of Arts and Sciences, Moscow. She is also a coauthor (with Y. V. Gankovsky) of *A History of Pakistan* (Moscow, 1964) and *A Modern History of India* (Moscow, 1960).

RIFFAT HASSAN holds a Ph.D. degree in philosophy from Durham University. Her doctoral dissertation was "An Analysis of the Philosophical Ideas in the Works of Iqbal". She is currently Deputy Director of the Bureau of National Research, Pakistan.

JAN MAREK is Research Fellow in the Department of Indian Studies of the Oriental Institute, Czechoslovak Academy of Science, Prague. In 1958, he obtained a Ph.D. degree from Charles University, Prague, for his dissertation, "Life and Work of Muhammad Iqbal". He has translated and published the Persian and Urdu poetry of Iqbal into Czech.

FREELAND ABBOTT is Professor of History at Tufts University. From 1953–1955 he was a Ford Foundation Research Fellow in Pakistan, and in 1959–1960 a Fulbright Research Scholar in Pakistan.

B. A. DAR is Director of the Iqbal Academy, Karachi, and Chief Editor of *The Pakistan Philosophical Journal* (of the Pakistan Philosophical Congress) and *The Iqbal Review* (Karachi). He is the author of *A Study in Iqbal's Philosophy* (Lahore, 1950) and *Iqbal and Post-Kantian Voluntarism* (Lahore, 1956).

A. H. KAMALI, formerly Chairman of the Department of Philosophy, S. M. College, Karachi, is currently Deputy Director of the Iqbal Academy, Karachi. He is also Assistant Editor of *The Iqbal Review*.

S. ALAM KHUNDMIRI is Reader in Philosophy at Osmania University, Andhra Pradesh, India. He specializes in the development of Indic Muslim philosophy.

NIKOLAY PETROVITCH ANIKEYEV is Research Fellow at the Institute of Philosophy, USSR Academy of Arts and Sciences, Moscow. He is the author of *The Materialistic Traditions in Indian Philosophy* (Moscow, 1965) and *Muhammad Iqbal: An Outstanding Thinker and Poet* (Moscow, 1959).

ABU SAYEED NUR-UD-DIN is Assistant Secretary of the East Pakistan Industrial Development Corporation. He obtained a Ph.D. degree in 1958 from the University of Karachi for his dissertation "Iqbal's Attitude toward Sufism" (Urdu) which was published by the Iqbal Academy in 1959.

M. T. STEPANYANTS, a Soviet specialist on Indo-Pakistani Islam, is the author of *Philosophy and Sociology in Pakistan* (Moscow, 1967). She has contributed several articles on Urdu literature and Islamic ethics to *Voprosy Philosophy* (Moscow).

ANNEMARIE SCHIMMEL is Professor of Comparative Religious Studies at the University of Bonn. She is the author of *Gabriel's Wing: A Study in the Religious Ideas of Sir Muhammad Iqbal* (Leiden, 1963) and has translated Iqbal's *Javid-Namah* into German.

HADI HUSSAIN joined the Indian Civil Service in 1931 and was transferred to the Civil Service of Pakistan in 1947. He retired from the C.S.P. in 1961. He is currently engaged in translating Iqbal's Persian and Urdu poems into English.

S. A. VAHID, a *doyen* of scholars on Iqbal, has written numerous articles and six books on Iqbal, including *Iqbal: His Art and Thought* (London, 1958) and *Introduction to Iqbal* (Karachi, 1964).

# Index

Al-abduhu (divine vice-regent), 209–210
'Abdullah, Mawlana Abu, 8
'Abdullah, Dr. S. M., xiii
*Abr-i Gawher Bār* (Blessed Showers), 16
Abyssinia, 160–62
*Abyssinia*, quoted, 161
Adareh Thaqafat-i Islamia (Lahore), 389*n*55
Adawiyyāh, Rabiha Al-, 214, 310
Afghani, Jamal-ud-Din, 115–16, 126, 244, 276
Afghanistan, 31–32, 35, 47, 165
*Ahl al-Hadith*, 49
Ahl al-Qur'ān, xii, 36, 50
Ahmad, Aziz, quoted, 219, 220
Ahmad, Maulana Nazīr, 16
Ahmad, Mian Bashīr, 44, 50
Ahmad, Mirza Ghulam, 54
Ahmadi movement, 15–16, 392*n*20
Ahrār, Majlis-i, 96
Akbar of Allahabad, 39
*Al-Arḍ l-Allah* (Earth is God's), 85
Alexander, Samuel, 254, 255, 256
Al-Hamra Palace, 40, 55
Ali, Amīr, 20
Ali, Amjad, 29
Ali, Bakhsh, 59, 62
Ali, Malik Barkat, 96, 97, 98, 104, 106
Ali, Maulana Muhammad, 89, 91, 116, 118, 
Aligarh movement, 5, 6, 8, 197
Aligarh Muslim University, 25, 109, 117;
Anglo-Muhammadan College, 8, 12
*Allah Ahsan-al Khaleqīn* (God, the best of creators), 298
All-India Muslim Conference, 90, 93
All-India Muslim League, xi, 20, 76, 80, 82, 104–105, 106, 383–84
All-India National Congress, 76, 80, 82, 87, 88, 95, 116, 133, 165
All-India Radio, xii

All-Parties' Muslim Conference, 88, 90
*'Ama* (insignia of the individual), 229, 230, 231, 233
Ana'l-Haqq (I am the Creative Truth), 311, 317, 318
*Anjuman-i-Halqa-i-Naqd-o-Nazar* (Society of Critics and Observers), 37
*Anjuman-i-Himāyat-i-Islam* (Society for the Support of Islam), 109, 110–11, 140; sessions, 16, 27, 39
Anjuman Kashmiri Musalmanan, 11–12
Ansari, Hadrat Ayyub, 42
'Arabi, Ibn al-, 54, 56, 71, 72, 212, 213, 222, 230, 290–91, 295–96, 301, 312, 314, 316, 372
Aristotelians, 227–28, 246
*Armaghān-i Hijaz* (Gift of Hijaz), 318, 355, 394*n*46, 420; quoted, 176–77
Arnold, Sir Thomas, 12–13, 17
'Arshi, Mohammad Husain, 37, 40–41, 48–49, 50–51
Art for life, 168–170
Arya Samaj, 82
Ash'ari, Abū al-Hassan, 235
Ashraf, Muhammad, 99
Asín Palacios, Miguel, 30, 371
*Asrār-i Khudi* (Secrets of the Self), 18, 19–20, 72, 118, 121, 127, 148–49, 197, 212, 250–51, 292, 394*n*46, 410*n*1; Nicholson, translation, 27; quoted, 7–8, 18, 127, 128, 191, 193, 198, 200, 202, 269, 270, 271, 272, 273, 292–93, 294, 297, 323, 336, 338–39, 377, 378; *see also* Individual; Personality; Self
Ataturk, Mustafa Kemal, 132
Atomists and atomism, 122, 234–36, 247–48, 304
'Attār, Farid-ud-Din, 311
Aurangzeb, Emperor, 75–76, 396*n*12

Avicenna, 234–35, 247
Awliya, Nizām-ud Din, 15, 391n18–19
A'yān thābitah (pre-existence of things in God's knowledge), 290, 291
Ayk Bahrī Qazzāq Awr Sikander, 163
Azad, Abul Kalam, 116, 133
Azad, Maulana Muhammad Hussain, 6

Bāl-i Jibrīl (Gabriel's Wing), 30, 170, 252, 299, 394n46, 399n74; quoted, 41, 85, 174, 199, 298, 356, 360, 365, 367
Balshewīyk Rūs (Bolshevik Russia), 172
Bandagi Namah, 330–31, 333–35, 337
Bāng-i-Dara (Call of the Highway), 14, 16, 18, 22, 37, 44, 111, 136–37, 138, 175, 250, 394n46; quoted, 22, 122, 131, 143, 144, 165, 207, 275, 347, 349
Baqli, Ruzbihān, 320
Baquilani, Abū Bakr, 235
Basri, Hasan-al, 310
Batalavi, Dr. 'Ashiq Husain, 36, 96, 97, 105, 106; quoted, 36, 100–101
Bazm (sedentary companionship), 43
Bazm-i-Iqbal (Iqbal Society), xiii
Begum, Rufi'ah Sultan, 22
Beidil, Mirza 'Abdul Qādir, 54, 212, 219–23
Bengali language: translations of Iqbal in, xiii
Berg-i Gul, 15
Bergson, Henri, 29, 30, 113, 199–203, 212, 233, 254, 255, 256–59, 302
Bilgrami, Mīr'Abdul Wāhid, 71
Billah, Khawja Bāqī, 240
Browning, Robert, 377–79

Capitalism, x, 155
Carlyle, Thomas, 342, 344
Central Institute of Islamic Research (Karachi), 398n55
Chahār Enātir (Beidil's autobiography), 221; Mathnavi, Mohit-i'Azam, 222
Chishti, Professor Yusuf Salim, 28
Chopra, H. L., quoted, 137
Cleugh, M. F., 256
Communal Award, 92, 93
Communist Party of India, 170
Curzon, Lord, 15, 83

Dāgh, Nawab Mirza Khan, 9, 363
Dante Alighieri, 369–77, 379
Daraz, Gasū, 213, 214
Darb-i Kalīm (Rod of Moses), 29, 31, 159–70 passim, 355, 394n46; quoted, 119, 161, 162, 163, 164, 166, 167, 168, 169, 170, 171, 172, 173, 209, 271
Dard, Khawaja Mīr, 236–38
Darwin, Charles, 73
Democracy, 155–58, 165–67, 174–83
Development of Metaphysics in Persia, 19, 123–24, 310, 313
Dhāt (the Divine Being), 203, 220
Dhu'l-Nun, 289, 290
Din-i Ilahi, 75
Dīn-o-Dunyā (Religion and the World), 16, 141
Diwān, quoted, 323
Douglas, Justice William O., ix–x, xii

Ecology, 73–76
Ego (khudi), xi–xii 113, 150–51, 192–93, 203, 223–26, 230–32, 259, 262, 270, 279, 287, 291, 296, 304–305; and non-ego, 191–92; definition of, 296–300
Emerson, Ralph Waldo, 175, 178

Faizee, Miss 'Atiya Begum, 10, 20–24, 39
Fanā fil haq (union with Reality), 71, 224, 290, 312
Faqr (poverty, mystic term), 208, 220
Fatalism, 307–309
Father's Prayer, quoted, 64–65
Fatimah binat 'Abdūllah, 27
Fauq, Muhammad Din, 11, 14
Fazli-i Husain, Mian, 43, 45, 70, 81, 82, 83–85, 88, 90, 94, 95–96, 97, 100
Fichte, Johann, 113, 190–93, 228, 357
Flah-i Qawn (Welfare of the Nation), 12
Forster, E. M., quoted, 141, 144
Fuṣūṣ al-Hikām (The Bezels of Wise Precepts), 54, 212–13, 290

Gandhi, Mahatma, 42, 91–92, 171
Ganjha-i-Garañmayā (Siddiqi), 36
Ghālib, Asadūllah Khan, 214–19, 347, 366; Mathnavi Dar Beyān-i-shān-i-Nabuwat (Splendor of Prophethood), 218, 219

Ghazzali, Abū Hamid al-, 212, 235, 243–44, 301, 305–306, 315, 321, 371
*Ghulāmuñ Key Nimāz* (Prayer of the Slaves), 167
Gilāni, 'Abdūl Qādir, quoted, 315–16
Girāmi, Maulana, 38, 43
God, 122–23, 127, 129, 158, 178, 209, 213, 224–26, 248, 251–52, 253, 262, 288–89, 295–96, 299, 304–305, 307–308
Goethe, Johann Wolfgang von, 194, 357–69, 379
Good and evil, 129–30, 307–309, 347, 364–65
Gorgani, Mirza Arshad, 11
Government College (Lahore), 10–13, 116
Grief, 38–42
*Gulshan-i Rāz-i Jadīd* (A Rose Garden of a New Secret), quoted, 188, 189, 192, 200, 201, 240, 242, 327, 328, 329, 335, 378

Haeckel, Ernest, 73
Hāfiz, Khāwja, 293–95, 335
Hakīm, Khalīfah 'Abdūl, xiii, 305; quoted, 7, 22, 152–53, 295
Hali, Altaf Husain, 6, 42, 61, 346
Hallaj, Mansūr al-, 49, 290, 310–24, 366
*Hama az Ust* (All is from Him), 288
Hamadani, Mir Ali, 213
*Hama Ust* (All is He), 288–89
Harith, Anwar, 295
Harith, b. Asad al-Muhasībi al-, 310
Harmayn, Imam al-, 235
Hasan, Sayyid Mīr, 8–9, 38, 43
Hasan, Shaikh Muhammad, 97
Heidelberg University, 20
*Himalā* (Home of Snow), 137
Hindu-Muslim conflict, 8–83, 87, 138–39, 148–49
Hindus, Hinduism, xi, 3, 17, 76; in the Punjab, 77, 78–79, 80, 82, 83, 85–87, 92
*Hindustani Bachoñ Kā Qawmi Gīt* (National Anthem of Indian Children), 17, 139
Hommel, Professor F., 19
Houben, J. J., quoted, 156
*Houri and the Poet, The*, 359
Hujwari, Ali Makhadūm, 224
*Humayūñ*, periodical, 44
Humayūñ, Justice Shah Din

*Hunerwaran-i Hind* (The Indian Artist), 169–70
Husain, Mīr Nazīr, 11
Husain, Sayyid Altaf, 42, 48, 49–50
Husain, Sayyid Tasaddaq, 97
Hussain, Chaudhari Muhammad, 62

*Iblīs Kā Farmān Apany Farzanduñ Kay Nām* (Injunction of the Devil), 164–65, 355
*Iblīs Ki Majlis*, 355
Ibn-Khaldun, 245
Iftikhār al-Din, Faqīr Sayyid, 37
*Ijtihād*, 28, 49, 125
*'Ilm-i Iqtisād*, 13
*Iltajā Masafer* (Request of the Traveler), 15
Imperialism, 162–65
*Imtenae'al-Nazir* (the impossibility of replica), 217
India: Iqbal's hope for unity and self-government, 137–38, 139, 145, 147, 151–52, 166
Indian Councils Act of *1892*, 79
Individual, 272–74, 280–82; see also Personality
*Insān-i kamil* (perfect man), 207–210, 332–35
Institute of Advanced Research in the Punjab (Adarah Darul Islam), 33
Intellect, 142, 143
Inter-Collegiate Muslim Brotherhood (Lahore), 103
Intuition, 279–80
*Iqbal*, periodical, xiii
Iqbal, Aftab (son), 10
Iqbal, Atta Muhammad (brother), 4, 5, 15–16
Iqbal, Imam Bibi (mother), 4, 197
Iqbal, Javid (son), 25, 52; writings about father, 37, 56–65
Iqbal, Karīm Bibi (wife), 9–10
Iqbal, Mi'raj Begum (daughter), 9–10
Iqbal, Muhammad
  influences on: early school days, 9, 11; Sir Thomas Arnold, 12–13, 17; Western philosophers, 30, 113, 187–210, 213, 255–60; Qur'ān, 32, 171, 261–62; al-'Arabi, 54, 72, 230, 301; Sayyid Ahmad Khan, 109–110, 126; Leibnitz, 113, 122, 248, 259, 303, 305;

Iqbal, Muhammad—(*Contd.*)
Kant, 113, 129, 187–90, 302, 306, 357; Fichte, 113, 190–93, 357; Bergson, 113, 199–203, 212, 256–59, 302; Nietzsche, 113, 157, 204–210, 212, 303–304, 323, 342–43, 357; Afghani, 115–16, 126, 276; Russian Revolution, 118–21, 153, 170, 172, 275–76; Shah Waliullah, 124–26; Schopenhauer, 193–99, 212; Persian, 211–34; Ghālib, 212, 214–19; Beidil, 212, 219–23; al-Junayd, 212, 223–26; Suhurwardi, 226–29, al-Jili, 229–33, 301; Dard, 236–38; Rumi, 238–39, 251, 301; Thani, 240–42; al-Ghazzali, 243–44, 301, 305–306; Milton, 272, 352–57, 379; Hallaj, 310, 317–24; Wordsworth, 347, 348–51, 363, 379; Western poets, 347–79; Goethe, 357–69, 379; Dante, 369–77, 379; Browning, 377–79

life; 3–65; mausoleum, ix, 35; death, 3, 34–35, 62–63; ancestors, 3–4; birth, 3, 391*n*1; parents, 4–5, 197; childhood, 5–8; education, 8–9, 10–13, 19, 111; marriages, 9–10, 24–25; children, 10, 25; academic degree, 11, 12, 13, 19, 20, 37; appointment as Macleod-Punjab Reader, 13; career as college and university teacher, 13–14, 116; failure to enter Punjab civil service, 14–15; studies and activities in Europe, 17–25, 28–31, 113, 141–44, 275, 370; law studies, 19; philosophical studies, 19; law career, 25–26, 28, 44, 45–46, 116; knighthood, 27; mission to Afghanistan, 31–32, 47; last five years, 33–35, 45; reminiscences, 36–55; memoir of son Javid, 56–65; opposition to Jinnah, 87–92; reorganization of Muslim League in the Punjab, 94–98; cooperation with Jinnah, 99–107

personal characteristics, 38–55

philosophy, ix, xiv, 114, 122–23, 125–29, 185–284 *passim;* development of political, 136–58 *passim;* sources of, 187–210 *passim*

poetry, 327–79 *passim;* in Urdu language, 9, 11, 13, 14, 15, 16, 17, 18, 37–38, 43, 159, 352, 363, 418, 420; recitations and readings of, 11, 15, 16, 27, 34, 39, 41, 44; in Persian language, 17–18, 43, 118, 352, 417–18, 419–20; nationalistic, 137; love, 143; style in, 347; *see also* titles of poems

politics, 69–183 *passim;* and relations with Jinnah, xi, 43, 61, 88–94, 96–98, 100, 102–103, 107, 383–88; two-nation theory of, xi, 90–91, 92, 107, 114–15, 116, 134–35; and contribution to founding of Pakistan, xi–xii, 36, 90–91, 93–94, 107, 108, 174; and Muslim nationalism, 16–17, 108, 110–11, 112, 114, 118, 131, 132–35, 144, 145–51; as member of Punjab Legislative Council, 28, 69, 81–83, 84–87, 145; at Round Table Conferences, 28–29, 40, 58, 91–92, 176; as President of Punjab Muslim League, 95, 100, 102–103, 133; and sociopolitical views, 109–110, 118, 128–32, 133–35, 152–55; and national unity, 110–12, 130; international, 159–73

popularity: as poet-philosopher of Pakistan, ix, xii–xiii, 44, 268–69; government honours, xiii, 27; in India, 11, 16–17, 44, 264; in Muslim world, 19, 44, 118, 264

religious views: liberalism, 48–51; and religious traditions of Islam, 108, 112–13, 114, 116, 118, 119, 133–35; and reformation of Islam, 121–26

works: translations of, xiii, 36, 420–41; political, 137–41, 159–73; statistics on book sales of, 393*n*46; *see also* titles

Iqbal, Mukhtar Begum (wife), 24

Iqbal, Munirah ([Munīra] daughter), 25, 58–59, 61–62

Iqbal, Sardar Begum (wife), 24–25, 35, 46, 58

Iqbal, Shaikh Nūr Muhammad (father), 4–5, 6, 38

Iqbal Academy (Karachi), xiii

Iqbal Academy (Lahore), xiii; *see also* Bazm-i Iqbal

*Iqbal aur Qur'ān* (Parvaiz), 36

Iqbal Day, xii, 103

*Iqbal Review*, periodical, xiii
'*Ishq* (dynamic love), 314
*Ishraqi* (theory of knowledge), 226–29
*Ishtrakīyat* (Socialism), 171
Islam, xi, 53, 71–72, 116, 140, 144, 145–46, 164–65, 172–73; and Iqbal's proposed *Islam As I Understand It*, 33; religious traditions of, 112–13; reformation and revival of, Iqbal's ideas on, 121–26, 145–46, 211–12, 302–303; *millat* (community), 147–48; Persian influence on, 211–12
*Islam as a Moral and Political Ideal*, quoted, 157–58
Islamia College, 13, 103
*Islamia College Kā Khatāb Punjab Kay Musalmānu sāy* (Islamia College's Address to the Muslims of the Punjab), 16
Islamic Reformation, 121–23
Islamic Research Institute, 398–55
Islamic Thought, 211–42; Iqbal's influence on, 244–63
Iyengar, Srinivasa, 88

Jairajpūri, Maulana Aslam, 313
Jalāl-ud-Din, Mirza, 26, 37, 44, 45, 49, 53
Jamā 'at-i Islami, xiii, 398n55
Jamia'-i Milliyā-i-Islamiyā (Delhi), 36
Jammu and Kashmir, 3–4
Jārullah, Mūsa, 51
*Javid-Namah* (Book of Eternity), 37, 62, 121, 130, 252, 276–77, 318–19, 348, 369, 370–77, 394n46; quoted, 64–65, 205, 210, 218, 225, 275, 308, 314, 320, 324, 350, 367, 374, 375
*Jawab Shikwah* (Answer), 27
*Jawher-i-fard* (atom-like substance), 232
Jili, 'Abdūl Karīm al-, 229–33, 301
Jinnah, Muhammad Ali, xi, 63, 76, 89, 183; and relations with Iqbal, xi, 43, 61, 88–94, 96–98, 100, 102–103, 107, 383–88
Junayd, Abu'l-Qāsim al-, 212, 223–36

Kant, Immanuel, 113, 129, 187–90, 249, 302, 306, 357
*Karl Marx Key Awāz* (Voice of Karl Marx), 171
Kermatians, 311, 411n3

Kashmir, 3–4
Kemal Ataturk, 132, 168
Khafif, Shaikh Ibn al-, 311
Khan, Aga, 90, 91
Khan, Ghulam Rasūl, 96, 97, 103, 104, 105
Khan, Hamīd Ahmad, 54
Khan, Khizer Hayat, 107
Khan, Liaquat Ali, 105, 106–107
Khan, Malik Zamān Mahdi, 97
Khan, Maulana Zafar Ali, 27, 96
Khan, Muhammad 'Azīm, 97
Khan, King Nādir, 31, 47
Khan, Nawab Isma'īl, 105, 106
Khan, Nawab Zulfiqar Ali, 26, 45, 89
Khan, Raja Ghazanfar Ali, 97, 98
Khan, Shah Nawaz, 104
Khan, Sir Sayyid Ahmad, xi, 5, 16, 109–110, 126–27, 141, 244, 268; quoted, xii
Khan, Sir Sikandar Hayāt, 43, 94, 97–98, 99, 100–107
Khan, Zafarullah, 70
Khilafat, Khilafatists, 27, 82
*Khizr-i-Rah* (The Guide), 39–40, 250; quoted, 155
*Khuftagān-i Khāk Say Istafsār* (A Land Asleep), 111
Kiernan, V. G., quoted, xiii
Kindi, Abū Yūsuf Ya'qūb, al-, 247, 289
Knowledge: Ishraqi theory of, 226–27
Kohn, Hans, quoted, ix
Koran; *see* Qur'ān
Korbel, Joseph, quoted, 3

Lahore, 3, 6, 10–11, 38
'*La ila ill-Allah*, quoted, 262
Lal, Lala Mohan, 83
Lal, Monohar, 86
Land Alienation Act (*1900*), 77–78; consequences of, 78–80
Land ownership, 83–85, 396n24
Leibnitz, Gottfried von, 113, 122, 248, 259, 303, 305
*Lenin Khudā Hadhūr Mein* (Lenin Before God), 170; quoted, 153, 275–76
Love, 40, 139, 144, 152, 178, 214–17, 238–39, 241–42, 252, 314, 323–24; lack of, 142–43; legend of Hallaj, 311–12
Lucknow Pact of *1916*, 76, 80–81, 86, 88

Madras Muslim Association, 28
*Mahawārah Ma-bayen Khudā Wa Insān* (God's Talk with man), quoted, 274, 307
Mahayani, Sheikh Ali, 214
Mahdi, Malik Zamān, 105, 106
Mahmud, Wāhid, 72
Majīd, Miam 'Abdūl, 96
Majithia, Sardar Umrao Singh, 26, 29
*Makhzan*, periodical, 37
*Malfūzat-i-Iqbal* (Conversational Discourses), 36–38, 39, 44, 45–46, 51, 53, 55
Malik, Hafeez, quoted, 110
Man, 181–82, 204–210, 221–23, 230–31, 274, 306–309
Marx, Karl, 171, 239
*Masafer* (The Traveler), 31–32, 419; quoted, 32
*Masjid-i Qirtabāh* (Mosque of Cordoba), 252; quoted, 30–31, 174, 299
Massignon, Louis, 29–30, 313–14
Mas'ud, Sir Sayyid Ross, 34
*Mathnawi* (Rumi), 41–42
Maudūdi, Abul, 'Alā, 33
McTaggart, John, 249, 297, 317
Mehr, Maulana Ghulām Rasūl, 46
Mercy-upon-the world, 218, 219
Metaphysics: Iqbal's proposed *Book of an Unknown Prophet*, 33
*Millat* (religious community), 133, 147–48
Millat, Ittahād-i, 96
Milton, John, 272, 352–57, 379
Minto-Morley Reforms, 80
*Momin* (believer), 71
Moneylenders in the Punjab, 77, 78
Monotheism, 131
Montagu-Chelmsford Reforms, 28, 69, 80, 81, 85
Muhammad the Prophet, ix, 7, 12, 16, 30, 42, 51, 61, 124, 144, 164, 179, 198, 217, 219, 233, 291, 348, 372, 392n20; Ascension of, 72, 233
Mujaddid Alf Thāni, *see* Sarhindi, Shaikh Ahmad
Mujīb, M., 36
Munich University, 19
Murtada, Mawlana Ghulam, 8
*Musaddas* (Hali), 42, 61
Muslim League, 63, 69, 82, 90–91, 95, 98, 102, 105, 107, 116, 133, 151; British Committee of, 20
Muslims, xi, xii, 5, 6, 16, 17, 40, 48–49; cultural identity of, 16, 27, 85–86, 109, 110–11, 140, 151–52, 172–73, 212–14; in India, 70–72, 74–76, 81, 112, 132–34, 138, 140, 146, 281, 346; in the Punjab, 77, 78–79, 80, 81, 82–83, 85–87, 92, 110; political identity of, 87–107, 140, 145; demand of, for separate state, 90–91, 92, 132–35, 151–52, 383–88
Mussolini, Benito, 31, 162
*Mussolini*, 162
*Mutakallimūn* (dialectical theologians), 246, 247, 248, 304, 305
Muzammal, Mawlana, Muhammad, 8
Mysticism, Islamic, 287–324 *passim*

*Nachariā* (Naturalist philosophy), 126
Nadir, Shah (the Afghan king), 32, 47
Najim-ud-Din, Faqīr, 58
*Nalā-i Firaq* (Lament of Separation), 13
*Nalā'-i Yatīm* (Orphan's Cry), 16
Napoleon's tomb, 29
Narang, Gokal Chand, 86
Nationalism: Iqbal's repudiation of, 146–47, 149, 165–68
Nationalism, Afro-Asian, 265–69
Nationalism, Muslim, 63, 108–135 *passim*, 145–51, 167–68; and self-determination as a basis of formation of Pakistan, xi, 90, 115, 132–135; Iqbal's definition of, 134–35, 144
Navaz, Mian Shah, 45
*Nawa-i Mazdūr* (Song of the Worker), quoted, 119
*Nawā-i Waqt* (Melody of Time), 252
*Nayā Shiwalā* (New Temple), 17; quoted, 138
*Nazar* (glance), 50
Nehru, Jawaharlal, 43, 151, 399n62; quoted, 99
Nehru Report, 88, 397n41
Neo-Platonism, 216–17, 219, 225, 227–28, 246, 289–90; defined, 288–89; *see also* Plato
Nicholson, Reynold A., 27, 49–50; quoted, 19
Nietzsche, Friedrich, 113, 157, 204–210, 212, 239, 273, 303–304, 322, 342–43, 357

Niyāzi, Sayyid Nazīr, xiii
Nizāmi, Khawja Hasan, 15

October Socialist Revolution, 118, 119, 120

Pahlāvī, Reza Shāh, 168, 404*n*22
Pakistan: Iqbal's contribution to creation of, xi–xii, 36, 90–91, 93–94, 107, 108, 174; as outgrowth of Muslim nationalism, 132–35, 151–52; first Constituent Assembly of, 398*n*55
Pan-Islamism, 115–18
Pantheism, 53–54, 112, 213, 232, 287–91, 299, 300, 312
*Parinde ke Faryād* (Bird's Lament), 111, 139
Parvaiz, Maulana Ghulam Ahmad, 36
*Pas Chā Bayad Kard Ay Aqwām-i* (What Is To Be Done?), 160, 209, 394*n*46; quoted, 50, 160, 161, 208
Pashto Language: translations of Iqbal into, xiii
*Payām-i Mashriq* (Message of the East), 119, 120–21, 251–52, 272, 274, 355, 261–62, 394*n*46; quoted, 120, 175, 198–99, 270, 298, 394, 350, 356–57, 357–58, 359, 360, 365, 368
Persian encrustation of Islam, 211, 242
Persian language, 9; Iqbal's works in, 17–18, 43, 118, 352, 417–18, 419–20
Personality: Iqbal's concept of, 127, 269–83; reality of, 269–72; and political society, 274–77; religion in development of, 277–79; intuition and, 279–80; *see also Asrār-i-khudi*; Individual, Self
Philosophy, Hindu, 195–96
Plato, 246;47, 271, 338–41; and Iqbal's rejection of theory of, 292–96; *see also* Neo-Platonism
Poetry: Iqbal's conception of the poet, 327–38, 340–41; and poetic passion, 329–32; decadent, 335–37; conceptions of, 338–46; didactic, 345–46
Poverty, 220
*Preaching of Islam, The* (Arnold), 12
*Principles of Movement in the Structure of Islam*, 121
Punjab, the, 3, 5, 28, 69–70; political life (1900–1940), 76–107; population, 77, 80; British rule in 77–80, 83–87; revenue system, 83–85; educational system, 85–87
*Punjab Kāy Pīr Zaduñ Say* (To the Punjab Pīrs), 399*n*74
Punjab Legislative Council, 28, 69, 80, 81–83, 86
Punjab Muslim League, 88, 94–107 *passim*, 133
Punjab National Unionist Party, 69, 81, 82, 84, 95, 97, 98, 99–100, 101–102, 107
Punjab University, 13, 19
Punjab Zamindara League, 102–103, 105

Qādir, Sir 'Abdūl, 9, 17–18, 37–39
Qadūs, 'Abdul, of Gangoh
Qarshi, Hakīm Muhammad, 37, 39
*Qawm* (nation), 133
Qizilbash, Muzaffar Ali Khan, 97, 98
Qur'ān (Koran), 4, 28, 32, 39, 50, 61, 71, 113, 159, 165, 171, 208, 219, 224, 246, 255, 260, 261–62, 281, 354, 413*n*15; Hasan's *Tafsīr*, 8; and Iqbal's proposed *Aids to the Study of*, 33; *Tarjmān al-Qur'ān*, periodical, 33; quoted, 41, 48, 50, 123, 125, 141, 171, 191, 198, 226, 291, 298, 300, 305, 307, 321

Rahmān, Justice S. A., xiii
*Ramūz-i-Bekhudi* (Mysteries of Selflessness), 118, 121, 128, 224; quoted, 76, 128
Razi, Imām, 212, 248
*Razm* (epic adventure), 43
Reason, limits of, 187–89
*Reconstruction of Religious Thought in Islam*, 121, 144, 190, 191, 203, 245, 253, 278, 306; quoted, 121, 128, 181, 191, 198, 201, 202, 232, 233, 234, 236, 259, 260, 261, 270, 274, 277, 278, 279, 280, 301, 302, 305, 306, 307, 317, 318, 354
Religion, 149–50, 172, 182; and Afro-Asian nationalism, 265–69; in personality development, 277–79
Revolution, 172
Round Table Conferences, 28–29, 40, 58, 91–92, 176
Rudhbari, Ali, 311
Rumi, Maulana Jalāl-ud-Din, 41, 42, 238–39, 251, 278, 301, 311, 314, 346; quoted, 296, 316

Russell, Bertrand, 235, 249, 253
Russia: Revolution in, 118–21; see also Socialism
Rūzgār-i-Faqīr (Wahīd al-Dīn), 37

Sadā'i Dard (Cry of Pain), 112
Sadr Bazaar (street in Sialkot renamed Iqbal Street), 8–9
Sālik, Maulana Abdūl Majīd, 46; quoted, 6–7, 43
Saqari, Sari-al, 310
Sarhindi, Shaikh Ahmad (Mujaddid Alf Thani), 54, 56, 57, 72, 75, 240–42, 299, 319
Sarhindi, Nāsir 'Ali, 54
Sarmad of Delhi, 42
Sawarj party, 82
Schopenhauer, Arthur, 193–99, 212, 239
Science, attitude toward, ix, x
Scotch Mission College (Murray College), Sialkot, 5, 9, 10
Secrets of the Self, see Asrār-i Khudi
Self, 223; see also Asrār-i Khudi; Individual; Personality
Self-determination for Muslims, 132, 134
Shafi', Mawlavi Muhammad, xiii
Shafi', Mian Muhammad, 70, 82, 88, 89, 91, 97
Shahāb-ud-Dīn, Chaudhary, 70
Shahīd, Sayyid Ahmad, xi
Sha'ir, 11; quoted, 112, 117
Shamā' Awr Shā'ir (Candle and the Poet), 116
Sharani, 'Abdūl Wahhab al-, 222
Shari'a, 113, 290
Sharīf, M. M., xiii, 305
Shibli Nu'mani, Muhammad, 12, 13
Shikwah (Complaint), 39, 54
Shuja'-ud-Din, Khalifah, 96, 97, 106
Sialkot, 3, 4, 5, 8, 38
Siddiqi, Rashīd Ahmad, 36
Sikhs, 30; in the Punjab, 76, 77, 80, 85–87, 92, 98
Simnani, 'Alā al-Daulah, 71
Simon Commission, 88–89
Sindhi language: translations of Iqbal into, xiii
Singh, Iqbal, 282–83; quoted, 281
Singh, Sir Jogendera, 26, 45
Singh, Raja Gulab, 3
Singh, Sardar Ujjal, 87
Six Lectures, 239
Slavery, 167
Socialism, 118–21, 152–55, 170–73, 277
Society: individual in, 272–74; interrelation among people in, 274–77
Soviet Academy of Arts and Sciences, xiv
Sturm und Drang school, aesthetic theories of, 341–42
Struggle, as the essence of man, 302, 303
Sufis, Sufism (Tasawwuf), 4, 20, 37, 51–55, 56, 71, 112, 129, 207, 211–12, 213, 220, 222–23, 232, 246, 251, 256, 269, 287; Iqbal's attitude toward, 53–55, 123–24, 287–300, 301–303, 305
Suhurwardi, Shabab-al-Din (al-Maqtūl), 213, 226–29
Sunna (Conduct of the Prophet), 125
Superman, the, 204–206
Sūyūti, Jalāl al-Dīn al, 222

Tagore, Rabindranath, 18, 268
Tahdhib al-Akhlaq, 8
Tahira, Qurat-ul-'Ain, 411–n1
Taimiyya, Ibn, 71, 72
Tāj-ud-Din, Pīr, 97, 106
Tārāna-i Hindi (Song of India), 17, 139–40
Tāriq, 'Abd al-Rashīd, 46, 47–48
Tarjmān al-Qur'ān, periodical, 33
Taskhīr-i Fitrat, 272, 355
Taswīr-i-Dard (Portrait of Anguish), 16, 111; quoted, 138–39
Tawhid (Unity of God), 53, 131, 288, 289, 290, 291, 300, 310, 311
Temple of Love, 137–41
Thani, Mujaddid Alf, 54, 56–58, 72, 75, 240–42, 299, 319
Tiger and Sheep, quoted, 292–93
Time, concepts of, 232–38; of Iqbal, 244–63; God and, 262–63
To Javid on Receiving His First Letter, quoted, 58
Trinity College, 19
Tughrayee, Feruz-ud-Din Ahmad, 295
Tulbā'-i Aligarh College Kay Nām (To the Students of Aligarh College), quoted, 117
Turkish Red Crescent, 167

Union, 240-42
Unionist Party, see Punjab National Unionist Party
University Oriental College, Lahore, 13, 14
Upanishads, 71, 195-97, 313
Urdu language, 6, 346; Iqbal's works in, 9, 11, 13, 14, 15, 16, 17, 18, 37-38, 43, 159, 352, 363, 418, 420; poetry in, 9, 11, 169, 363; translations by Iqbal into, 347

Wahdat al-Shahūd theory, 71-72, 73
Wahdat al-Wujūd (unity of being), see Pantheism
Wahid, 'Abdul, 44, 45
Wahīd al-Din, Faqīr Sayyid, 37
Wajeb al-Wujūd (Divine existence), 288
Walidāh Marhūmā key yād Meiñ (In Memory of My Blessed Mother), 197
Walīullah, Shah, xi, 124-26, 244, 407n1

Wasāl (Union), 22
Web of life, Darwinian concept of, 73
Weightage for minorities, 81
West: democracy of, 155-58, 176-83
West and East, 130, 142-43; Iqbal quoted on, x, 143
Whitehead, Alfred North, 254, 255, 256, 257, 258-59, 260, 262-63
Whitman, Walt, 177, 178, 183
Will, Schopenhauer's and Iqbal's philosophies of, 193-99
Wordsworth, William, 347, 348-51, 363, 379

Yatīm kā Khatāb Hilāl-i 'Id Sāy (Orphan's Plaint to the Crescent of 'Id), 16

Zabūr-i 'Ajam, quoted, 313, 327-38, 330-31, 333-35, 337, 353, 360, 394n46